Adventures in Theory

Adventures in Theory

A Compact Anthology

Edited by
Calvin Thomas

BLOOMSBURY ACADEMIC
NEW YORK · LONDON · OXFORD · NEW DELHI · SYDNEY

BLOOMSBURY ACADEMIC
Bloomsbury Publishing Inc
1385 Broadway, New York, NY 10018, USA
50 Bedford Square, London, WC1B 3DP, UK

BLOOMSBURY, BLOOMSBURY ACADEMIC and the Diana logo are trademarks
of Bloomsbury Publishing Plc

First published in the United States of America 2019

Copyright © Calvin Thomas, 2019

For legal purposes the Credits on p. ix constitute an extension of this
copyright page.

Cover design: Alice Marwick
Cover image © iStock

Bloomsbury Publishing Inc does not have any control over, or responsibility for,
any third-party websites referred to or in this book. All internet addresses given
in this book were correct at the time of going to press. The author and publisher
regret any inconvenience caused if addresses have changed or sites have ceased
to exist, but can accept no responsibility for any such changes.

A catalog record for this book is available from the Library of Congress.

ISBN: HB: 978-1-5013-3633-1
PB: 978-1-5013-3632-4
ePDF: 978-1-5013-3635-5
eBook: 978-1-5013-3634-8

Typeset by Deanta Global Publishing Services, Chennai, India
Printed and bound in Great Britain

To find out more about our authors and books visit www.bloomsbury.com
and sign up for our newsletters.

In Memory of Ihab and Sally Hassan

Contents

Credits

Editor's Introduction: Gearing Up for *Adventures*

There are times in life when the question of knowing if one can think differently than one thinks and perceive differently than one sees is absolutely necessary if one is to go on looking and reflecting at all.

Michel Foucault

1 Disturbances

The purpose of art, according to the artist known as Banksy, is to comfort the disturbed and disturb the comfortable. The purpose of that craft or sullen art called "theory" is to disturb *everybody*—to abrade all our staid assumptions, disrupt all our fixed understandings, undermine all our normalized meanings, and alienate us from all our familiarized identities. Writing becomes or remains adventurously "theoretical" only to the extent that it serves this purpose, this perpetual disturbance of our all-too-human realities.

Adventures in Theory: A Compact Anthology gathers a comparatively small group of writings, each driven in its own way by theory's subversive purpose. And while *all* theory anthologies are similarly "purpose-driven," *most* are anything *but* compact; most are in fact massively crammed with more agitation than any reader could productively manage in a single academic term. *Adventures* offers an alternative: a short collection of critical statements crucial to the understanding of theory, a relatively brief but steadily unsettling trek spanning some of the most significant (and still-startling) thought-provocations in the history of theoretical writing.

In a moment, I will relate the (short) story of how these *Adventures* got started. And eventually I will offer a few (big) words concerning the specific disturbances in which theoretical writings conspire to involve us. First, however, I will trumpet the news that *Adventures in Theory* was from the get-go conceived and intended as a lean and mean companion to another guidebook I've ventured to publish, called *Ten Lessons in Theory*.[1] If all has gone according to plan, you should have full access to both of these unsettling texts.

---

[1] Calvin Thomas, *Ten Lessons in Theory: An Introduction to Theoretical Writing* (New York and London: Bloomsbury Academic, 2013). As its title indicates, and to quote from its preface,

For with one significant (and perhaps telling) exception—namely, Frantz Fanon—all of the theoretical writers whose works are marshaled here in *Adventures* are encountered, if not discussed extensively, in *Ten Lessons*. And, without exception, all of the writers whose works are gathered here confirm what one articulates in the epigraph above: in the militant spirit of Michel Foucault, these writers all challenge and encourage us to disturb and discomfort ourselves and each other, to think about ourselves differently than we've gotten used to thinking and to see our worlds otherwise than we've grown accustomed to seeing them. On the other hand, for editorial and economic reasons that will presently be explained, there are a few hugely looming theoretical figures—Hegel, Freud, and, particularly, Jacques Lacan—whose arguments permeate *Ten Lessons* but whose actual works are *not* sampled directly (though they are amply mentioned) in *Adventures*. The strong presence of this trio throughout *Ten Lessons* should compensate for their fairly ironic absence in *Adventures*—all the more reason for you to have both texts at your disposal.[2]

Moreover, the fact that I've already provided a pretty long (and pretty good) intro to theory elsewhere, in *Ten Lessons*, permits me—in the interests of

---

This book proceeds in the form of ten "lessons," each based on an axiomatic sentence or "truth-claim" selected from the more or less established canon of theoretical writing. Each lesson works by extensively "unpacking" its featured sentence, exploring the sentence's conditions of possibility and most radical implications, asking what it means to say that "the world must be made to mean" (Stuart Hall), that "meaning is the polite word for pleasure" (Adam Philips), and "language is by nature fictional" (Roland Barthes), and so on. In the course of exploring the conditions and consequences of these sentences, the ten lessons work and play together to articulate the most basic assumptions and motivations supporting theoretical writing, from its earliest stirrings to its most current turbulences. (xii)

2   The absence in *Adventures* of direct writing samples from Hegel, Freud, and, particularly, Lacan is ironic only in so far as *Adventures* is meant to serve as a companion to *Ten Lessons*, but the irony increases when we consider the first two of *Ten Lessons*' three underlying premises. "The first premise," to quote again from the book's preface,

is that a genuinely productive understanding of theoretical activities depends upon a much more sustained encounter with the foundational writings of Hegel, Marx, Nietzsche, and Freud than any reader is likely to get from the standardized introductions to theory currently available; discourse concerning these four writers thus pervades *Ten Lessons in Theory*. The second premise involves what Fredric Jameson describes as "the conviction that of all the writing called theoretical, Lacan's is the richest"; holding to this conviction pretty much throughout, *Ten Lessons* pays more (and more careful) attention to the richness of Lacan's psychoanalytic writings than does any other introduction to theory (that isn't specifically an introduction to Lacan). The book's third premise is that "literary theory" isn't simply highfalutin speculation "about" literature, but that theory fundamentally *is* literature . . . . The book not only argues but attempts to demonstrate that "the writing called theoretical" is nothing if not a specific type of "creative writing," a particular way of engaging with the *art* of the sentence, the art of making sentences that make *trouble*—sentences that articulate the desire to make radical *changes* in the very fabric, or fabrication, of social reality. (xii) maximal compactness—to provide only a very brief introduction here, and to omit even a minimal headnote for each of *Adventures'* individual selections. In other words, unlike in other and longer anthologies (with editors far more industrious than I), in this one there won't be any contextualizing previews, any comforting words at the beginning of any piece explaining in advance what you're about to read for yourself, sparing you the work of diligently reading it or telling you up front what your "takeaway" from the reading should optimally be. No, all you're going to get from me at the outset of each selection in *Adventures* is the writer's name, nationality, years of birth and death (or just birth, if the writer hasn't yet lost the battle), the year of the original publication or composition of the selection, and a brief epigraph taken from the selection that—however tersely, cryptically, or even profanely—should help to illuminate it.[3]

The selections themselves are arranged in mostly chronological order, with a couple of strategic exceptions: Barbara Johnson's 1983 "Critique of Metaphysics" precedes Jacques Derrida's 1967 "Différance" because Johnson's later work introduces Derrida's general project to English-speaking readers (and remains in my view the single best brief preface to Derrida ever written), while Slavoj Žižek's 2002 contribution "The Real of Sexual Difference" gets situated before Lee Edelman's 1998 intervention simply because I've grown loath to the idea of giving Žižek any final words, particularly on the topic of sexual difference, and prefer to let Lee Edelman have them, as I more or less did in *Ten Lessons*.

Actually, Edelman's exuberant f-bombs are the last words only of the tenth lesson of *Ten*, while *Ten Lessons'* very last words come from Foucault and, not coincidentally, are the *same* words that appear in our opening epigraph here, while the *final* words in *Adventures* will have come from Derrida and—spoiler alert—they read as follows:
"Let us begin again."

2 Origins and acknowledgments

But as for the story of how *Adventures* itself began: a few years ago I was teaching a grad course in contemporary theory at my home institution, Georgia State University in downtown Atlanta. The required texts for the class were my own *Ten Lessons* and one of those aforementioned

---

[3] Regarding the epigraphs, the one exception to my general practice of taking each one from the selection in this volume (as it appears in this volume) is the epigraph to Gayle Rubin's "The Traffic in Women." You will find the explanation for this anomaly in Footnote 6.

massive theory anthologies (a textbook with, let's say, "global" aspirations exceedingly well met). Now, my university has a nice program called "GSU-62," which allows people who have reached that age to take or audit classes of their choice without having to fork over any tuition. One such individual audited my theory class that semester: his name was **Laurence Fennelly**, and I would like to acknowledge and thank him by name here, for without one of his sagacious observations, *Adventures in Theory* might never have happened.

It was the end of the semester. We were reviewing what all had worked well or not so well in the course, and, when it came to the question of the use-value of the required texts and assigned readings therefrom, I found myself apologizing for having made everyone pony up for a "doorstop" textbook that cost so much and from which we actually read so little—a text that, assessed realistically, could be "used" in its *entirety* in a *single* semester only *as* a doorstop. My apologies accepted, Mr. Fennelly pointed to his own dearly purchased copy of the "global" reader and remarked: "It would be good if there could be a more *compact* version of this."

The rest of the class assented, as did I, disclosing that to my knowledge such an edition *n'existait pas* and wondering to myself why no enterprising editor had ever thought of it before. I immediately (well, OK, eventually) set to work on a proposal and shortly persuaded **Haaris Naqvi**, my superb editor at Bloomsbury Academic, whom I warmly thank here for having been keen on the project, to agree to put the proposal through Bloomsbury's standard process of external review and scholarly evaluation. I also happily thank the scholars of theory involved in this review process—**Mari Ruti**, Distinguished Professor of Critical Theory and of Gender and Sexuality Studies at the University of Toronto, **Jean-Michel Rabaté**, Professor of English and Comparative Literature at the University of Pennsylvania, and **Russell Smith**, Lecturer in English at Australia National University—for all their kind support and helpful suggestions. Warm thanks also go to **Katherine De Chant**, senior editorial assistant at Bloomsbury, and to **Drew Wright**, my expert editorial assistant here at Georgia State.

But, as always, my greatest and warmest thanks go to **Liz Stoehr**, without whom none of my greatest adventures in theory, or in life, would ever have been possible.

3 Complications

Once *Adventures* had won its contract, my immediate editorial task was to start working my way through a professional terrain that I would soon come to take sick pleasure in calling *permissions hell*, a job involving the complicated and often long-drawn-out process of securing permissions, from various publishers holding various rights, to reprint, for a sometimes modest but occasionally quite hefty fee, all the desired selections in *Adventures* (and, yes, I am indeed trying to make this sentence as long and as tedious as the process it describes). Now, since the plan was to make this anthology not only *compact* but *affordable*, the initial budget for permissions fees was kept pretty tight; this strategic constriction, along with the occasional utter unresponsiveness or lack of cooperation on the part of certain publishing outfits (thanks a lot, you holders of the rights to Adorno's "On Popular Music"!), caused me to ratchet down the already small number of selections (from the initial twenty-four to the present eighteen) and, sadly, to let go of a few of my most strongly desired inclusions.

And here's where we return to the aforementioned trio of Hegel, Freud, and Lacan. Like many apologists for theory, I consider Hegel an indispensable figure, perhaps *the* indispensable figure, a philosopher so crucial to the grasp of our subject that I devote an entire "lesson" to his restless writing in *Ten Lessons*. Hegel is the *only* theoretical writer to receive a whole chapter's devotion in that book (and that book is the *only* introduction to theory to feature a whole chapter devoted to Hegel). But a single short excerpt from Hegel's notoriously gnarly work in an anthology such as *Adventures* would, I thought, be unworkable—or, to allude to a splendid phrase you'll encounter in Gayatri Spivak's selection in this volume, such an excerpt, situated smackdab at the chronologically appropriate outset of the text, would be *un*productively baffling, not at all the best way to begin. So what I initially wanted to kick *Adventures* off with was the entirety of Alexander Kojève's influential 1947 essay "An Introduction to the Reading of Hegel," with its lucidly Marxist gloss on so-called "anthropogenetic" desire and on the famous "master-slave dialectic" from Hegel's *Phenomenology of Spirit*. But, as things *dispiritingly* turned out, even a measly six-page extract from the Kojève piece (including the putative origins of specifically human desire but excluding the whole master-slave scenario) would have cost us more than a *third* of the initial permissions budget. And so so much for Kojève's Hegel's being in *Adventures* (though, again, a great big helping of Hegel does get ladled out in Lesson Six of *Ten Lessons*).

In Freud's case, mainly due to my tight focus on the famous "fort-da" game in *Ten Lessons*, Lesson Four, I had very much wanted to pull into *Adventures* an extract from *Beyond the Pleasure Principle*, where Freud elaborates on that game, on repetition compulsion, the death drive, and much of greatly unsettling significance besides. When it became clear that for reasons involving time and money this plan wasn't going to pan out, I opted instead for Peter Brooks's great 1977 essay "Freud's Masterplot," which effectively folds some of the tales Freud unfolds in *Beyond the Pleasure Principle* into a critical examination of the narrative dimensions of our human desires and the fatal trajectories of our narrative fictions.

As for Jacques Lacan, here's that *petite histoire*: even a casual glance at the blurbs on the back cover of *Ten Lessons* will tell you that that book is heavily steeped in Lacanese. It only stands to reason, then, that I would want to include a substantial or at least distinctive excerpt from Lacan's *oeuvre* in *Adventures*, something like the oft-anthologized "Instance of the Letter in the Unconscious" coupled with "The Signification of the Phallus," for example, or, better, the as-yet un-anthologized ass-kick to ego-coherence called "Aggressiveness in Psychoanalysis." When these more extended jabs of Lacanian aggression turned out to be unaffordable (the longer the piece, the heftier the permissions fee), I felt forced to scale back to the considerably briefer old reliable "The Mirror Stage as Formative of the *I* Function, as Revealed in Psychoanalytic Experience," which essay, truth be told, has been included in just about every other theory anthology on the planet (though I had planned to set *Adventures* somewhat apart by copping the most recent translation of the work). But after a series of delays and re-routings and re-initiations of my request to reprint even the briefest of Lacan's *écrits*, it eventually became evident that for time-and-money reasons I wasn't going be able to include in *Adventures* any Lacan at all and would have to settle for the discussions of his work in the selections from Brooks, Gayle Rubin, Lee Edelman, and of course Slavoj Žižek.

Meanwhile, in the midst of this particular frustration, I received from **Jeffrey R. di Leo** a very kind invitation to contribute a short entry on—guess what?—Lacan's "The Mirror Stage as Formative of the *I* Function, as Revealed in Psychoanalytic Experience" to *The Bloomsbury Handbook to Literary and Cultural Theory*, a guidebook that he was busy putting together and which was scheduled be published around the same time as *Adventures*. Long story short: I worked it out with Professor di Leo to "double-dip" and use the "Mirror Stage" entry that I'd submitted to the *Bloomsbury Handbook* as a substitute for the actual "Mirror Stage" essay in *Adventures*.[4] I'll brazenly add (in the spirit of academic advertising) that I offer ample discussion of Lacan's

---

4   Then I decided, very late in the process, that, if I was going to reprint, or pre-reprint, my brief "Mirror Stage" entry here in *Adventures*, in lieu of any actual Lacan, I might as well go ahead and reprint the even briefer entry on "Symbolic Castration" that I wrote some years ago for the *Routledge International Encyclopedia of Men and Masculinities*, eds. M. Flood, J. K. Gardiner, B. Pease, and K. Pringle (New York: Routledge, 2007). Both entries appear here under the heading "Editor's Interlude: Two Brief Pieces on Lacanian Psychoanalytic Theory."

"Mirror Stage," and of Louis Althusser's related fragment "On Ideology" (the Althusser entry in *Adventures*), in Lesson Five of *Ten Lessons*. And I'll even tread so heavily on the toes of Bloomsbury's marketing department as to bruit that if you can get your hands on all *three* of these disturbers of your ideational peace—*Adventures in Theory, Ten Lessons in Theory,* and *The Bloomsbury Handbook to Literary and Cultural Theory*—you'll be pretty well set as an unsettled student of theory.

But regarding the logic behind the other selections: for the most part, I'll admit, I've simply rounded up the usual suspects and offered up their greatest hits, aiming for maximal impact as well as compactness (not to mention the intended compatibility with *Ten Lessons*). In my view, no responsible theory anthology of any size, scope, or serviceability would lack writings from the posse assembled here, and in some cases, I've done no more than reprint the particular writer's most prominent piece of work (Derrida's "Différance," for example, or the extract on performativity from Judith Butler's *Gender Trouble*) rather than trying, for novelty's sake, to trot out some alternative theoretical pony much less frequently ridden. In cases where the logic of compatibility with *Ten Lessons* ruled, I went with selections reflecting that book's emphasis on Nietzsche, Freud, and Marx as the founding figures of anti-foundationalism, thus favoring Foucault's "Nietzsche, Freud, Marx" over that much more famous intervention he authored called "What is an Author?"[5] In an instance where the logic of compatibility with *Ten Lessons* lost out, I followed Mari Ruti's directions and dropped Chandra Mohanty's "Under Western Eyes: Feminist Scholarship and Colonial Discourses"— which I had wanted to include *not* because I think all that highly of the piece

---

[5]   Actually, my original and quite naïve desire was to run *both* Foucault essays and somehow stay within budget, just as I started off planning to include as our Nietzschean adventures both "On Truth and Lie in a Nonmoral Sense" (which appears here) and, because of the way it adumbrates Viktor Shklovsky's concept of "defamiliarization" in the essay "Art as Technique" (which also appears here), a two-page excerpt from Book Five of Nietzsche's *Gay Science* called "Origin of Our Concept of Knowledge" (which ended up *not* appearing here, though you can find an excerpt therefrom in the "Editor's Afterword" to *Adventures,* Footnote 11). And so, part of the reason I decided to run a revised version of my own piece "No Kingdom of the Queer" as the "Editor's Afterword" to *Adventures* is that this piece (written by invitation in 2008 to be included in the volume *Derrida and Queer Theory,* which wasn't published until 2017) helps compensate for the loss of that last little bit from Nietzsche. This afterword—here called "(Still) No Kingdom (of the Queer)"—in fact gathers a number of queerly theoretical threads together, including references to *both* Nietzsche selections, to Shklovsky, Derrida, Lee Edelman, Carla Freccero, and a few other hearty adventurers, all in order to end on the happy note of what Madhavi Menon calls "queer universalism" and to keep on the table Freccero's strong suggestion that all our "adventures in theory" are "always already" (still) disturbingly "queer." See Madhavi Menon, *Indifference to Difference: On Queer Universalism* (Minneapolis and London: University of Minnesota Press, 2015).

but because I subject it to an extensive (and perhaps ill-considered) critique in the tenth of *Ten Lessons*—and opted instead for Gayatri Spivak's better and better-known "Can the Subaltern Speak?" I also followed Ruti's ruling and jettisoned the (arguably) more belletristic business about Shakespeare's sister excerpted from Virginia Woolf's 1929 *A Room of One's Own* and adopted the entirety (or what I thought was the entirety) of Gayle Rubin's more heavily theoretical and more helpfully bellicose 1975 essay "The Traffic in Women: Notes on the Political Economy of Sex."[6]

Other logics of inclusion: the Saussure, Fanon, and Said selections are basically the standards, and I offer no apologies here for the fact that these pieces appear in just about these forms in just about every other theory anthology on earth. With Roland Barthes, I wanted the specific bit from "Myth Today" rather than the briefer (and presumably cheaper) "Death of the Author" because of the importance of the former in the history of postcolonial and cultural studies and because of the way Barthes's treatment of what he calls "myth" in this essay aligns with Althusser's analysis of "ideology in general" in the excerpt from *Lenin and Philosophy* reprinted here. With Lee Edelman's exquisitely negative "The Future is Kid Stuff," I went with the original publication as it appeared in the journal *Narrative*, rather than the expanded version that stands as the opening chapter of his book *No Future*, because the journal version, like the book, features the aforementioned fusillade of f-bombs that I've rudely included as the epigraph to Edelman's "Kid Stuff" here, *and* because I rightly figured that it would be easier (i.e., quicker and cheaper) to get permission for the journal version from the journal than to get permission for the longer book version from the university press that published the book (actually, *Narrative* was the only publishing outfit good enough to respond to my permission request *on the*

---

[6]   The selection from Woolf's *Room* is compatible with *Ten Lessons* in that I mention Woolf a few times in that text—in Lesson Seven, on literary formalism (which Woolf tacitly opposed, at least in what would become its dominant Anglo-American version), and in Lesson Ten, on feminism, gender studies, and queer theory (all of which, arguably, Woolf's *Room* helped make possible). Rubin's "Traffic," however, is *more* compatible with *Ten Lessons* than is Woolf's *Room* because it's more theoretically grounded, because Rubin's work includes extended discussions of *Ten Lessons'* major figures—Marx, Freud, and Lacan—and because I actually quote directly from Rubin's works more frequently in *Ten Lessons* than I do from Woolf's. Please note, however, that the version of "Traffic" that I got permission to reprint here in *Adventures* is *not* exactly the same, and not exactly as long, as the version that I quote from in *Ten Lessons*, as I realized only when it was too late to do anything about it except feel stupid. And so, awkwardly, a crucial formulation from Rubin's "Traffic" that appears in *Ten Lessons* (p. 251), and which I had planned to use as the epigraph to Rubin's "Traffic" in *Adventures*, appears *as* the epigraph to Rubin's "Traffic" in *Adventures* anyway, even though it doesn't show up in the version of Rubin's "Traffic" that is reprinted here in *Adventures*.

same day, and charging only a relatively modest fee; other outfits took too long and/or charged too much, while some, as I've already whined about above, never bothered to respond at all—so extra and sincere thanks go to our friends at the great journal *Narrative.*).

But speaking, all too briefly, of friends: I have passed over some of the more obvious contenders (Fredric Jameson, Jean-François Lyotard, Jürgen Habermas) for the single selection on postmodernism in *Adventures* and chosen to reprint here Ihab Hassan's 1987 essay "Toward a Concept of Postmodernism" for a number of reasons, but I'm not embarrassed to say that the most personal of these is that Ihab Hassan was my teacher; he was my dissertation director; and he was my friend. And I have chosen the specific sentence that appears as the epigraph to Ihab's essay because (and there's irony here, given that the epigraph precedes a discussion of *postmodernism*, the late-twentieth-century intellectual/aesthetic movement that some scorn as a sort of historical stage-setting for our current, corrupted, Trumped-up, post-veridical era of "alternative facts") *that* sentence's particular truth-claim rings categorically, universally, and transhistorically *true*: all writers and all teachers at all times are on some level absolutely convinced that this "battle of the books" in which we are engaged—our battle to *write* books, and our battle for others to *read* books, our struggle to *see* (and help others see) nothing that isn't there as well as the nothing that is—*is* nothing other than what Hassan calls our "ontic battle against death."[7] In asking you to read *this* book, I'm asking you to enlist, to sign up, to join me, to join us, in this unwinnable *agon*. And in asking you to read this book's ontic reincarnation of the creative writing of Ihab Hassan, I'm asking nothing more and nothing less than for you to help me keep my old friend alive.

4 "These are words with a *d* this time!"[8]

At a particular juncture in "Towards a Concept," Ihab Hassan lays out a list of big words, all beginning with the letter "d," words that for him pertain to what he calls the radical "*indetermanance*" of the postmodern moment. At the beginning of this introduction, I promised eventually to discuss a few big words concerning the specific ways theoretical writing disturbs us. Postmodernism and theory are of course intimately related activities, but

---

[7] See Hassan's contribution to this volume. See also Wallace Stevens's great poem "The Snow Man," to the last lines of which I have alluded here.

[8] A line lifted from the tune "Elephant Talk" by the band King Crimson, on their 1981 album *Discipline* (another word that begins with the letter "d").

they are not exactly the same animal, and so Hassan's list does not correspond, word for word, with mine. My big words, however, like Hassan's, do all begin with the fourth letter of the English alphabet. And here, as promised, or threatened, they are: *defamiliarization, denaturalization, desedimentation, decolonization, disidentification,* and *dereification.*

Now, in the interests of keeping my introduction brief, and our anthology compact, I'm not about to start belaboring each one of these cumbersome nuggets of jargon here, as much as I would enjoy the exercise. But assuming that 1) you're already familiar with *familiarity, nature, sediment, colony,* and *identity,* and so 2) could readily recognize the verbs *familiarize, naturalize, sediment, colonize,* and *identify,* and so 3) might have at least a vague idea of what plopping down a negativizing *"de"* or *"dis"* in front of *those* verbs does for us, but that 4) you're probably not yet up to speed with the meaning or *de*-meaning of the word *reification,* I will confine myself to defining this particular bit of terminology and to explaining why the difficult work of *dereification* remains a crucial part of what theoretical writing hopes to accomplish.

The word *reification* is based on the Latin *res,* for "thing." So *reification* pretty much means "thingification," making things thingy—or, rather, making *non*-things thingy, turning entities that, strictly (or ethically) speaking, *aren't* things *into* things. Or, to make a fairly big jump, let's say that *reification* in the largest sense involves *globally* misrecognizing an actively and elusively non-thingy *world* as a passively graspable *planet* of things, there for the taking, treating non-thingy entities (like, say, living breathing human beings) as if they were nothing but things, or objects, or property, or dirt. In one reading, *reification* goes hand in hand with *dehumanization*—specifically, *monetized* dehumanization—with figurative or literal *slavery,* with the profitable *objectification,* economic *exploitation,* and mechanically (or digitally) mass-reproduced *commodification* of living breathing human beings. Here *reification* involves our failing or refusing to recognize all the processes of *productive labor* that make our great big "socially constructed" world possible; it involves what Fredric Jameson productively calls the forced "removal of traces of production from the product"[9]; it involves our forgetting or never realizing that or how our "things" (our commodities, our concepts, our identities, our gods) are all humanly *manufactured*—laboriously, performatively, sometimes even aesthetically *made.* On an ideational or ideological level (a "superstructural" level supported by and reciprocally reinforcing the economic "base" just described), *reification* involves the ways

---

[9]   Fredric Jameson, *The Hegel Variations: On the Phenomenology of Sprit* (New York: Verso, 2010), 124.

we allow our perceptions and sensations, our metaphors and metonymies, our assumptions and projections, to congeal and harden into dense bricks of certainty. In this sense, *reification* is a word that names what happens when we allow ourselves to form too firm a "belief in the stability and substantiality of what is"[10]—when we buy into the inevitability of any given *status quo*. In another sense, *reification* is a word that names what happens when we forget that *words* and *names* are not stable and substantial things, or that no individual word can "mean" all by itself, indifferent to its social relations with all other words, that words cannot be free-standing things-in-themselves.

But here's the thing about the word *reification*: because it's all too easy for us to think of certain *familiar* words, certain so-called "facts" of *nature*, certain *sedimented* foundations, certain settled *colonies* and positive *identities* precisely as stable, static, and substantial *things* (rather than as, say, slippery socio-symbolic signifying *processes*), *reification* would seem to be the overarching logic drily lubricating *familiarization, naturalization, sedimentation, colonization*, and *identification* to boot. But if all this is the case, if *reification* really rules the socioeconomic/ideological roost, then *dereification*—the struggle *against* thingification, particularly *as* this *agon* plays itself out in the *history* of *re*sistant and *re*silient theoretical *writing*— might end up being the most subversively encompassing, intellectually radical "adventure" of them all.

Thus do two giants of critical theory, Max Horkheimer and Theodor Adorno, write that "intellect's true concern is a negation of reification," and that truly concerned critical intellect can only "perish when it is solidified into a cultural asset and handed out for consumption purposes."[11] Thus does the aforementioned theory-giant Fredric Jameson write "that theory is to be grasped as the perpetual . . . attempt to dereify the language of thought," that the "aim of theoretical writing" is to try "to escape the reifications [and] commodifications of the intellectual marketplace today"; thus does Jameson urge us thinkers to think against "reified thinking" and "commodified thoughts" and "to wage persistent and local guerilla warfare against their hegemony."[12] Thus does a key initiator of postcolonial theory, Edward Said, gather the discursive armies of *defamiliarization, denaturalization, decolonialization*, and *disidentification* together with his *de-reifying* observation that "the Orient is not an inert fact of nature."[13] Thus

---

[10] Jameson, *The Hegel Variations*, 25.

[11] Max Horkheimer and Theodor Adorno, *Dialectic of Enlightenment: Philosophical Fragments*, edited by Gunzelin Schmid Noerr, translated by Edmund Jephcott (Stanford, CA: Stanford University Press, 2002), xvii.

[12] Fredric Jameson, *Valences of the Dialectic* (New York: Verso, 2009), 9, 61.

[13] See Said's contribution to this volume.

does an earlier leader of postcolonial resistance, Frantz Fanon, painfully explain what it feels like to be sealed into a crushing thingness, to be on the business end of *reification* at its most pervasively racist. Thus does the founder of structural linguistics, Ferdinand de Saussure, pull the proverbial rug out from under *reification* by giving us the message that "language is a form and not a substance" and by insisting that *in* language "there are only differences *without positive terms*."[14] Thus does the putative granddaddy of postmodernism, Friedrich Nietzsche, argue that it is only by our forgetting that there *are* only differences that we petrify our perceptions into *reified* concepts, that it is only by forgetting that we ourselves are the artistically productive subjects of our objectively produced worlds that we allow ourselves to settle into our veridical easy-chairs of consistency, security, and repose. Thus does a still-reigning queen of feminist/queer theory, Judith Butler, drag *reification* through the rough by insisting on the *performativity*, rather than the naturally expressive *substantiality*, of supposedly hard-wired gender identity.

And thus does the editor of this volume, yours truly, attempt to do his best to do his duty to *dereification* by laying bare as many of the "traces of production" in this particular textual "product" as he can, tediously rehearsing all the base monetary matters of permissions-getting underlying his editorial decisions and selections for *Adventures in Theory* and meticulously over-narrating (even here) how this whole "thing" came to be an inevitably commodified "thing" circulating in today's "intellectual marketplace" in the first place.

But it's arguably the arch-disturber Karl Marx who, by standing Hegel on his feet and terminally *de-deifying* the Hegelian dialectic, really gets theory's *de-reifying* ball rolling with his empathetic analyses of alienated labor and his ruthless criticism of the power of money in capitalist society, not to mention his critically irreligious reminder—eternally undermining all fundamentalist fantasies whatsoever (wherever such fine products are sold)—that *people* create deities; deities don't create people. And so it is with Marx, of all people, that we begin these *Adventures* (and not simply because we couldn't book Hegel).

A couple of last notes, though, before we begin adventuring—one hopefully helpful, the other helpfully hopeful.

The helpful note just concerns *notes*, specifically *footnotes*: please note that I haven't added any of my own to any of the selections you're about to read. The notes you'll see at the bottom of the following pages correspond pretty

---

[14] See Saussure's contribution to this volume.

much to what shows up in all the selections as they appeared in the original venues (journals or books) from which I was granted permission to take and reprint them here. I have, that is, let stand all footnotes from authors, editors, and translators as they appeared in the original venues *except* in those cases, and there were a few, where certain editorial or translator's footnotes were unhelpfully cluttering or potentially confusing.[15]

The hopeful note concerns our opening quotation from Michel Foucault, which actually appears three times in *Ten Lessons in Theory*.[16] As you'll have read here, and as you can also read there, Foucault thinks that there are times in our lives when the question of whether or not we can think and see *differently* than we have heretofore thought and seen must necessarily arise.

I'll close this introduction by expressing my hope that *Adventures in Theory* will have been one of those times.

---

[15] When, for example, the editor's footnote read "see such and such in this volume" when "this volume" was something other than *Adventures in Theory*. I deleted quite a few footnotes in the Nietzsche selection for this reason.

[16] See Thomas, *Ten Lessons*, 5, 15, 274.

Karl Marx

German (1818-1883)

Three Excerpts from *Early Writings* (1844)

*The abolition of religion as the illusory happiness of the people is the demand
for their real happiness. To call on them to give up their illusions about their
condition is to call on them to give up a condition that requires illusions.*

1 From "A Contribution to the Critique
of Hegel's Philosophy of Right"

For Germany, the *criticism of religion* has been essentially completed, and the
criticism of religion is the prerequisite of all criticism.

The *profane* existence of error is compromised as soon as its *heavenly oratio
pro aris et focis*[1] has been refuted. Man, who has found only the *reflection* of
himself in the fantastic reality of heaven, where he sought a superman, will
no longer feel disposed to find the mere *appearance* of himself, the non-man,
where he seeks and must seek his true reality.

The foundation of irreligious criticism is: *Man makes religion,* religion
does not make man. Religion is indeed the self-consciousness and self-
esteem of man who has either not yet won through to himself or has already
lost himself again. But *man* is no abstract being squatting outside the world.
Man is *the world of man,* state, society. This state and this society produce
religion, which is an *inverted consciousness of the world,* because they are an
inverted world. Religion is the general theory of this world, its encyclopedic
compendium, its logic in popular form, its spiritual *point d'honneur,* its
enthusiasm, its moral sanction, its solemn complement and its universal
basis of consolation and justification. It is the *fantastic realization* of the
human essence since the human essence has not acquired any true reality.

---

[1] Plea on behalf of hearth and home.

The struggle against religion is therefore indirectly the struggle against *that world* whose spiritual *aroma* is religion.

Religious suffering is at one and the same time the *expression* of real suffering and a protest against real suffering. Religion is the sigh of the oppressed creature, the heart of a heartless world and the soul of soulless conditions. It is the *opium* of the people.

The abolition of religion as the *illusory* happiness of the people is the demand for their *real* happiness. To call on them to give up their illusions about their condition is to *call on them to give up a condition that requires illusions*. The criticism of religion is therefore in *embryo* the *criticism of that vale of tears* of which religion is the *halo*.

Criticism has plucked the imaginary flowers on the chain not in order that man shall continue to bear that chain without fantasy or consolation but so that he shall throw off the chain and pluck the living flower. The criticism of religion disillusions man, so that he will think, act and fashion his reality like a man who has discarded his illusions and regained his senses, so that he will move around himself as his own true sun. Religion is only the illusory sun which revolves around man as long as he does not revolve around himself.

It is therefore the *task of history*, once the *other-world of truth* has vanished, to establish the *truth of this world*. It is the immediate *task of philosophy*, which is in the service of history, to unmask self-estrangement in its *unholy forms* once the *holy form* of human self-estrangement has been unmasked. Thus the criticism of heaven turns into the criticism of earth, the *criticism of religion* into the *criticism of law* and the *criticism of theology* into the *criticism of politics*.

2 "Estranged Labour" (from *Economic and Philosophical Manuscripts*)

If the product of labour is alien to me and confronts me as an alien power, to whom does it then belong?
    To a being other than me.
    Who is this being?

We have started out from the premises of political economy. We have accepted its language and its laws. We presupposed private property; the separation of labour, capital and land, and likewise of wages, profit and capital; the division of labour; competition; the concept of exchange value, etc. From political economy itself, using its own words, we have shown that the worker sinks to the level of a commodity, and moreover the most wretched commodity of all; that the misery of the worker is in inverse proportion to the power and volume of his production; that the necessary consequence of competition is the accumulation of capital in a few hands and hence the restoration of monopoly in a more terrible form; and that finally the distinction between capitalist and landlord, between agricultural worker and industrial worker, disappears and the whole of society must split into the two classes of *property owners* and propertyless *workers*.

Political economy proceeds from the fact of private property. It does not explain it. It grasps the *material* process of private property, the process through which it actually passes, in general and abstract formulae which it then takes as *laws*. It does not *comprehend* these laws, i.e. it does not show how they arise from the nature of private property. Political economy fails to explain the reason for the division between labour and capital, between capital and land. For example, when it defines the relation of wages to profit it takes the interests of the capitalists as the basis of its analysis; i.e. it assumes what it is supposed to explain. Similarly, competition is frequently brought into the argument and explained in terms of external circumstances. Political economy teaches us nothing about the extent to which these external and apparently accidental circumstances are only the expression of a necessary development. We have seen how exchange itself appears to political economy as an accidental fact. The only wheels which political economy sets in motion are *greed* and the *war of the avaricious—competition*.

Precisely because political economy fails to grasp the interconnections within the movement, it was possible to oppose, for example, the doctrine of competition to the doctrine of monopoly, the doctrine of craft freedom to the doctrine of the guild and the doctrine of the division of landed property to the doctrine of the great estate; for competition, craft freedom and division of landed property were developed and conceived only as accidental, deliberate, violent consequences of monopoly, of the guilds and of feudal property and not as their necessary, inevitable and natural consequences.

We now have to grasp the essential connection between private property, greed, the separation of labour, capital and landed property, exchange and competition, value and the devaluation [*Entwertung*] of man, monopoly and competition, etc.—the connection between this entire system of estrangement [*Entfremdung*] and the *money* system.

We must avoid repeating the mistake of the political economist, who bases his explanations on some imaginary primordial condition. Such a primordial condition explains nothing. It simply pushes the question into the grey and nebulous distance. It assumes as facts and events what it is supposed to deduce, namely the necessary relationship between two things, between, for example, the division of labour and exchange. Similarly, theology explains the origin of evil by the fall of man, i.e. it assumes as a fact in the form of history what it should explain.

We shall start out from a *present-day* economic fact.

The worker becomes poorer the more wealth he produces, the more his production increases in power and extent. The worker becomes an ever cheaper commodity the more commodities he produces. The *devaluation* of the human world grows in direct proportion to the *increase in value* of the world of things. Labour not only produces commodities; it also produces itself and the workers as a *commodity* and it does so in the same proportion in which it produces commodities in general.

This fact simply means that the object that labour produces, its product, stands opposed to it as *something alien*, as a *power independent* of the producer. The product of labour is labour embodied and made material in an object, it is the *objectification* of labour. The realization of labour is its objectification. In the sphere of political economy this realization of labour appears as a *loss of reality* for the worker, objectification as *loss of and bondage to the object*, and appropriation as *estrangement*, as *alienation* [*Entäusserung*].

So much does the realization of labour appear as loss of reality that the worker loses his reality to the point of dying of starvation. So much does objectification appear as loss of the object that the worker is robbed of the objects he needs most not only for life but also for work. Work itself becomes an object which he can only obtain through an enormous effort and with spasmodic interruptions. So much does the appropriation of the object appear as estrangement that the more objects the worker produces the fewer can he possess and the more he falls under the domination of his product, of capital.

All these consequences are contained in this characteristic, that the worker is related to the *product of his labour* as to an *alien* object. For it is clear that, according to this premise, the more the worker exerts himself in his work, the more powerful the alien, objective world becomes which he brings into being over against himself, the poorer he and his inner world become, and the less they belong to him. It is the same in religion. The more man puts into God, the less he retains within himself. The worker places his life in the object; but now it no longer belongs to him, but to the object. The greater his activity, therefore, the fewer objects the worker possesses. What the product of his labour is, he is not. Therefore, the greater this product, the less is he himself. The externalization [*Entäusserung*] of the worker in his product means not only that his labour becomes an object, an *external* existence, but that it exists *outside him*, independently of him and alien to him, and begins to confront him as an autonomous power; that the life which he has bestowed on the object confronts him as hostile and alien.

Let us now take a closer look at *objectification*, at the production of the worker, and the *estrangement*, the *loss* of the object, of his product, that this entails.

The worker can create nothing without *nature*, without the *sensuous external world*. It is the material in which his labour realizes itself, in which it is active and from which and by means of which it produces.

But just as nature provides labour with the *means of life* in the sense that labour cannot *live* without objects on which to exercise itself, so also it provides the *means of life* in the narrower sense, namely the means of physical subsistence of the *worker*.

The more the worker *appropriates* the external world, sensuous nature, through his labour, the more he deprives himself of the *means of life* in two respects: firstly, the sensuous external world becomes less and less an object belonging to his labour, a *means of life* of his labour; and secondly, it becomes less and less a *means of life* in the immediate sense, a means for the physical subsistence of the worker.

In these two respects, then, the worker becomes a slave of his object; firstly in that he receives an *object of labour*, i.e. he receives work, and secondly in that he receives *means of subsistence*. Firstly, then, so that he can exist as a *worker*, and secondly as a *physical subject*. The culmination of this slavery is that it is only as a *worker* that he can maintain himself as a *physical subject* and only as a *physical subject* that he is a worker.

(The estrangement of the worker in his object is expressed according to the laws of political economy in the following way: the more the worker produces, the less he has to consume; the more values he creates, the more worthless he becomes; the more his product is shaped, the more misshapen the worker; the more civilized his object, the more barbarous the worker; the more powerful the work, the more powerless the worker; the more intelligent the work, the duller the worker and the more he becomes a slave of nature.)

Political economy conceals the estrangement in the nature of labour by ignoring the direct relationship between the worker (labour) and production. It is true that labour produces marvels for the rich, but it produces privation for the worker. It produces palaces, but hovels for the worker. It produces beauty, but deformity for the worker. It replaces labour by machines, but it casts some of the workers back into barbarous forms of labour and turns others into machines. It produces intelligence, but it produces idiocy and cretinism for the worker.

The direct relationship of labour to its products is the relationship of the worker to the objects of his production. The relationship of the rich man to the objects of production and to production itself is only a *consequence* of this first relationship, and confirms it. Later we shall consider this second aspect. Therefore when we ask what is the essential relationship of labour, we are asking about the relationship of the worker to production.

Up to now we have considered the estrangement, the alienation of the worker only from one aspect, i.e. his *relationship to the products of his labour*. But estrangement manifests itself not only in the result, but also in the *act of production*, within the *activity of production* itself. How could the product of the worker's activity confront him as something alien if it were not for the fact that in the act of production he was estranging himself from himself? After all, the product is simply the résumé of the activity, of the production. So if the product of labour is alienation, production itself must be active alienation, the alienation of activity, the activity of alienation. The estrangement of the object of labour merely summarizes the estrangement, the alienation in the activity of labour itself.

What constitutes the alienation of labour?

Firstly, the fact that labour is *external* to the worker, i.e. does not belong to his essential being; that he therefore does not confirm himself in his work, but denies himself, feels miserable and not happy, does not develop free mental and physical energy, but mortifies his flesh and ruins his mind. Hence the worker feels himself only when he is not working; when he is working he does not feel himself. He is at home when he is not working, and not at home when he is working. His labour is therefore not voluntary but forced, it is *forced labour*. It is therefore not the satisfaction of a need but a mere *means* to satisfy needs outside itself. Its alien character is clearly demonstrated by the fact that as soon as no physical or other compulsion exists it is shunned like the plague. External labour, labour in which man alienates himself, is a labour of self-sacrifice, of mortification. Finally, the external character of labour for the worker is demonstrated by the fact that it belongs not to him but to another, and that in it he belongs not to himself but to another. Just as in religion the spontaneous activity of the human imagination, the human brain and the human heart detaches itself from the individual and reappears as the alien activity of a god or of a devil, so the activity of the worker is not his own spontaneous activity. It belongs to another, it is a loss of his self.

The result is that man (the worker) feels that he is acting freely only in his animal functions—eating, drinking and procreating, or at most in his dwelling and adornment—while in his human functions he is nothing more than an animal.

It is true that eating, drinking and procreating, etc., are also genuine human functions. However, when abstracted from other aspects of human activity and turned into final and exclusive ends, they are animal.

We have considered the act of estrangement of practical human activity, of labour, from two aspects: (1) the relationship of the worker to the *product of labour* as an alien object that has power over him. This relationship is at the same time the relationship to the sensuous external world, to natural objects, as an alien world confronting him in hostile opposition. (2) The relationship of labour to the *act of production* within *labour*. This relationship is the relationship of the worker to his own activity as something which is alien and does not belong to him, activity as passivity [*Leiden*], power as impotence, procreation as emasculation, the worker's *own* physical and mental energy, his personal life—for what is life but activity?—as an activity directed against himself, which is independent of him and does not belong to him. *Self-estrangement*, as compared with the estrangement of the *object* [*Sache*] mentioned above.

We now have to derive a third feature of *estranged labour* from the two we have already looked at.

Man is a species-being, not only because he practically and theoretically makes the species—both his own and those of other things—his object, but also—and this is simply another way of saying the same thing—because he looks upon himself as the present, living species, because he looks upon himself as a *universal* and therefore free being.

Species-life, both for man and for animals, consists physically in the fact that man, like animals, lives from inorganic nature; and because man is more universal than animals, so too is the area of inorganic nature from which he lives more universal. Just as plants, animals, stones, air, light, etc., theoretically form a part of human consciousness, partly as objects of science and partly as objects of art—his spiritual inorganic nature, his spiritual means of life, which he must first prepare before he can enjoy and digest them—so too in practice they form a part of human life and human activity. In a physical sense man lives only from these natural products, whether in the form of nourishment, heating, clothing, shelter, etc. The universality of man manifests itself in practice in that universality which makes the whole of nature his *inorganic* body, (1) as a direct means of life and (2) as the matter, the object and the tool of his life activity. Nature is man's *inorganic body*, that is to say nature in so far as it is not the human body. Man *lives* from nature, i.e. nature is his *body*, and he must maintain a continuing dialogue with it if he is not to die. To say that man's physical and mental life is linked to nature simply means that nature is linked to itself, for man is a part of nature.

Estranged labour not only (1) estranges nature from man and (2) estranges man from himself, from his own active function, from his vital activity; because of this it also estranges man from his *species*. It turns his *species-life* into a means for his individual life. Firstly it estranges species-life and individual life, and secondly it turns the latter, in its abstract form, into the purpose of the former, also in its abstract and estranged form.

For in the first place labour, *life activity, productive life* itself appears to man only as a *means* for the satisfaction of a need, the need to preserve physical existence. But productive life is species-life. It is life-producing life. The whole character of a species, its species-character, resides in the nature of its life activity, and free conscious activity constitutes the species-character of man. Life itself appears only as a *means of life*.

The animal is immediately one with its life activity. It is not distinct from that activity; it *is* that activity. Man makes his life activity itself an object of his will and consciousness. He has conscious life activity. It is not a determination with which be directly merges. Conscious life activity directly distinguishes man from animal life activity. Only because of that is he a species-being. Or rather, he is a conscious being, i.e. his own life is an object for him, only because he is a species-being. Only because of that is his activity free activity. Estranged labour reverses the relationship so that man, just because he is a conscious being, makes his life activity, his *being* [*Wesen*], a mere means for his *existence*.

The practical creation of an *objective world*, the *fashioning* of inorganic nature, is proof that man is a conscious species-being, i.e. a being which treats the species as its own essential being or itself as a species-being. It is true that animals also produce. They build nests and dwellings, like the bee, the beaver, the ant, etc. But they produce only their own immediate needs or those of their young; they produce one-sidedly, while man produces universally; they produce only when immediate physical need compels them to do so, while man produces even when he is free from physical need and truly produces only in freedom from such need; they produce only themselves, while man reproduces the whole of nature; their products belong immediately to their physical bodies, while man freely confronts his own product. Animals produce only according to the standards and needs of the species to which they belong, while man is capable of producing according to the standards of every species and of applying to each object its inherent standard; hence man also produces in accordance with the laws of beauty.

It is therefore in his fashioning of the objective that man really proves himself to be a *species-being*. Such production is his active species-life. Through it nature appears as *his* work and his reality. The object of labour is therefore the *objectification of the species-life of man*: for man reproduces himself not only intellectually, in his consciousness, but actively and actually, and he can therefore contemplate himself in a world he himself has created. In tearing away the object of his production from man, estranged labour therefore tears away from him his *species-life*, his true species-objectivity, and transforms his advantage over animals into the disadvantage that his inorganic body, nature, is taken from him.

In the same way as estranged labour reduces spontaneous and free activity to a means, it makes man's species-life a means of his physical existence.

Consciousness, which man has from his species, is transformed through estrangement so that species-life becomes a means for him.

(3) Estranged labour therefore turns *man's species-being*—both nature and his intellectual species-powers—into a being *alien* to him and a *means* of his *individual existence*. It estranges man from his own body, from nature as it exists outside him, from his spiritual essence [*Wesen*], his *human* essence.

(4) An immediate consequence of man's estrangement from the product of his labour, his life activity, his species-being, is the *estrangement of man from man*. When man confronts himself, he also confronts *other* men. What is true of man's relationship to his labour, to the product of his labour and to himself, is also true of his relationship to other men, and to the labour and the object of the labour of other men.

In general, the proposition that man is estranged from his species-being means that each man is estranged from the others and that all are estranged from man's essence.

Man's estrangement, like all relationships of man to himself, is realized and expressed only in man's relationship to other men.

In the relationship of estranged labour each man therefore regards the other in accordance with the standard and the situation in which he as a worker finds himself.

We started out from an economic fact, the estrangement of the worker and of his production. We gave this fact conceptual form: *estranged, alienated* labour. We have analysed this concept, and in so doing merely analysed an economic fact.

Let us now go on to see how the concept of estranged, alienated labour must express and present itself in reality.

If the product of labour is alien to me and confronts me as an alien power, to whom does it then belong?

To a being *other* than me.

Who is this being?

The *gods*? It is true that in early times most production—e.g. temple building, etc., in Egypt, India and Mexico—was in the service of the gods, just as the product belonged to the gods. But the gods alone were never the masters of labour. The same is true of *nature*. And what a paradox it would be if the more man subjugates nature through his labour and the more divine miracles are made superfluous by the miracles of industry, the more he is forced to forgo the joy of production and the enjoyment of the product out of deference to these powers.

The *alien* being to whom labour and the product of labour belong, in whose service labour is performed and for whose enjoyment the product of labour is created, can be none other than *man* himself.

If the product of labour does not belong to the worker, and if it confronts him as an alien power, this is only possible because it belongs to *a man other than the worker*. If his activity is a torment for him, it must provide *pleasure* and enjoyment for someone else. Not the gods, not nature, but only man himself can be this alien power over men.

Consider the above proposition that the relationship of man to himself becomes *objective* and *real* for him only through his relationship to other men. If therefore he regards the product of his labour, his objectified labour, as an *alien, hostile* and powerful object which is independent of him, then his relationship to that object is such that another man—alien, hostile, powerful and independent of him—is its master. If he relates to his own activity as unfree activity, then he relates to it as activity in the service, under the rule, coercion and yoke of another man.

Every self-estrangement of man from himself and nature is manifested in the relationship he sets up between other men and himself and nature. Thus religious self-estrangement is necessarily manifested in the relationship between layman and priest, or, since we are here dealing with the spiritual world, between layman and mediator, etc. In the practical, real world, self-estrangement can manifest itself only in the practical, real relationship to other men. The medium through which estrangement progresses is itself a *practical* one. So through estranged labour man not only produces his relationship to the object and to the act of production as to alien and hostile powers; he also produces the relationship in which other men stand to his production and product, and the relationship in which he stands to these other men. Just as he creates his own production as a loss of reality, a punishment, and his own product as a loss, a product which does not belong to him, so he creates the domination of the non-producer over production and its product. Just as he estranges from himself his own activity, so he confers upon the stranger an activity which does not belong to him.

Up to now we have considered the relationship only from the side of the worker. Later on we shall consider it from the side of the non-worker.

Thus through *estranged, alienated labour* the worker creates the relationship of another man, who is alien to labour and stands outside it, to that labour. The relation of the worker to labour creates the relation of the capitalist—or whatever other word one chooses for the master of labour—to that labour. *Private property* is therefore the product, result and necessary consequence of *alienated labour*, of the external relation of the worker to nature and to himself.

Private property thus derives from an analysis of the concept of *alienated labour*, i.e. *alienated man*, estranged labour, estranged life, *estranged man*.

It is true that we took the concept of *alienated labour* (*alienated life*) from political economy as a result of the *movement of private property*. But it is clear from an analysis of this concept that, although private property appears as the basis and cause of alienated labour, it is in fact its consequence, just as the gods were *originally* not the cause but the effect of the confusion in men's minds. Later, however, this relationship becomes reciprocal.

It is only when the development of private property reaches its ultimate point of culmination that this its secret re-emerges; namely, that it is (a) the *product* of alienated labour and (b) the *means* through which labour is alienated, the *realization of this alienation*.

This development throws light upon a number of hitherto unresolved controversies.

(1) Political economy starts out from labour as the real soul of production, and yet gives nothing to labour and everything to private property. Proudhon has dealt with this contradiction by deciding for labour and against private property. But we have seen that this apparent contradiction is the contradiction of *estranged labour* with itself and that political economy has merely formulated the laws of estranged labour.

It therefore follows for us that *wages* and *private property* are identical: for where the product, the object of labour, pays for the labour itself, wages are only a necessary consequence of the estrangement of labour; similarly, where wages are concerned, labour appears not as an end in itself but as the servant of wages. We intend to deal with this point in more detail later on: for the present we shall merely draw a few conclusions.

An enforced *rise in wages* (disregarding all other difficulties, including the fact that such an anomalous situation could only be prolonged by force) would therefore be nothing more than better *pay for slaves* and would not mean an increase in human significance or dignity for either the worker or the labour.

Even the *equality of wages*, which Proudhon demands, would merely transform the relation of the present-day worker to his work into the relation of all men to work. Society would then be conceived as an abstract capitalist.

Wages are an immediate consequence of estranged labour, and estranged labour is the immediate cause of private property. If the one falls, then the other must fall too.

(2) It further follows from the relation of estranged labour to private property that the emancipation of society from private property, etc., from

servitude, is expressed in the *political* form of the *emancipation of the workers*. This is not because it is only a question of their emancipation, but because in their emancipation is contained universal human emancipation. The reason for this universality is that the whole of human servitude is involved in the relation of the worker to production, and all relations of servitude are nothing but modifications and consequences of this relation.

Just as we have arrived at the concept of *private property* through an *analysis* of the concept of *estranged, alienated labour*, so with the help of these two factors it is possible to evolve all economic *categories*, and in each of these categories, e.g. trade, competition, capital, money, we shall identify only a *particular* and *developed expression* of these basic constituents.

But before we go on to consider this configuration let us try to solve two further problems.

1. We have to determine the general *nature* of *private property*, as it has arisen out of estranged labour, in its relation to *truly human* and *social property*.
2. We have taken the *estrangement of labour*, its *alienation*, as a fact and we have analysed that fact. How, we now ask, does *man* come *to alienate his labour*, to estrange it? How is this estrangement founded in the nature of human development? We have already gone a long way towards solving this problem by *transforming* the question of the *origin* of *private property* into the question of the relationship of *alienated labour* to the course of human development. For in speaking of *private property* one imagines that one is dealing with something external to man. In speaking of labour one is dealing immediately with man himself. This new way of formulating the problem already contains its solution.

ad (1): The general nature of private property and its relationship to truly human property.

Alienated labour has resolved itself for us into two component parts which mutually condition one another, or which are merely different expressions of one and the same relationship. *Appropriation* appears as *estrangement*, as *alienation*; and *alienation* appears as *appropriation, estrangement* as true *admission to citizenship.*

We have considered the one aspect, *alienated* labour in relation to the *worker* himself, i.e. the *relation of alienated labour to itself.* And as product, as necessary consequence of this relationship we have found the *property relation of the non-worker* to the *worker and to labour*. Private property as the material, summarized expression of alienated labour embraces both relations— the *relation of the worker to labour and to the product of his labour and the non-worker* and the relation of the *non-worker to the worker* and to *the product of his labour.*

We have already seen that, in relation to the worker who *appropriates* nature through his labour, appropriation appears as estrangement, self-activity as activity for another and of another, vitality as a sacrifice of life, production of an object as loss of that object to an alien power, to an *alien* man. Let us now consider the relation between this man, who is *alien* to labour and to the worker, and the worker, labour, and the object of labour.

The first thing to point out is that everything which appears for the worker as an *activity of alienation, of estrangement,* appears for the non-worker as a *situation of alienation, of estrangement.*

Secondly, the *real, practical attitude* of the worker in production and to the product (as a state of mind) appears for the non-worker who confronts him as a *theoretical* attitude.

Thirdly, the non-worker does everything against the worker which the worker does against himself, but he does not do against himself what he does against the worker.

3 "Money" (from *Economic and Philosophical Manuscripts*)

If we assume man to be man, and his relation to the world to be a human one, then …

If man's *feelings*, passions, etc., are not merely anthropological characteristics in the narrower sense, but are truly *ontological* affirmations of his essence (nature), and if they only really affirm themselves in so far as their *object* exists *sensuously* for them, then it is clear:

1. That their mode of affirmation is by no means one and the same, but rather that the different modes of affirmation constitute the particular character of their existence, of their life. The mode in which the object exists for them is the characteristic mode of their *gratification*.
2. Where the sensuous affirmation is a direct annulment [*Aufheben*] of the object in its independent form (eating, drinking, fashioning of objects, etc.), this is the affirmation of the object.
3. In so far as man, and hence also his feelings, etc., are *human*, the affirmation of the object by another is also his own gratification.

4. Only through developed industry, i.e. through the mediation of private property, does the ontological essence of human passion come into being, both in its totality and in its humanity; the science of man is therefore itself a product of the self-formation of man through practical activity.
5. The meaning of private property, freed from its estrangement, is the *existence* of *essential objects* for man, both as objects of enjoyment and of activity.

Money, inasmuch as it possesses the *property* of being able to buy everything and appropriate all objects, is the *object* most worth possessing. The universality of this *property* is the basis of money's omnipotence; hence it is regarded as an omnipotent being . . . Money is the *pimp* between need and object, between life and man's means of life. But *that* which mediates *my* life also *mediates* the existence of other men for me. It is for me the *other* person.

> What, man! confound it, hands and feet
> And head and backside, all are yours!
> And what we take while life is sweet,
> Is that to be declared not ours?
> Six stallions, say, I can afford,
> Is not their strength my property?
> I tear along, a sporting lord,
> As if their legs belonged to me.

(Goethe, *Faust*—Mephistopheles)[2]

Shakespeare in *Timon of Athens*:

> Gold? Yellow, glittering, precious gold? No, gods,
> I am no idle votarist: roots, you clear heavens!
> Thus much of this will make black, white; foul, fair;
> Wrong, right; base, noble; old, young; coward, valiant.
> . . . Why, this
> Will lug your priests and servants from your sides;
> Pluck stout men's pillows from below their heads:
> This yellow slave
> Will knit and break religions; bless th'accurst;
> Make the hour leprosy adored; place thieves,
> And give them title, knee, and approbation,

---

[2] Part I, scene 4. Tr. P. Wayne, Harmondsworth, 1949.

With senators on the bench: this is it
That makes the wappen'd widow wed again;
She whom the spital-house and ulcerous sores
Would cast the gorge at, this embalms and spices
To th' April day again. Come, damned earth,
Thou common whore of mankind, that putt'st odds
Among the rout of nations, I will make thee
Do thy right nature.[3]

And later on:

O thou sweet king-killer, and dear divorce
'Twixt natural son and sire! Thou bright defiler
Of Hymen's purest bed! Thou valiant Mars!
Thou ever young, fresh, loved and delicate wooer,
Whose blush doth thaw the consecrated snow
That lies on Dian's lap! Thou *visible god,*
That solder'st close *impossibilities,*
And mak'st them kiss! That speak'st with every tongue,
To every purpose! O thou touch of hearts!
Think, thy slave man rebels; and by thy virtue
Set them into confounding odds, that beasts
May have the world in empire![4]

Shakespeare paints a brilliant picture of the nature of *money*. To understand him, let us begin by expounding the passage from Goethe.

That which exists for me through the medium of *money*, that which I can pay for, i.e. which money can buy, that *am I*, the possessor of the money. The stronger the power of my money, the stronger am I. The properties of money are my, the possessor's, properties and essential powers. Therefore what I *am* and what I *can do* is by no means determined by my individuality. I *am* ugly, but I can buy the *most beautiful* woman. Which means to say that I am not *ugly*, for the effect of *ugliness*, its repelling power, is destroyed by money. As an individual, I am *lame*, but money procures me twenty-four legs. Consequently, I am not lame. I am a wicked, dishonest, unscrupulous and stupid individual, but money is respected, and so also is its owner. Money is the highest good, and consequently its owner is also good. Moreover, money spares me the trouble of being dishonest, and I am therefore presumed to be

---

[3]   Act IV, scene 3.
[4]   ibid.

honest. I am *mindless*, but if money is the *true mind* of all things, how can its owner be mindless? What is more, he can buy clever people for himself, and is not he who has power over clever people cleverer than them? Through money I can have anything the human heart desires. Do I not therefore possess all human abilities? Does not money therefore transform all my incapacities into their opposite?

If *money* is the bond which ties me to *human* life and society to me, which links me to nature and to man, is money not the bond of all *bonds*? Can it not bind and loose all bonds? Is it therefore not the universal *means of separation*? It is the true *agent of separation* and the true *cementing agent*, it is the *chemical* power of society.

Shakespeare brings out two properties of money in particular:

1. It is the visible divinity, the transformation of all human and natural qualities into their opposites, the universal confusion and inversion of things; it brings together impossibilities.
2. It is the universal whore, the universal pimp of men and peoples.

The inversion and confusion of all human and natural qualities, the bringing together of impossibilities, the *divine* power of money lies in its *nature* as the estranged and alienating *species-essence* of man which alienates itself by selling itself. It is the alienated *capacity* of *mankind*.

What I as a man cannot do, i.e. what all my individual powers cannot do, I can do with the help of *money*. Money therefore transforms each of these essential powers into something which it is not, into its *opposite*.

If I desire a meal or want to take the mail coach because I am not strong enough to make the journey on foot, money can procure me both the meal and the mail coach, i.e. it transfers my wishes from the realm of imagination, it translates them from their existence as thought, imagination and desires into their *sensuous, real* existence, from imagination into life, and from imagined being into real being. In this mediating role money is the *truly creative* power.

Demand also exists for those who have no money, but their demand is simply a figment of the imagination. For me or for any other third party it has no effect, no existence. For me it therefore remains *unreal* and *without an object*. The difference between effective demand based on money and ineffective demand based on my need, my passion, my desire, etc., is the difference between *being* and *thinking*, between a representation which merely *exists* within me and one which exists outside me as a *real object*.

If I have no money for travel, I have no *need*, i.e. no real and self-realizing need, to travel. If I have a vocation to study, but no money for it, I have *no* vocation to study, i.e. no *real, true* vocation. But if I really do not have any vocation to study, but have the will *and* the money, then I have an *effective* vocation to do so. *Money*, which is the external, universal *means* and *power*—derived not from man as man and not from human society as society—to turn *imagination into reality* and *reality into mere imagination*, similarly turns *real human and natural powers* into purely abstract representations, and therefore *imperfections* and tormenting phantoms, just as it turns *real imperfections and phantoms*—truly impotent powers which exist only in the individual's fantasy—into *real essential powers* and *abilities*. Thus characterized, money is the universal inversion of *individualities*, which it turns into their opposites and to whose qualities it attaches contradictory qualities.

Money therefore appears as an *inverting* power in relation to the individual and to those social and other bonds which claim to be *essences* in themselves. It transforms loyalty into treason, love into hate, hate into love, virtue into vice, vice into virtue, servant into master, master into servant, nonsense into reason and reason into nonsense.

Since money, as the existing and active concept of value, confounds and exchanges everything, it is the universal *confusion* and *exchange* of all things, an inverted world, the confusion and exchange of all natural and human qualities.

He who can buy courage is brave, even if he is a coward. Money is not exchanged for a particular quality, a particular thing, or for any particular one of the essential powers of man, but for the whole objective world of man and of nature. Seen from the standpoint of the person who possesses it, money exchanges every quality for every other quality and object, even if it is contradictory; it is the power which brings together impossibilities and forces contradictions to embrace.

If we assume *man* to be *man*, and his relation to the world to be a human one, then love can be exchanged only for love, trust for trust, and so on. If you wish to enjoy art you must be an artistically educated person; if you wish to exercise influence on other men you must be the sort of person who has a truly stimulating and encouraging effect on others. Each one of your relations to man—and to nature—must be a *particular expression*, corresponding to the object of your will, of your *real individual* life. If you love unrequitedly, i.e. if your love as love does not call forth love in return, if through the *vital expression* of yourself as a loving person you fail to become a *loved person*, then your love is impotent, it is a misfortune.

Friedrich Nietzsche

German (1844-1900)

On Truth and Lies in a Nonmoral Sense (1873)

What then is truth? A moveable host of metaphors, metonymies,
and anthropomorphisms.

1

Once upon a time, in some out of the way corner of that universe which
is dispersed into numberless twinkling solar systems, there was a star
upon which clever beasts invented knowing. That was the most arrogant
and mendacious minute of "world history," but nevertheless, it was only
a minute. After nature had drawn a few breaths, the star cooled and
congealed, and the clever beasts had to die. —One might invent such a
fable, and yet he still would not have adequately illustrated how miserable,
how shadowy and transient, how aimless and arbitrary the human intellect
looks within nature. There were eternities during which it did not exist.
And when it is all over with the human intellect, nothing will have
happened. For this intellect has no additional mission which would lead it
beyond human life. Rather, it is human, and only its possessor and begetter
takes it so solemnly—as though the world's axis turned within it. But if we
could communicate with the gnat, we would learn that he likewise flies
through the air with the same solemnity, that he feels the flying center
of the universe within himself. There is nothing so reprehensible and
unimportant in nature that it would not immediately swell up like a balloon
at the slightest puff of this power of knowing. And just as every porter
wants to have an admirer, so even the proudest of men, the philosopher,
supposes that he sees on all sides the eyes of the universe telescopically
focused upon his action and thought.

It is remarkable that this was brought about by the intellect, which was certainly allotted to these most unfortunate, delicate, and ephemeral beings merely as a device for detaining them a minute within existence.

For without this addition they would have every reason to flee this existence as quickly as Lessing's son. The pride connected with knowing and sensing lies like a blinding fog over the eyes and senses of men, thus deceiving them concerning the value of existence. For this pride contains within itself the most flattering estimation of the value of knowing. Deception is the most general effect of such pride, but even its most particular effects contain within themselves something of the same deceitful character.

As a means for the preserving of the individual, the intellect unfolds its principle powers in dissimulation, which is the means by which weaker, less robust individuals preserve themselves—since they have been denied the chance to wage the battle for existence with horns or with the sharp teeth of beasts of prey. This art of dissimulation reaches its peak in man. Deception, flattering, lying, deluding, talking behind the back, putting up a false front, living in borrowed splendor, wearing a mask, hiding behind convention, playing a role for others and for oneself—in short, a continuous fluttering around the *solitary* flame of vanity—is so much the rule and the law among men that there is almost nothing which is less comprehensible than how an honest and pure drive for truth could have arisen among them. They are deeply immersed in illusions and in dream images; their eyes merely glide over the surface of things and see "forms." Their senses nowhere lead to truth; on the contrary, they are content to receive stimuli and, as it were, to engage in a groping game on the backs of things. Moreover, man permits himself to be deceived in his dreams every night of his life. His moral sentiment does not even make an attempt to prevent this, whereas there are supposed to be men who have stopped snoring through sheer will power. What does man actually know about himself? Is he, indeed, ever able to perceive himself completely, as if laid out in a lighted display case? Does nature not conceal most things from him—even concerning his own body—in order to confine and lock him within a proud, deceptive consciousness, aloof from the coils of the bowels, the rapid flow of the blood stream, and the intricate quivering of the fibers! She threw away the key. And woe to that fatal curiosity which might one day have the power to peer out and down through a crack in the chamber of consciousness and then suspect that man is sustained in the indifference of his ignorance by that which is pitiless, greedy, insatiable, and murderous—as if hanging in dreams on the back of a tiger. Given this situation, where in the world could the drive for truth have come from?

Insofar as the individual wants to maintain himself against other individuals, he will under natural circumstances employ the intellect mainly for dissimulation. But at the same time, from boredom and necessity, man wishes to exist socially and with the herd; therefore, he needs to make peace and strives accordingly to banish from his world at least the most flagrant *bellum omni contra omnes*. This peace treaty brings in its wake something which appears to be the first step toward acquiring that puzzling truth drive: to wit, *that* which shall count as "truth" from now on is established. That is to say, a uniformly valid and binding designation is invented for things, and this legislation of language likewise establishes the first laws of truth. For the contrast between truth and lie arises here for the first time. The liar is a person who uses the valid designations, the words, in order to make something which is unreal appear to be real. He says, for example, "I am rich," when the proper designation for his condition would be "poor." He misuses fixed conventions by means of arbitrary substitutions or even reversals of names. If he does this in a selfish and moreover harmful manner, society will cease to trust him and will thereby exclude him. What men avoid by excluding the liar is not so much being defrauded as it is being harmed by means of fraud. Thus, even at this stage, what they hate is basically not deception itself, but rather the unpleasant, hated consequences of certain sorts of deception. It is in a similarly restricted sense that man now wants nothing but truth: he desires the pleasant, life-preserving consequences of truth. He is indifferent toward pure knowledge which has no consequences; toward those truths which are possibly harmful and destructive he is even hostilely inclined. And besides, what about these linguistic conventions themselves? Are they perhaps products of knowledge, that is, of the sense of truth? Are designations congruent with things? Is language the adequate expression of all realities?

It is only by means of forgetfulness that man can ever reach the point of fancying himself to possess a "truth" of the grade just indicated. If he will not be satisfied with truth in the form of tautology, that is to say, if he will not be content with empty husks, then he will always exchange truths for illusions. What is a word? It is the copy in sound of a nerve stimulus. But the further inference from the nerve stimulus to a cause outside of us is already the result of a false and unjustifiable application of the principle of sufficient reason. If truth alone had been the deciding factor in the genesis of language, and if the standpoint of certainty had been decisive for designations, then how could we still dare to say "the stone is hard," as if "hard" were something otherwise familiar to us, and not merely a totally subjective stimulation! We separate things according to gender, designating the tree as masculine and the plant as feminine. What arbitrary assignments! How far this oversteps the canons of certainty! We speak of a "snake": this designation touches only upon its ability to twist itself and could therefore also fit a worm. What arbitrary

differentiations! What one-sided preferences, first for this, then for that
property of a thing! The various languages placed side by side show that with
words it is never a question of truth, never a question of adequate expression;
otherwise, there would not be so many languages.[1] The "thing in itself"
(which is precisely what the pure truth, apart from any of its consequences,
would be) is likewise something quite incomprehensible to the creator of
language and something not in the least worth striving for. This creator only
designates the relations of things to men, and for expressing these relations
he lays hold of the boldest metaphors. To begin with, a nerve stimulus is
transferred into an image: first metaphor. The image, in turn, is imitated in
a sound: second metaphor. And each time there is a complete overleaping of
one sphere, right into the middle of an entirely new and different one. One
can imagine a man who is totally deaf and has never had a sensation of sound
and music. Perhaps such a person will gaze with astonishment at Chladni's
sound figures; perhaps he will discover their causes in the vibrations of the
string and will now swear that he must know what men mean by "sound."
It is this way with all of us concerning language: we believe that we know
something about the things themselves when we speak of trees, colors,
snow, and flowers; and yet we possess nothing but metaphors for things—
metaphors which correspond in no way to the original entities. In the same
way that the sound appears as a sand figure, so the mysterious X of the thing
in itself first appears as a nerve stimulus, then as an image, and finally as a
sound. Thus the genesis of language does not proceed logically in any case,
and all the material within and with which the man of truth, the scientist, and
the philosopher later work and build, if not derived from never-never land, is
at least not derived from the essence of things.

   In particular, let us further consider the formation of concepts. Every
word instantly becomes a concept precisely insofar as it is not supposed to
serve as a reminder of the unique and entirely individual original experience
to which it owes its origin; but rather, a word becomes a concept insofar as it
simultaneously has to fit countless more or less similar cases—which means,
purely and simply, cases which are never equal and thus altogether unequal.
Every concept arises from the equation of unequal things. Just as it is certain
that one leaf is never totally the same as another, so it is certain that the
concept "leaf" is formed by arbitrarily discarding these individual differences
and by forgetting the distinguishing aspects. This awakens the idea that, in
addition to the leaves, there exists in nature the "leaf": the original model

[1]   What Nietzsche is rejecting here is the theory that there is a sort of "naturally appropriate"
     connection between certain words (or sounds) and things. Such a theory is defended by
     Socrates in Plato's *Cralylus*.

according to which all the leaves were perhaps woven, sketched, measured, colored, curled, and painted—but by incompetent hands, so that no specimen has turned out to be a correct, trustworthy, and faithful likeness of the original model. We call a person "honest," and then we ask "why has he behaved so honestly today?" Our usual answer is, "on account of his honesty." Honesty! This in turn means that the leaf is the cause of the leaves. We know nothing whatsoever about an essential quality called "honesty"; but we do know of countless individualized and consequently unequal actions which we equate by omitting the aspects in which they are unequal and which we now designate as "honest" actions. Finally we formulate from them a *qualitas occulta* which has the name "honesty." We obtain the concept, as we do the form, by overlooking what is individual and actual; whereas nature is acquainted with no forms and no concepts, and likewise with no species, but only with an X which remains inaccessible and undefinable for us. For even our contrast between individual and species is something anthropomorphic and does not originate in the essence of things; although we should not presume to claim that this contrast does not correspond to the essence of things: that would of course be a dogmatic assertion and, as such, would be just as indemonstrable as its opposite.

What then is truth? A movable host of metaphors, metonymies, and anthropomorphisms: in short, a sum of human relations which have been poetically and rhetorically intensified, transferred, and embellished, and which, after long usage, seem to a people to be fixed, canonical, and binding. Truths are illusions which we have forgotten are illusions; they are metaphors that have become worn out and have been drained of sensuous force, coins which have lost their embossing and are now considered as metal and no longer as coins.

We still do not yet know where the drive for truth comes from. For so far we have heard only of the duty which society imposes in order to exist: to be truthful means to employ the usual metaphors. Thus, to express it morally, this is the duty to lie according to a fixed convention, to lie with the herd and in a manner binding upon everyone. Now man of course forgets that this is the way things stand for him. Thus he lies in the manner indicated, unconsciously and in accordance with habits which are centuries' old; and precisely *by means of this unconsciousness* and forgetfulness he arrives at his sense of truth. From the sense that one is obliged to designate one thing as "red," another as "cold," and a third as "mute," there arises a moral impulse in regard to truth. The venerability, reliability, and utility of truth is something which a person demonstrates for himself from the contrast with the liar, whom no one trusts and everyone excludes. As a *"rational"* being, he now places his behavior under the control of abstractions. He will no longer tolerate being carried away by sudden impressions, by intuitions. First he universalizes all these impressions into less colorful, cooler concepts, so that he can entrust the guidance of his life and conduct to them. Everything which distinguishes man from the animals depends upon this ability to volatilize perceptual metaphors in a schema, and thus to dissolve an image into a concept. For something is possible in the realm of these schemata which could never be achieved with the vivid first impressions: the construction of a pyramidal order according to castes and degrees, the creation of a new world of laws, privileges, subordinations, and clearly marked boundaries—a new world, one which now confronts that other vivid world of first impressions as more solid, more universal, better known, and more human than the immediately perceived world, and thus as the regulative and imperative world. Whereas each perceptual metaphor is individual and without equals and is therefore able to elude all classification, the great edifice of concepts displays the rigid regularity of a Roman columbarium and exhales in logic that strength and coolness which is characteristic of mathematics. Anyone who has felt this cool breath [of logic] will hardly believe that even the concept—which is as bony, foursquare, and transposable as a die—is nevertheless merely the *residue of a metaphor*, and that the illusion which is involved in the artistic transference of a nerve stimulus into images is, if not the mother, then the grandmother of every single concept. But in this conceptual crap game "truth" means using every die in the designated manner, counting its spots accurately, fashioning the right categories, and never violating the order of caste and class rank. Just as the Romans and Etruscans cut up the heavens with rigid mathematical lines and confined a god within each of the spaces thereby delimited, as within a *templum*, so every people has a similarly mathematically divided conceptual heaven above themselves and henceforth thinks that truth demands that each conceptual god be sought only within *his own* sphere. Here one may certainly admire man as a mighty genius of construction, who succeeds in piling up an infinitely complicated dome of concepts upon an unstable foundation, and, as it were, on running water. Of course, in order to be supported by such a foundation, his construction must be like one constructed of spiders' webs: delicate enough to be carried along by the waves, strong enough not to be blown apart by every wind. As a genius of construction man raises himself far above the bee in the following way: whereas the bee builds with wax that he gathers from nature, man builds with the far more delicate conceptual material which he first has to manufacture from himself. In this he is greatly to be admired, but not on account of his drive for truth or for pure knowledge of things. When someone hides something behind a bush and looks for it again in the same place and finds it there as well, there is not much to praise in such seeking and finding. Yet this is how matters stand regarding seeking and finding "truth" within the realm of reason. If I make up the definition of a mammal, and then, after inspecting a camel, declare "look, a mammal," I have indeed brought a truth to light in this way, but it is a truth of limited value. That is to say, it is a thoroughly anthropomorphic truth which contains not a single point which would be "true in itself" or really and universally valid apart from man. At bottom, what the investigator of such truths is seeking is only the metamorphosis of the world into man. He strives to understand the world as something analogous to man, and at best he achieves by his struggles the feeling of assimilation. Similar to the way in which astrologers considered the stars to be in man's service and connected with his happiness and sorrow, such an investigator considers the entire universe in connection with man: the entire universe as the infinitely fractured echo of one original sound—man; the entire universe as the infinitely multiplied copy of one original picture— man. His method is to treat man as the measure of all things, but in doing so he again proceeds from the error of believing that he has these things [which he intends to measure] immediately before him as mere objects. He forgets that the original perceptual metaphors are metaphors and takes them to be the things themselves.

Only by forgetting this primitive world of metaphor can one live with any repose, security, and consistency: only by means of the petrification and coagulation of a mass of images which originally streamed from the primal faculty of human imagination like a fiery liquid, only in the invincible faith that *this* sun, *this* window, *this* table is a truth in itself, in short, only by forgetting that he himself is an *artistically creating* subject, does man live with any repose, security, and consistency. If but for an instant he could escape from the prison walls of this faith, his "self consciousness" would be immediately destroyed. It is even a difficult thing for him to admit to himself that the insect or the bird perceives an entirely different world from the one that man does, and that the question of which of these perceptions of the world is the more correct one is quite meaningless, for this would have to have been decided previously in accordance with the criterion of the *correct perception*, which means, in accordance with a criterion which is *not available*. But in any case it seems to me that "the correct perception"— which would mean "the adequate expression of an object in the subject"—is a contradictory impossibility. For between two absolutely different spheres, as between subject and object, there is no causality, no correctness, and no expression; there is, at most, an *aesthetic* relation: I mean, a suggestive transference, a stammering translation into a completely foreign tongue— for which there is required, in any case, a freely inventive intermediate sphere and mediating force. "Appearance" is a word that contains many temptations, which is why I avoid it as much as possible. For it is not true that the essence of things "appears" in the empirical world. A painter without hands who wished to express in song the picture before his mind would, by means of this substitution of spheres, still reveal more about the essence of things than does the empirical world. Even the relationship of a nerve stimulus to the generated image is not a necessary one. But when the same image has been generated millions of times and has been handed down for many generations and finally appears on the same occasion every time for all mankind, then it acquires at last the same meaning for men it would have if it were the sole necessary image and if the relationship of the original nerve stimulus to the generated image were a strictly causal one. In the same manner, an eternally repeated dream would certainly be felt and judged to be reality. But the hardening and congealing of a metaphor guarantees absolutely nothing concerning its necessity and exclusive justification.

Every person who is familiar with such considerations has no doubt felt a deep mistrust of all idealism of this sort: just as often as he has quite clearly convinced himself of the eternal consistency, omnipresence, and infallibility of the laws of nature. He has concluded that so far as we can penetrate here—from the telescopic heights to the microscopic depths—everything is secure, complete, infinite, regular, and without any gaps. Science will be able to dig successfully in this shaft forever, and all the things that are discovered will harmonize with and not contradict each other. How little does this resemble a product of the imagination, for if it were such, there should be some place where the illusion and unreality can be divined. Against this, the following must be said: if each of us had a different kind of sense perception—if we could only perceive things now as a bird, now as a worm, now as a plant, or if one of us saw a stimulus as red, another as blue, while a third even heard the same stimulus as a sound—then no one would speak of such a regularity of nature, rather, nature would be grasped only as a creation which is subjective in the highest degree. After all, what is a law of nature as such for us? We are not acquainted with it in itself, but only with its effects, which means in its relation to other laws of nature—which, in turn, are known to us only as sums of relations. Therefore all these relations always refer again to others and are thoroughly incomprehensible to us in their essence. All that we actually know about these laws of nature is what we ourselves bring to them—time and space, and therefore relationships of succession and number. But everything marvelous about the laws of nature, everything that quite astonishes us therein and seems to demand our explanation, everything that might lead us to distrust idealism: all this is completely and solely contained within the mathematical strictness and inviolability of our representations of time and space. But we produce these representations in and from ourselves with the same necessity with which the spider spins. If we are forced to comprehend all things only under these forms, then it ceases to be amazing that in all things we actually comprehend nothing but these forms. For they must all bear within themselves the laws of number, and it is precisely number which is most astonishing in things. All that conformity to law, which impresses us so much in the movement of the stars and in chemical processes, coincides at bottom with those properties which we bring to things. Thus it is we who impress ourselves in this way. In conjunction with this, it of course follows that the artistic process of metaphor formation with which every sensation begins in us already presupposes these forms and thus occurs within them. The only way in which the possibility of subsequently constructing a new conceptual edifice from metaphors themselves can be explained is by the firm persistence of these original forms. That is to say, this conceptual edifice is an imitation of temporal, spatial, and numerical relationships in the domain of metaphor.

2

We have seen how it is originally *language* which works on the construction of concepts, a labor taken over in later ages by *science*. Just as the bee simultaneously constructs cells and fills them with honey, so science works unceasingly on this great columbarium of concepts, the graveyard of perceptions. It is always building new, higher stories and shoring up, cleaning, and renovating the old cells; above all, it takes pains to fill up this monstrously towering framework and to arrange therein the entire empirical world, which is to say, the anthropomorphic world. Whereas the man of action binds his life to reason and its concepts so that he will not be swept away and lost, the scientific investigator builds his hut right next to the tower of science so that he will be able to work on it and to find shelter for himself beneath those bulwarks which presently exist. And he requires shelter, for there are frightful powers which continuously break in upon him, powers which oppose scientific "truth" with completely different kinds of "truths" which bear on their shields the most varied sorts of emblems.

The drive toward the formation of metaphors is the fundamental human drive, which one cannot for a single instant dispense with in thought, for one would thereby dispense with man himself. This drive is not truly vanquished and scarcely subdued by the fact that a regular and rigid new world is constructed as its prison from its own ephemeral products, the concepts. It seeks a new realm and another channel for its activity, and it finds this in *myth* and in *art* generally. This drive continually confuses the conceptual categories and cells by bringing forward new transferences, metaphors, and metonymies. It continually manifests an ardent desire to refashion the world which presents itself to waking man, so that it will be as colorful, irregular, lacking in results and coherence, charming, and eternally new as the world of dreams. Indeed, it is only by means of the rigid and regular web of concepts that the waking man clearly sees that he is awake; and it is precisely because of this that he sometimes thinks that he must be dreaming when this web of concepts is torn by art. Pascal is right in maintaining that if the same dream came to us every night we would be just as occupied with it as we are with the things that we see every day. "If a workman were sure to dream for twelve straight hours every night that he was king," said Pascal, "I believe that he would be just as happy as a king who dreamt for twelve hours every night that he was a workman."[2] In fact, because of the way that myth takes it for granted that miracles are always happening, the waking life of a mythically inspired people—the ancient Greeks, for instance—more closely resembles a dream than it does the waking world of a scientifically disenchanted thinker. When every tree can suddenly speak as a nymph, when a god in the shape of a bull can drag away maidens, when even the goddess Athena herself is suddenly seen in the company of Peisastratus driving through the market place of Athens with a beautiful team of horses—and this is what the honest Athenian believed—then, as in a dream, anything is possible at each moment, and all of nature swarms around man as if it were nothing but a masquerade of the gods, who were merely amusing themselves by deceiving men in all these shapes.

But man has an invincible inclination to allow himself to be deceived and is, as it were, enchanted with happiness when the rhapsodist tells him epic fables as if they were true, or when the actor in the theater acts more royally than any real king. So long as it is able to deceive without *injuring*, that master of deception, the intellect, is free; it is released from its former slavery and celebrates its Saturnalia. It is never more luxuriant, richer, prouder, more clever and more daring. With creative pleasure it throws metaphors into confusion and displaces the boundary stones of abstractions, so that, for example, it designates the stream as "the moving path which carries man where he would otherwise walk." The intellect has now thrown the token of bondage from itself. At other times it endeavors, with gloomy officiousness, to show the way and to demonstrate the tools to a poor individual who covets existence; it is like a servant who goes in search of booty and prey for his master. But now it has become the master and it dares to wipe from its face the expression of indigence. In comparison with its previous conduct, everything

---

[2] *Pensées*, number 386. Actually, Pascal says that the workman would be "almost as happy" as the king in this case!

that it now does bears the mark of dissimulation, just as that previous conduct did of distortion. The free intellect copies human life, but it considers this life to be something good and seems to be quite satisfied with it. That immense framework and planking of concepts to which the needy man clings his whole life long in order to preserve himself is nothing but a scaffolding and toy for the most audacious feats of the liberated intellect. And when it smashes this framework to pieces, throws it into confusion, and puts it back together in an ironic fashion, pairing the most alien things and separating the closest, it is demonstrating that it has no need of these makeshifts of indigence and that it will now be guided by intuitions rather than by concepts. There is no regular path which leads from these intuitions into the land of ghostly schemata, the land of abstractions. There exists no word for these intuitions; when man sees them he grows dumb, or else he speaks only in forbidden metaphors and in unheard of combinations of concepts. He does this so that by shattering and mocking the old conceptual barriers he may at least correspond creatively to the impression of the powerful present intuition.

There are ages in which the rational man and the intuitive man stand side by side, the one in fear of intuition, the other with scorn for abstraction. The latter is just as irrational as the former is inartistic. They both desire to rule over life: the former, by knowing how to meet his principle needs by means of foresight, prudence, and regularity; the latter, by disregarding these needs and, as an "overjoyed hero," counting as real only that life which has been disguised as illusion and beauty. Whenever, as was perhaps the case in ancient Greece, the intuitive man handles his weapons more authoritatively and victoriously than his opponent, then, under favorable circumstances, a culture can take shape and art's mastery over life can be established. All the manifestations of such a life will be accompanied by this dissimulation, this disavowal of indigence, this glitter of metaphorical intuitions, and, in general, this immediacy of deception: neither the house, nor the gait, nor the clothes, nor the clay jugs give evidence of having been invented because of a pressing need. It seems as if they were all intended to express an exalted happiness, an Olympian cloudlessness, and, as it were, a playing with seriousness. The man who is guided by concepts and abstractions only succeeds by such means in warding off misfortune, without ever gaining any happiness for himself from these abstractions. And while he aims for the greatest possible freedom from pain, the intuitive man, standing in the midst of a culture, already reaps from his intuition a harvest of continually inflowing illumination, cheer, and redemption—in addition to obtaining a defense against misfortune. To be sure, he suffers more intensely, *when* he suffers; he even suffers more frequently, since he does not understand how to learn from experience and keeps falling over and over again into the same ditch. He is then just as irrational in sorrow as he is in happiness: he cries aloud and will not be consoled. How differently the stoical man who learns from experience and governs himself by concepts is affected by the same misfortunes! This man, who at other times seeks nothing but sincerity, truth, freedom from deception, and protection against ensnaring surprise attacks, now executes a masterpiece of deception: he executes his masterpiece of deception in misfortune, as the other type of man executes his in times of happiness. He wears no quivering and changeable human face, but, as it were, a mask with dignified, symmetrical features. He does not cry; he does not even alter his voice. When a real storm cloud thunders above him, he wraps himself in his cloak, and with slow steps he walks from beneath it.

Ferdinand de Saussure

Swiss (1857-1913)

The Sign Considered in Its Totality (1916)

Putting it another way, language is a form and not a substance. This truth could not be overstressed.

Everything that has been said up to this point boils down to this: in language there are only differences. Even more important: a difference generally implies positive terms between which the difference is set up; but in language there are only differences *without positive terms*. Whether we take the signified or the signifier, language has neither ideas nor sounds that existed before the linguistic system, but only conceptual and phonic differences that have issued from the system. The idea or phonic substance that a sign contains is of less importance than the other signs that surround it. Proof of this is that the value of a term may be modified without either its meaning or its sound being affected, solely because a neighboring term has been modified.

But the statement that everything in language is negative is true only if the signified and the signifier are considered separately; when we consider the sign in its totality, we have something that is positive in its own class. A linguistic system is a series of differences of sound combined with a series of differences of ideas; but the pairing of a certain number of acoustical signs with as many cuts made from the mass of thought engenders a system of values; and this system serves as the effective link between the phonic and psychological elements within each sign. Although both the signified and the signifier are purely differential and negative when considered separately, their combination is a positive fact; it is even the sole type of facts that language has, for maintaining the parallelism between the two classes of differences is the distinctive function of the linguistic institution.

Certain diachronic facts are typical in this respect. Take the countless instances where alteration of the signifier occasions a conceptual change and where it is obvious that the sum of the ideas distinguished corresponds in principle to the sum of the distinctive signs. When two words are confused through phonetic alteration (e.g. French *décrépit* from *dēcrepitus* and *décrépi* from *crispus*), the ideas that they express will also tend to become confused if only they have something in common. Or a word may have different forms (cf. *chaise* 'chair' and *chaire* 'desk'). Any nascent difference will tend invariably to become significant but without always succeeding or being successful on the first trial. Conversely, any conceptual difference perceived by the mind seeks to find expression through a distinct signifier, and two ideas that are no longer distinct in the mind tend to merge into the same signifier.

When we compare signs—positive terms—with each other, we can no longer speak of difference; the expression would not be fitting, for it applies only to the comparing of two sound-images, e.g. *father* and *mother*, or two ideas, e.g. the idea "father" and the idea "mother"; two signs, each having a signified and signifier, are not different but only distinct. Between them there is only *opposition*. The entire mechanism of language, with which we shall be concerned later, is based on oppositions of this kind and on the phonic and conceptual differences that they imply.

What is true of value is true also of the unit. A unit is a segment of the spoken chain that corresponds to a certain concept; both are by nature purely differential.

Applied to units, the principle of differentiation can be stated in this way: *the characteristics of the unit blend with the unit itself.* In language, as in any semiological system, whatever distinguishes one sign from the others constitutes it. Difference makes character just as it makes value and the unit.

Another rather paradoxical consequence of the same principle is this: in the last analysis what is commonly referred to as a "grammatical fact" fits the definition of the unit, for it always expresses an opposition of terms; it differs only in that the opposition is particularly significant (e.g. the formation of German plurals of the type *Nacht: Nächte*). Each term present in the grammatical fact (the singular without umlaut or final *e* in opposition to the plural with umlaut and *-e*) consists of the interplay of a number of oppositions within the system. When isolated, neither *Nacht* nor *Nächte* is anything: thus everything is opposition. Putting it another way, the *Nacht: Nächte* relation can be expressed by an algebraic formula *a/b* in which *a* and *b* are not simple terms but result from a set of relations. Language, in a manner of speaking, is a type of algebra consisting solely of complex terms. Some of its oppositions are more significant than others; but units and grammatical facts are only different names for designating diverse aspects of the same general fact: the functioning of linguistic oppositions. This statement is so true that we might very well approach the problem of units by starting from grammatical facts. Taking an opposition like *Nacht: Nächte*, we might ask what are the units involved in it. Are they only the two words, the whole series of similar words, *a* and *ä,* or all singulars and plurals, etc.?

Units and grammatical facts would not be confused if linguistic signs were made up of something besides differences. But language being what it is, we shall find nothing simple in it regardless of our approach; everywhere and always there is the same complex equilibrium of terms that mutually condition each other. Putting it another way, *language is a form and not a substance.* This truth could not be overstressed, for all the mistakes in our terminology, all our incorrect ways of naming things that pertain to language, stem from the involuntary supposition that the linguistic phenomenon must have substance.

Viktor Shklovsky

Russian (1893-1984)

Art as Technique (1917)

Art is a way of experiencing the artfulness of an object;
the object is not important.

"Art is thinking in images." This maxim, which even high school students parrot, is nevertheless the starting point for the erudite philologist who is beginning to put together some kind of systematic literary theory. The idea, originated in part by Potebnya, has spread. "Without imagery there is no art, and in particular no poetry," Potebnya writes.[1] And elsewhere, "Poetry, as well as prose, is first and foremost a special way of thinking and knowing."[2]

Poetry is a special way of thinking; it is, precisely, a way of thinking in images, a way which permits what is generally called "economy of mental effort," a way which makes for "a sensation of the relative case of the process." Aesthetic feeling is the reaction to this economy. This is how the academician Ovsyaniko-Kulikovsky,[3] who undoubtedly read the works of Potebnya attentively, almost certainly understood and faithfully summarized the ideas of his teacher. Potebnya and his numerous disciples consider poetry a special kind of thinking—thinking by means of images; they feel that the purpose of imagery is to help channel various objects and activities into groups and to clarify the unknown by means of the known. Or, as Potebnya wrote:

The relationship of the image to what is being clarified is that: (a) the image is the fixed predicate of that which undergoes change—the

---

[1] Alexander Potcbnya, *tz zapisok po teorli stovesnosti* [*Notes on the Theory of Language*] (Kharkov, 1905), p. 83.

[2] *Ibid.*, p. 97.

[3] Dmitry Ovsyaniko-Kulikovsky (1835–1920), a leading Russian scholar, was an early contributor to Marxist periodicals and a literary conservative, antagonistic towards the deliberately meaningless poems of the Futurists. *Ed. note.*

unchanging means of attracting what is perceived as changeable. . . . (b) the image is far clearer and simpler than what it clarifies.[4]

In other words:

> Since the purpose of imagery is to remind us, by approximation, of those meanings for which the image stands, and since, apart from this, imagery is unnecessary for thought, we must be more familiar with the image than with what it clarifies.[5]

It would be instructive to try to apply this principle to Tyutchev's comparison of summer lightning to deaf and dumb demons or to Gogol's comparison of the sky to the garment of God.[6]

"Without imagery there is no art"—"Art is thinking in images." These maxims have led to far-fetched interpretations of individual works of art. Attempts have been made to evaluate even music, architecture, and lyric poetry as imagistic thought. After a quarter of a century of such attempts Ovsyaniko-Kulikovsky finally had to assign lyric poetry, architecture, and music to a special category of imageless art and to define them as lyric arts appealing directly to the emotions. And thus he admitted an enormous area of art which is not a mode of thought. A part of this area, lyric poetry (narrowly considered), is quite like the visual arts; it is also verbal. But, much more important, visual art passes quite imperceptibly into nonvisual art; yet our perceptions of both are similar.

Nevertheless, the definition "Art is thinking in images," which means (I omit the usual middle terms of the argument) that art is the making of symbols, has survived the downfall of the theory which supported it. It survives chiefly in the wake of Symbolism, especially among the theorists of the Symbolist movement.

Many still believe, then, that thinking in images—thinking in specific scenes of "roads and landscape" and "furrows and boundaries"[7]—is the chief characteristic of poetry. Consequently, they should have expected the history of "imagistic art," as they call it, to consist of a history of changes in imagery.

---

[4] Potebnya, *Iz zapisok po teorii slovesnosti*, p. 314.

[5] *Ibid.*, p. 291.

[6] Fyodor Tyutchev (1803–73), a poet, and Nicholas Gogol (1809–52), a master of prose fiction and satire, are mentioned here because their bold use of imagery cannot be accounted for by Potebnya's theory. Shklovsky is arguing that writers frequently gain their effects by comparing the commonplace to the exceptional rather than vice versa. *Ed. note.*

[7] This is an allusion to Vyacheslav Ivanov's *Borozdy i mezhi* [*Furrows and Boundaries*] (Moscow, 1916), a major statement of Symbolist theory. *Ed. note.*

But we find that images change little; from century to century, from nation to nation, from poet to poet, they flow on without changing. Images belong to no one: they are "the Lord's." The more you understand an age, the more convinced you become that the images a given poet used and which you thought his own were taken almost unchanged from another poet. The works of poets are classified or grouped according to the new techniques that poets discover and share, and according to their arrangement and development of the resources of language; poets are much more concerned with arranging images than with creating them. Images are given to poets; the ability to remember them is far more important than the ability to create them.

Imagistic thought does not, in any case, include all the aspects of art nor even all the aspects of verbal art. A change in imagery is not essential to the development of poetry. We know that frequently an expression is thought to be poetic, to be created for aesthetic pleasure, although actually it was created without such intent—e.g., Annensky's opinion that the Slavic languages are especially poetic and Andrey Bely's ecstasy over the technique of placing adjectives after nouns, a technique used by eighteenth-century Russian poets. Bely joyfully accepts the technique as something artistic, or more exactly, as intended, if we consider intention as art. Actually, this reversal of the usual adjective-noun order is a peculiarity of the language (which had been influenced by Church Slavonic). Thus a work may be (1) intended as prosaic and accepted as poetic, or (2) intended as poetic and accepted as prosaic. This suggests that the artistry attributed to a given work results from the way we perceive it. By "works of art," in the narrow sense, we mean works created by special techniques designed to make the works as obviously artistic as possible.

Potebnya's conclusion, which can be formulated "poetry equals imagery," gave rise to the whole theory that "imagery equals symbolism," that the image may serve as the invariable predicate of various subjects. (This conclusion, because it expressed ideas similar to the theories of the Symbolists, intrigued some of their leading representatives—Andrey Bely, Merezhkovsky and his "eternal companions" and, in fact, formed the basis of the theory of Symbolism.) The conclusion stems partly from the fact that Potebnya did not distinguish between the language of poetry and the language of prose. Consequently, he ignored the fact that there are two aspects of imagery: imagery as a practical means of thinking, as a means of placing objects within categories; and imagery as poetic, as a means of reinforcing an impression. I shall clarify with an example. I want to attract the attention of a young child who is eating bread and butter and getting the butter on her fingers. I call, "Hey, butterfingers!" This is a figure of speech, a clearly prosaic trope. Now a different example. The child is playing with my glasses and drops them. I call, "Hey, butterfingers!"[8] This figure of speech is a poetic trope. (In the first example, "butterfingers" is metonymic; in the second, metaphoric—but this is not what I want to stress.)

Poetic imagery is a means of creating the strongest possible impression. As a method it is, depending upon its purpose, neither more nor less effective than other poetic techniques; it is neither more nor less effective than ordinary or negative parallelism, comparison, repetition, balanced structure, hyperbole, the commonly accepted rhetorical figures, and all those methods which emphasize the emotional effect of an expression (including words or even articulated sounds).[9] But poetic imagery only externally resembles either the stock imagery of tables and ballads or thinking in images—e.g., the example in Ovsyaniko-Kulikovsky's *Language and Art* in which a little girl calls a ball a little watermelon. Poetic imagery is but one of the devices of poetic language. Prose imagery is a means of abstraction: a little watermelon instead of a lampshade, or a little watermelon instead of a head, is only the abstraction of one of the object's characteristics, that of roundness. It is no different from saying that the head and the melon are both round. This is what is meant, but it has nothing to do with poetry.

The law of the economy of creative effort is also generally accepted. [Herbert] Spencer wrote:

> On seeking for some clue to the law underlying these current maxims, we may see shadowed forth in many of them, the importance of economizing the reader's or the hearer's attention. To so present ideas that they may he apprehended with the least possible mental effort, is the desideratum towards which most of the rules above quoted point. . . . Hence, carrying out the metaphor that language is the vehicle of thought, there seems reason to think that in all cases the friction and inertia of the vehicle deduct from its efficiency; and that in composition, the chief, if not the sole thing to be done, is to reduce this friction and inertia to the smallest possible amount.[10]

---

[8] The Russian text involves a play on the word for "hat," colloquial for "clod," "duffer," etc. *Ed. note.*

[9] Shklovsky is here doing two things of major theoretical importance; (1) he argues that different techniques serve a single function, and that (2) no single technique is all-important. The second permits the Formalists to be concerned with any and all literary devices; the first permits them to discuss the devices from a single consistent theoretical position. *Ed. note.*

[10] Herbert Spencer, *The Philosophy of Style* [(Humboldt Library, Vol. XXXIV; New York, 1882), pp. 2–3. Shklovsky's quoted reference, in Russian, preserves the idea of the original but shortens it].

And R[ichard] Avenarius:

> If a soul possess inexhaustible strength, then, of course, it would
> be indifferent to how much might be spent from this inexhaustible
> source; only the necessarily expended time would be important. But
> since its forces are limited, one is led to expect that the soul hastens to
> carry out the apperceptive process as expediently as possible—that is,
> with comparatively the least expenditure of energy, and, hence, with
> comparatively the best result.

Petrazhitsky, with only one reference to the general law of mental effort,
rejects [William] James's theory of the physical basis of emotion, a theory
which contradicts his own. Even Alexander Veselovsky acknowledged the
principle of the economy of creative effort, a theory especially appealing
in the study of rhythm, and agreed with Spencer: "A satisfactory style is
precisely that style which delivers the greatest amount of thought in the
fewest words." And Andrey Bely, despite the fact that in his better pages
he gave numerous examples of "roughened" rhythm[11] and (particularly in
the examples from Baratynsky) showed the difficulties inherent in poetic
epithets, also thought it necessary to speak of the law of the economy of
creative effort in his book[12]—a heroic effort to create a theory of art based
on unverified facts from antiquated sources, on his vast knowledge of the
techniques of poetic creativity, and on Krayevich's high school physics
text.

These ideas about the economy of energy, as well as about the law
and aim of creativity, are perhaps true in their application to "practical"
language; they were, however, extended to poetic language. Hence they
do not distinguish properly between the laws of practical language and
the laws of poetic language. The fact that Japanese poetry has sounds not
found in conversational Japanese was hardly the first factual indication of
the differences between poetic and everyday language. Leo Jakubinsky has
observed that the law of the dissimilation of liquid sounds does not apply
to poetic language.[13] This suggested to him that poetic language tolerated
the admission of hard-to-pronounce conglomerations of similar sounds.
In his article, one of the first examples of scientific criticism, he indicates

[11] The Russian *zatrudyonny* means "made difficult." The suggestion is that poems with "easy" or smooth rhythms slip by unnoticed; poems that are difficult or "roughened" force the reader to attend to them. *Ed. note.*

[12] *Simvolizm*, probably. *Ed. note.*

[13] Leo Jakubinsky, "O zvukakh poeticheskovo yazyka" ["On the Sounds of Poetic Language"], *Shorniki*, 1 (1916), p. 38.

inductively the contrast (I shall say more about this point later) between the laws of poetic language and the laws of practical language.[14]

We must, then, speak about the laws of expenditure and economy in poetic language not on the basis of an analogy with prose, but on the basis of the laws of poetic language.

If we start to examine the general laws of perception, we see that as perception becomes habitual, it becomes automatic. Thus, for example, all of our habits retreat into the area of the unconsciously automatic; if one remembers the sensations of holding a pen or of speaking in a foreign language for the first time and compares that with his feeling at performing the action for the ten thousandth time, he will agree with us. Such habituation explains the principles by which, in ordinary speech, we leave phrases unfinished and words half expressed. In this process, ideally realized in algebra, things are replaced by symbols. Complete words are not expressed in rapid speech; their initial sounds are barely perceived. Alexander Pogodin offers the example of a boy considering the sentence "The Swiss mountains are beautiful" in the form of a series of letters: *T, S, m, a, b*.[15]

This characteristic of thought not only suggests the method of algebra, but even prompts the choice of symbols (letters, especially initial letters). By this "algebraic" method of thought we apprehend objects only as shapes with imprecise extensions; we do not see them in their entirety but rather recognize them by their main characteristics. We see the object as though it were enveloped in a sack. We know what it is by its configuration, but we see only its silhouette. The object, perceived thus in the manner of prose perception, fades and does not leave even a first impression; ultimately even the essence of what it was is forgotten. Such perception explains why we fail to hear the prose word in its entirety (see Leo Jakubinsky's article[16]) and, hence, why (along with other slips of the tongue) we fail to pronounce it. The process of "algebrization," the over-automatization of an object, permits the greatest economy of perceptive effort. Either objects are assigned only one proper feature—a number, for example—or else they function as though by formula and do not even appear in cognition:

---

[14] Leo Jakubinsky, "Skopleniye odinakovykh plavnykh v prakticheskom i poeticheskom yazykakh" ["The Accumulation of Identical Liquids in Practical and Poetic Language"], *Sborniki*, 11(1917), pp. 13–21.

[15] Alexander Pogodin, *Yazyk, kak trorchestvo [Language as Art]* (Kharkov, 1913), p. 42. [The original sentence was in French, *"Les montaignes de la Suisse sont belles,"* with the appropriate initials.]

[16] Jakubinsky, *Sborniki*, I (1916).

I was cleaning a room and, meandering about, approached the divan and couldn't remember whether or not I had dusted it. Since these movements are habitual and unconscious, I could not remember and felt that it was impossible to remember—so that if I had dusted it and forgot—that is, had acted unconsciously, then it was the same as if I had not. If some conscious person had been watching, then the fact could be established. If, however, no one was looking, or looking on unconsciously, if the whole complex lives of many people go on unconsciously, then such lives are as if they had never been.[17]

And so life is reckoned as nothing. Habitualization devours works, clothes, furniture, one's wife, and the fear of war. "If the whole complex lives of many people go on unconsciously, then such lives are as if they had never been." And art exists that one may recover the sensation of life; it exists to make one feel things, to make the stone *stony*. The purpose of art is to impart the sensation of things as they are perceived and not as they are known. The technique of art is to make objects "unfamiliar," to make forms difficult, to increase the difficulty and length of perception because the process of perception is an aesthetic end in itself and must be prolonged. *Art is a way of experiencing the artfulness of an object; the object is not important.*

The range of poetic (artistic) work extends from the sensory to the cognitive, from poetry to prose, from the concrete to the abstract: from Cervantes's Don Quixote—scholastic and poor nobleman, half consciously bearing his humiliation in the court of the duke—to the broad but empty Don Quixote of Turgenev; from Charlemagne to the name "king" [in Russian "Charles" and "king" obviously derive from the same root, *korol*]. The meaning of a work broadens to the extent that artfulness and artistry diminish; thus a fable symbolizes more than a poem, and a proverb more than a fable. Consequently, the least self-contradictory part of Potebnya's theory is his treatment of the fable, which, from his point of view, he investigated thoroughly. But since his theory did not provide for "expressive" works of art, he could not finish his book. As we know, *Notes on the Theory of Literature* was published in 1905, thirteen years after Potebnya's death. Potebnya himself completed only the section on the table.[18]

After we see an object several times, we begin to recognize it. The object is in front of us and we know about it, but we do not see it[19]—hence we cannot

17 Leo Tolstoy's *Diary*, entry dated February 29, 1897. [The date is transcribed incorrectly; it should read March 1, 1897.]
18 Alexander Potcbnya, *lz lektsy po teorii sloresnosti* [*Lectures on the Theory of Language*] (Kharkov, 1914).
19 Viktor Shklovsky, *Voskreshentye slova* [*The Resurrection of the Word*] (Petersburg, 1914).

say anything significant about it. Art removes objects from the automatism of perception in several ways. Here I want to illustrate a way used repeatedly by Leo Tolstoy, that writer who, for Merezhkovsky at least, seems to present things as if he himself saw them, saw them in their entirety, and did not alter them.

Tolstoy makes the familiar seem strange by not naming the familiar object. He describes an object as if he were seeing it for the first time, an event as if it were happening for the first time. In describing something he avoids the accepted names of its parts and instead names corresponding parts of other objects. For example, in "Shame" Tolstoy "defamiliarizes" the idea of flogging in this way: "to strip people who have broken the law, to hurl them to the floor, and to rap on their bottoms with switches," and, after a few lines, "to lash about on the naked buttocks." Then he remarks:

> Just why precisely this stupid, savage means of causing pain and not any other—why not prick the shoulders or any part of the body with needles, squeeze the hands or the feet in a vise, or anything like that?

I apologize for this harsh example, but it is typical of Tolstoy's way of pricking the conscience. The familiar act of flogging is made unfamiliar both by the description and by the proposal to change its form without changing its nature. Tolstoy uses this technique of "defamiliarization" constantly. The narrator of "Kholstomer," for example, is a horse, and it is the horse's point of view (rather than a person's) that makes the content of the story seem unfamiliar. Here is how the horse regards the institution of private property:

> I understood well what they said about whipping and Christianity. But then I was absolutely in the dark. What's the meaning of "his own," "his colt"? From these phrases I saw that people thought there was some sort of connection between me and the stable. At the time I simply could not understand the connection. Only much later, when they separated me from the other horses, did I begin to understand. But even then I simply could not see what it meant when they called me "man's property." The words "my horse" referred to me, a living horse, and seemed as strange to me as the words "my land," "my air," "my water."
>
> But the words made a strong impression on me. I thought about them constantly, and only after the most diverse experiences with people did I understand, finally, what they meant. They meant this: In life people are guided by words, not by deeds. It's not so much that they love the possibility of doing or not doing something as it is the possibility of speaking with words, agreed on among themselves, about various topics. Such are the words "my" and "mine," which they apply to different things,

creatures, objects, and even to land, people, and horses. They agree that only one may say "mine" about this, that, or the other thing. And the one who says "mine" about the greatest number of things is, according to the game which they've agreed to among themselves, the one they consider the most happy. I don't know the point of all this, but it's true. For a long time I tried to explain it to myself in terms of some kind of real gain, but I had to reject that explanation because it was wrong.

Many of those, for instance, who called me their own never rode on me—although others did. And so with those who fed me. Then again, the coachman, the veterinarians, and the outsiders in general treated me kindly, yet those who called me their own did not. In due time, having widened the scope of my observations, I satisfied myself that the notion "my," not only in relation to us horses, has no other basis than a narrow human instinct which is called a sense of or right to private property. A man says "this house is mine" and never lives in it; he only worries about its construction and upkeep. A merchant says "my shop," "my dry goods shop," for instance, and does not even wear clothes made from the better cloth he keeps in his own shop.

There are people who call a tract of land their own, but they never set eyes on it and never take a stroll on it. There are people who call others their own, yet never see them. And the whole relationship between them is that the so-called "owners" treat the others unjustly.

There are people who call women their own, or their "wives," but their women live with other men. And people strive not for the good in life, but for goods they can call their own.

I am now convinced that this is the essential difference between people and ourselves. And therefore, not even considering the other ways in which we are superior, but considering just this one virtue, we can bravely claim to stand higher than men on the ladder of living creatures. The actions of men, at least those with whom I have had dealings, are guided by *words*—ours, by deeds.

The horse is killed before the end of the story, but the manner of the narrative, its technique, does not change:

Much later they put Serpukhovsky's body, which had experienced the world, which had eaten and drunk, into the ground. They could profitably send neither his hide, nor his flesh, nor his bones anywhere.

But since his dead body, which had gone about in the world for twenty years, was a great burden to everyone, its burial was only a superfluous embarrassment for the people. For a long time no one had needed him;

for a long time he had been a burden on all. But nevertheless, the dead who buried the dead found it necessary to dress this bloated body, which immediately began to rot, in a good uniform and good boots; to lay it in a good new coffin with new tassels at the four corners, then to place this new coffin in another of lead and ship it to Moscow; there to exhume ancient bones and at just that spot, to hide this putrefying body, swarming with maggots, in its new uniform and clean boots, and to cover it over completely with dirt.

Thus we see that at the end of the story Tolstoy continues to use the technique even though the motivation for it [the reason for its use] is gone.

In *War and Peace* Tolstoy uses the same technique in describing whole battles as if battles were something new. These descriptions are too long to quote; it would be necessary to extract a considerable part of the four-volume novel. But Tolstoy uses the same method in describing the drawing room and the theater:

The middle of the stage consisted of flat boards; by the sides stood painted pictures representing trees, and at the back a linen cloth was stretched down to the floor boards. Maidens in red bodices and white skirts sat on the middle of the stage. One, very fat, in a white silk dress, sat apart on a narrow bench to which a green pasteboard box was glued from behind. They were all singing something. When they had finished, the maiden in white approached the prompter's box. A man in silk with tight-fitting pants on his fat legs approached her with a plume and began to sing and spread his arms in dismay. The man in the tight pants finished his song alone; then the girl sang. After that both remained silent as the music resounded; and the man, obviously waiting to begin singing his part with her again, began to run his fingers over the hand of the girl in the white dress. They finished their song together, and everyone in the theater began to clap and shout. But the men and women on stage, who represented lovers, started to bow, smiling and raising their hands.

In the second act there were pictures representing monuments and openings in the linen cloth representing the moonlight, and they raised lamp shades on a frame. As the musicians started to play the bass horn and counter-bass, a large number of people in black mantles poured onto the stage from right and left. The people, with something like daggers in their hands, started to wave their arms. Then still more people came running out and began to drag away the maiden who had been wearing a white dress but who now wore one of sky blue. They did not drag her off immediately, but sang with her for a long time before dragging her away. Three times they struck on something metallic behind the side scenes, and everyone got down on his knees and began to chant a prayer. Several times all of this activity was interrupted by enthusiastic shouts from the spectators.

The third act is described:

> . . . But suddenly a storm blew up. Chromatic scales and chords of diminished sevenths were heard in the orchestra. Everyone ran about and again they dragged one of the bystanders behind the scenes as the curtain fell.

In the fourth act, "There was some sort of devil who sang, waving his hands, until the boards were moved out from under him and he dropped down."[20]

In *Resurrection* Tolstoy describes the city and the court in the same way; he uses a similar technique in "Kreutzer Sonata" when he describes marriage— "Why, if people have an affinity of souls, must they sleep together?" But he did not defamiliarize only those things he sneered at:

> Pierre stood up from his new comrades and made his way between the campfires to the other side of the road where, it seemed, the captive soldiers were held. He wanted to talk with them. The French sentry stopped him on the road and ordered him to return. Pierre did so, but not to the campfire, not to his comrades, but to an abandoned, unharnessed carriage. On the ground, near the wheel of the carriage, he sat cross-legged in the Turkish fashion, and lowered his head. He sat motionless for a long time, thinking. More than an hour passed. No one disturbed him. Suddenly he burst out laughing with his robust, good natured laugh—so loudly that the men near him looked around, surprised at his conspicuously strange laughter.
>
> "Ha, ha, ha," laughed Pierre. And he began to talk to himself. "The soldier didn't allow me to pass. They caught me, barred me. Me—me— my immortal soul. Ha, ha, ha," he laughed with tears starting in his eyes.
>
> Pierre glanced at the sky, into the depths of the departing, playing stars. "And all this is mine, all this is in me, and all this is I," thought Pierre. "And all this they caught and put in a planked enclosure." He smiled and went off to his comrades to lie down to sleep.[21]

---

[20] The Tolstoy and Gogol translations are ours. The passage occurs in Vol. II, Part 8, Chap. 9 of the edition of *War and Peace* published in Boston by the Dana Estes Co. in 1904–12. *Ed. note.*

[21] Leo Tolstoy, *War and Peace*, IV, Part 13. Chap. 14. *Ed. note.*

Anyone who knows Tolstoy can find several hundred such passages in his work. His method of seeing things out of their normal context is also apparent in his last works. Tolstoy described the dogmas and rituals he attacked as if they were unfamiliar, substituting everyday meanings for the customarily religious meanings of the words common in church ritual. Many persons were painfully wounded; they considered it blasphemy to present as strange and monstrous what they accepted as sacred. Their reaction was due chiefly to the technique through which Tolstoy perceived and reported his environment. And after turning to what he had long avoided, Tolstoy found that his perceptions had unsettled his faith.

The technique of defamiliarization is not Tolstoy's alone. I cited Tolstoy because his work is generally known.

Now, having explained the nature of this technique, let us try to determine the approximate limits of its application. I personally feel that defamiliarization is found almost everywhere form is found. In other words, the difference between Potebnya's point of view and ours is this: An image is not a permanent referent for those mutable complexities of life which are revealed through it; its purpose is not to make us perceive meaning, but to create a special perception of the object—*it creates a "vision" of the object instead of serving as a means for knowing it.*

The purpose of imagery in erotic art can be studied even more accurately; an erotic object is usually presented as if it were seen for the first time. Gogol, in "Christmas Eve," provides the following example:

> Here he approached her more closely, coughed, smiled at her, touched her plump, bare arm with his fingers, and expressed himself in a way that showed both his cunning and his conceit.
>
> "And what is this you have, magnificent Solokha?" and having said this, he jumped back a little.
>
> "What? An arm, Osip Nikiforovich!" she answered. "Hmm, an arm! *He, he, he!*" said the secretary cordially, satisfied with his beginning. He wandered about the room.
>
> "And what is this you have, dearest Solokha?" he said in the same way, having approached her again and grasped her lightly by the neck, and in the very same way he jumped back.
>
> "As if you don't see, Osip Nikiforovich!" answered Solokha, "a neck, and on my neck a necklace."
>
> "Hmm! On the neck a necklace! *He, he, he!*" and the secretary again wandered about the room, rubbing his hands.
>
> "And what is this you have, incomparable Solokha?" . . . It is not known to what the secretary would stretch his long fingers now.

And Knut Hamsun has the following in "Hunger": "Two white prodigies appeared from beneath her blouse."

Erotic subjects may also be presented figuratively with the obvious purpose of leading us away from their "recognition." Hence sexual organs are referred to in terms of lock and key,[22] or quilting tools,[23] or bow and arrow, or rings and marlinspikes, as in the legend of Stavyor, in which a married man does not recognize his wife, who is disguised as a warrior. She proposes a riddle:

> "Remember, Stavyor, do you recall
> How we little ones walked to and fro in the street?
> You and I together sometimes played with a marlinspike—
> You had a silver marlinspike,
> But I had a gilded ring?
> I found myself at it just now and then,
> But you fell in with it ever and always."
> Says Stavyor, son of Godinovich,
> "What! I didn't play with you at marlinspikes!"
> Then Vasilisa Mikulichna: "So he says.
> Do you remember, Stavyor, do you recall,
> Now must you know, you and I together learned to read and write;
> Mine was an ink-well of silver,
> And yours a pen of gold?
> But I just moistened it a little now and then,
> And I just moistened it ever and always."[24]

In a different version of the legend we find a key to the riddle:

> Here the formidable envoy Vasilyushka
> Raised her skirts to the very navel,
> And then the young Stavyor, son of Godinovich,
> Recognized her gilded ring. . . .[25]

But defamiliarization is not only a technique of the erotic riddle—a technique of euphemism—it is also the basis and point of all riddles. Every riddle

---

[22] [Dimitry] Savodnikov, *Zagadki russkovo naroda* [*Riddles of the Russian People*] (St. Petersburg, 1901), Nos. 102–7.

[23] *Ibid.*, Nos. 588–91.

[24] A. E. Gruzinsky, ed., *Pesnt, sobrannye P[avel] N. Rybnikovym* [*Songs Collected by P. N. Rybnikov*] (Moscow, 1909–10), No. 30.

[25] *Ibid.*, No. 171.

pretends to show its subject either by words which specify or describe it but which, during the telling, do not seem applicable (the type: "black and white and 'red'—read—all over") or by means of odd but imitative sounds ("'Twas brillig, and the slithy toves/Did gyre and gimble in the wabe").[26]

Even erotic images not intended as riddles are defamiliarized ("boobies," "tarts," "piece," etc.). In popular imagery there is generally something equivalent to "trampling the grass" and "breaking the guelder-rose." The technique of defamiliarization is absolutely clear in the widespread image—a motif of erotic affectation—in which a bear and other wild beasts (or a devil, with a different reason for nonrecognition) do not recognize a man.[27]

The lack of recognition in the following tale is quite typical:

A peasant was plowing a field with a piebald mare. A bear approached him and asked, "Uncle, what's made this mare piebald for you?"

"I did the piebalding myself."

"But how?"

"Let me, and I'll do the same for you."

The bear agreed. The peasant tied his feet together with a rope, took the ploughshare from the two-wheeled plough, heated it on the fire, and applied it to his flanks. He made the bear piebald by scorching his fur down to the hide with the hot ploughshare. The man untied the bear, which went off and lay down under a tree.

A magpie flew at the peasant to pick at the meat on his shirt. He caught her and broke one of her legs. The magpie flew off to perch in the same tree under which the bear was lying. Then, after the magpie, a horsefly landed on the mare, sat down, and began to bite. The peasant caught the fly, took a stick, shoved it up its rear, and let it go. The fly went to the tree where the bear and the magpie were. There all three sat.

The peasant's wife came to bring his dinner to the field. The man and his wife finished their dinner in the fresh air, and he began to wrestle with her on the ground.

[26] We have supplied familiar English examples in place of Shklovsky's wordplay. Shklovsky is saying that we create words with no referents or with ambiguous referents in order to force attention to the objects represented by the similar-sounding words. By making the reader go through the extra step of interpreting the nonsense word, the writer prevents an automatic response. A toad is a toad, but "tove" forces one to pause and think about the beast. *Ed. note.*

[27] E. R. Romanov, "Besstrashny barin," *Velikorusskiye skazki* (Zapiski Imperskovo Russkovo Geograficheskovo Obshcstva, XLII, No. 52). Belorussky Sbornik, "Spravyadlivy soklat" ["The Intrepid Gentleman," *Great Russian Tales* (Notes of the Imperial Russian Geographical Society, XLII, No. 52). White Russian Anthology, "The Upright Soldier" (1886–1912)].

The bear saw this and said to the magpie and the fly, "Holy priests! The peasant wants to piebald someone again." The magpie said, "No, he wants to break someone's legs." The fly said, "No, he wants to shove a stick up someone's rump."[28]

The similarity of technique here and in Tolstoy's "Kholstomer," is, I think, obvious.

Quite often in literature the sexual act itself is defamiliarized; for example, the *Decameron* refers to "scraping out a barrel," "catching nightingales," "gay wool-beating work" (the last is not developed in the plot). Defamiliarization is often used in describing the sexual organs.

A whole series of plots is based on such a lack of recognition; for example, in Afanasyev's *Intimate Tales* the entire story of "The Shy Mistress" is based on the fact that an object is not called by its proper name—or, in other words, on a game of nonrecognition. So too in Onchukov's "Spotted Petticoats," tale no. 525, and also in "The Bear and the Hare" from *Intimate Tales,* in which the bear and the hare make a "wound."

Such constructions as "the pestle and the mortar," or "Old Nick and the infernal regions" (*Decameron*), are also examples of the technique of defamiliarization. And in my article on plot construction I write about defamiliarization in psychological parallelism. Here, then, I repeat that the perception of disharmony in a harmonious context is important in parallelism. The purpose of parallelism, like the general purpose of imagery, is to transfer the usual perception of an object into the sphere of a new perception—that is, to make a unique semantic modification.

In studying poetic speech in its phonetic and lexical structure as well as in its characteristic distribution of words and in the characteristic thought structures compounded from the words, we find everywhere the artistic trademark—that is, we find material obviously created to remove the automatism of perception; the author's purpose is to create the vision which results from that deautomatized perception. A work is created "artistically" so that its perception is impeded and the greatest possible effect is produced through the slowness of the perception. As a result of this lingering, the object is perceived not in its extension in space, but, so to speak, in its continuity. Thus "poetic language" gives satisfaction. According to Aristotle, poetic language must appear strange and wonderful; and, in fact, it is often actually foreign: the Sumerian used by the Assyrians, the Latin of Europe during the Middle Ages, the Arabisms of the Persians, the Old Bulgarian of

---

[28] D[mitry] S. Zelenin, *Velikorusskiye skazki Permskoy gubernii* [*Great Russian Tales of the Permian Province* (St. Petersburg, 1913)], No. 70.

Russian literature, or the elevated, almost literary language of folk songs. The common archaisms of poetic language, the intricacy of the sweet new style [*dolce stil nuovo*],[29] the obscure style of the language of Arnaut Daniel with the "roughened" [*harte*] forms *which make pronunciation difficult*—these are used in much the same way. Leo Jakubinsky has demonstrated the principle of phonetic "roughening" of poetic language in the particular case of the repetition of identical sounds. The language of poetry is, then, a difficult, roughened, impeded language. In a few special instances the language of poetry approximates the language of prose, but this does not violate the principle of "roughened" form.

> Her sister was called Tatyana.
> For the first time we shall
> Wilfully brighten the delicate
> Pages of a novel with such a name.

wrote Pushkin. The usual poetic language for Pushkin's contemporaries was the elegant style of Derzhavin; but Pushkin's style, because it seemed trivial then, was unexpectedly difficult for them. We should remember the consternation of Pushkin's contemporaries over the vulgarity of his expressions. He used the popular language as a special device for prolonging attention, just as his contemporaries generally used Russian words in their usually French speech (see Tolstoy's examples in *War and Peace*).

Just now a still more characteristic phenomenon is under way. Russian literary language, which was originally foreign to Russia, has so permeated the language of the people that it has blended with their conversation. On the other hand, literature has now begun to show a tendency towards the use of dialects (Remizov, Klyuycv, Essenin, and others,[30] so unequal in talent and so alike in language, are intentionally provincial) and of barbarisms (which gave rise to the Severyanin group[31]). And currently Maxim Gorky is changing his diction from the old literary language to the new literary colloquialism of Leskov.[32] Ordinary speech and literary

---

[29] Dante, *Purgatorio*, 24:56. Dante refers to the new lyric style of his contemporaries. *Ed. note.*

[30] Alexy Remizov (1877–1957) is best known as a novelist and satirist; Nicholas Klyuyev (1885–1937) and Sergey Esscnin (1895–1925) were "peasant poets." All three were noted for their faithful reproduction of Russian dialects and colloquial language. *Ed. note.*

[31] A group noted for its opulent and sensuous verse style. *Ed. note.*

[32] Nicholas Leskov (1831–95), novelist and short story writer, helped popularize the *skaz*, or yarn, and hence, because of the part dialect peculiarities play in the *skaz*, also altered Russian literary language. *Ed. note.*

language have thereby changed places (see the work of Vyacheslav Ivanov and many others). And finally, a strong tendency, led by Khlebnikov, to create a new and properly poetic language has emerged. In the light of these developments we can define poetry as *attenuated, tortuous* speech. Poetic speech is *formed speech*. Prose is ordinary speech—economical, easy, proper, the goddess of prose [*dea prosae*] is a goddess of the accurate, facile type, of the "direct" expression of a child. I shall discuss roughened form and retardation as the general *law* of art at greater length in an article on plot construction.[33]

Nevertheless, the position of those who urge the idea of the economy of artistic energy as something which exists in and even distinguishes poetic language seems, at first glance, tenable for the problem of rhythm. Spencer's description of rhythm would seem to be absolutely incontestable:

> Just as the body in receiving a series of varying concussions, must keep the muscles ready to meet the most violent of them, as not knowing when such may come: so, the mind in receiving unarranged articulations, must keep its perspectives active enough to recognize the least easily caught sounds. And as, if the concussions recur in definite order, the body may husband its forces by adjusting the resistance needful for each concussion; so, if the syllables be rhythmically arranged, the mind may economize its energies by anticipating the attention required for each syllable.[34]

This apparently conclusive observation suffers from the common fallacy, the confusion of the laws of poetic and prosaic language. In *The Philosophy of Style* Spencer failed utterly to distinguish between them. But rhythm may have two functions. The rhythm of prose, or of a work song like "Dubinushka," permits the members of the work crew to do their necessary "groaning together" and also eases the work by making it automatic. And, in fact, it is easier to march with music than without it, and to march during an animated conversation is even easier, for the walking is done unconsciously. Thus the rhythm of prose is an important automatizing element; the rhythm of poetry is not. There is "order" in art, yet not a single column of a Greek temple stands exactly in its proper order; poetic rhythm is similarly disordered rhythm. Attempts to systematize the irregularities have been made, and such attempts

---

[33] Shklovsky is probably referring to his *Razvyortyvantye syuzheta* [*Plot Development*] (Petrograd, 1921). *Ed. note.* Viktor Shklovsky, "Iskusstvo, kak priyom," *Sborniici*, II (1917).

[34] Spencer, [p. 169. Again the Russian text is shortened from Spencer's original].

are part of the current problem in the theory of rhythm. It is obvious that the systematization will not work, for in reality the problem is not one of complicating the rhythm but of disordering the rhythm—a disordering which cannot be predicted. Should the disordering of rhythm become a convention, it would be ineffective as a device for the roughening of language.

Frantz Fanon

Martinician (1925-1961)

The Fact of Blackness (1952)

"Kiss the handsome Negro's ass, madame!"

I came into the world imbued with the will to find a meaning in things, my spirit filled with the desire to attain to the source of the world, and then I found that I was an object in the midst of other objects.

Sealed into that crushing objecthood, I turned beseechingly to others. Their attention was a liberation, running over my body suddenly abraded into nonbeing, endowing me once more with an agility that I had thought lost, and by taking me out of the world, restoring me to it. But just as I reached the other side, I stumbled, and the movements, the attitudes, the glances of the other fixed me there, in the sense in which a chemical solution is fixed by a dye. I was indignant; I demanded an explanation. Nothing happened. I burst apart. Now the fragments have been put together again by another self.

As long as the black man is among his own, he will have no occasion, except in minor internal conflicts, to experience his being through others. There is of course the moment of "being for others," of which Hegel speaks, but every ontology is made unattainable in a colonized and civilized society. It would seem that this fact has not been given sufficient attention by those who have discussed the question. In the *Weltanschauung* of a colonized people there is an impurity, a flaw that outlaws any ontological explanation. Someone may object that this is the case with every individual, but such an objection merely conceals a basic problem. Ontology—once it is finally admitted as leaving existence by the wayside—does not permit us to understand the being of the black man. For not only must the black man be black; he must be black in relation to the white man. Some critics will take it on themselves to remind us that this proposition has a converse. I say that this is false. The black man has no ontological resistance in the eyes of the white man. Overnight the Negro has been given two frames of reference within which he has had to place himself. His metaphysics, or, less pretentiously, his customs and the sources on which they were based, were wiped out because they were in conflict with a civilization that he did not know and that imposed itself on him.

The black man among his own in the twentieth century does not know at what moment his inferiority comes into being through the other. Of course I have talked about the black problem with friends, or, more rarely, with American Negroes. Together we protested, we asserted the equality of all men in the world. In the Antilles there was also that little gulf that exists among the almost-white, the mulatto, and the nigger. But I was satisfied with an intellectual understanding of these differences. It was not really dramatic. And then. . . .

And then the occasion arose when I had to meet the white man's eyes. An unfamiliar weight burdened me. The real world challenged my claims. In the white world the man of color encounters difficulties in the development of his bodily schema. Consciousness of the body is solely a negating activity. It is a third-person consciousness. The body is surrounded by an atmosphere of certain uncertainty. I know that if I want to smoke, I shall have to reach out my right arm and take the pack of cigarettes lying at the other end of the table. The matches, however, are in the drawer on the left, and I shall have to lean back slightly. And all these movements are made not out of habit but out of implicit knowledge. A slow composition of my *self* as a body in the middle of a spatial and temporal world—such seems to be the schema. It does not impose itself on me; it is, rather, a definitive structuring of the self and of the world—definitive because it creates a real dialectic between my body and the world.

For several years certain laboratories have been trying to produce a serum for "denegrification"; with all the earnestness in the world, laboratories have sterilized their test tubes, checked their scales, and embarked on researches that might make it possible for the miserable Negro to whiten himself and thus to throw off the burden of that corporeal malediction. Below the corporeal schema I had sketched a historico-racial schema. The elements that I used had been provided for me not by "residual sensations and perceptions primarily of a tactile, vestibular, kinesthetic, and visual character,"[1] but by the other, the white man, who had woven me out of a thousand details, anecdotes, stories. I thought that what I had in hand was to construct a physiological self, to balance space, to localize sensations, and here I was called on for more.

"Look, a Negro!" It was an external stimulus that flicked over me as I passed by. I made a tight smile.

"Look, a Negro!" It was true. It amused me.

"Look, a Negro!" The circle was drawing a bit tighter. I made no secret of my amusement.

---

[1]   Jean Lhermitte, *L'Image de notre corps* (Paris, Nouvelle Revue critique, 1939), p. 17.

"Mama, see the Negro! I'm frightened!" Frightened! Frightened! Now they were beginning to be afraid of me. I made up my mind to laugh myself to tears, but laughter had become impossible.

I could no longer laugh, because I already knew that there were legends, stories, history, and above all *historicity*, which I had learned about from Jaspers. Then, assailed at various points, the corporeal schema crumbled, its place taken by a racial epidermal schema. In the train it was no longer a question of being aware of my body in the third person but in a triple person. In the train I was given not one but two, three places. I had already stopped being amused. It was not that I was finding febrile coordinates in the world. I existed triply: I occupied space. I moved toward the other . . . and the evanescent other, hostile but not opaque, transparent, not there, disappeared. Nausea. . . .

I was responsible at the same time for my body, for my race, for my ancestors. I subjected myself to an objective examination, I discovered my blackness, my ethnic characteristics; and I was battered down by tom-toms, cannibalism, intellectual deficiency, fetishism, racial defects, slave-ships, and above all else, above all: "Sho' good eatin.'"

On that day, completely dislocated, unable to be abroad with the other, the white man, who unmercifully imprisoned me, I took myself far off from my own presence, far indeed, and made myself an object. What else could it be for me but an amputation, an excision, a hemorrhage that spattered my whole body with black blood? But I did not want this revision, this thematization. All I wanted was to be a man among other men. I wanted to come lithe and young into a world that was ours and to help to build it together.

But I rejected all immunization of the emotions. I wanted to be a man, nothing but a man. Some identified me with ancestors of mine who had been enslaved or lynched: I decided to accept this. It was on the universal level of the intellect that I understood this inner kinship—I was the grandson of slaves in exactly the same way in which President Lebrun was the grandson of tax-paying, hard-working peasants. In the main, the panic soon vanished.

In America, Negroes are segregated. In South America, Negroes are whipped in the streets, and Negro strikers are cut down by machine-guns. In West Africa, the Negro is an animal. And there beside me, my neighbor in the university, who was born in Algeria, told me: "As long as the Arab is treated like a man, no solution is possible."

"Understand, my dear boy, color prejudice is something I find utterly foreign. . . . But of course, come in, sir, there is no color prejudice among us. . . . Quite, the Negro is a man like ourselves. . . . It is not because he is black that he is less intelligent than we are. . . . I had a Senegalese buddy in the army who was really clever. . . ."

Where am I to be classified? Or, if you prefer, tucked away?

"A Martinican, a native of 'our' old colonies."

Where shall I hide?

"Look at the nigger! . . . Mama, a Negro! . . . Hell, he's getting mad. . . . Take no notice, sir, he does not know that you are as civilized as we. . . ."

My body was given back to me sprawled out, distorted, recolored, clad in mourning in that white winter day. The Negro is an animal, the Negro is bad, the Negro is mean, the Negro is ugly; look, a nigger, it's cold, the nigger is shivering, the nigger is shivering because he is cold, the little boy is trembling because he is afraid of the nigger, the nigger is shivering with cold, that cold that goes through your bones, the handsome little boy is trembling because he thinks that the nigger is quivering with rage, the little white boy throws himself into his mother's arms: Mama, the nigger's going to eat me up.

All round me the white man, above the sky tears at its navel, the earth rasps under my feet, and there is a white song, a white song. All this whiteness that burns me. . . .

I sit down at the fire and I become aware of my uniform. I had not seen it. It is indeed ugly. I stop there, for who can tell me what beauty is?

Where shall I find shelter from now on? I felt an easily identifiable flood mounting out of the countless facets of my being. I was about to be angry. The fire was long since out, and once more the nigger was trembling.

"Look how handsome that Negro is! . . ."

"Kiss the handsome Negro's ass, madame!"

Shame flooded her face. At last I was set free from my rumination. At the same time I accomplished two things: I identified my enemies and I made a scene. A grand slam. Now one would be able to laugh.

The field of battle having been marked out, I entered the lists.

What? While I was forgetting, forgiving, and wanting only to love, my message was flung back in my face like a slap. The white world, the only honorable one, barred me from all participation. A man was expected to behave like a man. I was expected to behave like a black man—or at least like a nigger. I shouted a greeting to the world and the world slashed away my joy. I was told to stay within bounds, to go back where I belonged.

They would see, then! I had warned them, anyway. Slavery? It was no longer even mentioned, that unpleasant memory. My supposed inferiority? A hoax that it was better to laugh at. I forgot it all, but only on condition that the world not protect itself against me any longer. I had incisors to test. I was sure they were strong. And besides. . . .

What! When it was I who had every reason to hate, to despise, I was rejected? When I should have been begged, implored, I was denied the slightest recognition? I resolved, since it was impossible for me to get away from an *inborn complex*, to assert myself as a BLACK MAN. Since the other hesitated to recognize me, there remained only one solution: to make myself known.

In *Anti-Semite and Jew* (p. 95), Sartre says: "They [the Jews] have allowed themselves to be poisoned by the stereotype that others have of them, and they live in fear that their acts will correspond to this stereotype. . . . We may say that their conduct is perpetually overdetermined from the inside."

All the same, the Jew can be unknown in his Jewishness. He is not wholly what he is. One hopes, one waits. His actions, his behavior are the final determinant. He is a white man, and, apart from some rather debatable characteristics, he can sometimes go unnoticed. He belongs to the race of those who since the beginning of time have never known cannibalism. What an idea, to eat one's father! Simple enough, one has only not to be a nigger. Granted, the Jews are harassed—what am I thinking of? They are hunted down, exterminated, cremated. But these are little family quarrels. The Jew is disliked from the moment he is tracked down. But in my case everything takes on a *new* guise. I am given no chance. I am overdetermined from without. I am the slave not of the "idea" that others have of me but of my own appearance.

I move slowly in the world, accustomed now to seek no longer for upheaval. I progress by crawling. And already I am being dissected under white eyes, the only real eyes. I am *fixed*. Having adjusted their microtomes, they objectively cut away slices of my reality. I am laid bare. I feel, I see in those white faces that it is not a new man who has come in, but a new kind of man, a new genus. Why, it's a Negro!

I slip into corners, and my long antennae pick up the catch-phrases strewn over the surface of things—nigger underwear smells of nigger—nigger teeth are white—nigger feet are big—the nigger's barrel chest—I slip into corners, I remain silent, I strive for anonymity, for invisibility. Look, I will accept the lot, as long as no one notices me!

"Oh, I want you to meet my black friend. . . . Aimé Césaire, a black man and a university graduate. . . . Marian Anderson, the finest of Negro singers. . . . Dr. Cobb, who invented white blood, is a Negro. . . . Here, say hello to my friend from Martinique (be careful, he's extremely sensitive). . . ."

Shame. Shame and self-contempt. Nausea. When people like me, they tell me it is in spite of my color. When they dislike me, they point out that it is not because of my color. Either way, I am locked into the infernal circle. I turn away from these inspectors of the Ark before the Flood and I attach myself to my brothers, Negroes like myself. To my horror, they too reject me. They are almost white. And besides they are about to marry white women. They will have children faintly tinged with brown. Who knows, perhaps little by little. . . .

I had been dreaming.

"I want you to understand, sir, I am one of the best friends the Negro has in Lyon."

The evidence was there, unalterable. My blackness was there, dark and unarguable. And it tormented me, pursued me, disturbed me, angered me.

Negroes are savages, brutes, illiterates. But in my own case I knew that these statements were false. There was a myth of the Negro that had to be destroyed at all costs. The time had long since passed when a Negro priest was an occasion for wonder. We had physicians, professors, statesmen. Yes, but something out of the ordinary still clung to such cases. "We have a Senegalese history teacher. He is quite bright. . . . Our doctor is colored. He is very gentle."

It was always the Negro teacher, the Negro doctor; brittle as I was becoming, I shivered at the slightest pretext. I knew, for instance, that if the physician made a mistake it would be the end of him and of all those who came after him. What could one expect, after all, from a Negro physician? As long as everything went well, he was praised to the skies, but look out, no nonsense, under any conditions! The black physician can never be sure how close he is to disgrace. I tell you, I was walled in: No exception was made for my refined manners, or my knowledge of literature, or my understanding of the quantum theory.

I requested, I demanded explanations. Gently, in the tone that one uses with a child, they introduced me to the existence of a certain view that was held by certain people, but, I was always told, "We must hope that it will very soon disappear." What was it? Color prejudice.

> It [colour prejudice] is nothing more than the unreasoning hatred of one race for another, the contempt of the stronger and richer peoples for those whom they consider inferior to themselves, and the bitter resentment of those who are kept in subjection and are so frequently insulted. As colour is the most obvious outward manifestation of race it has been made the criterion by which men are judged, irrespective of their social or educational attainments. The light-skinned races have come to despise all those of a darker colour, and the dark-skinned peoples will no longer accept without protest the inferior position to which they have been relegated.[2]

I had read it rightly. It was hate; I was hated, despised, detested, not by the neighbor across the street or my cousin on my mother's side, but by an entire race. I was up against something unreasoned. The psychoanalysts say that

---

[2]   Sir Alan Burns, *Colour Prejudice* (London, Allen and Unwin, 1948), p. 16.

nothing is more traumatizing for the young child than his encounters with what is rational. I would personally say that for a man whose only weapon is reason there is nothing more neurotic than contact with unreason.

I felt knife blades open within me. I resolved to defend myself. As a good tactician, I intended to rationalize the world and to show the white man that he was mistaken.

In the Jew, Jean-Paul Sartre says, there is

a sort of impassioned imperialism of reason: for he wishes not only to convince others that he is right; his goal is to persuade them that there is an absolute and unconditioned value to rationalism. He feels himself to be a missionary of the universal; against the universality of the Catholic religion, from which he is excluded, he asserts the "catholicity" of the rational, an instrument by which to attain to the truth and establish a spiritual bond among men.[3]

And, the author adds, though there may be Jews who have made intuition the basic category of their philosophy, their intuition

has no resemblance to the Pascalian subtlety of spirit, and it is this latter—based on a thousand imperceptible perceptions—which to the Jew seems his worst enemy. As for Bergson, his philosophy offers the curious appearance of an anti-intellectualist doctrine constructed entirely by the most rational and most critical of intelligences. It is through argument that he establishes the existence of pure duration, of philosophic intuition; and that very intuition which discovers duration or life, is itself universal, since anyone may practice it, and it leads toward the universal, since its objects can be named and conceived.[4]

With enthusiasm I set to cataloguing and probing my surroundings. As times changed, one had seen the Catholic religion at first justify and then condemn slavery and prejudices. But by referring everything to the idea of the dignity of man, one had ripped prejudice to shreds. After much reluctance, the scientists had conceded that the Negro was a human being; *in vivo* and *in vitro* the Negro had been proved analogous to the white man: the same morphology, the same histology. Reason was confident of victory on every level. I put all the parts back together. But I had to change my tune.

[3] *Anti-Semite and Jew* (New York, Grove Press, 1960), pp. 112–113.
[4] *Ibid.*, p. 115.

That victory played cat and mouse; it made a fool of me. As the other put it, when I was present, it was not; when it was there, I was no longer. In the abstract there was agreement: The Negro is a human being. That is to say, amended the less firmly convinced, that like us he has his heart on the left side. But on certain points the white man remained intractable. Under no conditions did he wish any intimacy between the races, for it is a truism that "crossings between widely different races can lower the physical and mental level. . . . Until we have a more definite knowledge of the effect of race-crossings we shall certainly do best to avoid crossings between widely different races."[5]

For my own part, I would certainly know how to react. And in one sense, if I were asked for a definition of myself, I would say that I am one who waits; I investigate my surroundings, I interpret everything in terms of what I discover, I become sensitive.

In the first chapter of the history that the others have compiled for me, the foundation of cannibalism has been made eminently plain in order that I may not lose sight of it. My chromosomes were supposed to have a few thicker or thinner genes representing cannibalism. In addition to the *sex-linked*, the scholars had now discovered the *racial-linked*.[6] What a shameful science!

But I understand this "psychological mechanism." For it is a matter of common knowledge that the mechanism is only psychological. Two centuries ago I was lost to humanity, I was a slave forever. And then came men who said that it all had gone on far too long. My tenaciousness did the rest; I was saved from the civilizing deluge. I have gone forward.

Too late. Everything is anticipated, thought out, demonstrated, made the most of. My trembling hands take hold of nothing; the vein has been mined out. Too late! But once again I want to understand.

Since the time when someone first mourned the fact that he had arrived too late and everything had been said, a nostalgia for the past has seemed to persist. Is this that lost original paradise of which Otto Rank speaks? How many such men, apparently rooted to the womb of the world, have devoted their lives to studying the Delphic oracles or exhausted themselves in attempts to plot the wanderings of Ulysses! The pan-spiritualists seek to prove the existence of a soul in animals by using this argument: A dog lies down on the grave of his master and starves to death there. We had to wait for

---

[5] Jon Alfred Mjoen, "Harmonic and Disharmonic Race-crossings," The Second International Congress of Eugenics (1921), *Eugenics in Race and State*, vol. 11, p. 60, quoted in Sir Alan Burns, *op. cit.*, p. 120.

[6] In English in the original. (Translator's note.)

Janet to demonstrate that the aforesaid dog, in contrast to man, simply lacked the capacity to liquidate the past. We speak of the glory of Greece, Artaud says; but, he adds, if modern man can no longer understand the *Choephoroi* of Aeschylus, it is Aeschylus who is to blame. It is tradition to which the anti-Semites turn in order to ground the validity of their "point of view." It is tradition, it is that long historical past, it is that blood relation between Pascal and Descartes, that is invoked when the Jew is told, "There is no possibility of your finding a place in society." Not long ago, one of those good Frenchmen said in a train where I was sitting: "Just let the real French virtues keep going and the race is safe. Now more than ever, national union must be made a reality. Let's have an end of internal strife! Let's face up to the foreigners (here he turned toward my corner) no matter who they are."

It must be said in his defense that he stank of cheap wine; if he had been capable of it, he would have told me that my emancipated-slave blood could not possibly be stirred by the name of Villon or Taine.

An outrage!

The Jew and I: Since I was not satisfied to be racialized, by a lucky turn of fate I was humanized. I joined the Jew, my brother in misery.

An outrage!

At first thought it may seem strange that the anti-Semite's outlook should be related to that of the Negrophobe. It was my philosophy professor, a native of the Antilles, who recalled the fact to me one day: "Whenever you hear anyone abuse the Jews, pay attention, because he is talking about you." And I found that he was universally right—by which I meant that I was answerable in my body and in my heart for what was done to my brother. Later I realized that he meant, quite simply, an anti-Semite is inevitably anti-Negro.

You come too late, much too late. There will always be a world—a white world—between you and us. . . . The other's total inability to liquidate the past once and for all. In the face of this affective ankylosis of the white man, it is understandable that I could have made up my mind to utter my Negro cry. Little by little, putting out pseudopodia here and there, I secreted a race. And that race staggered under the burden of a basic element. What was it? *Rhythm!* Listen to our singer, Léopold Senghor:

> It is the thing that is most perceptible and least material. It is the archetype of the vital element. It is the first condition and the hallmark of Art, as breath is of life: breath, which accelerates or slows, which becomes even or agitated according to the tension in the individual, the degree and the nature of his emotion. This is rhythm in its primordial purity, this is rhythm in the masterpieces of Negro art, especially sculpture. It is composed of a theme—sculptural form—which is set in opposition

to a sister theme, as inhalation is to exhalation, and that is repeated. It is
not the kind of symmetry that gives rise to monotony; rhythm is alive,
it is free. . . . This is how rhythm affects what is least intellectual in us,
tyrannically, to make us penetrate to the spirituality of the object; and
that character of abandon which is ours is itself rhythmic.[7]

Had I read that right? I read it again with redoubled attention. From the
opposite end of the white world a magical Negro culture was hailing me.
Negro sculpture! I began to flush with pride. Was this our salvation?

I had rationalized the world and the world had rejected me on the basis
of color prejudice. Since no agreement was possible on the level of reason, I
threw myself back toward unreason. It was up to the white man to be more
irrational than I. Out of the necessities of my struggle I had chosen the method
of regression, but the fact remained that it was an unfamiliar weapon; here I
am at home; I am made of the irrational; I wade in the irrational. Up to the
neck in the irrational. And now how my voice vibrates!

[7]   "Ce que l'homme noir apporte," in Claude Nordey, *L'Homme de couleur* (Paris, Plon, 1939), pp. 309–310.

Roland Barthes

French (1915-1980)

Myth Today (1957)

Myth is constituted by the loss of the historical quality of things: in it, things lose the memory that they once were made. The world enters language as a dialectical relation between activities, between human actions; it comes out of myth as a harmonious display of essences.

What is a myth, today? I shall give at the outset a first, very simple answer, which is perfectly consistent with etymology: myth is a type of speech.[1]

Myth is a type of speech

Of course, it is not any type: language needs special conditions in order to become myth: we shall see them in a minute. But what must be firmly established at the start is that myth is a system of communication, that it is a message. This allows one to perceive that myth cannot possibly be an object, a concept, or an idea; it is a mode of signification, a form. Later, we shall have to assign to this form historical limits, conditions of use, and reintroduce society into it: we must nevertheless first describe it as a form.

It can be seen that to purport to discriminate among mythical objects according to their substance would be entirely illusory: since myth is a type of speech, everything can be a myth provided it is conveyed by a discourse. Myth is not defined by the object of its message, but by the way in which it utters this message: there are formal limits to myth, there are no 'substantial' ones. Everything, then, can be a myth? Yes, I believe this, for the universe is infinitely fertile in suggestions. Every object in the world can pass from a closed, silent existence to an oral state, open to appropriation by society, for

---

[1] Innumerable other meanings of the word 'myth' can be cited against this. But I have tried to define things, not words.

there is no law, whether natural or not, which forbids talking about things. A tree is a tree. Yes, of course. But a tree as expressed by Minou Drouet is no longer quite a tree, it is a tree which is decorated, adapted to a certain type of consumption, laden with literary self-indulgence, revolt, images, in short with a type of social usage which is added to pure matter.

Naturally, everything is not expressed at the same time: some objects become the prey of mythical speech for a while, then they disappear, others take their place and attain the status of myth. Are there objects which are inevitably a source of suggestiveness, as Baudelaire suggested about Woman? Certainly not: one can conceive of very ancient myths, but there are no eternal ones; for it is human history which converts reality into speech, and it alone rules the life and the death of mythical language. Ancient or not, mythology can only have an historical foundation, for myth is a type of speech chosen by history: it cannot possibly evolve from the 'nature' of things.

Speech of this kind is a message. It is therefore by no means confined to oral speech. It can consist of modes of writing or of representations; not only written discourse, but also photography, cinema, reporting, sport, shows, publicity, all these can serve as a support to mythical speech. Myth can be defined neither by its object nor by its material, for any material can arbitrarily be endowed with meaning: the arrow which is brought in order to signify a challenge is also a kind of speech. True, as far as perception is concerned, writing and pictures, for instance, do not call upon the same type of consciousness; and even with pictures, one can use many kinds of reading: a diagram lends itself to signification more than a drawing, a copy more than an original, and a caricature more than a portrait.

But this is the point: we are no longer dealing here with a theoretical mode of representation: we are dealing with this particular image, which is given for this particular signification. Mythical speech is made of a material which has already been worked on so as to make it suitable for communication: it is because all the materials of myth (whether pictorial or written) presuppose a signifying consciousness, that one can reason about them while discounting their substance. This substance is not unimportant: pictures, to be sure, are more imperative than writing, they impose meaning at one stroke, without analyzing or diluting it. But this is no longer a constitutive difference. Pictures become a kind of writing as soon as they are meaningful: like writing, they call for a lexis.

We shall therefore take language, discourse, speech, etc., to mean any significant unit or synthesis, whether verbal or visual: a photograph will be a kind of speech for us in the same way as a newspaper article; even objects will become speech, if they mean something. This generic way of conceiving language is in fact justified by the very history of writing: long before the invention of our alphabet, objects like the Inca quipu, or drawings, as in pictographs, have been accepted as speech. This does not mean that one must treat mythical speech like language; myth in fact belongs to the province of a general science, coextensive with linguistics, which is semiology.

Myth as a semiological system

For mythology, since it is the study of a type of speech, is but one fragment of this vast science of signs which Saussure postulated some forty years ago under the name of semiology. Semiology has not yet come into being. But since Saussure himself, and sometimes independently of him, a whole section of contemporary research has constantly been referred to the problem of meaning: psychoanalysis, structuralism, eidetic psychology, some new types of literary criticism of which Bachelard has given the first examples, are no longer concerned with facts except inasmuch as they are endowed with significance. Now to postulate a signification is to have recourse to semiology. I do not mean that semiology could account for all these aspects of research equally well: they have different contents. But they have a common status: they are all sciences dealing with values. They are not content with meeting the facts: they define and explore them as tokens for something else.

Semiology is a science of forms, since it studies significations apart from their content. I should like to say one word about the necessity and the limits of such a formal science. The necessity is that which applies in the case of any exact language. Zhdanov made fun of Alexandrov the philosopher, who spoke of 'the spherical structure of our planet.' 'It was thought until now', Zhdanov said, 'that form alone could be spherical.' Zhdanov was right: one cannot speak about structures in terms of forms, and vice versa. It may well be that on the plane of 'life', there is but a totality where structures and forms cannot be separated. But science has no use for the ineffable: it must speak about 'life' if it wants to transform it. Against a certain quixotism of synthesis, quite platonic incidentally, all criticism must consent to the ascesis, to the artifice of analysis; and in analysis, it must match method and language. Less terrorized by the specter of 'formalism', historical criticism might have been less sterile; it would have understood that the specific study of forms does not in any way contradict the necessary principles of totality and History. On the contrary: the more a system is specifically defined in its forms, the more amenable it is to historical criticism. To parody a well-known saying, I shall say that a little formalism turns one away from History, but that a lot brings one back to it. Is there a better example of total criticism than the description of saintliness, at once formal and historical, semiological and ideological, in Sartre's Saint-Genet? The danger, on the contrary, is to consider forms as ambiguous objects, half- form and half-substance, to endow form with a substance of form, as was done, for instance, by Zhdanovian realism. Semiology, once its limits are settled, is not a metaphysical trap: it is a science among others, necessary but not sufficient. The important thing is to see that the unity of an explanation cannot be based on the amputation of one or other of its approaches, but, as Engels said, on the dialectical co-ordination of the particular sciences it makes use of. This is the case with mythology: it is a part both of semiology inasmuch as it is a formal science, and of ideology inasmuch as it is an historical science: it studies ideas-in-form.[2]

Let me therefore restate that any semiology postulates a relation between two terms, a signifier and a signified. This relation concerns objects which belong to different categories, and this is why it is not one of equality but one of equivalence. We must here be on our guard for despite common parlance which simply says that the signifier expresses the signified, we are dealing, in any semiological system, not with two, but with three different terms. For what we grasp is not at all one term after the other, but the correlation which unites them: there are, therefore, the signifier, the signified and the sign, which is the associative total of the first two terms. Take a bunch of roses: I use it to signify my passion. Do we have here, then, only a signifier and a signified, the roses and my passion? Not even that: to put it accurately, there are here only 'passionified' roses. But on the plane of analysis, we do have three terms; for these roses weighted with passion perfectly and correctly allow themselves to be decomposed into roses and passion: the former and the latter existed before uniting and forming this third object, which is the sign. It is as true to say that on the plane of experience I cannot dissociate the roses from the message they carry, as to say that on the plane of analysis I cannot confuse the roses as signifier and the roses as sign: the signifier is empty, the sign is full, it is a meaning. Or take a black pebble: I can make it signify in several ways, it is a mere signifier; but if I weigh it with a definite signified (a death sentence, for instance, in an anonymous vote), it will become a sign. Naturally, there are between the signifier, the signified and the sign, functional implications (such as that of the part to the whole) which are so close that to analyse

---

[2] The development of publicity, of a national press, of radio, of illustrated news, not to speak of the survival of a myriad rites of communication which rule social appearances makes the development of a semiological science more urgent than ever. In a single day, how many really non-signifying fields do we cross? Very few, sometimes none. Here I am, before the sea; it is true that it bears no message. But on the beach, what material for semiology! Flags, slogans, signals, sign-boards, clothes, suntan even, which are so many messages to me.

them may seem futile; but we shall see in a moment that this distinction has a capital importance for the study of myth as semiological schema.

Naturally these three terms are purely formal, and different contents can be given to them. Here are a few examples: for Saussure, who worked on a particular but methodologically exemplary semiological system—the language or *langue*—the signified is the concept, the signifier is the acoustic image (which is mental) and the relation between concept and image is the sign (the word, for instance), which is a concrete entity.[3] For Freud, as is well known, the human psyche is a stratification of tokens or representatives. One term (I refrain from giving it any precedence) is constituted by the manifest meaning of behavior, another, by its latent or real meaning (it is, for instance, the substratum of the dream); as for the third term, it is here also a correlation of the first two: it is the dream itself in its totality, the parapraxis (a mistake in speech or behavior) or the neurosis, conceived as compromises, as economies effected thanks to the joining of a form (the first term) and an intentional function (the second term). We can see here how necessary it is to distinguish the sign from the signifier: a dream, to Freud, is no more its manifest datum than its latent content: it is the functional union of these two terms. In Sartrean criticism, finally (I shall keep to these three well known examples), the signified is constituted by the original crisis in the subject (the separation from his mother for Baudelaire, the naming of the theft for Genet); Literature as discourse forms the signifier; and the relation between crisis and discourse defines the work, which is a signification. Of course, this tri-dimensional pattern, however constant in its form, is actualized in different ways: one cannot therefore say too often that semiology can have its unity only at the level of forms, not contents; its field is limited, it knows only one operation: reading, or deciphering.

In myth, we find again the tri-dimensional pattern which I have just described: the signifier, the signified and the sign. But myth is a peculiar system, in that it is constructed from a semiological chain which existed before it: it is a second-order semiological system. That which is a sign (namely the associative total of a concept and an image) in the first system, becomes a mere signifier in the second. We must here recall that the materials of mythical speech (the language itself, photography, painting, posters, rituals, objects, etc.), however different at the start, are reduced to a pure signifying function as soon as they are caught by myth. Myth sees in them only the same raw material; their unity is that they all come down to the status of a mere language. Whether it deals with alphabetical or pictorial

---

[3] The notion of word is one of the most controversial in linguistics. I keep it here for the sake of simplicity.

writing, myth wants to see in them only a sum of signs, a global sign, the final term of a first semiological chain. And it is precisely this final term which will become the first term of the greater system which it builds and of which it is only a part. Everything happens as if myth shifted the formal system of the first significations sideways. As this lateral shift is essential for the analysis of myth, I shall represent it in the following way, it being understood, of course, that the spatialization of the pattern is here only a metaphor:

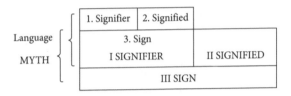

It can be seen that in myth there are two semiological systems, one of which is staggered in relation to the other: a linguistic system, the language (or the modes of representation which are assimilated to it), which I shall call the language-object, because it is the language which myth gets hold of in order to build its own system; and myth itself, which I shall call metalanguage, because it is a second language, in which one speaks about the first. When he reflects on a metalanguage, the semiologist no longer needs to ask himself questions about the composition of the language object, he no longer has to take into account the details of the linguistic schema; he will only need to know its total term, or global sign, and only inasmuch as this term lends itself to myth. This is why the semiologist is entitled to treat in the same way writing and pictures: what he retains from them is the fact that they are both signs, that they both reach the threshold of myth endowed with the same signifying function, that they constitute, one just as much as the other, a language-object.

It is now time to give one or two examples of mythical speech. I shall borrow the first from an observation by Valery.[4] I am a pupil in the second form in a French lycee. I open my Latin grammar, and I read a sentence, borrowed from Aesop or Phaedrus: *quia ego nominor leo*. I stop and think. There is something ambiguous about this statement: on the one hand, the words in it do have a simple meaning: because my name is lion. And on the other hand, the sentence is evidently there in order to signify something else to me. Inasmuch as it is addressed to me, a pupil in the second form, it tells me clearly: I am a grammatical example meant to illustrate the rule

---

[4] *Tel Quel*, II, p. 191.

about the agreement of the predicate. I am even forced to realize that the sentence in no way signifies its meaning to me, that it tries very little to tell me something about the lion and what sort of name he has; its true and fundamental signification is to impose itself on me as the presence of a certain agreement of the predicate. I conclude that I am faced with a particular, greater, semiological system, since it is coextensive with the language: there is, indeed, a signifier, but this signifier is itself formed by a sum of signs, it is in itself a first semiological system (my name is lion). Thereafter, the formal pattern is correctly unfolded: there is a signified (I am a grammatical example) and there is a global signification, which is none other than the correlation of the signifier and the signified; for neither the naming of the lion nor the grammatical example are given separately.

And here is now another example: I am at the barber's, and a copy of *Paris-Match* is offered to me. On the cover, a young Negro in a French uniform is saluting, with his eyes uplifted, probably fixed on a fold of the tricolour. All this is the meaning of the picture. But, whether naively or not, I see very well what it signifies to me: that France is a great Empire, that all her sons, without any color discrimination, faithfully serve under her flag, and that there is no better answer to the detractors of an alleged colonialism than the zeal shown by this Negro in serving his so-called oppressors. I am therefore again faced with a greater semiological system: there is a signifier, itself already formed with a previous system (a black soldier is giving the French salute); there is a signified (it is here a purposeful mixture of Frenchness and militariness); finally, there is a presence of the signified through the signifier.

Before tackling the analysis of each term of the mythical system, one must agree on terminology. We now know that the signifier can be looked at, in myth, from two points of view: as the final term of the linguistic system, or as the first term of the mythical system. We therefore need two names. On the plane of language, that is, as the final term of the first system, I shall call the signifier: meaning (my name is lion, a Negro is giving the French salute); on the plane of myth, I shall call it: form. In the case of the signified, no ambiguity is possible: we shall retain the name concept. The third term is the correlation of the first two: in the linguistic system, it is the sign; but it is not possible to use this word again without ambiguity, since in myth (and this is the chief peculiarity of the latter), the signifier is already formed by the signs of the language. I shall call the third term of myth the signification. This word is here all the better justified since myth has in fact a double function: it points out and it notifies, it makes us understand something and it imposes it on us.

[...]

However paradoxical it may seem, myth hides nothing: its function is to distort, not to make disappear. There is no latency of the concept in relation to the form: there is no need of an unconscious in order to explain myth. Of course, one is dealing with two different types of manifestation: form has a literal, immediate presence; moreover, it is extended. This stems—this cannot be repeated too often—from the nature of the mythical signifier, which is already linguistic: since it is constituted by a meaning which is already outlined, it can appear only through a given substance (whereas in language, the signifier remains mental). In the case of oral myth, this extension is linear (for my name is lion); in that of visual myth, it is multidimensional (in the center, the Negro's uniform, at the top, the blackness of his face, on the left, the military salute, etc.). The elements of the form therefore are related as to place and proximity: the mode of presence of the form is spatial. The concept, on the contrary, appears in global fashion, it is a kind of nebula, the condensation, more or less hazy, of a certain knowledge. Its elements are linked by associative relations: it is supported not by an extension but by a depth (although this metaphor is perhaps still too spatial): its mode of presence is memorial.

The relation which unites the concept of the myth to its meaning is essentially a relation of deformation. We find here again a certain formal analogy with a complex semiological system such as that of the various types of psychoanalysis. Just as for Freud the manifest meaning of behavior is distorted by its latent meaning, in myth the meaning is distorted by the concept. Of course, this distortion is possible only because the form of the myth is already constituted by a linguistic meaning. In a simple system like the language, the signified cannot distort anything at all because the signifier, being empty, arbitrary, offers no resistance to it. But here, everything is different: the signifier has, so to speak, two aspects: one full, which is the meaning (the history of the lion, of the Negro soldier), one empty, which is the form (for my name is lion; Negro-French- soldier-saluting-the-tricolor). What the concept distorts is of course what is full, the meaning: the lion and the Negro are deprived of their history, changed into gestures. What Latin exemplarity distorts is the naming of the lion, in all its contingency; and what French imperiality obscures is also a primary language, a factual discourse which was telling me about the salute of a Negro in uniform. But this distortion is not an obliteration: the lion and the Negro remain here, the concept needs them; they are half-amputated, they are deprived of memory, not of existence: they are at once stubborn, silently rooted there, and garrulous, a speech wholly at the service of the concept. The concept, literally, deforms, but does not abolish the meaning; a word can-perfectly render this contradiction: it alienates it.

What must always be remembered is that myth is a double system; there occurs in it a sort of ubiquity: its point of departure is constituted by the arrival of a meaning. To keep a spatial metaphor, the approximative character of which I have already stressed, I shall say that the signification of the myth is constituted by a sort of constantly moving turnstile which presents alternately the meaning of the signifier and its form, a language object and a metalanguage, a purely signifying and a purely imagining consciousness. This alternation is, so to speak, gathered up in the concept, which uses it like an ambiguous signifier, at once intellective and imaginary, arbitrary and natural.

[...]

And it is again this duplicity of the signifier which determines the characters of the signification. We now know that myth is a type of speech defined by its intention (I am a grammatical example) much more than by its literal sense (my name is lion); and that in spite of this, its intention is somehow frozen, purified, eternalized, made absent by this literal sense (The French Empire? It's just a fact: look at this good Negro who salutes like one of our own boys). This constituent ambiguity of mythical speech has two consequences for the signification, which henceforth appears both like a notification and like a statement of fact.

Myth has an imperative, buttonholing character: stemming from an historical concept, directly springing from contingency (a Latin class, a threatened Empire), it is I whom it has come to seek. It is turned towards me, I am subjected to its intentional force, it summons me to receive its expansive ambiguity.

[...]

For this interpellant speech is at the same time a frozen speech: at the moment of reaching me, it suspends itself, turns away and assumes the look of a generality: it stiffens, it makes itself look neutral and innocent. The appropriation of the concept is suddenly driven away once more by the literalness of the meaning. This is a kind of arrest, in both the physical and the legal sense of the term: French imperiality condemns the saluting Negro to be nothing more than an instrumental signifier, the Negro suddenly hails me in the name of French imperiality; but at the same moment the Negro's salute thickens, becomes vitrified, freezes into an eternal reference meant to establish French imperiality. On the surface of language something has stopped moving: the use of the signification is here, hiding behind the fact, and conferring on it a notifying look; but at the same time, the fact paralyses the intention, gives it something like a malaise producing immobility: in order to make it innocent, it freezes it. This is because myth is speech stolen and restored. Only, speech which is restored is no longer quite that which was stolen: when it was brought back, it was not put exactly in its place. It is this brief act of larceny, this moment taken for a surreptitious faking, which gives mythical speech its benumbed look.

One last element of the signification remains to be examined: its motivation. We know that in a language, the sign is arbitrary: nothing compels the acoustic image tree 'naturally' to mean the concept tree: the sign, here, is unmotivated. Yet this arbitrariness has limits, which come from the associative relations of the word: the language can produce a whole fragment of the sign by analogy with other signs (for instance one says amiable in French, and not amable, by analogy with aime). The mythical signification, on the other hand, is never arbitrary; it is always in part motivated, and unavoidably contains some analogy. For Latin exemplarity to meet the naming of the lion, there must be an analogy, which is the agreement of the predicate; for French imperiality to get hold of the saluting Negro, there must be identity between the Negro's salute and that of the French soldier. Motivation is necessary to the very duplicity of myth: myth plays on the analogy between meaning and form, there is no myth without motivated form.[5]

[...]

Motivation is unavoidable. It is none the less very fragmentary. To start with, it is not 'natural': it is history which supplies its analogies to the form.

[...]

We reach here the very principle of myth: it transforms history into nature. We now understand why, in the eyes of the myth consumer, the intention, the adhomination of the concept can remain manifest without however appearing to have an interest in the matter: what causes mythical speech to be uttered is perfectly explicit, but it is immediately frozen into something natural; it is not read as a motive, but as a reason. If I read the Negro-saluting as symbol pure and simple of imperiality, I must renounce the reality of the picture, it discredits itself in my eyes when it becomes an instrument. Conversely, if I decipher the Negro's salute as an alibi of coloniality, I shatter the myth even more surely by the obviousness of its motivation. But for the myth-reader, the outcome is quite different: everything happens as if the picture naturally

---

[5]   From the point of view of ethics, what is disturbing in myth is precisely that its form is motivated. For if there is a 'health' of language, it is the arbitrariness of the sign which is its grounding. What is sickening in myth is its resort to a false nature, its superabundance of significant forms, as in these objects which decorate their usefulness with a natural appearance. The will to weigh the signification with the full guarantee of nature causes a kind of nausea; myth is too rich, and what is in excess is precisely its motivation. This nausea is like the one I feel before the arts which refuse to choose between physis and anti-physis, using the first as an ideal and the second as an economy.

Ethically, there is a kind of baseness in hedging one's bets.

conjured up the concept, as if the signifier gave a foundation to the signified: the myth exists from the precise moment when French imperiality achieves the natural state: myth is speech justified *in excess*.

[...]

[In myth], causality is artificial, false; but it creeps, so to speak, through the back door of Nature. This is why myth is experienced as innocent speech: not because its intentions are hidden—if they were hidden, they could not be efficacious—but because they are naturalized.

[...]

The status of the bourgeoisie is particular, historical: man as represented by it is universal, eternal. The bourgeois class has precisely built its power on technical, scientific progress, on an unlimited transformation of nature: bourgeois ideology yields in return an unchangeable nature. The first bourgeois philosophers pervaded the world with significations, subjected all things to an idea of the rational, and decreed that they were meant for man: bourgeois ideology is of the scientistic or the intuitive kind, it records facts or perceives values, but refuses explanations; the order of the world can be seen as sufficient or ineffable, it is never seen as significant. Finally, the basic idea of a perfectible mobile world, produces the inverted image of an unchanging humanity, characterized by an indefinite repetition of its identity. In a word, in the contemporary bourgeois society, the passage from the real to the ideological is defined as that from an *anti-physis* to a *pseudo-physis*.

Myth is depoliticized speech

And this is where we come back to myth. Semiology has taught us that myth has the task of giving an historical intention a natural justification, and making contingency appear eternal. Now this process is exactly that of bourgeois ideology. If our society is objectively the privileged field of mythical significations, it is because formally myth is the most appropriate instrument for the ideological inversion which defines this society: at all the levels of human communication, myth operates the inversion of anti-physis into pseudo-physis.

What the world supplies to myth is an historical reality, defined, even if this goes back quite a while, by the way in which men have produced or used it; and what myth gives in return is a natural image of this reality. And just as bourgeois ideology is defined by the abandonment of the name 'bourgeois', myth is constituted by the loss of the historical quality of things: in it, things lose the memory that they once were made. The world enters language as a dialectical relation between activities, between human actions; it comes out of myth as a harmonious display of essences. A conjuring trick has taken place; it has turned reality inside out, it has emptied it of history and has filled it with nature, it has removed from things their human meaning so as to make them signify a human insignificance. The function of myth is to empty reality: it is, literally, a ceaseless flowing out, a hemorrhage, or perhaps an evaporation, in short a perceptible absence.

It is now possible to complete the semiological definition of myth in a bourgeois society: myth is depoliticized speech. One must naturally understand political in its deeper meaning, as describing the whole of human relations in their real, social structure, in their power of making the world; one must above all give an active value to the prefix de-: here it represents an operational movement, it permanently embodies a defaulting. In the case of the soldier-Negro, for instance, what is got rid of is certainly not French imperiality (on the contrary, since what must be actualized is its presence); it is the contingent, historical, in one word: fabricated, quality of colonialism. Myth does not deny things, on the contrary, its function is to talk about them; simply, it purifies them, it makes them innocent, it gives them a natural and eternal justification, it gives them a clarity which is not that of an explanation but that of a statement of fact. If I state the fact of French imperiality without explaining it, I am very near to finding that it is natural and goes without saying: I am reassured. In passing from history to nature, myth acts economically: it abolishes the complexity of human acts, it gives them the simplicity of essences, it does away with all dialectics, with any going back beyond what is immediately visible, it organizes a world which is without contradictions because it is without depth, a world wide open and wallowing in the evident, it establishes a blissful clarity: things appear to mean something by themselves.[6]

---

[6] To the pleasure-principle of Freudian man could be added the clarity-principle of mythological humanity. All the ambiguity of myth is there: its clarity is euphoric.

Michel Foucault

French (1926-1984)

Nietzsche, Freud, Marx (1967)

If interpretation can never be brought to an end, it is simply because there is nothing to interpret. There is nothing absolutely primary to interpret, because at bottom everything is already interpretation. Each sign is in itself not the thing that presents itself to interpretation, but the interpretation of other signs.

This plan for a "round table,"[1] when it was proposed to me, appeared very interesting, but clearly quite puzzling. I suggest a subterfuge: some themes concerning *the techniques of interpretation* in Marx, Nietzsche, and Freud.

In reality, behind these themes there is a dream that one day it will be possible to make a kind of general corpus, an encyclopedia of all the techniques of interpretation that we can know from the Greek grammarians to our time. I think that few of the chapters of this great corpus of all the techniques of interpretation have thus far been drawn up. It seems to me that one could say, as a general introduction to this idea of a history of techniques of interpretation, that language, at least language in Indo-European cultures, has always given rise to two kinds of suspicions.

- First of all, the suspicion that language does not say exactly what it means [*le langage ne dit pas exactement ce qu'il dit*]. The meaning [*sens*] that one grasps, and that is immediately manifest, is perhaps in reality only a lesser meaning [*moindre sens*] that shields, restrains, and despite everything transmits another meaning, the meaning "underneath it" [*"d'en dessous"*]. This is what the Greeks called *allegoria* and *hyponoïa*.

---

[1] The "round table" Foucault refers to was a discussion held during the Seventh International Philosophical Colloquium at Royaumont, July 4–8, 1964. At the Colloquium on Nietzsche, papers were presented by Foucault, Jean Beaufret, Henri Birault, Giorgio Colli and Mazzino Montinari, Gilles Deleuze, Edouard Gaéde, Danko Grlic, Pierre Klossowski, Karl Löwith, Gabriel Marcel, Herbert W. Reichert, Boris de Schloezer, Gianni Vattimo, and Jean Wahl.—TRANS.

- On the other hand, language gives rise to another suspicion: that in some way it overflows its properly verbal form, and that there are many other things in the world that speak, and that are not language. After all, it might be that nature, the sea, rustling trees, animals, faces, masks, crossed swords all speak. Perhaps there is some language articulating itself in a way that would not be verbal. This would be, if you wish, very crudely, the *semaïnon* of the Greeks.

These two suspicions, which we see appearing already in Greek texts, have not disappeared. They are still our contemporaries, as once again we have come to believe, precisely since the nineteenth century, that mute gestures, illnesses, all the confusion around us can speak as well. More than ever we are at the listening post of all this possible language, trying to overhear, beneath the words, a discourse that would be more essential.

I think that each culture, I mean each cultural form in Western civilization, has had its system of interpretation, its techniques, its methods, its way of suspecting that language means something other than what it says, and of suspecting that there is language elsewhere than in language. It seems in fact that there was an attempt to establish the system or the table, as they used to say in the seventeenth century, of all these systems of interpretation.

To understand what sort of system of interpretation the nineteenth century founded and, as a result, to what sort of system of interpretation we others, even now, belong, it seems to me that it would be necessary to take a distant reference, a type of technique as may have existed, for example, in the sixteenth century. At that time, resemblance was what gave *rise* to interpretation, at one and the same time its general site and the minimal unity that interpretation had to treat. There, where things were like each other, there, where *interpretation* would resemble itself, something wanted to be said and could be deciphered. The important role played by resemblance and all the notions that revolved like satellites around it in the cosmology, the botany, the zoology, and the philosophy of the sixteenth century are well known. To tell the truth, to our eyes as people of the twentieth century, this whole network of similitudes is fairly confused and entangled. In fact, this corpus of resemblance in the sixteenth century was perfectly organized. There were at least five exactly defined notions:

- The notion of convenience [*convenance*, propriety, expediency, fitness], *convenentia*, which is agreement (for example, of the soul to the body, or the animal series to the vegetable series).
- The notion of *sympatheïa*, sympathy, which is the identity of accidents in distinct substances.

- The notion of *emulatio,* which is the very curious parallelism of attributes in substances or in distinct beings, such that the attributes of one being are like the reflection of the other's attributes. (Thus Porta explains that the human face, with the seven parts that distinguish it, is the emulation of the sky with its seven planets.)
- The notion of *signatura,* the signature, which is the image of an invisible and hidden property among the visible properties of an individual.
- And then, of course, the notion of *analogie,* which is the identity of the relations between two or more distinct substances.

At that time, the theory of the sign and the techniques of interpretation rested in fact on a perfectly clear definition of all the possible types of resemblance, and they had established two types of completely distinct knowledge: *cognitio,* which was the passage, in some way lateral, from one resemblance to another; and *divinatio,* which was the deep knowledge [*connaissance en profondeur*], going from a superficial resemblance to a more profound resemblance. All these resemblances manifest the *consensus* of the world that lays their foundation; they resist the *simulacrum,* the false resemblance which rests on the discord between God and the Devil.

If these techniques of interpretation of the sixteenth century were left suspended by the evolution of Western thought in the seventeenth and eighteenth centuries, if the Baconian and Cartesian critique of resemblance certainly played a large part in their being put in parentheses, the nineteenth century, and quite singularly Marx, Nietzsche, and Freud, placed us once again in the presence of a new possibility of interpretation. They founded anew the possibility of a hermeneutic.

The first book of *Capital* and texts like *The Birth of Tragedy, On the Genealogy of Morals,* and the *Interpretation of Dreams* place us in the presence of these interpretive techniques. And the shock effect, the type of wound provoked in Western thought by these works, comes probably from something they reconstituted before our eyes that Marx, himself, moreover, called "hieroglyphs." This has put us in an uncomfortable situation, since these techniques of interpretation concern ourselves: since we interpret, we interpret ourselves according to these techniques. It is with these techniques of interpretation, in return, that we must question these interpreters who were Freud, Nietzsche, and Marx, so that we are always returned in a perpetual play of mirrors.

Freud says somewhere that there are three great narcissistic wounds in Western culture: the wound imposed by Copernicus; that made by Darwin, when he discovered that man was descended from the ape; and the wound made by Freud himself when he, in his turn, discovered that consciousness was based on the unconscious. I wonder whether we could not say that by involving us in an interpretive task that always reflects upon itself, Freud, Nietzsche, and Marx did not constitute around us, and for us, those mirrors which reflect to us the images whose inexhaustible wounds form our contemporary narcissism. In any case, and it is to this proposal that I would like to make some suggestions, it seems to me that Marx, Nietzsche, and Freud have not somehow multiplied the signs in the Western world. They have not given a new meaning to things which did not have any meaning. In reality they have changed the nature of the sign, and modified the way in which the sign in general could be interpreted.

The first question that I want to pose is this: have not Marx, Freud, and Nietzsche profoundly modified the distributive space [*répartition*, assessment] in which signs can be signs? At the time that I have taken for a point of reference, the sixteenth century, signs were disposed of in a homogeneous way in a space that was itself in all directions homogeneous. Signs of the earth turned back to the sky, but they turned back as well to the underground world; they turned back reciprocally, from man to animal, from animal to plant. From the nineteenth century on, that is, from Freud, Marx, and Nietzsche, signs are themselves stages in a much more differentiated space, according to a dimension that we could call depth, on the condition that one understand by that not interiority but, on the contrary, exteriority.

I am thinking in particular of the long debate with depth that Nietzsche never stopped maintaining. There is in the works of Nietzsche a critique of ideal depth, the depth of consciousness that he denounces as an invention of the philosophers. This depth would be a pure, interior search for truth. Nietzsche shows how depth implies resignation, hypocrisy, the mask, so that the interpreter, when he surveys signs in order to denounce them, must descend the length of the vertical line and show that this depth of interiority is in reality something other than what appears. It is necessary, therefore, that the interpreter descend, that he be, as he says, "the good excavator of the underworld."[2]

But when one interprets, one can in reality traverse this descending line only to restore the sparkling exteriority that has been covered up and buried. The fact is that whereas the interpreter must go himself to the bottom of things like an excavator, the movement of interpretation is, on the contrary, one that projects out over the depth, raised more and more above the depth, always leaving the depth below, exposed to ever greater visibility. The depth is now restored as an absolutely superficial secret, in such a way that the eagle's taking flight, the ascent of the mountain, all the verticality so important in *Zarathustra*, is, in the strict sense, the reversal of depth, the discovery that

---

[2] Cf. Friedrich Nietzsche, *Daybreak*, Section 446.

depth was only a game, and a crease [*pli*] in the surface. As the world becomes more profound under our gaze, one notices that everything that exercised the profundity of man was only child's play.

I wonder whether this spatiality, Nietzsche's play with profundity, could be compared to the apparently different game that Marx conducted with platitude. The concept of "platitude" is very important in the works of Marx. At the beginning of *Capital*,[3] he explains how, contrary to Perseus, he should bury himself in the uncertainty to show in fact that there are neither monsters nor profound enigmas. Instead one finds that all there is of profundity in the conception that the bourgeoisie have of money, of capital, of value, and so forth is in reality only platitude.

And, of course, it would be necessary to recall the interpretive space that Freud constituted, not only in the celebrated topology of Consciousness and the Unconscious, but equally in the rules that he formulated for psychoanalytic attention, and the deciphering by the analyst of what is said all along the spoken "chain." One should recall the spatiality, after all quite material, to which Freud attached so much importance, and which exposes the patient under the watchful gaze of the psychoanalyst.

The second theme I would like to propose to you, which is moreover somewhat tied to the former, would be to indicate that, beginning with these three men who now speak to us, interpretation at last became an endless task. To tell the truth, it was already that in the sixteenth century, but the signs were exchanged back and forth, quite simply because resemblance could only be limited. From the nineteenth century on, signs were linked in an inexhaustible as well as infinite network, not because they rested on a resemblance without border, but because there are irreducible gaps and openings.

The incompleteness of interpretation, the fact that it is always fragmented and initially remains suspended on itself, is met with again, I believe, in a sufficiently similar way in the works of Marx, Nietzsche, and Freud in the form of the denial of origination [*commencement*]: the denial of the "Robinsonade," said Marx; the distinction, so important in the works of Nietzsche, between the beginning and the origin; and the always incomplete character of the regressive and analytic practice in the works of Freud. It is above all in the works of Nietzsche and Freud, and to a lesser degree in those of Marx, that we see delineated this experience, which I believe to be so important for modern hermeneutics, that the further one goes in interpretation, the closer one approaches at the same time an absolutely dangerous region where interpretation is not only going to find its points of

---

[3] The reference to Perseus appears in the preface to the first German edition of *Capital*.—TRANS.

no return but where it is going to disappear itself as interpretation, bringing perhaps the disappearance of the interpreter himself. The existence that always approached some absolute point of interpretation would be at the same time that of a breaking point [*point de rupture*].

In the works of Freud, it is well known how progressively the discovery of this structurally open character of interpretation is forced structurally wide open. It was done first in a very allusive way, quite hidden by itself in the *Interpretation of Dreams*, when Freud analyzed his own dreams, and he invoked reasons of modesty or nondivulgence of a personal secret in order to interrupt himself. In the analysis of Dora, one sees appear this idea that interpretation must stop itself, unable to go to its conclusion in consideration of something that some years later will be called *transference*. And then, the inexhaustibility of analysis affirms itself across the entire study of transference in the infinite and infinitely problematic character of the relationship of the analyzed and the analyst, a relationship which is clearly constituent for psychoanalysis—one that opens the space in which it never stops deploying itself without ever being able to be finished.

In the works of Nietzsche also, it is clear that interpretation is always unfinished. What is philosophy for him if not a sort of philology always suspended, a philology without end, always further unfolded, a philology which would never be absolutely fixed? Why? It is, as he said in *Beyond Good and Evil*, because "to perish from absolute knowledge might be a basic characteristic of existence."[4] And yet he showed in *Ecce Homo* how he was near this absolute knowledge which makes up a part of the foundation of Being [*fondement de l'Etre*]—likewise, during Autumn, 1888 in Turin.

If one deciphers in the correspondence of Freud his constant anxiety from the moment when he discovered psychoanalysis, we can wonder whether the experience of Freud is not, at bottom, quite similar to that of Nietzsche. What is in question at the breaking point of interpretation, in this convergence of interpretation toward a point that renders it impossible, could well be something like the experience of madness—experience against which Nietzsche struggled and by which he was fascinated, experience against which Freud himself, all his life, had wrestled, not without anguish. This experience of madness would be the penalty for a movement of interpretation which approached the infinity of its center, and which collapsed, calcinated.

---

4   Cf. Friedrich Nietzsche, *Beyond Good and Evil*, Section 39. [The German text, which reads "*ja es könnte selbst zur Grundbeschaffenheit des Daseins gehören, dass man an seiner völligen Erkenntnis zugrunde ginge*," is quoted by Foucault from the French translation as "*périr par la connaissance absolue pourrait bien faire partie du fondement de l'être.*"—TRANS.]

I believe that this essential incompleteness of interpretation is linked to two other equally fundamental principles, and with the two former ones that I have just mentioned, would constitute the postulates of modern hermeneutics. This one first: if interpretation can never be brought to an end, it is simply because there is nothing to interpret. There is nothing absolutely primary to interpret, because at bottom everything is already interpretation [*tout est déjà interprétation*]. Each sign is in itself not the thing that presents itself to interpretation, but the interpretation of other signs.

There is never, if you will, an *interpretandum* which is not already an *interpretans*, so that there is established in interpretation a relation of violence as much as of elucidation. In fact, interpretation does not illuminate an interpretive topic that would offer itself passively to it; it can only violently seize an interpretation already there, which it must reverse, return, shatter with blows of a hammer. This is seen already in the works of Marx, which do not interpret the history of relations of production, but which interpret a relation that, inasmuch as it presents itself as nature, is already giving itself as an interpretation. Likewise, Freud does not interpret signs, but interpretations. Indeed, what does Freud discover under symptoms? He does not discover, as one says, "traumatisms"—he brings to light *fantasies*, with their burden of anguish, that is to say, a nucleus which is already itself, in its own being, an interpretation. Anorexia, for example, is not sent back [*renvoie*] to weaning, as the signifier would refer [*renverrait*] to the signified; but anorexia as sign, as symptom to interpret, refers to the fantasies of the false maternal breast, which is itself an interpretation, which is already in itself a speaking body. That is why Freud did not have to interpret what his patients offered to him as symptoms in language other than that of his patients; his interpretation is the interpretation of an interpretation, in the terms in which that interpretation is given. It is well known that Freud invented the "superego" [*"surmoi"*] the day when a patient said to him: "I sense a dog over me" [*"je sens un chien sur moi"*].

In the same way, Nietzsche makes himself master of interpretations which have already seized one another. There is no original signified for Nietzsche. Words themselves are nothing other than interpretations; throughout their history, they interpret before being signs, and in the long run they signify only because they are only essential interpretations. Look at the famous etymology of *agathos*.[5] This is also what Nietzsche says when he says that words have always been invented by the upper classes: they do not indicate a signified; they impose an interpretation. Therefore it is not because there are primary and enigmatic signs that we are now dedicated [*voués*] to the

---

[5] Cf. Friedrich Nietzsche, *On the Genealogy of Morals*, Essay One, Sections 4 and 5.

task of interpretation, but because there are interpretations, because beneath everything they never stop being that which expresses the great texture of violent interpretations. This is the reason that there are signs, signs which prescribe to us the interpretation of their interpretation, which prescribe to us their reversal as signs. In this sense, it can be said that *Allegoria, Hyponoïa,* are *at the foundation of language and before it,* not what are slid under the words afterwards [*non pas ce qui s'est glissé après coup sous les mots*] in order to displace them and make them vibrate, but what give birth to words, what cause them to shine with a brilliance that is never fixed. This is also why, in the works of Nietzsche, the interpreter is the "truthful one [*"véridique"*]; he is the "genuine one" [*"véritable"*], not because he makes himself master of a sleeping truth in order to utter it, but because he declares the interpretation that all truth has the function of concealing. Perhaps this preeminence of interpretation in relation to signs is what is most decisive in modern hermeneutics.

The idea that interpretation precedes the sign implies that the sign may not be simple and benevolent being, as was still the case in the sixteenth century, when the plethora of signs—the fact that things were alike—simply proved the benevolence of God, and only a transparent veil separated the sign from the signified. On the other hand, from the nineteenth century on, beginning with Freud, Marx, and Nietzsche, it seems to me that the sign is going to become malevolent. I mean that there is in the sign an ambiguous quality and a slight suspicion of ill will and "malice." Moreover, insofar as the sign is already an interpretation which is not given as such, signs are interpretations which try to justify themselves, and not the reverse.

Thus functions money as one sees it defined in the *Critique of Political Economy,* and above all in the first book of *Capital.* Symptoms also function in the same way in the works of Freud. And in the works of Nietzsche, words, justice, the binary classification of Good and Evil, that is to say, signs, are masks. By acquiring this new function of covering up [*recouvrement,* recovery] the interpretation, the sign loses its simple being as signifier that it still possessed at the time of the Renaissance. Its own thickness comes almost to open itself, and all the negative concepts which had until then remained foreign to the theory of the sign can rush into the opening. This theory had known only the transparent moment and the negative penalty [*peine*] of the veil. Now the whole play of negative concepts, contradictions, oppositions, in short, the ensemble of that play of reactive forces that Deleuze has analyzed so well in his book on Nietzsche[6] has the power to organize itself in the interior of the sign.

---

[6]   Gilles Deleuze, *Nietzsche et la philosophie* (Paris: Presses Universitaires de France, 1962). English translation: *Nietzsche and Philosophy,* translated by Hugh Tomlinson (New York: Columbia University Press, 1984).—TRANS.

"To put the dialectic back on its feet": if this expression must have a meaning, is it not to have justly replaced in the thickness of the sign, in that open, gaping space without end, in that space without real content or reconciliation, all this play of negativity that the dialectic finally uncapped in giving to it a positive sense?

Finally, the last characteristic of hermeneutics: interpretation finds itself before the obligation of interpreting itself endlessly, of always correcting itself. From here, two important consequences follow. The first is that interpretation will be henceforth always interpretation by the "who?": one does not interpret what there is in the signified, but one interprets, fundamentally, *who* has posed the interpretation. The origin [*principe*] of interpretation is nothing other than the interpreter, and this is perhaps the sense that Nietzsche gave to the word *"psychology."*[7] The second consequence is that interpretation always has to interpret itself, and it cannot fail to return to itself. In opposition to the age of signs, which is a time when payments fall due, and in opposition to the age of the dialectic, which despite everything is linear, one has an age of interpretation which is circular. This age is obliged to pass again where it has already passed, which on the whole makes that the only danger which interpretation really runs; but it is a supreme danger, for it is paradoxically the signs which make it run the risk. The death of interpretation is to believe that there are signs, signs that exist primarily, originally, actually, like coherent, pertinent, and systematic marks.

The life of interpretation, on the contrary, is to believe that there is nothing but interpretations. It seems to me that one must understand well that which many of our contemporaries forget, that *hermeneutics and semiology are two ferocious enemies.* A hermeneutic that in fact winds itself around a semiology, believing in the absolute existence of signs, gives up the violence, the incompleteness, the infinity of interpretations, so as to create a reign of terror where the mark rules [*régner la terreur de l'indice*] and suspects language— we recognize here Marxism after Marx. On the other hand, a hermeneutic that envelopes around itself this intermediate region of madness and pure language enters into the domain of languages that never stop implicating themselves—it is there that we recognize Nietzsche.

---

[7] See, for example, the definition of "psychology" as "morphology and *the doctrine of the development of the will to power"* in *Beyond Good and Evil,* Section 23.—TRANS.

Barbara Johnson

American (1947-2009)

A Critique of Western Metaphysics (1983)

*To mean, in other words, is automatically not to be. As soon as there is
meaning, there is difference.*

Best known in this country for having forged the term "deconstruction,"
Jacques Derrida follows Nietzsche and Heidegger in elaborating a critique
of "Western metaphysics," by which he means not only the Western
philosophical tradition but "everyday" thought and language as well. Western
thought, says Derrida, has always been structured in terms of dichotomies or
polarities: good vs. evil, being vs. nothingness, presence vs. absence, truth vs.
error, identity vs. difference, mind vs. matter, man vs. woman, soul vs. body,
life vs. death, nature vs. culture, speech vs. writing. These polar opposites do
not, however, stand as independent and equal entities. The second term in
each pair is considered the negative, corrupt, undesirable version of the first,
a fall away from it. Hence, absence is the lack of presence, evil is the fall from
good, error is a distortion of truth, etc. In other words, the two terms are not
simply opposed in their meanings, but are arranged in a hierarchical order
which gives the first term *priority,* in both the temporal and the qualitative
sense of the word. In general, what these hierarchical oppositions do is to
privilege unity, identity, immediacy, and temporal and spatial *presentness*
over distance, difference, dissimulation, and deferment. In its search for
the answer to the question of Being, Western philosophy has indeed always
determined Being as *presence.*

Derrida's critique of Western metaphysics focuses on its privileging of
the spoken word over the written word. The spoken word is given a higher
value because the speaker and listener are both present to the utterance
simultaneously. There is no temporal or spatial distance between speaker,
speech, and listener, since the speaker hears himself speak at the same moment
the listener does. This immediacy seems to guarantee the notion that in the
spoken word we know what we mean, mean what we say, say what we mean,

and know what we have said. Whether or not perfect understanding always occurs *in fact*, this image of perfectly self-present meaning is, according to Derrida, the underlying ideal of Western culture. Derrida has termed this belief in the self-presentation of meaning "Logocentrism," from the Greek word *Logos* (meaning speech, logic, reason, the Word of God). Writing, on the other hand, is considered by the logocentric system to be only a *representation* of speech, a secondary substitute designed for use only when speaking is impossible. Writing is thus a second-rate activity that tries to overcome distance by making use of it: the writer puts his thought on paper, distancing it from himself, transforming it into something that can be read by someone far away, even after the writer's death. This inclusion of death, distance, and difference is thought to be a corruption of the self-presence of meaning, to open meaning up to all forms of adulteration which immediacy would have prevented.

In the course of his critique, Derrida does not simply reverse this value system and say that writing is better than speech. Rather, he attempts to show that the very possibility of opposing the two terms on the basis of presence vs. absence or immediacy vs. representation is an illusion, since speech is *already* structured by difference and distance as much as writing is. The very fact that a word is divided into a phonic *signifier* and a mental *signified*, and that, as Saussure pointed out, language is a system of differences rather than a collection of independently meaningful units, indicates that language as such is already constituted by the very distances and differences it seeks to overcome. To mean, in other words, is automatically *not* to be. As soon as there is meaning, there is difference. Derrida's word for this lag inherent in any signifying act is *différance*, from the French verb *différer*, which means both "to differ" and "to defer." What Derrida attempts to demonstrate is that this *différance* inhabits the very core of what appears to be immediate and present. Even in the seemingly nonlinguistic areas of the structures of consciousness and the unconscious, Derrida analyzes the underlying necessity that induces Freud to compare the psychic apparatus to a structure of scriptural *différance*, a "mystic writing-pad."[1] The illusion of the self-presence of meaning or of consciousness is thus produced by the repression of the differential structures from which they spring.

Derrida's project in his early writings is to elaborate a science of writing called *grammatology*: a science that would study the effects of this *différance* which Western metaphysics has systematically repressed in its search for self-present Truth. But, as Derrida himself admits, the very notion of a perfectly

---

[1] See "Freud and the Scene of Writing," in *Writing and Difference*, trans. Alan Bass (Chicago: University of Chicago Press, 1978), pp. 196–231.

adequate *science* or *-logy* belongs to the logocentric discourse which the science of writing would try, precisely, to put in question. Derrida thus finds himself in the uncomfortable position of attempting to account for an error by means of tools derived from that very error. For it is not possible to show that the belief in truth is an error without implicitly believing in the notion of Truth. By the same token, to show that the binary oppositions of metaphysics are illusions is *also,* and perhaps most importantly, to show that such illusions cannot simply in turn *be opposed* without repeating the very same illusion. The task of undoing the history of logocentrism in order to disinter *différance* would thus appear to be a doubly impossible one: on the one hand, it can only be conducted by means of notions of revelation, representation, and rectification, which are *the* logocentric notions par excellence, and, on the other hand, it can only dig up something that is really nothing—a difference, a gap, an interval, a trace. How, then, can such a task be undertaken?

Jacques Derrida

French (1930-2004)

Différance (1967)

Not only is there no kingdom of différance, but différance instigates the subversion of every kingdom. Which makes it obviously threatening and infallibly dreaded by everything within us that desires a kingdom, the past or future presence of a kingdom.

I will speak, therefore, of a letter.

Of the first letter, if the alphabet, and most of the speculations which have ventured into it, are to be believed.

I will speak, therefore, of the letter *a*, this initial letter which it apparently has been necessary to insinuate, here and there, into the writing of the word *difference;* and to do so in the course of a writing on writing, and also of a writing within writing whose different trajectories thereby find themselves, at certain very determined points, intersecting with a kind of gross spelling mistake, a lapse in the discipline and law which regulate writing and keep it seemly. One can always, de facto or de jure, erase or reduce this lapse in spelling, and find it (according to situations to be analyzed each time, although amounting to the same), grave or unseemly, that is, to follow the most ingenuous hypothesis, amusing. Thus, even if one seeks to pass over such an infraction in silence, the interest that one takes in it can be recognized and situated in advance as prescribed by the mute irony, the inaudible misplacement, of this literal permutation. One can always act as if it made no difference. And I must state here and now that today's discourse will be less a justification of, and even less an apology for, this silent lapse in spelling, than a kind of insistent intensification of its play.

On the other hand, I will have to be excused if I refer, at least implicitly, to some of the texts I have ventured to publish. This is precisely because I would like to attempt, to a certain extent, and even though in principle and in the last analysis this is impossible, and impossible for essential reasons, to reassemble in a *sheaf* the different directions in which I have been able to utilize what I would call provisionally the word or concept of *différance*, or rather to let it impose itself upon me in its neographism, although as we shall see, *différance* is literally neither a word nor a concept. And I insist upon the word *sheaf* for two reasons. On the one hand, I will not be concerned, as I might have been, with describing a history and narrating its stages, text by text, context by context, demonstrating the economy that each time imposed this graphic disorder; rather, I will be concerned with the *general system of this economy*. On the other hand, the word *sheaf* seems to mark more appropriately that the assemblage to be proposed has the complex structure of a weaving, an interlacing which permits the different threads and different lines of meaning—or of force—to go off again in different directions, just as it is always ready to tie itself up with others.

Therefore, preliminarily, let me recall that this discreet graphic intervention, which neither primarily nor simply aims to shock the reader or the grammarian, came to be formulated in the course of a written investigation of a question about writing. Now it happens, I would say in effect, that this graphic difference (*a* instead of *e*), this marked difference between two apparently vocal notations, between two vowels, remains purely graphic: it is read, or it is written, but it cannot be heard. It cannot be apprehended in speech, and we will see why it also bypasses the order of apprehension in general. It is offered by a mute mark, by a tacit monument, I would even say by a pyramid, thinking not only of the form of the letter when it is printed as a capital, but also of the text in Hegel's *Encyclopedia* in which the body of the sign is compared to the Egyptian Pyramid. The *a* of *différance*, thus, is not heard; it remains silent, secret and discreet as a tomb: *oikēsis*. And thereby let us anticipate the delineation of a site, the familial residence and tomb of the proper[1] in which is produced, by *différance*, the *economy of death*. This stone—provided that one knows how to decipher its inscription—is not far from announcing the death of the tyrant.[2]

---

[1] TN. Throughout this book I will translate *le propre* as "the proper." Derrida most often intends all the senses of the word at once: that which is correct, as in *le sens propre* (proper, literal meaning), and that which is one's own, that which may be owned, that which is legally, correctly owned—all the links between proper, property, and propriety.

[2] TN. The last three sentences refer elliptically and playfully to the following ideas. Derrida first plays on the "silence" of the *a* in *différance* as being like a silent tomb, like a pyramid, like the pyramid to which Hegel compares the body of the sign. "Tomb" in Greek is *oikēsis*, which is akin to the Greek *oikos*—house—from which the word "economy" derives (*oikos*—house—and *nemein*—to manage). Thus Derrida speaks of the "economy of death" as the "familial residence and tomb of the proper." Further, and more elliptically still, Derrida speaks of the tomb, which always bears an inscription in stone, announcing the death of the tyrant. This seems to refer to Hegel's treatment of the Antigone story in the *Phenomenology*. It will be recalled that Antigone defies the tyrant Creon by burying her brother Polynices. Creon retaliates by having Antigone entombed. There she cheats

And it is a tomb that cannot even be made to resonate. In effect, I cannot let you know through my discourse, through the speech being addressed at this moment to the French Society of Philosophy, what difference I am talking about when I talk about it. I can speak of this graphic difference only through a very indirect discourse on writing, and on the condition that I specify, each time, whether I am referring to difference with an *e* or *différance* with an *a*. Which will not simplify things today, and will give us all, you and me, a great deal of trouble, if, at least, we wish to understand each other. In any event, the oral specifications that I will provide—when I say "with an *e*" or "with an *a*"—will refer uncircumventably to a *written text* that keeps watch over my discourse, to a text that I am holding in front of me, that I will read, and toward which I necessarily will attempt to direct your hands and your eyes. We will be able neither to do without the passage through a written text, nor to avoid the order of the disorder produced within it—and this, first of all, is what counts for me.

The pyramidal silence of the graphic difference between the *e* and the *a* can function, of course, only within the system of phonetic writing, and within the language and grammar which is as historically linked to phonetic writing as it is to the entire culture inseparable from phonetic writing. But I would say that this in itself—the silence that functions within only a so-called phonetic writing—quite opportunely conveys or reminds us that, contrary to a very widespread prejudice, there is no phonetic writing. There is no purely and rigorously phonetic writing. So-called phonetic writing, by all rights and in principle, and not only due to an empirical or technical insufficiency, can function only by admitting into its system nonphonetic "signs" (punctuation, spacing, etc.). And an examination of the structure and necessity of these nonphonetic signs quickly reveals that they can barely tolerate the concept of the sign itself. Better, the play of difference, which, as Saussure reminded us, is the condition for the possibility and functioning of every sign, is in itself a silent play. Inaudible is the difference between two phonemes which alone permits them to be and to operate as such. The inaudible opens up the apprehension of two present phonemes such as they present themselves. If there is no purely phonetic writing, it is that there is no purely phonetic *phōnē*. The difference which establishes phonemes and lets them be heard remains in and of itself inaudible, in every sense of the word.

---

the slow death that awaits her by hanging herself. The tyrant Creon has a change of heart too late, and—after the suicides of his son and wife, his *family*—kills himself. Thus family, death, inscription, tomb, law, economy. In a later work, *Glas,* Derrida analyzes Hegel's treatment of the *Antigone*.

It will be objected, for the same reasons, that graphic difference itself vanishes into the night, can never be sensed as a full term, but rather extends an invisible relationship, the mark of an inapparent relationship between two spectacles. Doubtless. But, from this point of view, that the difference marked in the "differ( )nce" between the *e* and the *a* eludes both vision and hearing perhaps happily suggests that here we must be permitted to refer to an order which no longer belongs to sensibility. But neither can it belong to intelligibility, to the ideality which is not fortuitously affiliated with the objectivity of *theorem* or understanding.[3] Here, therefore, we must let outselves refer to an order that resists the opposition, one of the founding oppositions of philosophy, between the sensible and the intelligible. The order which resists this opposition, and resists it because it transports it, is announced in a movement of *différance* (with an *a*) between two differences or two letters, a *différance* which belongs neither to the voice nor to writing in the usual sense, and which is located, as the strange space that will keep us together here for an hour, *between* speech and writing, and beyond the tranquil familiarity which links us to one and the other, occasionally reassuring us in our illusion that they are two.

What am I to do in order to speak of the *a* of *différance?* It goes without saying that it cannot be *exposed.* One can expose only that which at a certain moment can become *present,* manifest, that which can be shown, presented as something present, a being-present[4] in its truth, in the truth of a present or the presence of the present. Now if *différance* (and I also cross out the) what makes possible the presentation of the being-present, it is never presented as such. It is never offered to the present. Or to anyone. Reserving itself, not exposing itself, in regular fashion it exceeds the order of truth at a certain precise point, but without dissimulating itself as something, as a mysterious being, in the occult of a nonknowledge or in a hole with indeterminable

---

[3] TN. ". . . not fortuitously affiliated with the objectivity of *theôrein* or understanding." A play on words has been lost in translation here, a loss that makes this sentence difficult to understand. In the previous sentence Derrida says that the difference between the *e* and the *a* of *différenceldifférance* can neither be seen nor heard. It is not a sensible—that is, relating to the senses—difference. But, he goes on to explain, neither is this an intelligible difference, for the very names by which we conceive of objective intelligibility are already in complicity with sensibility. *Theôrein*—the Greek origin of "theory"—literally means "to look at," to *see;* and the word Derrida uses for "understanding" here is *entendement,* the noun form of *entendre,* to *hear.*

[4] TN. As in the past, *être* (*Sein*) will be translated as Being. *Etant* (*Seiendes*) will be either beings or being, depending on the context. Thus, here *étant-present* is "being-present." For a justification of this translation see Derrida, *Writing and Difference,* trans. Alan Bass (Chicago: University of Chicago Press, 1978), Translator's Introduction, p. xvii.

borders (for example, in a topology of castration).[5] In every exposition it would be exposed to disappearing as disappearance. It would risk appearing: disappearing.

So much so that the detours, locutions, and syntax in which I will often have to take recourse will resemble those of negative theology, occasionally even to the point of being indistinguishable from negative theology. Already we have had to delineate *that différance is not,* does not exist, is not a present-being (*on*) in any form; and we will be led to delineate also everything *that* it *is not,* that is, *everything;* and consequently that it has neither existence nor essence. It derives from no category of being, whether present or absent. And yet those aspects of *différance* which are thereby delineated are not theological, not even in the order of the most negative of negative theologies, which are always concerned with disengaging a superessentiality beyond the finite categories of essence and existence, that is, of presence, and always hastening to recall that God is refused the predicate of existence, only in order to acknowledge his superior, inconceivable, and ineffable mode of being. Such a development is not in question here, and this will be confirmed progressively. *Différance* is not only irreducible to any ontological or theological—ontotheological— reappropriation, but as the very opening of the space in which ontotheology— philosophy—produces its system and its history, it includes ontotheology, inscribing it and exceeding it without return.

For the same reason there is nowhere to *begin* to trace the sheaf or the graphics of *différance.* For what is put into question is precisely the quest for a rightful beginning, an absolute point of departure, a principal responsibility. The problematic of writing is opened by putting into question the value *arkhē.*[6] What I will propose here will not be elaborated simply as a philosophical discourse, operating according to principles, postulates, axioms or definitions, and proceeding along the discursive lines of a linear order of reasons. In the delineation of *différance* everything is strategic and adventurous. Strategic because no transcendent truth present outside the field of writing can govern theologically the totality of the field. Adventurous because this strategy is not a simple strategy in the sense that strategy orients tactics according to a final

[5] TN. ". . . a hole with indeterminable borders (for example, in a topology of castration)." This phrase was added to "La Différance" for its publication in the French edition of this volume and refers to the polemic Derrida had already engaged (in *Positions;* elaborated further in *le Facteur de la verité*) with Jacques Lacan. For Derrida, Lacan's "topology of castration," which assigns the "hole" or lack to a place—"a hole with determinable borders"—repeats the metaphysical gesture (albeit a negative one) of making absence, the lack, the hole, a transcendental principle that can be pinned down as such, and can thereby *govern* a theoretical discourse.

[6] TN. The Greek *arkhē* combines the values of a founding principle and of government by a controlling principle (e.g. *arch*eology, mon*arch*y).

goal, a *telos* or theme of domination, a mastery and ultimate reappropriation of the development of the field. Finally, a strategy without finality, what might be called blind tactics, or empirical wandering if the value of empiricism did not itself acquire its entire meaning in its opposition to philosophical responsibility. If there is a certain wandering in the tracing of *différance,* it no more follows the lines of philosophical-logical discourse than that of its symmetrical and integral inverse, empiricallogical discourse. The concept of *play* keeps itself beyond this opposition, announcing, on the eve of philosophy and beyond it, the unity of chance and necessity in calculations without end.

Also, by decision and as a rule of the game, if you will, turning these propositions back on themselves, we will be introduced to the thought of *différance* by the theme of strategy or the strategem. By means of this solely strategic justification, I wish to underline that the efficacity of the thematic of *différance* may very well, indeed must, one day be superseded, lending itself if not to its own replacement, at least to enmeshing itself in a chain that in truth it never will have governed. Whereby, once again, it is not theological.

I would say, first off, that *différance,* which is neither a word nor a concept, strategically seemed to me the most proper one to think, if not to master— thought, here, being that which is maintained in a certain necessary relationship with the structural limits of mastery—what is most irreducible about our "era." Therefore I am starting, strategically, from the place and the time in which "we" are, even though in the last analysis my opening is not justifiable, since it is only on the basis of *différance* and its "history" that we can allegedly know who and where "we" are, and what the limits of an "era" might be.

Even though *différance* is neither a word nor a concept, let us nevertheless attempt a simple and approximate semantic analysis that will take us to within sight of what is at stake.

We know that the verb *différer* (Latin verb *differre*) has two meanings which seem quite distinct;[7] for example in Littré they are the object of two separate articles. In this sense the Latin *differre* is not simply a translation of the Greek *diapherein,* and this will not be without consequences for us, linking our discourse to a particular language, and to a language that passes as less philosophical, less originally philosophical than the other. For the distribution of meaning in the Greek *diapherein* does not comport one of the two motifs of the Latin *differre,* to wit, the action of putting off until later, of taking into account, of taking account of time and of the forces of an operation that implies an economical calculation, a detour, a delay, a relay, a reserve, a representation—concepts that I would summarize here in a word I have

---

[7]   TN. In English the two distinct meanings of the Latin *differre* have become two separate words: to defer and to differ.

never used but that could be inscribed in this chain: *temporization.* *Différer* in this sense is to temporize, to take recourse, consciously or unconsciously, in the temporal and temporizing mediation of a detour that suspends the accomplishment or fulfillment of "desire" or "will," and equally effects this suspension in a mode that annuls or tempers its own effect. And we will see, later, how this temporization is also temporalization and spacing, the becoming-time of space and the becoming-space of time, the "originary constitution" of time and space, as metaphysics or transcendental phenomenology would say, to use the language that here is criticized and displaced.

The other sense of *différer* is the more common and identifiable one: to be not identical, to be other, discernible, etc. When dealing with *differen(ts)(ds)*, a word that can be written with a final *ts* or a final *ds*, as you will, whether it is a question of dissimilar otherness or of allergic and polemical otherness, an interval, a distance, *spacing*, must be produced between the elements other, and be produced with a certain perseverence in repetition.[8]

Now the word *différence* (with an *e*) can never refer either to *différer* as temporization or to *différends* as *polemos*.[9] Thus the word *différance* (with an *a*) is to compensate—economically—this loss of meaning, for *différance* can refer simultaneously to the entire configuration of its meanings. It is immediately and irreducibly polysemic, which will not be indifferent to the economy of my discourse here. In its polysemia this word, of course, like any meaning, must defer to the discourse in which it occurs, its interpretive context; but in a way it defers itself, or at least does so more readily than any other word, the *a* immediately deriving from the present participle (*différant*), thereby bringing us close to the very action of the verb *différer*, before it has even produced an effect constituted as something different or as *différence* (with an *e*).[10] In a conceptuality adhering to classical strictures "*différance*" would be said to

---

[8] TN. The next few sentences will require some annotation, to be found in this note and the next two. In this sentence Derrida is pointing out that two words that sound exactly alike in French (*différents, différends*) refer to the sense of *differre* that implies spacing, otherness—difference in its usual English sense. *Les différents* are different things; *les différends* are differences of opinion, grounds for dispute—whence the references to *allergy* (from the Greek *allos*, other) and polemics.

[9] TN. However, to continue the last note, *différence* (in French) does not convey the sense of active putting off, of deferring (*différance* in what would be its usual sense in French, if it were a word in common usage), or the sense of active polemical difference, actively differing with someone or something. ("Active" here, though, is not really correct, for reasons that Derrida will explain below.) The point is that there is no noun-verb, no gerund for either sense in French.

[10] TN. Such a gerund would normally be constructed from the present participle of the verb: *différant.* Curiously then, the noun *différance* suspends itself between the two senses of *différant*—deferring, differing. We might say that it defers differing, and differs from deferring, in and of itself.

designate a constitutive, productive, and originary causality, the process of scission and division which would produce or constitute different things or differences. But, because it brings us close to the infinitive and active kernel of *différer*, *différance* (with an *a*) neutralizes what the infinitive denotes as simply active, just as *mouvance* in our language does not simply mean the fact of moving, of moving oneself or of being moved. No more is resonance the act of resonating. We must consider that in the usage of our language the ending *-ance* remains undecided *between* the active and the passive. And we will see why that which lets itself be designated *différance* is neither simply active nor simply passive, announcing or rather recalling something like the middle voice, saying an operation that is not an operation, an operation that cannot be conceived either as passion or as the action of a subject on an object, or on the basis of the categories of agent or patient, neither on the basis of nor moving toward any of these *terms*. For the middle voice, a certain nontransitivity, may be what philosophy, at its outset, distributed into an active and a passive voice, thereby constituting itself by means of this repression.

Différance as temporization, *différance* as spacing. How are they to be joined?

Let us start, since we are already there, from the problematic of the sign and of writing. The sign is usually said to be put in the place of the thing itself, the present thing, "thing" here standing equally for meaning or referent. The sign represents the present in its absence. It takes the place of the present. When we cannot grasp or show the thing, state the present, the being-present, when the present cannot be presented, we signify, we go through the detour of the sign. We take or give signs. We signal. The sign, in this sense, is deferred presence. Whether we are concerned with the verbal or the written sign, with the monetary sign, or with electoral delegation and political representation, the circulation of signs defers the moment in which we can encounter the thing itself, make it ours, consume or expend it, touch it, see it, intuit its presence. What I am describing here in order to define it is the classically determined structure of the sign in all the banality of its characteristics—signification as the *différance* of temporization. And this structure presupposes that the sign, which defers presence, is conceivable only on the *basis* of the presence that it defers and *moving toward* the deferred presence that it aims to reappropriate. According to this classical semiology, the substitution of the sign for the thing itself is both *secondary* and *provisional*: secondary due to an original and lost presence from which the sign thus derives; provisional as concerns this final and missing presence toward which the sign in this sense is a movement of mediation.

In attempting to put into question these traits of the provisional secondariness of the substitute, one would come to see something like an originary *différance;* but one could no longer call it originary or final in the extent to which the values of origin, archi-, *telos, eskhaton,* etc. have always denoted presence—*ousia, parousia.*[11] To put into question the secondary and provisional characteristics of the sign, to oppose to them an "originary" *différance,* therefore would have two consequences.

1. One could no longer include *différance* in the concept of the sign, which always has meant the representation of a presence, and has been constituted in a system (thought or language) governed by and moving toward presence.
2. And thereby one puts into question the authority of presence, or of its simple symmetrical opposite, absence or lack. Thus one questions the limit which has always constrained us, which still constrains us—as inhabitants of a language and a system of thought—to formulate the meaning of Being in general as presence or absence, in the categories of being or beingness (*ousia*). Already it appears that the type of question to which we are redirected is, let us say, of the Heideggerian type, and that *différance seems* to lead back to the ontico-ontological difference. I will be permitted to hold off on this reference. I will note only that between difference as temporization-temporalization, which can no longer be conceived within the horizon of the present, and what Heidegger says in *Being and Time* about temporalization as the transcendental horizon of the question of Being, which must be liberated from its traditional, metaphysical domination by the present and the now, there is a strict communication, even though not an exhaustive and irreducibly necessary one.

But first let us remain within the semiological problematic in order to see *différance* as temporization and *différance* as spacing conjoined. Most of the semiological or linguistic researches that dominate the field of thought today, whether due to their own results or to the regulatory model that they find themselves acknowledging everywhere, refer genealogically to Saussure (correctly or incorrectly) as their common inaugurator. Now Saussure first of all is the thinker who put the *arbitrary character of the sign* and the *differential character* of the sign at the very foundation of general semiology, particularly linguistics. And, as we know, these two motifs—arbitrary and differential—are inseparable in his view. There can be arbitrariness only because the system of signs is constituted solely by the differences in terms,

---

[11] TN. *Ousia* and *parousia* imply presence as both origin and end, the founding principle (*arkhē-*) as that toward which one moves (*telos, eskhaton*).

and not by their plenitude. The elements of signification function due not to the compact force of their nuclei but rather to the network of oppositions that distinguishes them, and then relates them one to another. "Arbitrary and differential," says Saussure, "are two correlative characteristics."

Now this principle of difference, as the condition for signification, affects the *totality* of the sign, that is the sign as both signified and signifier. The signified is the concept, the ideal meaning; and the signifier is what Saussure calls the "image," the "psychical imprint" of a material, physical—for example, acoustical—phenomenon. We do not have to go into all the problems posed by these definitions here. Let us cite Saussure only at the point which interests us: "The conceptual side of value is made up solely of relations and differences with respect to the other terms of language, and the same can be said of its material side . . . Everything that has been said up to this point boils down to this: in language there are only differences. Even more important: a difference generally implies positive terms between which the difference is set up; but in language there are only differences *without positive terms.* Whether we take the signified or the signifier, language has neither ideas nor sounds that existed before the linguistic system, but only conceptual and phonic differences that have issued from the system. The idea or phonic substance that a sign contains is of less importance than the other signs that surround it."[12]

The first consequence to be drawn from this is that the signified concept is never present in and of itself, in a sufficient presence that would refer only to itself. Essentially and lawfully, every concept is inscribed in a chain or in a system within which it refers to the other, to other concepts, by means of the systematic play of differences. Such a play, *différance,* is thus no longer simply a concept, but rather the possibility of conceptuality, of a conceptual process and system in general. For the same reason, *différance,* which is not a concept, is not simply a word, that is, what is generally represented as the calm, present, and self-referential unity of concept and phonic material. Later we will look into the word in general.

The difference of which Saussure speaks is itself, therefore, neither a concept nor a word among others. The same can be said, a fortiori, of *différance.* And we are thereby led to explicate the relation of one to the other.

In a language, in the *system* of language, there are only differences. Therefore a taxonomical operation can undertake the systematic, statistical, and classificatory inventory of a language. But, on the one hand, these

---

[12] TN. Ferdinand de Saussure, *Course in General Linguistics,* trans. Wade Baskin (New York: Philosophical Library, 1959), pp. 117–18, 120.

differences *play:* in language, in speech too, and in the exchange between language and speech. On the other hand, these differences are themselves *effects.* They have not fallen from the sky fully formed, and are no more inscribed in a *topos noētos,* than they are prescribed in the gray matter of the brain. If the word "history" did not in and of itself convey the motif of a final repression of difference, one could say that only differences can be "historical" from the outset and in each of their aspects.

What is written as *différance,* then, will be the playing movement that "produces"—by means of something that is not simply an activity—these differences, these effects of difference. This does not mean that the *différance* that produces differences is somehow before them, in a simple and unmodified—in-different—present. *Différance* is the non-full, non-simple, structured and differentiating origin of differences. Thus, the name "origin" no longer suits it.

Since language, which Saussure says is a classification, has not fallen from the sky, its differences have been produced, are produced effects, but they are effects which do not find their cause in a subject or a substance, in a thing in general, a being that is somewhere present, thereby eluding the play of *différance.*

If such a presence were implied in the concept of cause in general, in the most classical fashion, we then would have to speak of an effect without a cause, which very quickly would lead to speaking of no effect at all. I have attempted to indicate a way out of the closure of this framework via the "trace," which is no more an effect than it has a cause, but which in and of itself, outside its text, is not sufficient to operate the necessary transgression.

Since there is no presence before and outside semiological difference, what Saussure has written about language can be extended to the sign in general: "Language is necessary in order for speech to be intelligible and to produce all of its effects; but the latter is necessary in order for language to be established; historically, the fact of speech always comes first."[13]

Retaining at least the framework, if not the content, of this requirement formulated by Saussure, we will designate as *différance* the movement according to which language, or any code, any system of referral in general, is constituted "historically" as a weave of differences. "Is constituted," "is produced," "is created," "movement," "historically," etc., necessarily being understood beyond the metaphysical language in which they are retained, along with all their implications. We ought to demonstrate why concepts like *production,* constitution, and history remain in complicity with what is at

---

[13] TN. Ibid., p. 18.

issue here. But this would take me too far today—toward the theory of the representation of the "circle" in which we appear to be enclosed—and I utilize such concepts, like many others, only for their strategic convenience and in order to undertake their deconstruction at the currently most decisive point. In any event, it will be understood, by means of the circle in which we appear to be engaged, that as it is written here, *différance* is no more static than it is genetic, no more structural than historical. Or is no less so; and to object to this on the basis of the oldest of metaphysical oppositions (for example, by setting some generative point of view against a structural-taxonomical point of view, or vice versa) would be, above all, not to read what here is missing from orthographical ethics. Such oppositions have not the least pertinence to *différance*, which makes the thinking of it uneasy and uncomfortable.

Now if we consider the chain in which *différance* lends itself to a certain number of nonsynonymous substitutions, according to the necessity of the context, why have recourse to the "reserve," to "archi-writing," to the "archi-trace," to "spacing," that is, to the "supplement," or to the *pharmakon,* and soon to the hymen, to the margin-mark-march, etc.[14]

Let us [begin again]. It is because of *différance* that the movement of signification is possible only if each so-called "present" element, each element appearing on the scene of presence, is related to something other than itself, thereby keeping within itself the mark of the past element, and already letting itself be vitiated by the mark of its relation to the future element, this trace being related no less to what is called the future than to what is called the past, and constituting what is called the present by means of this very relation to what it is not: what it absolutely is not, not even a past or a future as a modified present. An interval must separate the present from what it is not in order for the present to be itself, but this interval that constitutes it as present must, by the same token, divide the present in and of itself, thereby also dividing, along with the present, everything that is thought on the basis of the present, that is, in our metaphysical language, every being, and singularly substance or the subject. In constituting itself, in dividing itself

---

14 TN. All these terms refer to writing and inscribe *différance* within themselves, as Derrida says, according to the context. The supplement (*supplément*) is Rousseau's word to describe writing (analyzed in *Of Grammatology,* trans. Gayatri Spivak [Baltimore: Johns Hopkins University Press, 1976]). It means *both* the missing piece and the extra piece. The *pharmakon* is Plato's word for writing (analyzed in "Plato's Pharmacy" in *Dissemination,* trans. Barbara Johnson [Chicago: University of Chicago Press, 1981]), meaning *both* remedy and poison; the hymen (*l'hymen*) comes from Derrida's analysis of Mallarmé's writing and Mallarmé's reflections on writing ("The Double Session" in *Dissemination*) and refers *both* to virginity and to consummation; *marge-marque-marche* is the series *en différance* that Derrida applies to Sollers's *Nombres* ("Dissemination" in *Dissemination*).

dynamically, this interval is what might be called *spacing,* the becoming-space of time or the becoming-time of space *(temporization).* And it is this constitution of the present, as an "originary" and irreducibly nonsimple (and therefore, *stricto sensu* nonoriginary) synthesis of marks, or traces of retentions and protentions (to reproduce analogically and provisionally a phenomenological and transcendental language that soon will reveal itself to be inadequate), that I propose to call archi-writing, archi-trace, or *différance.* Which (is) (simultaneously) spacing (and) temporization.

Could not this (active) movement of (the production of) *différance* without origin be called simply, and without neographism, *differentiation?* Such a word, among other confusions, would have left open the possibility of an organic, original, and homogeneous unity that eventually would come to be divided, to receive difference as an event. And above all, since it is formed from the verb "to differentiate," it would negate the economic signification of the detour, the temporizing delay, "deferral." Here, a remark in passing, which I owe to a recent reading of a text that Koyré (in 1934, in *Revue d'histoire et de philosophic réligieuse,* and reprinted in his *Etudes d'histoire de la pensée philosophique)* devoted to "Hegel in Jena." In this text Koyré gives long citations, in German, of the Jena *Logic,* and proposes their translation. On two occasions he encounters the expression *differente Beziehung* in Hegel's text. This word *(different),* with its Latin root, is rare in German and, I believe, in Hegel, who prefers *verschieden* or *ungleich,* calling difference *Unterschied* and qualitative variety *Verschiedenheit.* In the Jena *Logic* he uses the word *different* precisely where he treats of time and the present. Before getting to a valuable comment of Koyré's, let us look at some sentences from Hegel, such as Koyré translates them: "The infinite, in this simplicity, is, as a moment opposed to the equal-to-itself, the negative, and in its moments, although it is (itself) presented to and in itself the totality, (it is) what excludes in general, the point or limit; but in its own (action of) negating, it is related immediately to the other and negates itself by itself. The limit or moment of the present *(der Gegen-wart),* the absolute 'this' of time, or the now, is of an absolutely negative simplicity, which absolutely excludes from itself all multiplicity, and, by virtue of this, is absolutely determined; it is not whole or a *quantum* which would be extended in itself (and) which, in itself, also would have an undetermined moment, a diversity which, as indifferent *(gleichgultig)* or exterior in itself, would be related to an other *(auf ein anderes bezöge),* but in this is a relation absolutely different from the simple *(sondern es ist absolut differente Beziehung)."* And Koyré most remarkably specifies in a note: "different Relation: *differente Beziehung.* One might say: 'differentiating relation.'" And on the next page, another text of Hegel's in which one can read this: *"Diese Beziehung ist Gegenwart, als eine differente Beziehung* (This relationship is [the] present as a different relationship)." Another note of Koyré's: "The term *different* here is taken in an active sense."[15]

Writing *"différant"*[16] or *"différance"* (with an *a*) would have had the advantage of making it possible to translate Hegel at that particular point—which is also an absolutely decisive point in his discourse—without further notes or specifications. And the translation would be, as it always must be, a transformation of one language by another. I contend, of course, that the word *différance* can also serve other purposes: first, because it marks not only the activity of "originary" difference, but also the temporizing detour of deferral; and above all because *différance* thus written, although maintaining relations of profound affinity with Hegelian discourse (such as it must be read), is also, up to a certain point, unable to break with that discourse (which has no kind of meaning or chance); but it can operate a kind of infinitesimal and radical displacement of it, whose space I attempt to delineate elsewhere but of which it would be difficult to speak briefly here.

Differences, thus, are "produced"—deferred—by *différance*. But *what* defers or *who* defers? In other words, *what is différance?* With this question we reach another level and another resource of our problematic.

What differs? Who differs? What is *différance?*

If we answered these questions before examining them as questions, before turning them back on themselves, and before suspecting their very form, including what seems most natural and necessary about them, we would immediately fall back into what we have just disengaged ourselves from. In effect, if we accepted the form of the question, in its meaning and its syntax ("what is?" "who is?" "who is it that?"), we would have to conclude that *différance* has been derived, has happened, is to be mastered and governed on the basis of the point of a present being, which itself could be some thing, a form, a state, a power in the world to which all kinds of names might be given, a *what*, or a present being as a *subject*, a *who*. And in this last case, notably, one would conclude implicitly that this present being, for example a

15 TN. Alexandre Koyré, "Hegel à lena," in *Etudes d'histoire de la pensée philosophique* (Paris: Armand Colin, 1961), pp. 153–54. In his translation of "La différance" (in *Speech and Phenomena* [Evanston: Northwestern University Press, 1973]), David Allison notes (p. 144) that the citation from Hegel comes from "Jensener Logik, Metaphysik, und Naturphilosophie" in *Sämtliche Werke* (Leipzig: F. Meiner, 1925), XVIII, 202. Allison himself translated Hegel's text, and I have modified his translation.

16 TN. The point here, which cannot be conveyed in English, is that Koyré's realization that Hegel is describing a "differentiating relation," or "different" in an active sense, is precisely what the formation of *différance* from the participle *différant* describes, as explained in notes 9 and 10 above. And that it is the *present* that is described as differing from and deferring itself helps clarify Derrida's argument (at the end of the essay) that presence is to be rethought as the trace of the trace, as *différance* differed-and-deferred.

being present to itself, as consciousness, eventually would come to defer or to differ: whether by delaying and turning away from the fulfillment of a "need" or a "desire," or by differing from itself. But in neither of these cases would such a present being be "constituted" by this *différance*.

Now if we refer, once again, to semiological difference, of what does Saussure, in particular, remind us? That "language [which only consists of differences] is not a function of the speaking subject." This implies that the subject (in its identity with itself, or eventually in its consciousness of its identity with itself, its self-consciousness) is inscribed in language, is a "function" of language, becomes a *speaking* subject only by making its speech conform—even in so-called "creation," or in so-called "transgression"—to the system of the rules of language as a system of differences, or at very least by conforming to the general law of *différance*, or by adhering to the principle of language which Saussure says is "spoken language minus speech." "Language is necessary for the spoken word to be intelligible and so that it can produce all of its effects."[17]

If, by hypothesis, we maintain that the opposition of speech to language is absolutely rigorous, then *différance* would be not only the play of differences within language but also the relation of speech to language, the detour through which I must pass in order to speak, the silent promise I must make; and this is equally valid for semiology in general, governing all the relations of usage to schemata, of message to code, etc. (Elsewhere I have attempted to suggest that this *différance* in language, and in the relation of speech and language, forbids the essential dissociation of speech and language that Saussure, at another level of his discourse, traditionally wished to delineate. The practice of a language or of a code supposing a play of forms without a determined and invariable substance, and also supposing in the practice of this play a retention and protention of differences, a spacing and a temporization, a play of traces—all this must be a kind of writing before the letter, an archi-writing without a present origin, without archi-. Whence the regular erasure of the archi-, and the transformation of general semiology into grammatology, this latter executing a critical labor on everything within semiology, including the central concept of the sign, that maintained metaphysical presuppositions incompatible with the motif of *différance*.)

One might be tempted by an objection: certainly the subject becomes a *speaking* subject only in its commerce with the system of linguistic differences; or yet, the subject becomes a *signifying* (signifying in general, by means of speech or any other sign) subject only by inscribing itself in the system of differences. Certainly in this sense the speaking or signifying

---

[17] TN. Saussure, *Course in General Linguistics*, p. 37.

subject could not be present to itself, as speaking or signifying, without the play of linguistic or semiological *différance*. But can one not conceive of a presence, and of a presence to itself of the subject before speech or signs, a presence to itself of the subject in a silent and intuitive consciousness?

Such a question therefore supposes that, prior to the sign and outside it, excluding any trace and any *différance*, something like consciousness is possible. And that consciousness, before distributing its signs in space and in the world, can gather itself into its presence. But what is consciousness? What does "consciousness" mean? Most often, in the very form of meaning, in all its modifications, consciousness offers itself to thought only as self-presence, as the perception of self in presence. And what holds for consciousness holds here for so-called subjective existence in general. Just as the category of the subject cannot be, and never has been, thought without the reference to presence as *hupokeimenon* or as *ousia*, etc., so the subject as consciousness has never manifested itself except as self-presence. The privilege granted to consciousness therefore signifies the privilege granted to the present; and even if one describes the transcendental temporality of consciousness, and at the depth at which Husserl does so, one grants to the "living present" the power of synthesizing traces, and of incessantly reassembling them.

This privilege is the ether of metaphysics, the element of our thought that is caught in the language of metaphysics. One can delimit such a closure today only by soliciting[18] the value of presence that Heidegger has shown to be the ontotheological determination of Being; and in thus soliciting the value of presence, by means of an interrogation whose status must be completely exceptional, we are also examining the absolute privilege of this form or epoch of presence in general that is consciousness as meaning[19] in self-presence.

Thus one comes to posit presence—and specifically consciousness, the being beside itself of consciousness—no longer as the absolutely central form of Being but as a "determination" and as an "effect." A determination or an effect within a system which is no longer that of presence but of *différance*, a system that no longer tolerates the opposition of activity and passivity, nor that of cause and effect, or of indetermination and determination, etc., such that in designating consciousness as an effect or a determination, one continues—for strategic reasons that can be more or less lucidly deliberated

---

[18] TN. The French *solliciter*, as the English *solicit*, derives from an Old Latin expression meaning to shake the whole, to make something tremble in its entirety. Derrida comments on this later, but is already using "to solicit" in this sense here.

[19] TN. "Meaning" here is the weak translation of *vouloir-dire*, which has a strong sense of willing (*voluntas*) to say, putting the attempt to mean in conjunction with speech, a crucial conjunction for Derrida.

and systematically calculated—to operate according to the lexicon of that which one is de-limiting.

Before being so radically and purposely the gesture of Heidegger, this gesture was also made by Nietzsche and Freud, both of whom, as is well known, and sometimes in very similar fashion, put consciousness into question in its assured certainty of itself. Now is it not remarkable that they both did so on the basis of the motif of *différance*?

Différance appears almost by name in their texts, and in those places where everything is at stake. I cannot expand upon this here; I will only recall that for Nietzsche "the great principal activity is unconscious," and that consciousness is the effect of forces whose essence, byways, and modalities are not proper to it. Force itself is never present; it is only a play of differences and quantities. There would be no force in general without the difference between forces; and here the difference of quantity counts more than the content of the quantity, more than absolute size itself. "Quantity itself, therefore, is not separable from the difference of quantity. The difference of quantity is the essence of force, the relation of force to force. The dream of two equal forces, even if they are granted an opposition of meaning, is an approximate and crude dream, a statistical dream, plunged into by the living but dispelled by chemistry."[20] Is not all of Nietzsche's thought a critique of philosophy as an active indifference to difference, as the system of adiaphoristic reduction or repression? Which according to the same logic, according to logic itself, does not exclude that philosophy lives *in* and *on différance*, thereby blinding itself to the *same*, which is not the identical. The same, precisely, is *différance* (with an *a*) as the displaced and equivocal passage of one different thing to another, from one term of an opposition to the other. Thus one could reconsider all the pairs of opposites on which philosophy is constructed and on which our discourse lives, not in order to see opposition erase itself but to see what indicates that each of the terms must appear as the *différance* of the other, as the other different and deferred in the economy of the same (the intelligible as differing-deferring the sensible, as the sensible different and deferred; the concept as different and deferred, differing-deferring intuition; culture as nature different and deferred, differing-deferring; all the others of *physis— tekhné, nomos, thesis,* society, freedom, history, mind, etc.—as *physis* different and deferred, or as *physis* differing and deferring. *Physis* in *différance*. And in this we may see the site of a reinterpretation of *mimēsis* in its alleged opposition to *physis*). And on the basis of this unfolding of the same as *différance*, we see announced the sameness of *différance* and repetition in the eternal return.

---

[20] Gilles Deleuze, *Nietzsche et la philosophie* (Paris: Presses Universitaires de France, 1970), p. 49.

Themes in Nietzsche's work that are linked to the symptomatology that always diagnoses the detour or ruse of an agency disguised in its *différance;* or further, to the entire thematic of active interpretation, which substitutes incessant deciphering for the unveiling of truth as the presentation of the thing itself in its presence, etc. Figures without truth, or at least a system of figures not dominated by the value of truth, which then becomes only an included, inscribed, circumscribed function.

Thus, *différance* is the name we might give to the "active," moving discord of different forces, and of differences of forces, that Nietzsche sets up against the entire system of metaphysical grammar, wherever this system governs culture, philosophy, and science.

It is historically significant that this diaphoristics, which, as an energetics or economics of forces, commits itself to putting into question the primacy of presence as consciousness, is also the major motif of Freud's thought: another diaphoristics, which in its entirety is both a theory of the figure (or of the trace) and an energetics. The putting into question of the authority of consciousness is first and always differential.

The two apparently different values of *différance* are tied together in Freudian theory: to differ as discernibility, distinction, separation, diastem, *spacing;* and to defer as detour, relay, reserve, *temporization.*

1. The concepts of trace (*Spur*), of breaching (*Bahnung*),²¹ and of the forces of breaching, from the *Project* on, are inseparable from the concept of difference. The origin of memory, and of the psyche as (conscious or unconscious) memory in general, can be described only by taking into account the difference between breaches. Freud says so overtly. There is no breach without difference and no difference without trace.

2. All the differences in the production of unconscious traces and in the processes of inscription (*Niederschrift*) can also be interpreted as moments of *différance,* in the sense of putting into reserve. According to a schema that never ceased to guide Freud's thought, the movement of the trace is described as an effort of life to protect itself by *deferring* the dangerous investment, by constituting a reserve (*Vorrat*). And all the oppositions that furrow Freudian thought relate each of his concepts one to another as moments of a detour in the economy of *différance.* One

---

²¹ TN. Derrida is referring here to his essay "Freud and the Scene of Writing" in *Writing and Difference.* "Breaching" is the translation for *Bahnung* that I adopted there: it conveys more of the sense of breaking open (as in the German *Bahnung* and the French *frayage*) than the Standard Edition's "facilitation." The *Project* Derrida refers to here is the *Project for a Scientific Psychology* (1895), in which Freud attempted to cast his psychological thinking in a neurological framework.

is but the other different and deferred, one differing and deferring the other. One is the other in *différance*, one is the *différance* of the other. This is why every apparently rigorous and irreducible *opposition* (for example the opposition of the secondary to the primary) comes to be qualified, at one moment or another, as a "theoretical fiction." Again, it is thereby, for example (but such an example governs, and communicates with, everything), that the difference between the pleasure principle and the reality principle is only *différance* as detour. In *Beyond the Pleasure Principle* Freud writes: "Under the influence of the ego's instincts of self-preservation, the pleasure principle is replaced by the reality principle. This latter principle does not abandon the intention of ultimately obtaining pleasure, but it nevertheless demands and carries into effect the postponement of satisfaction, the abandonment of a number of possibilities of gaining satisfaction and the temporary toleration of un-pleasure as a step on the long indirect road (*Aufschub*) to pleasure."[22]

Here we are touching upon the point of greatest obscurity, on the very enigma of *différance*, on precisely that which divides its very concept by means of a strange cleavage. We must not hasten to decide. How are we to think *simultaneously*, on the one hand, *différance* as the economic detour which, in the element of the same, always aims at coming back to the pleasure or the presence that have been deferred by (conscious or unconscious) calculation, and, on the other hand, *différance* as the relation to an impossible presence, as expenditure without reserve, as the irreparable loss of presence, the irreversible usage of energy, that is, as the death instinct, and as the entirely other relationship that apparently interrupts every economy? It is evident—and this is the evident itself—that the economical and the noneconomical, the same and the entirely other, etc., cannot be thought *together*. If *différance* is unthinkable in this way, perhaps we should not hasten to make it evident, in the philosophical element of evidentiality which would make short work of dissipating the mirage and illogicalness of *différance* and would do so with the infallibility of calculations that we are well acquainted with, having precisely recognized their place, necessity, and function in the structure of *différance*. Elsewhere, in a reading of Bataille, I have attempted to indicate what might come of a rigorous and, in a new sense, "scientific" *relating* of the "restricted economy" that takes no part in expenditure without reserve, death, opening itself to nonmeaning, etc., to a general economy that *takes into account* the nonreserve, that

---

[22] TN. *The Standard Edition of the Complete Psychological Works* (London: Hogarth Press, 1950 [hereafter cited as *SE*]), vol. 18, p. 10.

keeps in reserve the nonreserve, if it can be put thus. I am speaking of a relationship between a *différance* that can make a profit on its investment and a *différance* that misses its profit, the *investiture* of a presence that is pure and without loss here being confused with absolute loss, with death. Through such a relating of a restricted and a general economy the very project of philosophy, under the privileged heading of Hegelianism, is displaced and reinscribed. The *Aufhebung—la relève*—is constrained into writing itself otherwise. Or perhaps simply into writing itself. Or, better, into taking account of its consumption of writing.[23]

For the economic character of *différance* in no way implies that the deferred presence can always be found again, that we have here only an

---

[23] TN. Derrida is referring here to the reading of Hegel he proposed in "From Restricted to General Economy: A Hegelianism Without Reserve," in *Writing and Difference*. In that essay Derrida began his consideration of Hegel as the great philosophical *speculator;* thus all the economic metaphors of the previous sentences. For Derrida the deconstruction of metaphysics implies an endless confrontation with Hegelian concepts, and the move from a restricted, "speculative" philosophical economy—in which there is nothing that cannot be made to make sense, in which there is nothing *other* than meaning—to a "general" economy—which affirms that which exceeds meaning, the excess of meaning from which there can be no speculative profit—involves a reinterpretation of the central Hegelian concept: the *Aufhebung. Auflhebung* literally means "lifting up"; but it also contains the double meaning of conservation and negation. For Hegel, dialectics is a process of *Aufhebung:* every concept is to be negated and lifted up to a higher sphere in which it is thereby conserved. In this way, there is nothing from which the *Aufhebung* cannot profit. However, as Derrida points out, there is always an effect of *différance* when the same word has two contradictory meanings. Indeed it is this effect of *différance*— the excess of the trace *Aufhebung* itself—that is precisely what the *Aufhebung* can never *aufheben:* lift up, conserve, and negate. This is why Derrida wishes to constrain the *Aufhebung* to write itself otherwise, or simply to write itself, to take into account its consumption of writing. Without writing, the trace, there could be no words with double, contradictory meanings. As with *différance*, the translation of a word with a double meaning is particularly difficult, and touches upon the entire problematics of writing and *différance.* The best translators of Hegel usually cite Hegel's own delight that the most speculative of languages, German, should have provided this most speculative of words as the vehicle for his supreme speculative effort. Thus *Aufhebung* is usually best annotated and left untranslated. (Jean Hyppolite, in his French translations of Hegel, carefully annotates his rendering of *Aufheben* as both *supprimer* and *dépasser.* Baillie's rendering of *Aufhebung* as "sublation" is misleading.) Derrida, however, in his attempt to make *Aufhebung* write itself otherwise, has proposed a new translation of it that *does* take into account the effect of *différance* in its double meaning. Derrida's translation is *la relève.* The word comes from the verb *relever*, which means to lift up, as does *Aufheben.* But *relever* also means to relay, to relieve, as when one soldier on duty relieves another. Thus the conserving-and-negating lift has become *la relève*, a "lift" in which is inscribed an effect of substitution and difference, the effect of substitution and difference inscribed in the double meaning of *Aufhebung.* A. V. Miller's rendering of *Aufhebung* as "supersession" in his recent translation of the *Phenomenology* comes close to *relever* in combining the senses of raising up and replacement, although without the elegance of Derrida's maintenance of the verb meaning "to lift" (*heben, lever*) and change of prefix (*auf-, re-*). Thus we will leave *la relève* untranslated throughout, as with *différance.*

investment that provisionally and calculatedly delays the perception of its profit or the profit of its perception. Contrary to the metaphysical, dialectical, "Hegelian" interpretation of the economic movement of *différance,* we must conceive of a play in which whoever loses wins, and in which one loses and wins on every turn. If the displaced presentation remains definitively and implacably postponed, it is not that a certain present remains absent or hidden. Rather, *différance* maintains our relationship with that which we necessarily misconstrue, and which exceeds the alternative of presence and absence. A certain alterity—to which Freud gives the metaphysical name of the unconscious—is definitively exempt from every process of presentation by means of which we would call upon it to show itself in person. In this context, and beneath this guise, the unconscious is not, as we know, a hidden, virtual, or potential self-presence. It differs from, and defers, itself; which doubtless means that it is woven of differences, and also that it sends out delegates, representatives, proxies; but without any chance that the giver of proxies might "exist," might be present, be "itself" somewhere, and with even less chance that it might become conscious. In this sense, contrary to the terms of an old debate full of the metaphysical investments that it has always assumed, the "unconscious" is no more a "thing" than it is any other thing, is no more a thing than it is a virtual or masked consciousness. This radical alterity as concerns every possible mode of presence is marked by the irreducibility of the aftereffect, the delay. In order to describe traces, in order to read the traces of "unconscious" traces (there are no "conscious" traces), the language of presence and absence, the metaphysical discourse of phenomenology, is inadequate. (Although the phenomenologist is not the only one to speak this language.)

The structure of delay (*Nachträglichkeit*) in effect forbids that one make of temporalization (temporization) a simple dialectical complication of the living present as an originary and unceasing synthesis—a synthesis constantly directed back on itself, gathered in on itself and gathering—of retentional traces and protentional openings. The alterity of the "unconscious" makes us concerned not with horizons of modified—past or future—presents, but with a "past" that has never been present, and which never will be, whose future to come will never be a *production* or a reproduction in the form of presence. Therefore the concept of trace is incompatible with the concept of retention, of the becoming-past of what has been present. One cannot think the trace—and therefore, *différance*—on the basis of the present, or of the presence of the present.

A past that has never been present: this formula is the one that Emmanuel Levinas uses, although certainly in a nonpsychoanalytic way, to qualify the trace and enigma of absolute alterity: the Other.[24] Within these limits, and from this point of view at least, the thought of *différance* implies the entire critique of classical ontology undertaken by Levinas. And the concept of the trace, like that of *différance* thereby organizes, along the lines of these different traces and differences of traces, in Nietzsche's sense, in Freud's sense, in Levinas's sense—these "names of authors" here being only indices—the network which reassembles and traverses our "era" as the delimitation of the ontology of presence.

Which is to say the ontology of beings and beingness. It is the domination of beings that *différance* everywhere comes to solicit, in the sense that *sollicitare,* in old Latin, means to shake as a whole, to make tremble in entirety. Therefore, it is the determination of Being as presence or as beingness that is interrogated by the thought of *différance.* Such a question could not emerge and be understood unless the difference between Being and beings were somewhere to be broached. First consequence: *différance* is not. It is not a present being, however excellent, unique, principal, or transcendent. It governs nothing, reigns over nothing, and nowhere exercises any authority. It is not announced by any capital letter. Not only is there no kingdom of *différance,* but *différance* instigates the subversion of every kingdom. Which makes it obviously threatening and infallibly dreaded by everything within us that desires a kingdom, the past or future presence of a kingdom. And it is always in the name of a kingdom that one may reproach *différance* with wishing to reign, believing that one sees it aggrandize itself with a capital letter.

Can *différance,* for these reasons, settle down into the division of the ontico-ontological difference, such as it is thought, such as its "epoch" in particular is thought, "through," if it may still be expressed such, Heidegger's uncircumventable meditation?

There is no simple answer to such a question.

In a certain aspect of itself, *différance* is certainly but the historical and epochal *unfolding* of Being or of the ontological difference. The *a* of *différance* marks the *movement* of this unfolding.

And yet, are not the thought of the *meaning* or *truth* of Being, the determination of *différance* as the ontico-ontological difference, difference thought within the horizon of the question *of Being,* still intrametaphysical effects of *différance?* The unfolding of *différance* is perhaps not solely the truth of Being, or of the epochality of Being: Perhaps we must attempt to think this unheard-of thought, this silent tracing: that the history of Being,

---

[24] TN. On Levinas, and on the translation of his term *autrui* by "Other," see "Violence and Metaphysics," note 6, in *Writing and Difference.*

whose thought engages the Greco-Western *logos* such as it is produced via the ontological difference, is but an epoch of the *diapherein*. Henceforth one could no longer even call this an "epoch," the concept of epochality belonging to what is within history as the history of Being. Since Being has never had a "meaning," has never been thought or said as such, except by dissimulating itself in beings, then *différance*, in a certain and very strange way, (is) "older" than the ontological difference or than the truth of Being. When it has this age it can be called the play of the trace. The play of a trace which no longer belongs to the horizon of Being, but whose play transports and encloses the meaning of Being: the play of the trace, or the *différance*, which has no meaning and is not. Which does not belong. There is no maintaining, and no depth to, this bottomless chessboard on which Being is put into play.

Perhaps this is why the Heraclitean play of the *hen diapheron heautöi*, of the one differing from itself, the one in difference with itself, already is lost like a trace in the determination of the *diapherein* as ontological difference.

To think the ontological difference doubtless remains a difficult task, and any statement of it has remained almost inaudible. Further, to prepare, beyond our *logos*, for a *différance* so violent that it can be interpellated neither as the epochality of Being nor as ontological difference, is not in any way to dispense with the passage through the truth of Being, or to "criticize," "contest," or misconstrue its incessant necessity. On the contrary, we must stay within the difficulty of this passage, and repeat it in the rigorous reading of metaphysics, wherever metaphysics normalizes Western discourse, and not only in the texts of the "history of philosophy." As rigorously as possible we must permit to appear/ disappear the trace of what exceeds the truth of Being. The trace (of that) which can never be presented, the trace which itself can never be presented: that is, appear and manifest itself, as such, in its phenomenon. The trace beyond that which profoundly links fundamental ontology and phenomenology. Always differing and deferring, the trace is never as it is in the presentation of itself. It erases itself in presenting itself, muffles itself in resonating, like the *a* writing itself, inscribing its pyramid in *différance*.

The annunciating and reserved trace of this movement can always be disclosed in metaphysical discourse, and especially in the contemporary discourse which states, through the attempts to which we just referred (Nietzsche, Freud, Levinas), the closure of ontology. And especially through the Heideggerean text.

This text prompts us to examine the essence of the present, the presence of the present.

What is the present? What is it to think the present in its presence?

Let us consider, for example, the 1946 text entitled *Der Spruch des Anaximander* ("The Anaximander Fragment").[25] In this text Heidegger recalls that the forgetting of Being forgets the difference between Being and beings: ". . . to be the Being *of* beings is the matter of Being (*die Sache des Seins*). The grammatical form of this enigmatic, ambiguous genitive indicates a genesis (*Genesis*), the emergence (*Herkunft*) of what is present from presencing (*des Anwesenden aus dem Anwesen*). Yet the essence (*Wesen*) of this emergence remains concealed (*verbogen*) along with the essence of these two words. Not only that, but even the very relation between presencing and what is present (*Anwesen und Anwesenden*) remains unthought. From early on it seems as though presencing and what is present were each something for itself. Presencing itself unnoticeably becomes something present . . . The essence of presencing (*Das Wesen des Anwesens*), and with it the distinction between presencing and what is present, remains forgotten. *The oblivion of Being is oblivion of the distinction between Being and beings*" (p. 50).

In recalling the difference between Being and beings (the ontological difference) as the difference between presence and the present, Heidegger advances a proposition, a body of propositions, that we are not going to use as a subject for criticism. This would be foolishly precipitate; rather, what we shall try to do is to return to this proposition its power to provoke.

Let us proceed slowly. What Heidegger wants to mark is this: the difference between Being and beings, the forgotten of metaphysics, has disappeared without leaving a trace. The very trace of difference has been submerged. If we maintain that *différance* (is) (itself) other than absence and presence, if it *traces*, then when it is a matter of the forgetting of the difference (between Being and beings), we would have to speak of a disappearance of the trace of the trace. Which is indeed what the following passage from "The Anaximander Fragment" seems to imply: "Oblivion of Being belongs to the self-veiling essence of Being. It belongs so essentially to the destiny of Being that the dawn of this destiny rises as the unveiling of what is present in its presenting. This means that the history of Being begins with the oblivion of Being, since Being—together with its essence, its distinction from beings—keeps to itself. The distinction collapses. It remains forgotten. Although the two parties to the distinction, what is present and presencing (*das Anwesende und das Anwesen*), reveal

---

[25] TN. Martin Heidegger, *Holzwege* (Frankfurt: V. Klostermann, 1957). English translation ("The Anaximander Fragment") in *Early Greek Thinking,* trans. David Farrell Krell and Frank Capuzzi (New York: Harper and Row, 1975). All further references in the text.

themselves, they do not do so as distinguished. Rather, even the early trace (*die frühe Spur*) of the distinction is obliterated when presencing appears as something present (*das Anwesen wie ein Anwesendes erscheint*) and finds itself in the position of being the highest being present (*in einem höchsten Anwesenden*)" (pp. 50–51).

Since the trace is not a presence but the simulacrum of a presence that dislocates itself, displaces itself, refers itself, it properly has no site—erasure belongs to its structure. And not only the erasure which must always be able to overtake it (without which it would not be a trace but an indestructible and monumental substance), but also the erasure which constitutes it from the outset as a trace, which situates it as the change of site, and makes it disappear in its appearance, makes it emerge from itself in its production. The erasure of the early trace (*die frühe Spur*) of difference is therefore the "same" as its tracing in the text of metaphysics. This latter must have maintained the mark of what it has lost, reserved, put aside. The paradox of such a structure, in the language of metaphysics, is an inversion of metaphysical concepts, which produces the following effect: the present becomes the sign of the sign, the trace of the trace. It is no longer what every reference refers to in the last analysis. It becomes a function in a structure of generalized reference. It is a trace, and a trace of the erasure of the trace.

Thereby the text of metaphysics is *comprehended*. Still legible; and to be read. It is not surrounded but rather traversed by its limit, marked in its interior by the multiple furrow of its margin. Proposing *all at once* the monument and the mirage of the trace, the trace simultaneously traced and erased, simultaneously living and dead, and, as always, living in its simulation of life's preserved inscription. A pyramid. Not a stone fence to be jumped over but itself stonelike, on a wall, to be deciphered otherwise, a text without voice.

Thus one can think without contradiction, or at least without granting any pertinence to such a contradiction, what is perceptible and imperceptible in the trace. The "early trace" of difference is lost in an invisibility without return, and yet its very loss is sheltered, retained, seen, delayed. In a text. In the form of presence. In the form of the proper. Which itself is only an effect of writing.

Having stated the erasure of the early trace, Heidegger can therefore, in a contradiction without contradiction, consign, countersign, the sealing of the trace. A bit further on: "However, the distinction between Being and beings, as something forgotten, can invade our experience only if it has already unveiled itself with the presenting of what is present (*mit dem Anwesen des Anwesenden*); only if it has left a trace (*eine Spur geprägt hat*) which remains preserved (*gewahrt bleibt*) in the language to which Being comes" (p. 51).

Still further on, while meditating on Anaximander's *to khreon*, which he translates as *Brauch* (usage), Heidegger writes this: "Enjoining order and reck (*Fug und Ruch verfügend*), usage delivers to each present being (*Anwesende*) the while into which it is released. But accompanying this process is the constant danger that lingering will petrify into mere persistence (*in das blosse Beharren verhärtet*). Thus usage essentially remains at the same time the distribution (*Aushändigung*: dis-maintenance) of presenting (*des Anwesens*) into disorder (*in den Un-fug*). Usage conjoins the dis (*Der Brauch fügt das Un-*)" (p. 54).

And it is at the moment when Heidegger recognizes *usage* as *trace* that the question must be asked: can we, and to what extent, think this trace and the *dis* of *différance* as *Wesen des Seins*? Does not the *dis* of *différance* refer us beyond the history of Being, and also beyond our language, and everything that can be named in it? In the language of Being, does it not call for a necessarily violent transformation of this language by an entirely other language?

Let us make this question more specific. And to force the "trace" out of it (and has anyone thought that we have been tracking something down, something other than tracks themselves to be tracked down?), let us read this passage: 'The translation of *to khreon* as 'usage' has not resulted from a preoccupation with etymologies and dictionary meanings. The choice of the word stems from a prior crossing *over* (*Über-setzen*; trans-lation) of a thinking which tries to think the distinction in the essence of Being (*im Wesen des Seins*) in the fateful beginning of Being's oblivion. The word 'usage' is dictated to thinking in the experience (*Erfahrung*) of Being's oblivion. What properly remains to be thought in the word 'usage' has presumably left a trace (*Spur*) in *to khreon*. This trace quickly vanishes (*alsbald verschwindet*) in the destiny of Being which unfolds in world history as Western metaphysics" (p. 54).

How to conceive what is outside a text? That which is more or less than a text's *own, proper* margin? For example, what is other than the text of Western metaphysics? It is certain that the trace which "quickly vanishes in the destiny of Being (and) which unfolds . . . as Western metaphysics" escapes every determination, every name it might receive in the metaphysical text. It is sheltered, and therefore dissimulated, in these names. It does not appear in them as the trace "itself." But this is because it could never appear itself, *as such*. Heidegger also says that difference cannot appear as such: "Lichtung des Unterschiedes kann deshalb auch nicht bedeuten, class der Unterschied als der Unterschied erscheint." There is no essence of *différance*; it (is) that which not only could never be appropriated in the *as such* of its name or its appearing, but also that which threatens the authority of the *as such* in general, of the presence of the thing itself in its essence. That there is not a proper essence[26] of *différance* at this point, implies that there is neither a Being nor truth of the play of writing such as it engages *différance*.

For us, *différance* remains a metaphysical name, and all the names that it receives in our language are still, as names, metaphysical. And this is particularly the case when these names state the determination of *différance* as the difference between presence and the present (*Anwesen/Anwesend*), and above all, and is already the case when they state the determination of *différance* as the difference of Being and beings.

"Older" than Being itself, such a *différance* has no name in our language. But we "already know" that if it is unnameable, it is not provisionally so, not because our language has not yet found or received this *name*, or because we would have to seek it in another language, outside the finite system of our own. It is rather because there is no *name* for it at all, not even the name of essence or of Being, not even that of *"différance,"* which is not a name, which is not a pure nominal unity, and unceasingly dislocates itself in a chain of differing and deferring substitutions.

"There is no name for it": a proposition to be read in its *platitude*. This unnameable is not an ineffable Being which no name could approach: God,

---

[26] *Différance* is not a "species" of the genus *ontological difference*. If the "gift of presence is the property of Appropriating (*Die Cabe von Anwesen ist Eigentum des Erergnens*)" ["Time and Being," in *On Time and Being*, trans. Joan Stambaugh, New York: Harper and Row, 1972; p. 221, *différance* is not a process of propriation in any sense whatever. It is neither position (appropriation) nor negation (expropriation), but rather other. Hence it seems—but here, rather, we are marking the necessity of a future itinerary—that *différance* would be no more a species of the genus *Ereignis* than Being. Heidegger: ". . . then Being belongs into Appropriating (*Dann gehört das Sein in das Ereignen*). Giving and its gift receive their determination from Appropriating. In that case, Being would be a species of Appropriation (*Ereignis*), and not the other way around. To take refuge in such an inversion would be too cheap. Such thinking misses the matter at stake (*Sie denkt am Sachverhalt vorbei*). Appropriation (*Ereignis*) is not the encompassing general concept under which Being and time could be subsumed. Logical classifications mean nothing here. For as we think Being itself and follow what is its own (*seinem Eigenen folgen*). Being proves to be destiny's gift of presence (*gewahrte Gabe des Geschickes von Anwesenheit*), the gift granted by the giving (*Reichen*) of time. The gift of presence is the property of Appropriating (*Die Gabe von Anwesen ist Eigentum des Ereignens*)." (*On Time and Being*, pp. 21–22.)Without a displaced reinscription of this chain (Being, presence, -propriation, etc.) the relation between general or fundamental onto-logy and whatever ontology masters or makes subordinate under the rubric of a regional or particular science will never be transformed rigorously and irreversibly. Such regional sciences include not only political economy, psychoanalysis, semiolinguistics—in all of which, and perhaps more than elsewhere, the value of the *proper* plays an irreducible role—but equally all spiritualist or materialist metaphysics. The analyses articulated in this volume aim at such a preliminary articulation. It goes without saying that such a reinscription will never be contained in theoretical or philosophical discourse, or generally in any discourse or writing, but only on the scene of what I have called elsewhere the text in general (1972)

for example. This unnameable is the play which makes possible nominal effects, the relatively unitary and atomic structures that are called names, the chains of substitutions of names in which, for example, the nominal effect *différance* is itself *enmeshed,* carried off, reinscribed, just as a false entry or a false exit is still part of the game, a function of the system.

What we know, or what we would know if it were simply a question here of something to know, is that there has never been, never will be, a unique word, a master-name. This is why the thought of the letter *a* in *différance* is not the primary prescription or the prophetic annunciation of an imminent and as yet unheard-of nomination. There is nothing kerygmatic about this "word," provided that one perceives its decapita(liza)tion. And that one puts into question the name of the name.

There will be no unique name, even if it were the name of Being. And we must think this without *nostalgia,* that is, outside of the myth of a purely maternal or paternal language, a lost native country of thought. On the contrary, we must *affirm* this, in the sense in which Nietzsche puts affirmation into play, in a certain laughter and a certain step of the dance.

From the vantage of this laughter and this dance, from the vantage of this affirmation foreign to all dialectics, the other side of nostalgia, what I will call Heideggerian *hope,* comes into question. I am not unaware how shocking this word might seem here. Nevertheless I am venturing it, without excluding any of its implications, and I relate it to what still seems to me to be the metaphysical part of "The Anaximander Fragment": the quest for the proper word and the unique name. Speaking of the first word of Being (*das frühe Wort des Seins: to khreon*), Heidegger writes: "The relation to what is present that rules in the essence of presencing itself is a unique one (*ist eine einzige*), altogether incomparable to any other relation. It belongs to the uniqueness of Being itself (*Sie gehört zur Einzigkeit des Seins selbst*). Therefore, in order to name the essential nature of Being (*das wesende Seins*), language would have to find a single word, the unique word (*ein einziges, das einzige Wort*). From this we can gather how daring every thoughtful word (*denkende Wort*) addressed to Being is (*das dem Sein zugesprochen wird*). Nevertheless such daring is not impossible, since Being speaks always and everywhere throughout language" (p. 52).

Such is the question: the alliance of speech and Being in the unique word, in the finally proper name. And such is the question inscribed in the simulated affirmation of *différance.* It bears (on) each member of this sentence: "Being / speaks / always and everywhere / throughout / language."

Editor's Interlude: Two Brief Pieces on Lacanian Psychoanalytic Theory

> *Je est un autre.*
>
> Artur Rimbaud

1 The mirror stage

In his essay "The Mirror Stage as Formative of the I Function as Revealed in Psychoanalytic Experience," Jacques Lacan (1900–81) speculates about that signal event in which the human infant is propped up in front of a reflective surface and prompted by its betters to identify with what it sees.[1] Lacan argues that, prior to this event, the infant lacks (or is as yet unburdened by) any coherent sense of identity; upon the moment of the mirror stage, the young one leans in toward its own idealized reflection and psychically sets out on a path of morphological mimicry that allows (or compels) it to start getting its act together in order to function as an "I" in the larger socio-symbolic order.

On Lacan's view, this self-inaugurating spectacle—a disciplinary cultural intervention always implicated in the regnant protocols of libidinal normalization—is shot through with ambiguity and ambivalence. For the outside image that the infant takes in represents both *itself* and something *other*, an unfamiliar *thing*. Presenting the "I" to itself *as* an other, the mirror gives back the infant's *own* body as *some*body *else*, somebody *better*, superior in that the apparently free-standing figure singled out *by* the betters ("*there you are,*" they say, "*there's* our darling little one") seems to hang together seamlessly, in a unified and autonomous way that trumps the real beholder's experiential dehiscence, agential incompetence, and suckling dependence. Self-estranged at the get-go of subjectivity, the upstart ego only ever begins

---

[1] Lacan's essay was composed in 1949 but not published until the 1966 *Écrits*. For the most recent English translation, see *Écrits: The First Complete Translation in English*, translated by Bruce Fink (New York: Norton, 2006), 75–81. For an explanation of why you're getting these editorial interludes about Lacan here and not an actual excerpt from Lacan, see the Editor's Introduction.

to comprehend itself "extimately,"[2] in an unhappily ecstatic *mis*recognition, psychically registering if not actually becoming the very discrepancy between the sharper image of idealized coherence and corporeal wholeness that it *sees* and the abjectly mess-making, perceptually fragmented body that it *is*.

We might map the dynamics of this orthopedic encounter onto Freud's famous slogan *Wo Es war, soll Ich werden*—where id was, there *ego* must be, or, where it (*das Es*) was, there I (*das Ich*) must come into being.[3] But we should note the counterintuitive coordinates, the weirdly inverted where's and there's, of this ego-boosting cartography. If we apply our everyday understanding of the difference between an "I" and an "it" to the scene of the prelinguistic human situated before a mirror, we would normally place "child" on the "personological" side of the I/self/subject and "mirror" on the "material" side of the it/thing/object. In the mirror scenario, however, these "sides" are arguably reversed: the real living body of the child is the speechless "it," while the ego or "I" initially "resides" in a manufactured contraption of deadwood and glass. Paradoxically, the living *infant* exits the organically *real* and begins to enter that montage of the *imaginary* and *symbolic* that Lacan calls human reality by virtue of a formally *mortifying* experience: at the spectacular moment of the mirror stage, a *specter* of humanity, launched from the "dead" side of the mirror's surface, enters and inhabits/inhibits the dumb vitality of the *infant*, so that in a sense it's from the subjective position of the mirror-image that the Freudian slogan is articulated: where "it," that stupid, merely living body on *that* side *was*, there "I," the culturally endorsed, symbolically validated, and appropriately gendered form of personhood must be established, must move in, take over, plant the socio-symbolic's self-colonizing flag.[4]

---

[2] "Extimately" would be the adverbial form of the Lacanian neologism "extimacy," which mixes "exteriority" with "intimacy" and thereby "neatly expresses the way in which psychoanalysis problematizes the opposition between the inside and the outside, between container and contained" (Dylan Evans, *An Introductory Dictionary of Lacanian Psychoanalysis*, London and New York: Routledge, 1996, 58). The word "extimacy" signifies the always unsettling idea that "the innermost, intimate core of a person's psychical being is, at root, an alien, foreign 'thing.'" (Adrian Johnston, *Badiou, Žižek, and Political Transformations: The Cadence of Change*, Evanston: Northwestern University Press, 2009, 86).

[3] For Freud's *Wo Es war, soll Ich werden*, see Footnote 3 in the "Editor's Afterword" to *Adventures in Theory* below.

[4] Twice in that last long sentence I let the word "infant"—which means "incapable of speech"—appear as "*infant*," with the bookends *i* and *t* italicized, in order to emphasize the way the human infant is (enfolded in) the *it* and is not yet strictly speaking an *I*. This little bit of *linguistricks* works only in English, however: a singular French enfant would be ensconced in the *and*, even if the plural French *enfants* would be held within the German es—*n'est pas*?

Of course, there's next to nothing "natural" about this "planting." Like everything else in human reality, the mirror in question is always ever only artifice, an anthropogenetic product of labor, while the word "stage" in Lacan's phrase points less to some phase of biological development than to the subjective performance of political theater. Back behind the mirror (offstage, as it were) an endless panoply of socially produced and politically "interpellating" images—pretty pictures of ideal comportment and compliant identity—lies in wait, ready to capture any fledgling human subject's eye.[5] Stationed at what Lacan calls the threshold of the visible world, the mirror stage is our initial imaginary gateway to the ongoing operations of normativity that help put the "I" in ideology and keep ideology in the "I."

2 Symbolic castration

"I" remember my own castration quite clearly. It did involve a decisive "cut," but the castration of which I speak had nothing to do with real genitalia, something to do with *speaking*, and everything to do with being *severed* from—everything itself. Somewhere around four years old, unselfconsciously at play in a small backyard, I suddenly withdrew from myself in my own perception, looked down at myself as if from above, and heard myself being put into words, thinking: "No, you're not *all that*—you're only *that*."

As Lacanian psychoanalysis might parse this sentence: No (my own little echo of the prohibitory "no of the father"), you're not *all that* (with *that* being *everything*, the mythical plenitude of primary narcissism's nostalgia), you're only *that* (image or thing-presentation of small boy's body translated into even smaller pronoun, signifier constitutively exiled from its signified). In short, in other words, I remember being shortened, experientially diminished to a word, to *that* shrunken residue of an "I" that must be spoken but cannot complete itself by designating itself in any statement, that comes into linguistic being only at the cost of losing *everything*, being cut off from any oceanic *all that*. Identifying myself in language, I lost myself in it like an object—and it hurt like hell, I have to tell you.

But why regard this abrupt recognition of being *not all*, this small sacrifice of being to meaning, as a specifically *sexual* dismemberment?

---

[5] For a definition of "interpellating" and a description of the political operations of "interpellation," see Althusser's "On Ideology," the next selection in *Adventures*, and Lesson Five in *Ten Lessons*.

Why call this memory/event *castration*? There are splendid reasons not to.[6] For Lacanian psychoanalysis, however, castration is the correct word—the nonanatomically correct word—because of the way this alienating sense of losing/being lost (from) *everything* can be mapped onto a misinterpretation of the female body as castrated (*not all*), the mother's "lack" allegorizing the "incomplete" condition of the word as the presence of the absence of the thing. For psychoanalysis in general, *real* castration is completely insignificant. Castration *anxiety*, however, is for Freud the necessary condition for the normative resolution of the Oedipus complex for boys, while *symbolic* castration is for Lacan the universal condition of anyone who speaks, anyone who follows/enters/obeys the symbolic order. Subject of/to language/desire, I am castrated because I say so, or because I say "so," because I say anything at all, because language, desire, and subjectivity are all *not all*, all "no-thing," so *that* . . . .

But here I break off, allow myself to be broken off, consenting to my castration, leaving that sentence as incomplete as any "I" (that is an other) must be.

---

[6] For a lead on Derrida's various gripes against Lacan's deployment of the term "castration," see Footnote 5 in the version of "*Différance*" reprinted here in *Adventures*. See also the numerous references to/complaints against "castration" in Gayle Rubin's "Traffic in Women" in *Adventures*. See also *Ten Lessons in Theory*, Lesson Four, not to mention Dylan Evans's entry on the word in his *Introductory Dictionary of Lacanian Psychoanalysis*.

Louis Althusser

French (1918-1990)

On Ideology (1971)

"Hey, you there!"

When I put forward the concept of an Ideological State Apparatus, when I said that the ISAs 'function by ideology', I invoked a reality which needs a little discussion: ideology.

It is well known that the expression 'ideology' was invented by Cabanis, Destutt de Tracy and their friends, who assigned to it as an object the (genetic) theory of ideas. When Marx took up the term fifty years later, he gave it a quite different meaning, even in his Early Works. Here, ideology is the system of the ideas and representations which dominate the mind of a man or a social group. The ideologico-political struggle conducted by Marx as early as his articles in the *Rheinische Zeitung* inevitably and quickly brought him face to face with this reality and forced him to take his earliest intuitions further.

However, here we come upon a rather astonishing paradox. Everything seems to lead Marx to formulate a theory of ideology. In fact, *The German Ideology* does offer us, after the *1844 Manuscripts*, an explicit theory of ideology, but . . . it is not Marxist (we shall see why in a moment). As for *Capital*, although it does contain many hints towards a theory of ideologies (most visibly, the ideology of the vulgar economists), it does not contain that theory itself, which depends for the most part on a theory of ideology in general.

I should like to venture a first and very schematic outline of such a theory. The theses I am about to put forward are certainly not off the cuff, but they cannot be sustained and tested, i.e. confirmed or rejected, except by much thorough study and analysis.

Ideology has no history

One word first of all to expound the reason in principle which seems to me to found, or at least to justify, the project of a theory of ideology in general, and not a theory of particular ideologies, which, whatever their form (religious, ethical, legal, political), always express *class positions*.

It is quite obvious that it is necessary to proceed towards a theory of ideologies in the two respects I have just suggested. It will then be clear that a theory of ideologies depends in the last resort on the history of social formations, and thus of the modes of production combined in social formations, and of the class struggles which develop in them. In this sense it is clear that there can be no question of a theory of ideolog*ies in general*, since ideolog*ies* (defined in the double respect suggested above: regional and class) have a history, whose determination in the last instance is clearly situated outside ideologies alone, although it involves them.

On the contrary, if I am able to put forward the project of a theory of ideology *in general*, and if this theory really is one of the elements on which theories of ideologies depend, that entails an apparently paradoxical proposition which I shall express in the following terms: *ideology has no history.*

As we know, this formulation appears in so many words in a passage from *The German Ideology.* Marx utters it with respect to metaphysics, which, he says, has no more history than ethics (meaning also the other forms of ideology).

In *The German Ideology,* this formulation appears in a plainly positivist context. Ideology is conceived as a pure illusion, a pure dream, i.e. as nothingness. All its reality is external to it. Ideology is thus thought as an imaginary construction whose status is exactly like the theoretical status of the dream among writers before Freud. For these writers, the dream was the purely imaginary, i.e. null, result of 'day's residues', presented in an arbitrary arrangement and order, sometimes even 'inverted', in other words, in 'disorder'. For them, the dream was the imaginary, it was empty, null and arbitrarily 'stuck together' (*bricolé*), once the eyes had closed, from the residues of the only full and positive reality, the reality of the day. This is exactly the status of philosophy and ideology (since in this book philosophy is ideology *par excellence*) in *The German Ideology.*

Ideology, then, is for Marx an imaginary assemblage (*bricolage*), a pure dream, empty and vain, constituted by the 'day's residues' from the only full and positive reality, that of the concrete history of concrete material individuals materially producing their existence. It is on this basis that ideology has no history in *The German Ideology,* since its history is outside it, where the only existing history is, the history of concrete individuals, etc.

In *The German Ideology,* the thesis that ideology has no history is therefore a purely negative thesis, since it means both:

1. ideology is nothing insofar as it is a pure dream (manufactured by who knows what power: if not by the alienation of the division of labour, but that, too, is a *negative* determination);
2. ideology has no history, which emphatically does not mean that there is no history in it (on the contrary, for it is merely the pale, empty and inverted reflection of real history) but that it has no history *of its own.*

Now, while the thesis I wish to defend formally speaking adopts the terms of *The German Ideology* ('ideology has no history'), it is radically different from the positivist and historicist thesis of *The German Ideology.*

For on the one hand, I think it is possible to hold that ideologies *have a history of their own* (although it is determined in the last instance by the class struggle); and on the other, I think it is possible to hold that ideology *in general has no history,* not in a negative sense (its history is external to it), but in an absolutely positive sense.

This sense is a positive one if it is true that the peculiarity of ideology is that it is endowed with a structure and a functioning such as to make it a non-historical reality, i.e. an *omni-historical* reality, in the sense in which that structure and functioning are immutable, present in the same form throughout what we can call history, in the sense in which the *Communist Manifesto* defines history as the history of class struggles, i.e. the history of class societies.

To give a theoretical reference-point here, I might say that, to return to our example of the dream, in its Freudian conception this time, our proposition: ideology has no history, can and must (and in a way which has absolutely nothing arbitrary about it, but, quite the reverse, is theoretically necessary, for there is an organic link between the two propositions) be related directly to Freud's proposition that the *unconscious is eternal,* i.e. that it has no history.

If eternal means, not transcendent to all (temporal) history, but omnipresent, trans-historical and therefore immutable in form throughout the extent of history, I shall adopt Freud's expression word for word, and write *ideology is eternal,* exactly like the unconscious. And I add that I find this comparison theoretically justified by the fact that the eternity of the unconscious is not unrelated to the eternity of ideology in general.

That is why I believe I am justified, hypothetically at least, in proposing a theory of ideology *in general,* in the sense that Freud presented a theory of the unconscious *in general.*

To simplify the phrase, it is convenient, taking into account what has been said about ideologies, to use the plain term ideology to designate ideology in general, which I have just said has no history, or, what comes to the same thing, is eternal, i.e. omnipresent in its immutable form throughout history (= the history of social formations containing social classes). For the moment I shall restrict myself to 'class societies' and their history.

Ideology is a 'representation' of the imaginary relationship of individuals to their real conditions of existence

In order to approach my central thesis on the structure and functioning of ideology, I shall first present two theses, one negative, the other positive. The first concerns the object, which is 'represented' in the imaginary form of ideology, the second concerns the materiality of ideology.

Thesis I: Ideology represents the imaginary relationship of individuals to their real conditions of existence. We commonly call religious ideology, ethical ideology, legal ideology, political ideology, etc., so many 'world outlooks'. Of course, assuming that we do not live one of these ideologies as the truth (e.g. 'believe' in God, Duty, justice, etc. . . .), we admit that the ideology we are discussing from a critical point of view, examining it as the ethnologist examines the myths of a 'primitive society', that these 'world outlooks' are largely imaginary, i.e. do not 'correspond to reality'.

However, while admitting that they do not correspond to reality, i.e. that they constitute an illusion, we admit that they do make allusion to reality, and that they need only be 'interpreted' to discover the reality of the world behind their imaginary representation of that world (ideology = *illusion/allusion*).

There are different types of interpretation, the most famous of which are the *mechanistic* type, current in the eighteenth century (God is the imaginary representation of the real King), and the *'hermeneutic'* interpretation, inaugurated by the earliest Church Fathers, and revived by Feuerbach and the theologico-philosophical school which descends from him, e.g. the theologian Barth (to Feuerbach, for example, God is the essence of real Man). The essential point is that on condition that we interpret the imaginary transposition (and inversion) of ideology we arrive at the conclusion that in ideology 'men represent their real conditions of existence to themselves in an imaginary form'.

Unfortunately, this interpretation leaves one small problem unsettled: why do men 'need' this imaginary transposition of their real conditions of existence in order to 'represent to themselves' their real conditions of existence?

The first answer (that of the eighteenth century) proposes a simple solution: Priests or Despots are responsible. They 'forged' the Beautiful Lies so that, in the belief that they were obeying God, men would in fact obey the Priests and Despots, who are usually in alliance in their imposture, the Priests acting in the interests of the Despots or *vice versa*, according to the political positions of the 'theoreticians' concerned. There is therefore a cause for the imaginary transposition of the real conditions of existence: that cause is the existence of a small number of cynical men who base their domination and exploitation of the 'people' on a falsified representation of the world which they have imagined in order to enslave other minds by dominating their imaginations.

The second answer (that of Feuerbach, taken over word for word by Marx in his Early Works) is more 'profound', i.e. just as false. It, too, seeks and finds a cause for the imaginary transposition and distortion of men's real conditions of existence, in short, for the alienation in the imaginary of the representation of men's conditions of existence. This cause is no longer Priests or Despots, nor their active imagination and the passive imagination of their victims. This cause is the material alienation which reigns in the conditions of existence of men themselves. This is how, in *The Jewish Question* and elsewhere, Marx defends the Feuerbachian idea that men make themselves an alienated (= imaginary) representation of their conditions of existence because these conditions of existence are themselves alienating (in the *1844 Manuscripts:* because these conditions are dominated by the essence of alienated society—'alienated *labour*').

All these interpretations thus take literally the thesis, which they presuppose, and on which they depend, i.e. that what is reflected in the imaginary representation of the world found in an ideology is the conditions of existence of men, i.e. their real world.

Now I can return to a thesis which I have already advanced: it is not their real conditions of existence, their real world, that 'men' 'represent to themselves' in ideology, but above all it is their relation to those conditions of existence which is represented to them there. It is this relation, which is at the center of every ideological, i.e. imaginary, representation of the real world. It is this relation that contains the 'cause', which has to explain the imaginary distortion of the ideological representation of the real world. Or rather, to leave aside the language of causality it is necessary to advance the thesis that it is the *imaginary nature of this relation* which underlies all the imaginary distortion that we can observe (if we do not live in its truth) in all ideology.

To speak in a Marxist language, if it is true that the representation of the real conditions of existence of the individuals occupying the posts of agents of production, exploitation, repression, ideologization and scientific practice, does in the last analysis arise from the relations of production, and from relations deriving from the relations of production, we can say the following: all ideology represents in its necessarily imaginary distortion not the existing relations of production (and the other relations that derive from them), but above all the (imaginary) relationship of individuals to the relations of production and the relations that derive from them. What is represented in ideology is therefore not the system of the real relations which govern the existence of individuals, but the imaginary relation of those individuals to the real relations in which they live.

If this is the case, the question of the 'cause' of the imaginary distortion of the real relations in ideology disappears and must be replaced by a different question: why is the representation given to individuals of their (individual) relation to the social relations which govern their conditions of existence and their collective and individual life necessarily an imaginary relation? And what is the nature of this imaginariness? Posed in this way, the question explodes the solution by a 'clique',[1] by a group of individuals (Priests or Despots) who are the authors of the great ideological mystification, just as it explodes the solution by the alienated character of the real world. We shall see why later in my exposition. For the moment I shall go no further.

Thesis II: Ideology has a material existence. I have already touched on this thesis by saying that the 'ideas' or 'representations', etc., which seem to make up ideology do not have an ideal (*idéale or idéelle*) or spiritual existence, but a material existence. I even suggested that the ideal (*idéale, idéelle*) and spiritual existence of 'ideas' arises exclusively in an ideology of the 'idea' and of ideology, and let me add, in an ideology of what seems to have 'founded' this conception since the emergence of the sciences, i.e. what the practicians of the sciences represent to themselves in their spontaneous ideology as 'ideas', true or false. Of course, presented in affirmative form, this thesis is unproven. I simply ask that the reader be favourably disposed towards it, say, in the name of materialism. A long series of arguments would be necessary to prove it.

This hypothetical thesis of the not spiritual but material existence of 'ideas' or other 'representations' is indeed necessary if we are to advance in our analysis of the nature of ideology. Or rather, it is merely useful to us in order the better to reveal what every at all serious analysis of any ideology will immediately and empirically show to every observer, however critical.

While discussing the ideological State apparatuses and their practices, I said that each of them was the realization of an ideology (the unity of these

---

[1] I use this very modern term deliberately. For even in Communist circles, unfortunately, it is a commonplace to 'explain' some political deviation (left or right opportunism) by the action of a 'clique'.

different regional ideologies—religious, ethical, legal, political, aesthetic, etc.—being assured by their subjection to the ruling ideology). I now return to this thesis: an ideology always exists in an apparatus, and its practice, or practices. This existence is material.

Of course, the material existence of the ideology in an apparatus and its practices does not have the same modality as the material existence of a paving stone or a rifle. But, at the risk of being taken for a Neo-Aristotelian (NB Marx had a very high regard for Aristotle), I shall say that 'matter is discussed in many senses,' or rather that it exists in different modalities, all rooted in the last instance in 'physical' matter.

Having said this, let me move straight on and see what happens to the 'individuals' who live in ideology, i.e. in a determinate (religious, ethical, etc.), representation of the world whose imaginary distortion depends on their imaginary relation to their conditions of existence, in other words, in the last instance, to the relations of production and to class relations (ideology = an imaginary relation to real relations). I shall say that this imaginary relation is itself endowed with a material existence.

Now I observe the following.

An individual believes in God, or Duty, or justice, etc. This belief derives (for everyone, i.e. for all those who live in an ideological representation of ideology, which reduces ideology to ideas endowed by definition with a spiritual existence) from the ideas of the individual concerned, i.e. from him as a subject with a consciousness, which contains the ideas of his belief. In this way, i.e. by means of the absolutely ideological 'conceptual' device *(dispositif)* thus set up (a subject endowed with a consciousness in which he freely forms or freely recognizes ideas in which he believes), the (material) attitude of the subject concerned naturally follows.

The individual in question behaves in such and such a way, adopts such and such a practical attitude, and, what is more, participates in certain regular practices which are those of the ideological apparatus on which 'depend' the ideas which he has in all consciousness freely chosen as a subject. If he believes in God, he goes to Church to attend Mass, kneels, prays, confesses, does penance (once it was material in the ordinary sense of the term) and naturally repents and so on. If he believes in Duty, he will have the corresponding attitudes, inscribed in ritual practices 'according to the correct principles'. If he believes in justice, he will submit unconditionally to the rules of the Law, and may even protest when they are violated, sign petitions, take part in a demonstration, etc.

Throughout this schema we observe that the ideological representation of ideology is itself forced to recognize that every 'subject' endowed with a 'consciousness' and believing in the 'ideas' that his 'consciousness' inspires in him and freely accepts, must 'act according to his ideas', must therefore inscribe his own ideas as a free subject in the actions of his material practice. If he does not do so, 'that is wicked'.

Indeed, if he does not do what he ought to do as a function of what he believes, it is because he does something else, which, still as a function of the same idealist scheme, implies that he has other ideas in his head as well as those he proclaims, and that he acts according to these other ideas, as a man who is either 'inconsistent' ('no one is willingly evil') or cynical, or perverse.

In every case, the ideology of ideology thus recognizes, despite its imaginary distortion, that the 'ideas' of a human subject exist in his actions, or ought to exist in his actions, and if that is not the case, it lends him other ideas corresponding to the actions (however perverse) that he does perform. This ideology talks of actions: I shall talk of actions inserted into *practices*. *And* I shall point out that these practices are governed by the *rituals* in which these practices are inscribed, within the material existence of an *ideological apparatus,* be it only a small part of that apparatus: a small mass in a small church, a funeral, a minor match at a sports' club, a school day, a political party meeting, etc.

Besides, we are indebted to Pascal's defensive 'dialectic' for the wonderful formula which will enable us to invert the order of the notional schema of ideology. Pascal says more or less: 'Kneel down, move your lips in prayer, and you will believe.' He thus scandalously inverts the order of things, bringing, like Christ, not peace but strife, and in addition something hardly Christian (for woe to him who brings scandal into the world!)—scandal itself. A fortunate scandal which makes him stick with Jansenist defiance to a language that directly names the reality.

I will be allowed to leave Pascal to the arguments of his ideological struggle with the religious ideological State apparatus of his day. And I shall be expected to use a more directly Marxist vocabulary, if that is possible, for we are advancing in still poorly explored domains.

I shall therefore say that, where only a single subject (such and such an individual) is concerned, the existence of the ideas of his belief is material in that *his ideas are his material actions inserted into material practices governed by material rituals which are themselves defined by the material ideological apparatus from which derive the ideas of that subject.* Naturally, the four inscriptions of the adjective 'material' in my proposition must be affected by different modalities: the materialities of a displacement for going to mass, of kneeling down, of the gesture of the sign of the cross, or of the *mea culpa,* of a sentence, of a prayer, of an act of contrition, of a penitence, of a gaze, of a hand-shake, of an external verbal discourse or an 'internal' verbal discourse (consciousness), are not one and the same materiality. I shall leave on one side the problem of a theory of the differences between the modalities of materiality.

It remains that in this inverted presentation of things, we are not dealing with an 'inversion' at all, since it is clear that certain notions have purely and simply disappeared from our presentation, whereas others on the contrary survive, and new terms appear.

Disappeared: the term *ideas*.

Survive: the terms *subject, consciousness, belief, actions*.

Appear: the terms *practices, rituals, ideological apparatus*.

It is therefore not an inversion or overturning (except in the sense in which one might say a government or a glass is overturned), but a reshuffle (of a non-ministerial type), a rather strange reshuffle, since we obtain the following result.

Ideas have disappeared as such (insofar as they are endowed with an ideal or spiritual existence), to the precise extent that it has emerged that their existence is inscribed in the actions of practices governed by rituals defined in the last instance by an ideological apparatus. It therefore appears that the subject acts insofar as he is acted by the following system (set out in the order of its real determination): ideology existing in a material ideological apparatus, prescribing material practices governed by a material ritual, which practices exist in the material actions of a subject acting in all consciousness according to his belief.

But this very presentation reveals that we have retained the following notions: subject, consciousness, belief, actions. From this series I shall immediately extract the decisive central term on which everything else depends: the notion of the *subject*.

And I shall immediately set down two conjoint theses:

- there is no practice except by and in an ideology;
- there is no ideology except by the subject and for subjects.

I can now come to my central thesis.

Ideology interpellates individuals as subjects

This thesis is simply a matter of making my last proposition explicit: there is no ideology except by the subject and for subjects. Meaning, there is no ideology except for concrete subjects, and this destination for ideology is only made possible by the subject: meaning, *by the category of the subject* and its functioning.

By this I mean that, even if it only appears under this name (the subject) with the rise of bourgeois ideology, above all with the rise of legal ideology,[2] the category of the subject (which may function under other names: e.g., as the soul in Plato, as God, etc.) is the constitutive category of all ideology, whatever its determination (regional or class) and whatever its historical date—since ideology has no history.

I say: the category of the subject is constitutive of all ideology, but at the same time and immediately I add that *the category of the subject is only constitutive of all ideology insofar as all ideology has the function (which defines it) of 'constituting' concrete individuals as subjects.* In the interaction of this double constitution exists the functioning of all ideology, ideology being nothing but its functioning in the material forms of existence of that functioning.

In order to grasp what follows, it is essential to realize that both he who is writing these lines and the reader who reads them are themselves subjects, and therefore ideological subjects (a tautological proposition), i.e. that the author and the reader of these lines both live 'spontaneously' or 'naturally' in ideology in the sense in which I have said that 'man is an ideological animal by nature.'

That the author, insofar as he writes the lines of a discourse which claims to be scientific, is completely absent as a 'subject' from 'his' scientific discourse (for all scientific discourse is by definition a subject-less discourse, there is no 'Subject of science' except in an ideology of science) is a different question which I shall leave on one side for the moment.

As St Paul admirably put it, it is in the 'Logos', meaning in ideology, that we 'live, move and have our being'. It follows that, for you and for me, the category of the subject is a primary 'obviousness' (obviousnesses are always primary): it is clear that you and I are subjects (free, ethical, etc. . . .). Like all obviousnesses, including those that make a word 'name a thing' or 'have a meaning' (therefore including the obviousness of the 'transparency' of language), the 'obviousness' that you and I are subjects—and that that does not cause any problems—is an ideological effect, the elementary ideological effect.[3] It is indeed a peculiarity of ideology that it imposes (without appearing

---

[2] Which borrowed the legal category of 'subject in law' to make an ideological notion: man is by nature a subject.

[3] Linguists and those who appeal to linguistics for various purposes often run up against difficulties which arise because they ignore the action of the ideological effects in all discourses—including even scientific discourses.

to do so, since these are 'obviousnesses') obviousnesses as obviousnesses, which we cannot *fail to recognize* and before which we have the inevitable and natural reaction of crying out (aloud or in the 'still, small voice of conscience'): 'That's obvious! That's right! That's true!'

At work in this reaction is the ideological *recognition* function which is one of the two functions of ideology as such (its inverse being the function of *misrecognition—méconnaissance*).

To take a highly 'concrete' example, we all have friends who, when they knock on our door and we ask, through the door, the question 'Who's there?' answer (since 'it's obvious') 'It's me.' And we recognize that 'it is him,' or 'her'. We open the door, and 'it's true, it really was she who was there.' To take another example, when we recognize somebody of our (previous) acquaintance *((re)-connaissance)* in the street, we show him that we have recognized him (and have recognized that he has recognized us) by saying to him 'Hello, my friend', and shaking his hand (a material ritual practice of ideological recognition in everyday life—in France, at least; elsewhere, there are other rituals).

In this preliminary remark and these concrete illustrations, I only wish to point out that you and I are *always already* subjects, and as such constantly practice the rituals of ideological recognition, which guarantee for us that we are indeed concrete, individual, distinguishable and (naturally) irreplaceable subjects. The writing I am currently executing and the reading you are currently[4] performing are also in this respect rituals of ideological recognition, including the 'obviousness' with which the 'truth' or 'error' of my reflections may impose itself on you.

But to recognize that we are subjects and that we function in the practical rituals of the most elementary everyday life (the hand-shake, the fact of calling you by your name, the fact of knowing, even if I do not know what it is, that you 'have' a name of your own, which means that you are recognized as a unique subject, etc.)—this recognition only gives us the 'consciousness' of our incessant (eternal) practice of ideological recognition—its consciousness, i.e. its *recognition*—but in no sense does it give us the (scientific) *knowledge* of the mechanism of this recognition. Now it is this knowledge that we have to reach, if you will, while speaking in ideology, and from within ideology we have to outline a discourse which tries to break with ideology, in order to dare to be the beginning of a scientific (i.e. subject-less) discourse on ideology.

---

[4] NB: this double 'currently' is one more proof of the fact that ideology is 'eternal', since these two 'currentlys' are separated by an indefinite interval; I am writing these lines on 6 April 1969, you may read them at any subsequent time.

Thus in order to represent why the category of the 'subject' is constitutive of ideology, which only exists by constituting concrete subjects as subjects, I shall employ a special mode of exposition: 'concrete' enough to be recognized, but abstract enough to be thinkable and thought, giving rise to a knowledge.

As a first formulation I shall say: *all ideology hails or interpellates concrete individuals as concrete subjects,* by the functioning of the category of the subject.

This is a proposition which entails that we distinguish for the moment between concrete individuals, on the one hand and concrete subjects on the other, although at this level concrete subjects only exist insofar as they are supported by a concrete individual.

I shall then suggest that ideology 'acts' or 'functions' in such a way that it 'recruits' subjects among the individuals (it recruits them all), or 'transforms' the individuals into subjects (it transforms them all) by that very precise operation which I have called *interpellation* or hailing, and which can be imagined along the lines of the most commonplace everyday police (or other) hailing: 'Hey, you there!'[5]

Assuming that the theoretical scene I have imagined takes place in the street, the hailed individual will turn round. By this mere one-hundred-and-eighty-degree physical conversion, he becomes a *subject.* Why? Because he has recognized that the hail was 'really' addressed to him, and that 'it was *really him* who was hailed' (and not someone else). Experience shows that the practical telecommunication of hailings is such that they hardly ever miss their man: verbal call or whistle, the one hailed always recognizes that it is really him who is being hailed. And yet it is a strange phenomenon, and one which cannot be explained solely by 'guilt feelings', despite the large numbers who 'have something on their consciences'.

Naturally for the convenience and clarity of my little theoretical theatre I have had to present things in the form of a sequence, with a before and an after, and thus in the form of a temporal succession. There are individuals walking along. Somewhere (usually behind them) the hail rings out: 'Hey, you there!' One individual (nine times out of ten it is the right one) turns round, believing/suspecting knowing that it is for him, i.e. recognizing that 'it really is he' who is meant by the hailing. But in reality these things happen without any succession. The existence of ideology and the hailing or interpellation of individuals as subjects are one and the same thing.

I might add: what thus seems to take place outside ideology (to be precise, in the street), in reality takes place in ideology. What really takes place in

---

[5] Hailing as an everyday practice subject to a precise ritual takes a quite 'special' form in the policeman's practice of 'hailing' which concerns the hailing of 'suspects'.

ideology seems therefore to take place outside it. That is why those who are in ideology believe themselves by definition outside ideology: one of the effects of ideology is the practical *denegation* of the ideological character of ideology by ideology: ideology never says, 'I am ideological.' It is necessary to be outside ideology, i.e. in scientific knowledge, to be able to say: I am in ideology (a quite exceptional case) or (the general case): I was in ideology. As is well known, the accusation of being in ideology only applies to others, never to oneself (unless one is really a Spinozist or a Marxist, which, in this matter, is to be exactly the same thing). Which amounts to saying that ideology *has no outside* (for itself), but at the same time *that it is nothing but outside* (for science and reality).

Spinoza explained this completely two centuries before Marx, who practiced it but without explaining it in detail. But let us leave this point, although it is heavy with consequences, consequences which are not just theoretical, but also directly political, since, for example, the whole theory of criticism and self-criticism, the golden rule of the Marxist-Leninist practice of the class struggle, depends on it.

Thus ideology hails or interpellates individuals as subjects. As ideology is eternal, I must now suppress the temporal form in which I have presented the functioning of ideology, and say: ideology has always-already interpellated individuals as subjects, which amounts to making it clear that individuals are always-already interpellated by ideology as subjects, which necessarily leads us to one last proposition: *individuals are always-already subjects.* Hence individuals are 'abstract' with respect to the subjects, which they always-already are. This proposition might seem paradoxical.

That an individual is always-already a subject, even before he is born, is nevertheless the plain reality, accessible to everyone and not a paradox at all. Freud shows that individuals are always 'abstract' with respect to the subjects they always-already are, simply by noting the ideological ritual that surrounds the expectation of a 'birth', that 'happy event.' Everyone knows how much and in what way an unborn child is expected. Which amounts to saying, very prosaically, if we agree to drop the 'sentiments', i.e. the forms of family ideology (paternal/maternal/ conjugal/fraternal) in which the unborn child is expected: it is certain in advance that it will bear its Father's Name, and will therefore have an identity and be irreplaceable. Before its birth, the child is therefore always-already a subject, appointed as a subject in and by the specific familial ideological configuration in which it is 'expected' once it has been conceived. I hardly need add that this familial ideological configuration is, in its uniqueness, highly structured, and that it is in this implacable and more or less 'pathological' (presupposing that any meaning can be assigned to that term) structure that the former subject-to-be will have to 'find' 'its' place, i.e. 'become' the sexual subject (boy or girl) which it already is in advance. It is clear that this ideological constraint and pre-appointment, and all the rituals of rearing and then education in the family, have some relationship with what Freud studied in the forms of the pre-genital and genital 'stages' of sexuality, i.e. in the 'grip' of what Freud registered by its effects as being the unconscious.

Gayle Rubin

American (1949-)

The Traffic in Women: Notes on the "Political Economy" of Sex (1975)

Far from being an expression of natural differences, exclusive gender identity is the suppression of natural similarities. It requires repression: in men, of whatever is the local version of "feminine" traits; in women, of the local definition of "masculine" traits. The division of the sexes has the effect of repressing some of the personality characteristics of virtually everyone, men and women. The same social system which oppresses women in its relations of exchange, oppresses everyone in its insistence upon a rigid division of personality.

1

The literature on women—both feminist and antifeminist—is a long rumination on the question of the nature and genesis of women's oppression and social subordination. The question is not a trivial one, since the answers given it determine our visions for the future, and our evaluation of whether or not it is realistic to hope for a sexually egalitarian society. More important, the analysis of the causes of women's oppression forms the basis for any assessment of just what would have to be changed in order to achieve a society without gender hierarchy. Thus, if innate male aggression and dominance are at the root of female oppression, then the feminist program would logically require either the extermination of the offending sex, or else a eugenics project to modify its character. If sexism is a byproduct of capitalism's relentless appetite for profit, then sexism would wither away in the advent of a successful socialist revolution. If the world-historical defeat of women occurred at the hands of an armed patriarchal revolt, then it is time for Amazon guerrillas to start training in the Adirondacks.

It lies outside the scope of this paper to conduct a sustained critique of some of the currently popular explanations of the genesis of sexual inequality—theories such as the popular evolution exemplified by *The Imperial Animal*, the alleged overthrow of prehistoric matriarchies, or the attempt to extract all of the phenomena of social subordination from the first volume of *Capital*.[1] Instead, I want to sketch some elements of an alternate explanation of the problem.

Marx once asked: "What is a Negro slave? A man of the black race. The one explanation is as good as the other. A Negro is a Negro. He only becomes a slave in certain relations. A cotton spinning jenny is a machine for spinning cotton. It becomes *capital* only in certain relations. Torn from these relationships it is no more capital than gold in itself is money or sugar is the price of sugar."[2] One might paraphrase: what is a domesticated woman? A female of the species. The one explanation is as good as the other. A woman is a woman. She only becomes a domestic, a wife, a chattel, a playboy bunny, a prostitute, or a human Dictaphone in certain relations. Torn from these relationships, she is no more the helpmate of man than gold in itself is money . . . and so on. What, then, are these relationships by which a female becomes an oppressed woman?

The place to begin to unravel the system of relationships by which women become the prey of men is in the overlapping works of Claude Lévi-Strauss and Sigmund Freud. The domestication of women, under other names, is discussed at length in both of their oeuvres. In reading through these works, one begins to have a sense of a systematic social apparatus which takes up females as raw materials and fashions domesticated women as products. Neither Freud nor Lévi-Strauss sees his work in this light, and certainly neither turns a critical glance upon the processes he describes. Their analyses and descriptions must be read, therefore, in something like the way Marx read the classical political economists who preceded him.[3] Freud and Lévi-Strauss are in some sense analogous to Ricardo and Smith: they see neither the implications of what they are saying, nor the implicit critique that their work can generate when subjected to a feminist eye. Nevertheless, they provide conceptual tools with which one can build descriptions of the part of social life that is the locus of the oppression of women, of sexual minorities, and of certain aspects of human personality within individuals. I call that part of social life the "sex/gender system," for lack of a more elegant term. As a preliminary definition, a "sex/gender system" is the set of arrangements

---

[1] Tiger and Fox, *The Imperial Animal*.
[2] Marx, *Wage-Labor and Capital*, 28.
[3] On this, see Althusser and Balibar, *Reading Capital*, 11–69.

by which a society transforms biological sexuality into products of human activity, and in which these transformed sexual needs are satisfied.

The purpose of this essay is to arrive at a more fully developed definition of the sex/gender system, by way of a somewhat idiosyncratic and exegetical reading of Lévi-Strauss and Freud. I use the word *exegetical* deliberately. The dictionary defines *exegesis* as a "critical explanation or analysis; especially, interpretation of the Scriptures." At times, my reading of Lévi-Strauss and Freud is freely interpretive, moving from the explicit content of a text to its presuppositions and implications. My reading of certain psychoanalytic texts is filtered through a lens provided by Jacques Lacan, whose own interpretation of the Freudian scripture has been heavily influenced by Lévi-Strauss.[4]

I will return later to refine the definition of a sex/gender system. First, however, I will try to demonstrate the need for such a concept by discussing the failure of classical Marxism to fully express or conceptualize sex oppression. This failure results from the fact that Marxism, as a theory of social life, is relatively unconcerned with sex. In Marx's map of the social world, human beings are workers, peasants, or capitalists; that they are also men and women is not seen as very significant. By contrast, in the maps of social reality drawn by Freud and Lévi-Strauss, there is a deep recognition of the place of sexuality in society, and of the profound differences between the social experiences of men and women.

Marx

No theory accounts for the oppression of women—in its endless variety and monotonous similarity, cross-culturally and throughout history— with anything like the explanatory power of the Marxist theory of class oppression. Therefore, it is not surprising that there have been numerous attempts to apply Marxist analysis to the question of women. There are many ways of doing this. It has been argued that women are a reserve labor force for capitalism, that women's generally lower wages provide extra surplus to a capitalist employer, that women serve the ends of capitalist consumerism in

---

[4]   Moving between Marxism, structuralism, and psychoanalysis produces a certain clash of epistemologies. In particular, structuralism is a can from which worms crawl out all over the epistemological map. Rather than trying to cope with this problem, I have more or less ignored the fact that Lacan and Lévi-Strauss are among the foremost living ancestors of the contemporary French intellectual revolution (see Foucault, *The Order of Things*). It would be fun, interesting, and, if this were France, essential to start my argument from the center of the structuralist maze and work my way out from there, along the lines of a "dialectical theory of signifying practices" (see Hefner, "The *Tel Quel* Ideology").

their roles as administrators of family consumption, and so forth. However, a number of articles have tried to do something much more ambitious— to locate the oppression of women in the heart of the capitalist dynamic by pointing to the relationship between housework and the reproduction of labor.[5] To do this is to place women squarely in the definition of capitalism, the process in which capital is produced by the extraction of surplus value from labor by capital.

Briefly, Marx argued that capitalism is distinguished from all other modes of production by its unique aim: the creation and expansion of capital.

Whereas other modes of production might find their purpose in making useful things to satisfy human needs, or in producing a surplus for a ruling nobility, or in producing to insure sufficient sacrifice for the edification of the gods, capitalism produces capital. Capitalism is a set of social relations— forms of property, and so forth—in which production takes the form of turning money, things, and people into capital. And capital is a quantity of goods or money which, when exchanged for labor, reproduces and augments itself by extracting unpaid labor, or surplus value, from labor and into itself. "The result of the capitalist production process is neither a mere product (use-value) nor a *commodity*, that is, a use-value which has exchange value. Its result, its product, is the creation of *surplus-value* for capital, and consequently the actual *transformation* of money or commodity into capital."[6]

The exchange between capital and labor which produces surplus value, and hence capital, is highly specific. The worker gets a wage; the capitalist gets the things the worker has made during his or her time of employment. If the total value of the things the worker has made exceeds the value of his or her wage, the aim of capitalism has been achieved. The capitalist gets back the cost of the wage, plus an increment—surplus value. This can occur because the wage is determined not by the value of what the laborer makes, but by the value of what it takes to keep him or her going—to reproduce him or her from day to day, and to reproduce the entire workforce from one generation to the next. Thus, surplus value is the difference between what the laboring class produced as a whole, and the amount of that total which is recycled into maintaining the laboring class.

5   Benston, "The Political Economy of Women's Liberation"; Dalla Costa, *The Power of Women and the Subversion of the Community*; Larguia and Dumoulin, "Towards a Science of Women's Liberation"; Gerstein, "Domestic Work and Capitalism"; Vogel, "The Earthly Family"; Secombe, "Housework under Capitalism"; Gardiner, "Political Economy of Female Labor in Capitalist Society"; Rowntree and Rowntree, "More on the Political Economy of Women's Liberation."
6   Marx, *Theories of Surplus Value, Part 1*, 399.

The capital given in exchange for labour power is converted into necessaries, by the consumption of which the muscles, nerves, bones, and brains of existing labourers are reproduced, and new labourers are begotten. . . . [T]he individual consumption of the labourer, whether it proceed within the workshop or outside it, whether it be part of the process of production or not, forms therefore a factor of the production and reproduction of capital; just as cleaning machinery does.[7]

Given the individual, the production of labour-power consists in his reproduction of himself or his maintenance. For his maintenance he requires a given quantity of the means of subsistence. . . . Labour-power sets itself in action only by working. But thereby a definite quantity of human muscle, brain, nerve, etc., is wasted, and these require to be restored.[8]

The amount of difference between the reproduction of labor power and its products depends, therefore, on the determination of what it takes to reproduce that labor power. Marx tends to make that determination on the basis of the quantity of commodities—food, clothing, housing, fuel—that would be necessary to maintain the health, life, and strength of a worker. But these commodities must be consumed before they can be sustenance, and they are not immediately in consumable form when they are purchased by the wage. Additional labor must be performed upon these things before they can be turned into people. Food must be cooked, clothes cleaned, beds made, wood chopped. Housework is therefore a key element in the process of the reproduction of the laborer from whom surplus value is taken. Since it is usually women who do housework, it has been observed that it is through the reproduction of labor power that women are articulated into the surplus-value nexus which is the sine qua non of capitalism.[9] It can be further argued that since no wage is paid for housework, the labor of women in the home contributes to the ultimate quantity of surplus value realized by the capitalist. But to explain women's usefulness to capitalism is one thing. To argue that this usefulness explains the genesis of the oppression of women is quite

[7] Marx, *Capital*, 572.
[8] Ibid., 171.
[9] A lot of the debate on women and housework has centered around whether or not housework is "productive" labor. Strictly speaking, housework is not ordinarily "productive" in the technical sense of the term (Gough, "Marx and Productive Labour"; Marx, *Theories of Surplus Value, Part 1*, 387–413). But this distinction is irrelevant to the main line of the argument. Housework may not be "productive," in the sense of directly producing surplus value, capital, and yet be a crucial element in the production of surplus value and capital.

another. It is precisely at this point that the analysis of capitalism ceases to explain very much about women and the oppression of women.

Women are oppressed in societies which can by no stretch of the imagination be described as capitalist. In the Amazon Valley and the New Guinea Highlands, women are frequently kept in their place by gang rape when the ordinary mechanisms of masculine intimidation prove insufficient. "We tame our women with the banana," said one Mundurucu man.[10] The ethnographic record is littered with practices whose effect is to keep women "in their place"—men's cults, secret initiations, arcane male knowledge, and so on. And precapitalist, feudal Europe was hardly a society in which there was no sexism. Capitalism has taken over and rewired notions of male and female which predate it by centuries. No analysis of the reproduction of labor power under capitalism can explain foot-binding, chastity belts, or any of the incredible array of Byzantine, fetishized indignities—let alone the more ordinary ones—that have been inflicted upon women in various times and places. The analysis of the reproduction of labor power does not even explain why it is usually women rather than men who do domestic work in the home.

In this light it is interesting to return to Marx's discussion of the reproduction of labor. What is necessary to reproduce the worker is determined in part by the biological needs of the human organism, in part by the physical conditions of the place in which it lives, and in part by cultural tradition. Marx observed that beer is necessary for the reproduction of the English working class, and wine necessary for the French.

> The number and extent of his [the worker's] so-called necessary wants, as also the modes of satisfying them, are themselves the product of historical development, and depend therefore to a great extent on the degree of civilization of a country, more particularly on the conditions under which, and consequently on the habits and degree of comfort in which, the class of tree labourers has been formed. In contradistinction therefore to the case of other commodities, there enters into the determination of the value of labour-power a historical and moral element.[11]

It is precisely this "historical and moral element" which determines that a "wife" is among the necessities of a worker, that women rather than men do housework, and that capitalism is heir to a long tradition in which women do not inherit, in which women do not lead, and in which women do not talk to God. It is this "historical and moral element" that presented capitalism with

---

[10] Murphy, "Social Structure and Sex Antagonism," 195.
[11] Marx, *Capital*, 171, emphasis added.

a cultural heritage of forms of masculinity and femininity. It is within this "historical and moral element" that the entire domain of sex, sexuality, and sex oppression is subsumed. And the briefness of Marx's comment only serves to emphasize the vast area of social life that it covers and leaves unexamined. Only by subjecting this "historical and moral element" to analysis can the structures of sex oppression be delineated.

Engels

In *The Origin of the Family, Private Property, and the State,* Engels sees sex oppression as part of capitalism's heritage from prior social forms. Moreover, Engels integrates sex and sexuality into his theory of society. *Origin* is a frustrating book. Like the nineteenth-century tomes on the history of marriage and the family which it echoes, the state of the evidence in *Origin* renders it quaint to a reader familiar with more recent developments in anthropology. Nevertheless, it is a book whose considerable insight should not be overshadowed by its limitations. The idea that the "relations of sexuality" can and should be distinguished from the "relations of production" is not the least of Engels's intuitions.

> According to the materialistic conception, the determining factor in history is, in the final instance, the production and reproduction of immediate life. *This, again, is of a twofold character: on the one hand, the production of the means of existence, of food, clothing, and shelter and the tools necessary for that production; on the other side, the production of human beings themselves,* the propagation of the species. The social organization under which the people of a particular historical epoch and a particular country live is determined by both kinds of production: by the stage of development of labor, on the one hand, and of the family on the other.[12]

This passage indicates an important recognition—that a human group must do more than apply its activity to reshaping the natural world in order to clothe, feed, and warm itself. We usually call the system by which elements of the natural world are transformed into objects of human consumption the "economy." But the needs that are satisfied by economic activity even in the richest, Marxian sense do not exhaust fundamental human requirements. A

---

[12] Engels, *The Origin of the Family, Private Property, and the State,* 71–72, emphasis added.

human group must also reproduce itself from generation to generation. The needs of sexuality and procreation must be satisfied as much as the need to eat, and one of the most obvious deductions to he made from the data of anthropology is that these needs are hardly ever satisfied in any "natural" form, any more than are the needs for food. Hunger is hunger, but what counts as food is culturally determined and obtained. Every society has some form of organized economic activity. Sex is sex, but what counts as sex is equally culturally determined and obtained. Every society also has a sex/gender system—a set of arrangements by which the biological raw material of human sex and procreation is shaped by human, social intervention and satisfied in a conventional manner, no matter how bizarre some of the conventions may be.[13]

The realm of human sex, gender, and procreation has been subjected to, and changed by, relentless social activity for millennia. Sex as we know it—gender identity, sexual desire and fantasy, concepts of childhood—is itself a social product. We need to understand the relations of its production, and forget, for awhile, about food, clothing, automobiles, and transistor radios. In most Marxist tradition, and even in Engels's book, the concept of the

---

[13] That some of them are pretty bizarre from our point of view only demonstrates the point that sexuality is expressed through the intervention of culture (see Ford and Beach, *Patterns of Sexual Behaviour*). Some examples may be chosen from among the exotica in which anthropologists delight. Among the Banaro, marriage involved several socially sanctioned sexual partnerships. When a woman is married, she is initiated into intercourse by the sib-friend of her groom's father. After bearing a child by this man, she begins to have intercourse with her husband. She also has an institutionalized partnership with the sib-friend of her husband. A man's partners include his wife, the wife of his sib-friend, and the wife of his sib-friend's son (Thurnwald, "Banaro Society"). Multiple intercourse is a more pronounced custom among the Marind Anim. At the time of marriage, the bride has intercourse with all of the members of the groom's clan, the groom coming last. Every major festival is accompanied by a practice known as *otiv-bombari*, in which semen is collected for ritual purposes. A few women have intercourse with many men, and the resulting semen is collected in coconut-shell buckets. A Marind male is subjected to multiple homosexual intercourse during initiation (Van Baal, *Dema*). Among the Etoro, heterosexual intercourse is taboo for between 205 and 260 days a year (Kelly, "Witchcraft and Sexual Relations"). In much of New Guinea, men fear copulation and think that it will kill them if they engage in it without magical precautions (Glasse, "The Mask of Venery"; Meggitt, "Male-Female Relationships in the Highlands of Australian New Guinea"). Usually, such ideas of feminine pollution express the subordination of women. But symbolic systems contain internal contradictions, whose logical extensions sometimes lead to inversions of the propositions on which a system is based. In New Britain, men's fear of sex is so extreme that rape appears to be feared by men rather than women. Women run after men, who flee from them, women are the sexual aggressors, and it is bridegrooms who are reluctant (Goodale and Chowning, "The Contaminating Woman"). Other interesting sexual variations can be found in Yalmon, "On the Purity of Women in the Castes of Ceylon and Malabar," and Gough, "The Nayars and the Definition of Marriage."

"second aspect of material life" has tended to fade into the background or to be incorporated into the usual notions of "material life." Engels's suggestion has never been followed up and subjected to the refinement it needs. But he does indicate the existence and importance of the domain of social life that I want to call the sex/gender system.

Other names have been proposed for the sex/gender system. The most common alternatives are "mode of reproduction" and "patriarchy." It may be foolish to quibble about terms, but both of these can lead to confusion. All three proposals have been made in order to introduce a distinction between "economic" systems and "sexual" systems, and to indicate that sexual systems have a certain autonomy and cannot always be explained in terms of economic forces. "Mode of reproduction," for instance, has been proposed in opposition to the more familiar "mode of production." But this terminology links the "economy" to the production, and the sexual system to the "reproduction." It reduces the richness of either system, since "productions" and "reproductions" take place in both. Every mode of production involves reproduction—of tools, labor, and social relations. We cannot relegate all of the multifaceted aspects of social reproduction to the sex system. Replacement of machinery is an example of reproduction in the economy. On the other hand, we cannot limit the sex system to "reproduction" in either the social or biological sense of the term. A sex/gender system is not simply the reproductive moment of a "mode of production." The formation of gender identity is an example of production in the realm of the sexual system. And a sex/gender system involves more than the "relations of procreation," reproduction in a biological sense.

The term *patriarchy* was introduced to distinguish the forces maintaining sexism from other social forces, such as capitalism. But the use of *patriarchy* obscures other distinctions. Its use is analogous to using *capitalism* to refer to all modes of production, whereas the usefulness of the term *capitalism* lies precisely in that it distinguishes between the different systems by which societies are provisioned and organized. Any society will have some system of "political economy." Such a system may be egalitarian or socialist. It may be class stratified, in which case the oppressed class may consist of serfs, peasants, or slaves. The oppressed class may consist of wage laborers, in which case the system is properly labeled "capitalist." The power of the term lies in its implication that, in fact, there are alternatives to capitalism.

Similarly, any society will have some systematic ways to deal with sex, gender, and babies. Such a system may be sexually egalitarian, at least in theory, or it may be "gender stratified," as seems to be the case for most or all of the known examples. But it is important—even in the face of a depressing history—to maintain a distinction between the human capacity and necessity to create a sexual world, and the empirically oppressive ways in which sexual worlds have been organized. *Patriarchy* subsumes both meanings into the same term. *Sex/gender system*, on the other hand, is a neutral term that refers to the domain and indicates that oppression is not inevitable in that domain, but is the product of the specific social relations which organize it.

Finally, there are gender-stratified systems that are not adequately described as patriarchal. Many New Guinea societies are viciously oppressive to women.[14] But the power of males in these groups is founded not on their roles as fathers or patriarchs, but on their collective adult maleness, embodied in secret cults, men's houses, warfare, exchange networks, ritual knowledge, and various initiation procedures. Patriarchy is a specific form of male dominance, and the use of the term ought to be confined to the ecclesiastical offices and authorities to which the term initially referred, or to the Old Testament-type pastoral nomads and similar groups whose political structures the word usefully describes. Abraham was a Patriarch—one old man whose absolute power over wives, children, herds, and dependents was an aspect of the institution of fatherhood, as defined in the social group in which he lived.

Whichever term we use, what is important is to develop concepts to adequately describe the social organization of sexuality and the reproduction of the conventions of sex and gender. We need to pursue the project Engels abandoned when he located the subordination of women in a development within the mode of production.[15] To do this, we can imitate Engels in his method rather than in his results. Engels approached the task of analyzing the "second aspect of material life" by way of an examination of a theory of kinship systems. Kinship systems are and do many things. But they are made up of, and reproduce concrete forms of socially organized sexuality. Kinship systems are observable and empirical forms of sex/gender systems.

---

[14] See Enga, Maring, Bena Bena, Huli, Melpa, Kuma, Gahuku-Gama, Fore, Marind Anim, ad nauseam. See Berndt. *Excess and Restraint*; Langness, "Sexual Antagonism in the New Guinea Highlands"; Rappaport, *Pigs for the Ancestors*; Read, "The Nama Cult of the Central Highlands, New Guinea"; Meggitt, "Male-Female Relationships in the Highlands of Australian New Guinea"; Glasse, "The Mask of Venery"; Strathern, *Women in Between*; Reay, *The Kinna*; Van Baal, *Dema*; Lindenbaum, "A Wife Is the Hand of the Man."

[15] Engels thought men acquired wealth in the form of herds and, wanting to pass this wealth to their own children, overthrew "mother right" in favor of patrilineal inheritance. "The overthrow of mother right was the *world historical defeat of the female sex*. The man took command in the home also; the woman was degraded and reduced to servitude; she became the slave of his lust and a mere instrument for the production of children" (Engels, *The Origin of the Family, Private Property, and the State*, 120–21). As has been often pointed out, women do not necessarily have significant social authority in societies practicing matrilineal inheritance (Schneider and Gough, *Matrilineal Kinship*).

Kinship: On the part played by sexuality in the transition from Ape to "Man"

To an anthropologist, a kinship system is not a list of biological relatives. It is a system of categories and statuses which often contradict actual genetic relationships. There are dozens of examples in which socially defined kinship statuses take precedence over biology. The Nuer custom of "woman marriage" is a case in point. The Nuer define the status of fatherhood as belonging to the person in whose name cattle bridewealth is given for the mother. Thus, a woman can be married to another woman, and be husband to the wife and father of her children, despite the fact that she is not the inseminator.

In pre-state societies, kinship is often the idiom of social interaction, organizing economic, political, and ceremonial, as well as sexual activity. One's duties, responsibilities, and privileges vis-à-vis others are defined in terms of mutual kinship or lack thereof. The exchange of goods and services, production and distribution, hostility and solidarity, ritual and ceremony, all take place within the organizational structure of kinship. The ubiquity and adaptive effectiveness of kinship has led many anthropologists to consider its invention, along with the invention of language, to have been the developments that decisively marked the discontinuity between semihuman hominids and human beings.[16]

While the idea of kinship's importance enjoys the status of a first principle in anthropology, the internal workings of kinship systems have long been a focus of intense controversy. Kinship systems vary wildly from one culture to the next. They contain all sorts of bewildering rules which govern whom one may or may not marry. Their internal complexity is dazzling. Kinship systems have for decades provoked the anthropological imagination into trying to explain incest taboos, cross-cousin marriage, terms of descent, relationships of avoidance or forced intimacy, clans and sections, taboos on names—the diverse array of items found in descriptions of actual kinship systems. In the nineteenth century, several thinkers attempted to write comprehensive accounts of the nature and history of human sexual systems.[17] One of these was *Ancient Society*, by Lewis Henry Morgan. It was this book which inspired Engels to write *The Origin of the Family, Private Property, and the State.* Engels's theory is based upon Morgan's account of kinship and marriage.

---

[16] Sahlins, "The Origin of Society"; Livingstone, "Genetics, Ecology, and the Origins of Incest and Exogamy"; Lévi-Strauss, *The Elementary Structures of Kinship.*

[17] Fee, "The Sexual Politics of Victorian Social Anthropology."

In taking up Engels's project of extracting a theory of sex oppression from the study of kinship, we have the advantage of the maturation of ethnology since the nineteenth century. We also have the advantage of a peculiar and particularly appropriate book, Lévi-Strauss's *The Elementary Structures of Kinship* (1969). This is the boldest twentieth-century version of the nineteenth-century attempt to understand human marriage. It is a book in which kinship is explicitly conceived of as an imposition of cultural organization upon the facts of biological procreation. It is permeated with an awareness of the importance of sexuality in human society. It is a description of society that does not assume an abstract, genderless human subject. On the contrary, the human subject in Lévi-Strauss's work is always either male or female, and the divergent social destinies of the two sexes can therefore be traced. Since Lévi-Strauss sees the essence of kinship systems to lie in an exchange of women between men, he constructs an implicit theory of sex oppression. Aptly, the book is dedicated to the memory of Lewis Henry Morgan.

"Vile and precious merchandise."— Monique Wittig, *Les Guérillères*

The Elementary Structures of Kinship is a grand statement on the origin and nature of human society. It is a treatise on the kinship systems of approximately one-third of the ethnographic globe. Most fundamentally, it is an attempt to discern the structural principles of kinship. Lévi-Strauss argues that the application of these principles (summarized in the last chapter of *Elementary Structures*) to kinship data reveals an intelligible logic in the taboos and marriage rules that have perplexed and mystified Western anthropologists. He constructs a chess game of such complexity that it cannot be recapitulated here. But two of his chess pieces are particularly relevant to women—the "gift" and the incest taboo, whose dual articulation adds up to his concept of the exchange of women.

The Elementary Structures is in part a radical gloss on another famous theory of primitive social organization, Marcel Mauss's *Essay on the Gift* (1967).[18] It was Mauss who first theorized the significance of one of the most striking features of primitive societies: the extent to which giving, receiving, and reciprocating gifts dominate social intercourse. In such societies, all sorts of things circulate in exchange—food, spells, rituals, words, names, ornaments, tools, and powers: "Your own mother, your own sister, your own

---

[18] See also Sahlins, *Stone Age Economics*, chap. 4.

pigs, your own yams that you have piled up, you may not eat. Other people's mothers, other people's sisters, other people's pigs, other people's yams that they have piled up, you may eat."[19]

In a typical gift transaction, neither party gains anything. In the Trobriand Islands, each household maintains a garden of yams and each household eats yams. But the yams a household grows and the yams it eats are not the same. At harvest time, a man sends the yams he has cultivated to the household of his sister; the household in which he lives is provisioned by his wife's brother.[20] Since such a procedure appears to be a useless one from the point of view of accumulation or trade, its logic has been sought elsewhere. Mauss proposed that the significance of gift-giving is that it expresses, affirms, or creates a social link between the partners of an exchange. Gift-giving confers upon its participants a special relationship of trust, solidarity, and mutual aid. One can solicit a friendly relationship in the offer of a gift; acceptance implies a willingness to return a gift and a confirmation of the relationship. Gift exchange may also be the idiom of competition and rivalry. There are many examples in which one person humiliates another by giving more than can be reciprocated. Some political systems, such as the Big Man systems of highland New Guinea, are based on exchange that is unequal on the material plane. An aspiring Big Man wants to give away more goods than can be reciprocated. He gets his return in political prestige.

Although both Mauss and Lévi-Strauss emphasize the solidary aspects of gift exchange, the other purposes served by gift-giving only strengthen the point that it is a ubiquitous means of social commerce. Mauss proposed that gifts were the threads of social discourse, the means by which such societies were held together in the absence of specialized governmental institutions. "The gift is the primitive way of achieving the peace that in civil society is secured by the state. . . . Composing society, the gift was the liberation of culture."[21]

Lévi-Strauss adds to the theory of primitive reciprocity the idea that marriages are a most basic form of gift exchange, in which it is women who are the most precious gifts. He argues that the incest taboo should best be understood as a mechanism to insure that such exchanges take place between families and between groups. Since the existence of incest taboos is universal, but the content of their prohibitions variable, they cannot be explained as having the aim of preventing the occurrence of genetically close matings. Rather, the incest taboo imposes the social aim of exogamy and alliance upon

[19] Arapesh, cited in Lévi-Strauss, *The Elementary Structures of Kinship*, 27.
[20] Malinowski, *The Sexual Life of Savages*.
[21] Sahlins, *Stone Age Economics*, 169, 175.

the biological events of sex and procreation. The incest taboo divides the universe of sexual choice into categories of permitted and prohibited sexual partners. Specifically, by forbidding unions within a group it enjoins marital exchange between groups. "The prohibition on the sexual use of a daughter or a sister compels them to be given in marriage to another man, and at the same time it establishes a right to the daughter or sister of this other man. . . . The woman whom one does not take is, for that very reason, offered up. . . . The prohibition of incest is less a rule prohibiting marriage with the mother, sister, or daughter, than a rule obliging the mother, sister, or daughter to be given to others. It is the supreme rule of the gift."[22]

The result of a gift of women is more profound than the result of other gift transactions, because the relationship thus established is not just one of reciprocity, but one of kinship. The exchange partners have become affines, and their descendants will be related by blood: "Two people may meet in friendship and exchange gifts and yet quarrel and fight in later times, but intermarriage connects them in a permanent manner."[23] As is the case with other gift-giving, marriages are not always simply activities to make peace. Marriages may be highly competitive, and there are plenty of affines who fight each other. Nevertheless, in a general sense the argument is that the taboo on incest results in a wide network of relations, a set of people whose connections with one another compose a kinship structure. All other levels, amounts, and directions of exchange—including hostile ones—are ordered by this structure. The marriage ceremonies recorded in the ethnographic literature are moments in a ceaseless and ordered procession in which women, children, shells, words, cattle, names, fish, ancestors, whale's teeth, pigs, yams, spells, dances, mats, and so on, pass from hand to hand, leaving as their tracks the ties that bind. Kinship is organization, and organization gives power.

But who is organized? If it is women who are being transacted, then it is the men who give and take them who are linked, the woman being a conduit of a relationship rather than a partner of it.[24] The exchange of women does not necessarily imply that women are objectified, in the modern sense, since objects in the primitive world are imbued with highly personal qualities. But it does imply a distinction between gift and giver. If women are the gifts, then it is men who are the exchange partners. And it is the partners, not the

---

[22] Lévi-Strauss, *The Elementary Structures of Kinship*, 51, 481.

[23] Best, cited in ibid., 481.

[24] "What, would you like to marry your sister? What is the matter with you? Don't you want a brother-in-law? Don't you realize that if you marry another man's sister and another man marries your sister, you will have at least two brothers-in-law, while if you marry your own sister you will have none? With whom will you hunt, with whom will you garden, whom will you go visit?" (Arapesh, cited in ibid., 485).

presents, upon whom reciprocal exchange confers its quasi-mystical powers of social linkage. The relations of such a system are such that women are in no position to realize the benefits of their own circulation. As long as the relations specify that men exchange women, it is men who are the beneficiaries of the product of such exchanges—social organization. "The total relationship of exchange which constitutes marriage is not established between a man and a woman, but between two groups of men, and the woman figures only as one of the objects in the exchange, not as one of the partners. . . . This remains true even when the girl's feelings are taken into consideration, as, moreover, is usually the case. In acquiescing to the proposed union, she precipitates or allows the exchange to take place; she cannot alter its nature."[25]

To enter into a gift exchange as a partner, one must have something to give. If women are for men to dispose of, they are in no position to give themselves away.

> "What woman," mused a young Northern Melpa man, "is ever strong enough to get up and say, 'Let us make *moka*, let us find wives and pigs, let us give our daughters to men, let us wage war. Let us kill our enemies!' No, indeed not! . . . they are little rubbish things who stay at home simply, don't you see?"[26]

What women indeed! The Melpa women of whom the young man spoke cannot get wives; they *are* wives, and what they get are husbands, an entirely different matter. The Melpa women can't give their daughters to men, because they do not have the same rights in their daughters that their male kin have, rights of bestowal (although *not* of ownership).

The "exchange of women" is a seductive and powerful concept. It is attractive in that it places the oppression of women within social systems, rather than in biology. Moreover, it suggests that we look for the ultimate locus of women's oppression within the traffic in women, rather than within the traffic of merchandise. It is certainly not difficult to find ethnographic and historical examples of trafficking in women. Women are given in marriage, taken in battle, exchanged for favors, sent as tribute, traded, bought, and sold. Far from being confined to the "primitive" world, these practices seem only to become more pronounced and commercialized in more "civilized"

---

[25] Ibid., 115. This analysis of society as based on bonds between men by means of women makes the separatist responses of the women's movement thoroughly intelligible. Separatism can be seen as a mutation in social structure, as an attempt to form social groups based on unmediated bonds between women. It can also be seen as a radical denial of men's "rights" in women, and as a claim by women of rights in themselves.

[26] Strathern, *Women in Between*, 161.

societies. Men are of course also trafficked—but as slaves, hustlers, athletic stars, serfs, or as some other catastrophic social status, rather than as men. Women are transacted as slaves, serfs, and prostitutes, but also simply as women. And if men have been sexual subjects—exchangers—and women sexual semi objects—gifts—for much of human history, then many customs, clichés, and personality traits seem to make a great deal of sense (among others, the curious custom by which a father gives away the bride).

The "exchange of women" is also a problematic concept. Since Lévi-Strauss argues that the incest taboo and the results of its application constitute the origin of culture, his analysis implies that the world-historical defeat of women occurred with the origin of culture, and is a prerequisite of culture. If his analysis is adopted in its pure form, the feminist program must include a task even more onerous than the extermination of men; it must attempt to get rid of culture and substitute some entirely new phenomena on the face of the earth. However, it would be a dubious proposition at best to argue that if there were no exchange of women there would be no culture, if for no other reason than that culture is, by definition, inventive. It is even debatable that "exchange of women" adequately describes all of the empirical evidence of kinship systems. Some cultures, such as the Lele and the Kuma, exchange women explicitly and overtly. In other cultures, the exchange of women can be inferred. In some—particularly those hunters and gatherers excluded from Lévi-Strauss's sample—the efficacy of the concept becomes altogether questionable. What are we to make of a concept which seems so useful and yet so difficult?

The "exchange of women" is neither a definition of culture nor a system in and of itself. The concept is an acute, but condensed, apprehension of certain aspects of the social relations of sex and gender. A kinship system is an imposition of social ends upon a part of the natural world. It is therefore "production" in the most general sense of the term: a molding, a transformation of objects (in this case, people) to and by a subjective purpose.[27] It has its own relations of production, distribution, and exchange, which include certain "property" forms in people. These forms are not exclusive, private property rights, but rather different sorts of rights that various people have in other people. Marriage transactions—the gifts and material which circulate in the ceremonies marking a marriage—are a rich source of data for determining exactly who has which rights in whom. It is not difficult to deduce from such transactions that in most cases women's rights are considerably more residual than those of men.

---

[27] For this sense of production, see Marx, *Pre-capitalist Economic Formations*, 80–99.

Kinship systems do not merely exchange women. They exchange sexual access, genealogical statuses, lineage names and ancestors, rights, and *people*—men, women, and children—in concrete systems of social relationships. These relationships always include certain rights for men, others for women. "Exchange of women" is a shorthand expression for the social relations of kinship systems specifying that men have certain rights in their female kin, and that women do not have the same rights either to themselves or to their male kin. In this sense, the exchange of women is a profound perception of a system in which women do not have full rights to themselves. The exchange of women becomes an obfuscation if it is seen as a cultural necessity and when it is used as the single tool with which an analysis of a particular kinship system is approached.

If Lévi-Strauss is correct in seeing the exchange of women as a fundamental principle of kinship, the subordination of women can be seen as a product of the relationships by which sex and gender are organized and produced. The economic oppression of women is derivative and secondary. But there is an "economics" of sex and gender, and what we need is a political economy of sexual systems. We need to study each society to determine the exact mechanisms by which particular conventions of sexuality are produced and maintained. The "exchange of women" is an initial step toward building an arsenal of concepts with which sexual systems can be described.

Psychoanalysis and its discontents

The battle between psychoanalysis and the women's and gay movements has become legendary. In part, this confrontation between sexual revolutionaries and the clinical establishment has been due to the evolution of psychoanalysis in the United States, where clinical tradition has fetishized anatomy. The child is thought to travel through its organismic stages until it reaches its anatomical destiny and the missionary position. Clinical practice has often seen its mission as the repair of individuals who somehow have become derailed en route to their "biological" aim. Transforming moral law into scientific law, clinical practice has acted to enforce sexual convention upon unruly participants. In this sense, psychoanalysis has often become more than a theory of the mechanisms of the reproduction of sexual arrangements; it has been one of those mechanisms. Since the aim of the feminist and gay revolts is to dismantle the apparatus of sexual enforcement, a critique of psychoanalysis has been in order.

But the rejection of Freud by the women's and gay movement has deeper roots in the rejection by psychoanalysis of its own insights. Nowhere are the effects on women of male-dominated social systems better documented than within the clinical literature. According to the Freudian orthodoxy, the attainment of "normal" femininity extracts severe costs from women. The theory of gender acquisition could have been the basis of a critique of sex roles. Instead, the radical implications of Freud's theory have been radically repressed. This tendency is evident even in the original formulations of the theory, but it has been exacerbated over time until the potential for a critical psychoanalytic theory of gender is visible only in the symptomatology of its denial—an intricate rationalization of sex roles as they are. It is not the purpose of this paper to conduct a psychoanalysis of the psychoanalytic unconscious; but I do hope to demonstrate that it exists. Moreover, the salvage of psychoanalysis from its own motivated repression is not for the sake of Freud's good name. Psychoanalysis contains a unique set of concepts for understanding men, women, and sexuality. It is a theory of sexuality in human society. Most important, psychoanalysis provides a description of the mechanisms by which the sexes are divided and deformed, of how bisexual, androgynous infants are transformed into boys and girls.[28] Psychoanalysis is a feminist theory *manqué*.

The Oedipus hex

Until the late 1920s, the psychoanalytic movement did not have a distinctive theory of feminine development. Instead, variants of an "Electra" complex in women had been proposed, in which female experience was thought to be a mirror image of the Oedipal complex described for males. The boy loved his mother, but gave her up out of fear of the father's threat of castration. The girl, it was thought, loved her father, and gave him up out of fear of maternal vengeance. This formulation assumed that both children were

---

[28] "In studying women we cannot neglect the methods of a science of the mind, a theory that attempts to explain how women become women and men, men. The borderline between the biological and the social which finds expression in the family is the land psychoanalysis sets out to chart, the land where sexual distinction originates" (Mitchell, *Women's Estate*, 167), "What is the *object* of psychoanalysis? . . . but the *'effects,'* prolonged into the surviving adult, of the extraordinary adventure which from birth the liquidation of the Oedipal phase transforms a small animal conceived by a man and a woman into a small human child . . . the 'effects' still present in the survivors of the forced 'humanization' of the small human animal into a *man* or a *woman*" (Althusser, "Freud and Lacan," 57, 59).

subject to a biological imperative toward heterosexuality. It also assumed that the children were already, before the Oedipal phase, "little" men and women. Freud had voiced reservations about jumping to conclusions about women on the basis of data gathered from men. But his objections remained general until the discovery of the pre-Oedipal phase in women. The concept of the pre-Oedipal phase enabled both Freud and Jeanne Lampl de Groot to articulate the classic psychoanalytic theory of femininity.[29] The idea of the pre-Oedipal phase in women produced a dislocation of the biologically derived presuppositions which underlay notions of an "Electra" complex. In the pre-Oedipal phase, children of both sexes were psychically indistinguishable, which meant that their differentiation into masculine and feminine children had to be explained, rather than assumed. Pre-Oedipal children were described as bisexual. Both sexes exhibited the full range of libidinal attitudes, active and passive. And for children of both sexes, the mother was the object of desire.

The characteristics of the pre-Oedipal female challenged the ideas of a primordial heterosexuality and gender identity. Since the girl's libidinal activity was directed toward the mother, her adult heterosexuality had to be explained:

"It would be a solution of ideal simplicity if we could suppose that from a particular age onwards the elementary influence of the mutual attraction between the sexes makes itself felt and impels the small woman towards men. . . . But we are not going to find things so easy; we scarcely know whether we are to believe seriously in the power of which poets talk so much and with such enthusiasm but which cannot be further dissected analytically."[30]

---

[29] The psychoanalytic theories of femininity were articulated in the context of a debate which took place largely in the *International Journal of Psychoanalysis* and *The Psychoanalytic Quarterly*, in the late 1920s and early 1930s. Articles representing the range of discussion include: Freud, "Female Sexuality," "Some Psychical Consequences of the Anatomical Distinction between the Sexes," "Femininity"; Lampl de Groot, "Problems of Femininity," "The Evolution of the Oedipus Complex in Women"; Deutsch, "On Female Homosexuality," "The Significance of Masochism in the Mental Life of Women"; Horney, "The Denial of the Vagina"; Jones, "The Phallic Phase." Some of my dates are of reprints; for the original chronology, see Chasseguet-Smirgel (*Female Sexuality*, introduction).The debate was complex, and I have simplified it. Freud, Lampl de Groot, and Deutsch argued that femininity developed out of a bisexual, "phallic" girl-child; Horney and Jones argued for an innate femininity. The debate was not without its ironies. Horney defended women against penis envy by postulating that women are born and not made; Deutsch, who considered women to be made and not born, developed a theory of feminine masochism whose best rival is *Story of O*. I have attributed the core of the "Freudian" version of female development equally to Freud and to Lampl de Groot. In reading through the articles, it has seemed to me that the theory is as much (or more) hers as it is his.

[30] Freud, "Femininity," 119.

Moreover, the girl did not manifest a "feminine" libidinal attitude. Since her desire for the mother was active and aggressive, her ultimate accession to "femininity" had also to be explained: "In conformity with its peculiar nature, psychoanalysis does not try to describe what a woman is . . . but sets about enquiring how she comes into being, how a woman develops out of a child with a bisexual disposition."[31]

In short, feminine development could no longer be taken for granted as a reflex of biology. Rather, it had become immensely problematic. It is in explaining the acquisition of "femininity" that Freud employs the concepts of penis envy and castration, which have infuriated feminists since he first introduced them. According to Freud, the girl turns from the mother and represses the "masculine" elements of her libido as a result of her recognition that she is castrated. She compares her tiny clitoris to the larger penis, and in the face of its evident superior ability to satisfy the mother, falls prey to penis envy and a sense of inferiority. She gives up her struggle for the mother and assumes a passive feminine position vis-à-vis the father. Freud's account can be read as claiming that femininity is a consequence of the anatomical differences between the sexes. He has therefore been accused of biological determinism. Nevertheless, even in his most anatomically stated versions of the female castration complex, the "inferiority" of the woman's genitals is a product of the situational context: the girl feels less "equipped" to possess and satisfy the mother. If the pre-Oedipal lesbian were not confronted by the heterosexuality of the mother, she might draw different conclusions about the relative status of her genitals.

Freud was never as much of a biological determinist as some would have him. He repeatedly stressed that all adult sexuality resulted from psychic, not biologic, development. But his writing is often ambiguous, and his wording leaves plenty of room for the biological interpretations which have been so popular in American psychoanalysis. In France, on the other hand, the trend in psychoanalytic theory has been to de-biologize Freud, and to conceive of psychoanalysis as a theory of information rather than organs. Jacques Lacan, the instigator of this line of thinking, insists that Freud never meant to say anything about anatomy, and that Freud's theory was instead about language and the cultural meanings imposed upon anatomy. The debate over the "real" Freud is extremely interesting, but it is not my purpose here to contribute to it. Rather, I want to rephrase the classic theory of femininity in Lacan's terminology, after introducing some of the pieces on Lacan's conceptual chessboard.

[31] Ibid., 116

Kinship, Lacan, and the Phallus

Lacan suggests that psychoanalysis is the study of the traces left in the psyches of individuals as a result of their conscription into systems of kinship.

> Isn't it striking that Lévi-Strauss, in suggesting that implication of the structures of language with that part of the social laws which regulate marriage ties and kinship, is already conquering the very terrain in which Freud situates the unconscious?[32]
>
> For where on earth would one situate the determinations of the unconscious if it is not in those nominal cadres in which marriage ties and kinship are always grounded. . . . And how would one apprehend the analytical conflicts and their Oedipean prototype outside the engagements which have fixed, long before the subject came into the world, not only his destiny, but his identity itself?[33]
>
> This is precisely where the Oedipus complex . . . may be said, in this connection, to mark the limits which our discipline assigns to subjectivity: that is to say, what the subject can know of his unconscious participation in the movement of the complex structures of marriage ties, by verifying the symbolic effects in his individual existence of the tangential movement towards incest.[34]

Kinship is the culturalization of biological sexuality on the societal level; psychoanalysis describes the transformation of the biological sexuality of individuals as they are enculturated.

Kinship terminology contains information about the system. Kin terms demarcate statuses and indicate some of the attributes of those statuses. For instance, in the Trobriand Islands a man calls the women of his clan by the term for "sister." He calls women of clans into which he can marry by a term indicating their marriageability. When the young Trobriand male learns these terms, he learns which women he can safely desire. In Lacan's scheme, the Oedipal crisis occurs when a child learns of the sexual rules embedded in the terms for family and relatives. The crisis begins when the child comprehends the system and his or her place in it; the crisis is resolved when the child accepts that place and accedes to it. Even if the child refuses that place, he or she cannot escape the knowledge of it. Before the Oedipal phase, the sexuality of the child is labile and relatively unstructured. Each

---

[32] Lacan, *The Language of Self: The Function of Language in Psychoanalysis*, 48.
[33] Ibid., 126.
[34] Ibid., 40.

child contains all the sexual possibilities available to human expression. But in any given society, only some of these possibilities will be expressed, while others will be constrained. Upon leaving the Oedipal phase, the child's libido and gender identity have been organized in conformity with the rules of the culture which is domesticating it.[35]

The Oedipal complex is an apparatus for the production of sexual personality. It is a truism to say that societies will inculcate in their young the character traits appropriate to carrying on the business of society. For instance, E. P. Thompson speaks of the transformation of the personality structure of the English working class as artisans were changed into good industrial workers.[36] Just as the social forms of labor demand certain kinds of personality, the social forms of sex and gender demand certain kinds of people. In the most general terms, the Oedipal complex is a machine which fashions the appropriate forms of sexual individuals.[37]

In the Lacanian theory of psychoanalysis, it is the kin terms that indicate a structure of relationships that will determine the role of any individual or object within the Oedipal drama. For instance, Lacan makes a distinction between the "function of the father" and a particular father who embodies this function. In the same way, he makes a radical distinction between the penis and the "phallus," between organ and information. The phallus is a set of meanings conferred upon the penis. The differentiation between phallus and penis in contemporary French psychoanalytic terminology emphasizes the idea that the penis could not and does not play the role attributed to it in the classical terminology of the castration complex.[38]

---

[35] [Erotic desires and gender identities may of course deviate from their proscribed destinations. But even deviance is shaped within historically and socially available parameters.—G. R.]

[36] Thompson, *The Making of the English Working Class.*

[37] See also the discussion of different forms of "historical individuality" in Althusser and Balibar, *Reading Capital,* 112, 251–53.

[38] I have taken my position on Freud somewhere between the French structuralist interpretations and the American biologistic ones, because I think that Freud's wording is similarly somewhere in the middle. He does talk about penises, about the "inferiority" of the clitoris, and about the psychic consequences of anatomy. The Lacanians, on the other hand, argue from Freud's text that he is unintelligible if his words are taken literally, and that a thoroughly nonanatomical theory can be deduced as Freud's intention (see Althusser, "Freud and Lacan"). I think that they are right; the penis is walking around too much for its role to be taken literally. The detachability of the penis and its transformation in fantasy (e.g., penis = feces = child = gift) argue strongly for a symbolic interpretation. Nevertheless, 1 don't think that Freud was as consistent as either I or Lacan would like him to have been, and some gesture must be made to what he said, even as we play with what he must have meant.

In Freud's terminology, the Oedipal complex presents two alternatives to a child: to have a penis or to be castrated. In contrast, the Lacanian theory of the castration complex leaves behind all reference to anatomical reality.

The theory of the castration complex amounts to having the mate organ play a dominant role—this time as a symbol—*to the extent that its absence or presence transforms an anatomical difference into a major classification of humans, and to the extent that, for each subject, this presence or absence is not taken for granted, is not reduced purely and simply to a given, but is the problematical result of an intra- and intersubjective process* (the subject's assumption of his own sex).[39]

The alternative presented to the child may be rephrased as an alternative between having, or not having, the phallus. Castration is not having the (symbolic) phallus. Castration is not a real "lack," but a meaning conferred on the genitals of a woman: "Castration may derive support from . . . the apprehension in the Real of the absence of the penis in women—but even this supposes a symbolization of the object, since the Real is full, and 'lacks' nothing. Insofar as one finds castration in the genesis of neurosis, it is never real but symbolic."[40]

The phallus is, as it were, a distinctive feature differentiating "castrated" and "noncastrated." The presence or absence of the phallus carries the differences between two sexual statuses, "man" and "woman."[41] Since these are not equal, the phallus also carries a meaning of the dominance of men over women, and it may be inferred that "penis envy" is a recognition thereof. Moreover, as long as men have rights in women which women do not have in themselves, the phallus also carries the meaning of the difference between "exchanger" and "exchanged," gift and giver. Ultimately, neither the classical Freudian nor the rephrased Lacanian theories of the Oedipal process make sense unless at least this much of the Paleolithic relations of sexuality are still with us. We still live in a "phallic" culture.

Lacan also speaks of the phallus as a symbolic object which is exchanged within and between families.[42] It is interesting to think about this observation in terms of primitive marriage transactions and exchange networks. In those transactions, the exchange of women is usually one of many cycles of exchange. Usually, there are other objects circulating as well as women.

[39] Laplanche and Pontalis, in Mehlman, *French Freud*, 198–99, emphasis added.
[40] Wilden, "Lacan and the Discourse of the Other, 271.
[41] Jakobson and Halle, *Fundamentals of Language*, on distinctive features.
[42] Wilden, "Lacan and the Discourse of the Other," 303–5.

Women move in one direction, cattle, shells, or mats in the other. In one sense, the Oedipal complex is an expression of the circulation of the phallus in intrafamily exchange, an inversion of the circulation of women in interfamily exchange. In the cycle of exchange manifested by the Oedipal complex, the phallus passes through the medium of women from one man to another—from father to son, from mother's brother to sister's son, and so forth. In this family *Kula* ring, women go one way, the phallus the other. It is where we aren't. In this sense, the phallus is more than a feature which distinguishes the sexes: it is the embodiment of the male status, to which men accede, and in which certain rights inhere—among them, the right to a woman. It is an expression of the transmission of male dominance. It passes through women and settles upon men.[43] The tracks which it leaves include gender identity, the division of the sexes. But it leaves more than this. It leaves "penis envy," which acquires a rich meaning of the disquietude of women in a phallic culture.

Oedipus revisited

We return now to the two pre-Oedipal androgynes, sitting on the border between biology and culture. Lévi-Strauss places the incest taboo on that border, arguing that its initiation of the exchange of women constitutes the origin of society. In this sense, the incest taboo and the exchange of women are the content of the original social contract.[44] For individuals, the Oedipal crisis occurs at the same divide, when the incest taboo initiates the exchange of the phallus.

The Oedipal crisis is precipitated by certain items of information. The children discover the differences between the sexes, and that each child must become one or the other gender. They also discover the incest taboo, and that some sexuality is prohibited—in this case, the mother is unavailable to either

---

[43] The pre-Oedipal mother is the "phallic mother"; she is believed to possess the phallus. The Oedipal-inducing information is that the mother does not possess the phallus. In other words, the crisis is precipitated by the "castration" of the mother, by the recognition that the phallus only passes through her but does not settle on her. The "phallus" must pass through her, since the relationship of a male to every other male is defined through a woman. A man is linked to a son by a mother, to his nephew by virtue of a sister, and so on. Every relationship between male kin is defined by the woman between them. If power is a male prerogative, and must be passed on, it must go through the women-in-between. Marshall Sahlins (personal communication) once suggested that the reason women are so often defined as stupid, polluting, disorderly, silly, profane, or whatever, is that such categorizations define women as "incapable" of possessing the power which must be transferred through them.

[44] See Sahlins, *Stone Age Economics*, chap. 4.

child because she "belongs" to the father. Lastly, they discover that the two genders do not have the same sexual "rights" or futures.

In the normal course of events, the boy renounces his mother for fear that otherwise his father would castrate him (refuse to give him the phallus, and make him a girl). But by this act of renunciation, the boy affirms the relationships which have given mother to father and which will give him, if he becomes a man, a woman of his own. In exchange for the boy's affirmation of his father's right to his mother, the father affirms the phallus of his son (does not castrate him). The boy exchanges his mother for the phallus, the symbolic token which can later be exchanged for a woman. The only thing required of him is a little patience. He retains his initial libidinal organization and the sex of his original love object. The social contract to which he has agreed will eventually recognize his own rights and provide him with a woman of his own.

What happens to the girl is more complex. She, like the boy, discovers the taboo against incest and the division of the sexes. She also discovers some unpleasant information about the gender to which she is being assigned. For the boy, the taboo on incest is a taboo on certain women. For the girl, it is a taboo on all women. Since she is in a homosexual position vis-à-vis the mother, the rule of heterosexuality which dominates the scenario makes her position excruciatingly untenable. The mother, and all women by extension, can be properly beloved only by someone "with a penis" (phallus). Since the girl has no "phallus," she has no "right" to love her mother or another woman since she is herself destined to some man. She does not have the symbolic token which can be exchanged for a woman.

If Freud's wording of this moment of the female Oedipal crisis is ambiguous, Lampl de Groot's formulation makes the context which confers meaning upon the genitals explicit: "*If the little girl comes to the conclusion that such an organ is really indispensable to the possession of the mother, she experiences* in addition to the narcissistic insults common to both sexes still another blow, namely *a feeling of inferiority about her genitals.*"[45] The girl concludes that the "penis" is indispensable for the possession of the mother because only those who possess the phallus have a "right" to a woman, and the token of exchange. She does not come to her conclusion because of the natural superiority of the penis either in and of itself, or as an instrument for making love. The hierarchical arrangement of the male and female genitals is a result of the definitions of the situation—the rule of obligatory heterosexuality and the relegation of women (those without the phallus, castrated) to men (those with the phallus).

---

[45] Lampl de Groot, "Problems of Femininity," 497, emphasis added.

The girl then begins to turn away from the mother, and to the father. "To the girl, it [castration] is an accomplished fact, which is irrevocable, but the recognition of which compels her finally to renounce her first love object and to taste to the full the bitterness of its loss. . . . [T]he father is chosen as a love-object, the enemy becomes the beloved."[46] This recognition of "castration" forces the girl to redefine her relationship to herself, her mother, and her father.

She turns from the mother because she does not have the phallus to give her. She turns from the mother also in anger and disappointment, because the mother did not give her a "penis" (phallus). But the mother, a woman in a phallic culture, does not have the phallus to give away (having gone through the Oedipal crisis herself a generation earlier). The girl then turns to the father because only he can "give her the phallus," and it is only through him that she can enter into the symbolic exchange system in which the phallus circulates. But the father does not give her the phallus in the same way that he gives it to the boy. The phallus is affirmed in the boy, who then has it to give away. The girl never gets the phallus. It passes through her, and in its passage is transformed into a child. When she "recognizes her castration," she accedes to the place of a woman in a phallic exchange network. She can "get" the phallus—in intercourse, or as a child—but only as a gift from a man. She never gets to give it away.

When she turns to the father, she also represses the "active" portions of her libido.

> The turning away from her mother is an extremely important step in the course of a little girl's development. It is more than a mere change of object . . . hand in hand with it there is to be observed a marked lowering of the active sexual impulses and a rise of the passive ones. . . . The transition to the father object is accomplished with the help of the passive trends in so far as they have escaped the catastrophe. The path to the development of femininity now lies open to the girl.[47]

The ascendance of passivity in the girl is due to her recognition of the futility of realizing her active desire, and of the unequal terms of the struggle. Freud locates active desire in the clitoris and passive desire in the vagina, and thus describes the repression of active desire as the repression of clitoral eroticism in favor of passive vaginal eroticism. In this scheme, cultural stereotypes have been mapped onto the genitals. Since the work of Masters and Johnson, it is evident that this genital division is a false one. Any organ—penis, clitoris,

---

[46] Lampl de Groot, "The Evolution of the Oedipus Complex in Women," 213.
[47] Freud, "Some Psychical Consequences of the Anatomical Distinction between the Sexes," 239.

vagina—can be the locus of either active or passive eroticism. What is important in Freud's scheme, however, is not the geography of desire but its self-confidence. It is not an organ which is repressed but a segment of erotic possibility. Freud notes that "more constraint has been applied to the libido when it is pressed into the service of the feminine function."[48] The girl has been robbed.

If the Oedipal phase proceeds normally and the girl "accepts her castration," her libidinal structure and object choice are now congruent with the female gender role. She has become a little woman—feminine, passive, heterosexual. Actually. Freud suggests that there are three alternate routes out of the Oedipal catastrophe. The girl may simply freak out, repress sexuality altogether, and become asexual. She may protest, cling to her narcissism and desire, and become either "masculine" or homosexual. Or she may accept the situation, sign the social contract, and attain "normality."

Karen Horney is critical of the entire Freud/Lampl de Groot scheme. But in the course of her critique she articulates its implications.

> When she [the girl] first turns to a man (the father), it is in the main
> only by way of the narrow bridge of resentment. . . . We should feel it a
> contradiction if the relation of woman to man did not retain throughout
> life some tinge of this enforced substitute for that which was really
> desired. . . . The same character of something remote from instinct,
> secondary and substitutive, would, even in normal women, adhere to
> the wish for motherhood. . . . The special point about Freud's viewpoint
> is rather that it sees the wish for motherhood not as an innate formation,
> but as something that can be reduced psychologically to its ontogenetic
> elements and draws its energy originally from homosexual or phallic
> instinctual elements. . . . It would follow, finally, that women's whole
> reaction to life would be based on a strong subterranean resentment.[49]

Horney considers these implications to be so far-fetched that they challenge the validity of Freud's entire scheme. But it is certainly plausible to argue instead that the creation of "femininity" in women in the course of socialization is an act of psychic brutality, and that it leaves in women an immense resentment of the suppression to which they were subjected. It is also possible to argue that women have few means for realizing and expressing their residual anger. One can read Freud's essays on femininity as descriptions of how a group is prepared psychologically, at a tender age, to live with its oppression.

---

[48] Freud, "Femininity," 131.
[49] Horney, "The Denial of the Vagina," 148–49.

There is an additional element in the classic discussions of the attainment of womanhood. The girl first turns to the father, because she must, because she is "castrated" (a helpless woman). She then discovers that "castration" is a prerequisite to the father's love, that she must be a woman for him to love her. She therefore begins to desire "castration," and what had previously been a disaster becomes a wish. "Analytic experience leaves no room for doubt that the little girl's first libidinal relation to her father is masochistic, and the masochistic wish in its earliest distinctively feminine phase is: 'I want to be castrated by my father.'"[50] Deutsch argues that such masochism may conflict with the ego, causing some women to flee the entire situation in defense of their self-regard. Those women to whom the choice is "between finding bliss in suffering or peace in renunciation" will have difficulty in attaining a healthy attitude to intercourse and motherhood.[51] Why Deutsch appears to consider such women to be special cases, rather than the norm, is not clear from her discussion.

The psychoanalytic theory of femininity is one that sees female development based largely on pain and humiliation, and it takes some fancy footwork to explain why anyone ought to enjoy being a woman. At this point in the classic discussions biology makes a triumphant return. The fancy footwork consists in arguing that finding joy in pain is adaptive to the role of women in reproduction, since defloration and childbirth are "painful." Would it not make more sense to question the entire procedure? If women, in finding their place in a sexual system, are robbed of libido and forced into a masochistic eroticism, why did the analysts not argue for novel arrangements, instead of rationalizing the old ones?

Freud's theory of femininity has been subjected to feminist critique since it was first published. To the extent that the theory is a rationalization of female subordination, this critique has been justified. To the extent that it is a description of a process that subordinates women, this critique is a mistake. As a description of how phallic culture domesticates women, and the effects in women of their domestication, psychoanalytic theory has no parallel.[52] And since psychoanalysis is a theory of gender, dismissing it would be ill advised for a political movement dedicated to eradicating gender hierarchy (or gender itself). We cannot dismantle something that we underestimate or do not understand. The oppression of women is deep; equal pay, equal work, and all the female politicians in the world will not extirpate the

[50] Deutsch, "On Female Homosexuality," 228.
[51] Ibid., 231.
[52] See also Mitchell, *Women's Estate* and *Psychoanalysis and Feminism*; Lasch, "Freud and Women."

roots of sexism. Lévi-Strauss and Freud elucidate what would otherwise be poorly perceived parts of the deep structures of sex oppression. They serve as reminders of the intractability and magnitude of what we fight, and their analyses provide preliminary charts of the social machinery we must rearrange.

Women unite to off the Oedipal residue of culture

The precision of the fit between Freud and Lévi-Strauss is striking. Kinship systems require a division of the sexes. The Oedipal phase divides the sexes. Kinship systems include sets of rules governing sexuality. The Oedipal crisis is the assimilation of these rules and taboos. Compulsory heterosexuality is the product of kinship. The Oedipal phase constitutes heterosexual desire. Kinship rests on a radical difference between the rights of men and women. The Oedipal complex confers male rights upon the boy and forces the girl to accommodate herself to her lesser rights.

This fit between Lévi-Strauss and Freud is by implication an argument that our sex/gender system is still organized by the principles outlined by Lévi-Strauss, despite the entirely nonmodern character of his data. The more recent data on which Freud bases his theories testifies to the endurance of these sexual structures. If my reading of Freud and Lévi-Strauss is accurate, it suggests that the feminist movement must attempt to resolve the Oedipal crisis of culture by reorganizing the domain of sex and gender in such a way that each individual's Oedipal experience would be less destructive. The dimensions of such a task are difficult to imagine, but at least certain conditions would have to be met.

Several elements of the Oedipal situation would have to be altered in order that the phase not have such disastrous effects on the young female ego. The Oedipal phase institutes a contradiction in the girl by placing irreconcilable demands upon her. On the one hand, the girl's love for the mother is induced by the mother's job of child care. The girl is then forced to abandon this love because of the female sex role—to belong to a man. If the sexual division of labor were such that adults of both sexes cared for children equally, primary object choice would be bisexual. If heterosexuality were not obligatory, this early love would not have to be suppressed, and the penis would not be over-valued. If the sexual property system were reorganized in such a way that men did not have overriding rights in women (if there was no exchange of women) and if there were no gender, the entire Oedipal drama would be a relic. In short, feminism must call for a revolution in kinship.

The organization of sex and gender once had functions other than itself—it organized society. Now, it mainly organizes and reproduces itself. The kinds of relationships sexuality established in the dim human past still dominate our sexual lives, our ideas about men and women, and the ways we raise our children. But they lack the functional load they once carried. One of the most conspicuous features of kinship is that it has been systematically stripped of its functions—political, economic, educational, and organizational. It has been reduced to its barest bones—*sex and gender*.

Human sexual life will always be subject to convention and human intervention. It will never be completely "natural," if only because our species is social, cultural, and articulate. The wild profusion of infantile sexuality will always be tamed. The confrontation between immature and helpless infants and the developed social life of their elders will probably always leave some residue of disturbance. But the mechanisms and aims of this process need not he largely independent of conscious choice. Cultural evolution provides us with the opportunity to seize control of the means of sexuality, reproduction, and socialization, and to make conscious decisions to liberate human sexual life from the archaic relationships which deform it. Ultimately, a thoroughgoing feminist revolution would liberate more than women. It would liberate forms of sexual expression, and it would liberate human personality from the straightjacket of gender.

"Daddy, daddy, you bastard, I'm through."—Sylvia Plath

In the course of this essay I have tried to construct a theory of women's oppression by borrowing concepts from anthropology and psychoanalysis. But Lévi-Strauss and Freud write within intellectual traditions produced by a culture in which women are oppressed. The danger in my enterprise is that the sexism in the traditions of which they are a part tends to be dragged in with each borrowing. "We cannot utter a single destructive proposition which has not already slipped into the form, the logic, and the implicit postulations of precisely what it seeks to contest."[53] And what slips in is formidable. Both psychoanalysis and structural anthropology are, in one sense, the most sophisticated ideologies of sexism around.[54]

---

[53] Derrida, "Structure, Sign, and Play in the Discourse of the Human Sciences," 250.
[54] Parts of Wittig's *Les Guérillères* (1973) appear to be tirades against Lévi-Strauss and Lacan. For instance: "Has he not indeed written, power and the possession of women, leisure and the enjoyment of women: He writes that you are currency, an item of exchange. He

For instance, Lévi-Strauss sees women as being like words, which are misused when they are not "communicated" and exchanged. On the last page of a very long book, he observes that this creates something of a contradiction in women, since women are at the same time "speakers" and "spoken." His only comment on this contradiction is this.

> But woman could never become just a sign and nothing more, since even in a man's world she is still a person, and since insofar as she is defined as a sign she must be recognized as a generator of signs. In the matrimonial dialogue of men, woman is never purely what is spoken about; for if women in general represent a certain category of signs, destined to a certain kind of communication, each woman preserves a particular value arising from her talent, before and after marriage, for taking her part in a duet. In contrast to words, which have wholly become signs, woman has remained at once a sign and a value. *This explains why the relations between the sexes have preserved that affective richness, ardour and mystery which doubtless originally permeated the entire universe of human communications.*[55]

This is an extraordinary statement. Why is he not, at this point, denouncing what kinship systems do to women, instead of presenting one of the greatest rip-offs of all time as the root of romance?

A similar insensitivity is revealed within psychoanalysis by the inconsistency with which it assimilates the critical implications of its own theory. For instance, Freud did not hesitate to recognize that his findings posed a challenge to conventional morality: "We cannot avoid observing with critical eyes, and we have found that it is impossible to give our support to conventional sexual morality or to approve highly of the means by which society attempts to arrange the practical problems of sexuality in life. *We can demonstrate with ease that what the world calls its code of morals demands more sacrifices than it is worth*, and that its behavior is neither dictated by honesty nor instituted with wisdom."[56]

writes, barter, barter, possession and acquisition of women and merchandise. Better for you to see your guts in the sun and utter the death rattle than to live a life that anyone can appropriate. What belongs to you on this earth? Only death. No power on earth can take that away from you. And—consider explain tell yourself—if happiness consists in the possession of something, then hold fast to this sovereign happiness—to die" (Wittig, *Les Guérillères*, 115–16; see also 106–7, 113–14, 134). The awareness by French feminists of Lévi-Strauss and Lacan is most clearly evident in a group called Psychoanalyse et Politique, which defined its task as a feminist use and critique of Lacanian psychoanalysis.

[55] Lévi-Strauss, *The Elementary Structures of Kinship*, 496, emphasis added.

[56] Freud, *A General Introduction to Psychoanalysis*, 376–77, emphasis added.

Nevertheless, when psychoanalysis demonstrates with equal facility that the ordinary components of feminine personality are masochism, self-hatred, and passivity, a similar judgment is *not* made.[57] Instead, a double standard of interpretation is employed. Masochism is bad for men, essential to women. Adequate narcissism is necessary for men, impossible for women. Passivity is tragic in man, while lack of passivity is tragic in a woman.

It is this double standard which enables clinicians to try to accommodate women to a role whose destructiveness is so lucidly detailed in their own theories. It is the same inconsistent attitude which permits therapists to consider lesbianism as a problem to be cured, rather than as the resistance to the bad situation that their own theory suggests.[58] There are points within the analytic discussions of femininity where one might say, "This is oppression of women," or "We can demonstrate with ease that what the world calls femininity demands more sacrifices than it is worth." It is precisely at such points that the implications of the theory are ignored and are replaced with formulations whose purpose is to keep those implications firmly lodged in the theoretical unconscious. It is at these points that all sorts of mysterious chemical substances, joys in pain, and biological aims are substituted for a critical assessment of the costs of femininity. These substitutions are the symptoms of theoretical repression, in that they are not consistent with the usual canons of psychoanalytic argument. The extent to which these rationalizations of femininity go against the grain of psychoanalytic logic is strong evidence for the extent of the need to suppress the radical and feminist implications of the theory of femininity (Deutsch's discussions are excellent examples of this process of substitution and repression).

The argument which must be woven in order to assimilate Lévi-Strauss and Freud into feminist theory is somewhat tortuous. I have engaged it for several reasons. First, while neither Lévi-Strauss nor Freud questions the undoubted sexism endemic to the systems they describe, the questions which ought to be posed are blindingly obvious. Second, their work enables

---

[57] "Every woman adores a fascist" (Plath, "Daddy").

[58] One clinician, Charlotte Wolff (*Love between Women*) has taken the psychoanalytic theory of womanhood to its logical extreme and proposed that lesbianism is a healthy response to female socialization: "Women who do not rebel against the status of object have declared themselves defeated as persons in their own right" (65). "The lesbian girl is the one who, by all means at her disposal, will try to find a place of safety inside and outside the family, through her fight for equality with the male. She will not, like other women, play up to him: indeed, she despises the very idea of it" (ibid., 59). "The lesbian was and is unquestionably in the avant-garde of the fight for equality of the sexes, and for the psychical liberation of women" (ibid., 66). It is revealing to compare Wolff's discussion with the articles on lesbianism in Marmor, *Sexual Inversion*.

us to isolate sex and gender from "mode of production," and to counter a certain tendency to explain sex oppression as a reflex of economic forces. Their work provides a framework in which the full weight of sexuality and marriage can be incorporated into an analysis of sex oppression. It suggests a conception of the women's movement as analogous to, rather than isomorphic with, the working-class movement, each addressing a different source of human discontent. In Marx's vision, the working-class movement would do more than throw off the burden of its own exploitation. It also had the potential to change society, to liberate humanity, to create a classless society. Perhaps the women's movement has the task of effecting the same kind of social change for a system of which Marx had only an imperfect apperception. Something of this sort is implicit in Wittig—the dictatorship of the Amazon *guérillères* is a temporary means for achieving a genderless society.

The sex/gender system is not immutably oppressive and has lost much of its traditional function. Nevertheless, it will not wither away in the absence of opposition. It still carries the social burden of sex and gender, of socializing the young, and of providing ultimate propositions about the nature of human beings themselves. And it serves economic and political ends other than those it was originally designed to further.[59] The sex/gender system must be reorganized through political action.

Finally, the exegesis of Lévi-Strauss and Freud suggests a certain vision of feminist politics and the feminist utopia. It suggests that we should not aim for the elimination of men, but for the elimination of the social system which creates sexism and gender. I personally find a vision of an Amazon matriarchate, in which men are reduced to servitude or oblivion (depending on the possibilities for parthenogenetic reproduction), distasteful and inadequate. Such a vision maintains gender and the division of the sexes. It is a vision which simply inverts the arguments of those who base their case for inevitable male dominance on ineradicable and *significant* biological differences between the sexes. But we are not only oppressed *as* women; we are oppressed by having to *be* women—or men as the case may be. I personally feel that the feminist movement must dream of even more than the elimination of the oppression of women. It must dream of the elimination of obligatory sexualities and sex roles. The dream I find most compelling is one of an androgynous and gender-less (though not sexless) society, in which one's sexual anatomy is irrelevant to who one is, what one does, and with whom one makes love.

---

[59] Scott, "The Role of Collegiate Sororities in Maintaining Class and Ethnic Endogamy."

The political economy of sex

It would be nice to be able to conclude here with the implications for feminism and gay liberation of the overlap between Freud and Lévi-Strauss. But I must suggest, tentatively, a next step on the agenda: a Marxian analysis of sex/gender systems. Sex/gender systems are not ahistorical emanations of the human mind; they are products of historical human activity.

We need, for instance, an analysis of the evolution of sexual exchange along the lines of Marx's discussion in *Capital* of the evolution of money and commodities. There are an economics and a politics to sex/gender systems that are obscured by the concept of "exchange of women." For instance, a system in which women are exchangeable only for one another has different effects on women than one in which there is a commodity equivalent for women.

> That marriage in simple societies involves an "exchange" is a somewhat vague notion that has often confused the analysis of social systems. The extreme case is the exchange of "sisters," formerly practiced in parts of Australia and Africa. Here the term has the precise dictionary meaning of "to be received as an equivalent for," "to give and receive reciprocally." From quite a different standpoint the virtually universal incest prohibition means that marriage systems necessarily involve "exchanging" siblings for spouses, giving rise to a reciprocity that is purely notational. But in most societies marriage is mediated by a set of intermediary transactions. If we see these transactions as simply implying immediate or long-term reciprocity, then the analysis is likely to be blurred. . . . The analysis is further limited if one regards the passage of property simply as a symbol of the transfer of rights, for then the nature of the objects handed over . . . is of little importance. . . . Neither of these approaches is wrong; both are inadequate.[60]

There are systems in which there is no equivalent for a woman. To get a wife, a man must have a daughter, a sister, or other female kinswoman in whom he has a right of bestowal. He must have control over some female flesh. The Lele and Kuma are cases in point. Lele men scheme constantly in order to stake claims in some as yet unborn girl, and scheme further to make good their claims.[61] A Kuma girl's marriage is determined by an intricate web of debts, and she has little say in choosing her husband. A girl is usually married

[60] Goody and Tambiah, *Bridewealth and Dowry*, 2.
[61] Douglas, *The Lele of Kasai*.

against her will, and her groom shoots an arrow into her thigh to symbolically prevent her from running away. The young wives almost always do run away, only to be returned to their new husbands by an elaborate conspiracy enacted by their kin and affines.[62]

In other societies, there is an equivalent for women. A woman can be converted into bridewealth, and bridewealth can be in turn converted into a woman. The dynamics of such systems vary accordingly, as does the specific kind of pressure exerted upon women. The marriage of a Melpa woman is not a return for a previous debt. Each transaction is self-contained, in that the payment of a bridewealth in pigs and shells will cancel the debt. The Melpa woman therefore has more latitude in choosing her husband than does her Kuma counterpart; still, her destiny is linked to bridewealth. If her husband's kin are slow to pay, her kin may encourage her to leave him; on the other hand, if her consanguineal kin are satisfied with the balance of payments, they may refuse to back her in the event that she wants to leave her husband. Moreover, her male kinsmen use the bridewealth for their own purposes, in *moka* exchange and for their own marriages. If a woman leaves her husband, some or all of the bridewealth will have to be returned. If, as is usually the case, the pigs and shells have been distributed or promised, her kin will be reluctant to back her in the event of marital discord. And each time a woman divorces and remarries her value in bridewealth tends to depreciate. On the whole, her male consanguines will lose in the event of a divorce, unless the groom has been delinquent in his payments. While the Melpa woman is freer as a new bride than a Kuma woman, the bridewealth system makes divorce difficult or impossible.[63]

In some societies, like the Nuer, bridewealth can only be converted into brides. In others, bridewealth can be converted into something else, such as political prestige. In this case, a woman's marriage is implicated in a political system. In the Big Man systems of Highland New Guinea, the material which circulates for women also circulates in the exchanges on which political power is based. Within the political system men are in constant need of valuables to disburse, and they are dependent upon input. They depend not only upon their immediate partners, but upon the partners of their partners, to several degrees of remove. If a man has to return some bridewealth, he may not be able to give it to someone who planned to give it to someone else who intended to use it to give a feast upon which his status depends. Big Men are therefore concerned with the domestic affairs of others whose relationship with them may be extremely indirect. There are cases in which

---

[62] Reay, *The Kuma.*
[63] Strathern, *Women in Between.*

headmen intervene in marital disputes involving indirect trading partners in order that *moka* exchanges not be disrupted.[64] The weight of this entire system may come to rest upon one woman kept in a miserable marriage.

In short, there are other questions to ask of a marriage system than whether or not it exchanges women. Is the woman traded for a woman, or is there an equivalent? Is this equivalent only for women, or can it be turned into something else? If it can be turned into something else, is it turned into political power or wealth? On the other hand, can bridewealth be obtained only in marital exchange, or can it be obtained from elsewhere? Can women be accumulated through amassing wealth? Can wealth be accumulated by disposing of women? Is a marriage system part of a system of stratification?[65]

These last questions point to another task for a political economy of sex. Kinship and marriage are always parts of total social systems and are tied into economic and political arrangements.

> Lévi-Strauss . . . rightly argues that the structural implications of a marriage can only be understood if we think of it as one item in a whole series of transactions between kin groups. So far, so good. But in none of the examples which he provides in his book does he carry this principle far enough. The reciprocities of kinship obligation are not merely symbols of alliance, they are also economic transactions, political transactions, charters to rights of domicile and land use. No useful picture of "how a kinship system works" can be provided unless these several aspects or implications of the kinship organization are considered simultaneously.[66]

Among the Kachin, the relationship of a tenant to a landlord is also a relationship between a son-in-law and a father-in-law. "The procedure for acquiring land rights of any kind is in almost all cases tantamount to marrying a woman from the lineage of the lord."[67] In the Kachin system, bridewealth moves from commoners to aristocrats, women moving in the opposite direction.

> From an economic aspect the effect of the matrilateral cross-cousin marriage is that, on balance, the headman's lineage constantly pays

---

64 Bulmer, "Political Aspects of the Moka Ceremonial Exchange System among the Kyaka People of the Western Highlands of New Guinea," 11.
65 Another line of inquiry would compare bridewealth systems to dowry systems. Many of these questions are treated in Goody and Tambiah, *Bridewealth and Dowry*.
66 Leach, *Rethinking Anthropology*, 90.
67 Ibid., 88.

wealth to the chief's lineage in the form of bridewealth. The payment can also, from an analytical point of view, be regarded as a rent paid to the senior landlord by the tenant. The most important part of this payment is in the form of consumer goods—namely cattle. The chief converts this perishable wealth into imperishable prestige through the medium of spectacular feasting. The ultimate consumers of the goods are in this way the original producers, namely, the commoners who attend the feast.[68]

In another example, it is traditional in the Trobriands for a man to send a harvest gift—*urigubu*—of yams to his sister's household. For the commoners, this amounts to a simple circulation of yams. But the chief is polygamous, and marries a woman from each subdistrict within his domain. Each of these sub-districts therefore sends *urigubu* to the chief, providing him with a bulging storehouse out of which he finances feasts, craft production, and *kula* expeditions. This "fund of power" underwrites the political system and forms the basis for chiefly power.[69]

In some systems, position in a political hierarchy and position in a marriage system are intimately linked. In traditional Tonga, women married up in rank. Thus, low-ranking lineages would send women to higher-ranking lineages. Women of the highest lineage were married into the "house of Fiji," a lineage defined as outside the political system. If the highest-ranking chief gave his sister to a lineage other than one which had no part in the ranking system, he would no longer be the highest-ranking chief. Rather, the lineage of his sister's son would outrank his own. In times of political rearrangement, the demotion of the previous high-ranking lineage was formalized when it gave a wife to a lineage which it had formerly outranked. In traditional Hawaii, the situation was the reverse. Women married down, and the dominant lineage gave wives to junior lines. A paramount would either marry a sister or obtain a wife from a distant land. When a junior lineage usurped rank, it formalized its position by giving a wife to its former senior line.

There is even some tantalizing data suggesting that marriage systems may be implicated in the evolution of social strata and perhaps in the development of early states. The first round of the political consolidation which resulted in the formation of a state in Madagascar occurred when one chief obtained title to several autonomous districts through the vagaries of marriage and inheritance.[70] In Samoa, legends place the origin of the paramount title— the *Tafa'ifa*—as a result of intermarriage between ranking members of

---

[68] Ibid., 89.
[69] Malinowski, "The Primitive Economics of the Trobriand Islanders."
[70] Henry Wright, personal communication.

four major lineages. My thoughts are too speculative, my data too sketchy, to say much on this subject. But a search ought to be undertaken for data which might demonstrate how marriage systems intersect with large-scale political processes like state-making. Marriage systems might be implicated in a number of ways: in the accumulation of wealth and the maintenance of differential access to political and economic resources; in the building of alliances; in the consolidation of high-ranking persons into a single closed stratum of endogamous kin.

These examples—like the Kachin and Trobriand ones—indicate that sexual systems cannot, in the final analysis, be understood in isolation. A full-bodied analysis of women in a single society, or throughout history, must take *everything* into account: the evolution of commodity forms in women, systems of land tenure, political arrangements, subsistence technology, and so on. Equally important, economic and political analyses are incomplete if they do not consider women, marriage, and sexuality. The traditional concerns of anthropology and social science—such as the evolution of social stratification and the origin of the state—must be reworked to include the implications of matrilateral cross-cousin marriage, surplus extracted in the form of daughters, the conversion of female labor into male wealth, the conversion of female lives into marriage alliances, the contribution of marriage to political power, and the transformations that all of these varied aspects of society have undergone in the course of time.

This sort of endeavor is, in the final analysis, exactly what Engels tried to do in his effort to make coherent so many of the diverse aspects of social life. He tried to relate men and women, town and country, kinship and state, forms of property, systems of land tenure, convertibility of wealth, forms of exchange, the technology of food production, and forms of trade—to name a few—into a systematic historical account. Eventually, someone will have to write a new version of *The Origin of the Family, Private Property, and the State*, recognizing the mutual interdependence of sexuality, economics, and politics without underestimating the full significance of each in human society.

Works cited

Althusser, Louis. "Freud and Lacan." *New Left Review* 55 (May-June 1969): 48-66.
Althusser, Lous, and Etienne Balibar. *Reading Capital*. London: New Left, 1970.
Benston, Margaret. "The Political Economy of Women's Liberation." *Monthly Review* 21, no. 4 (1969): 13-27.
Berndt, Ronald. *Excess and Constraint*. Chicago: University of Chicago, 1962.

Bulmer, Ralph. "Political Aspects of the Moka Ceremonial Exchange System among the Kyaka People of the Western Highlands of New Guinea." *Oceania* 31, no. 1 (1960): 1-13.

Chasseguet-Smirgel, J. *Female Sexuality*. Ann Arbor: University of Michigan Press, 1970.

Dalla Costa, Mariarosa. *The Power of Women and the Subversion of the Community*. Bristol: Falling Wall, 1972.

Derrida, Jacques. "Structure, Sign, and Play in the Discourse of the Human Sciences." *The Structuralist Controversy*, ed. R. Macksey and E. Donato, 247-72. Baltimore: Johns Hopkins University Press, 1972.

Deutsch, Helene. "On Female Homosexuality." *The Psychoanalytic Reader*, ed. R. Fleiss, 237-60. New York: International Universities Press, 1948.

Deutsch, Helene. "The Significance of Masochism in the Mental Life of Women." *The Psychoanalytic Reader*, ed. R. Fleiss, 223-36. New York: International Universities Press, 1948.

Douglas, Mary. *The Lele of Kasia*. London: Oxford University Press, 1963.

Engels, Friedrich. *The Origin of the Family, Private Property, and the State*. 1942. Introduction by Eleanor Burke Leacock. New York: International Publishers, 1972.

Fee, Elizabeth. "The Sexual Politics of Victorian Social Anthropology." *Feminist Studies* 1 (winter-spring 1973): 23-29.

Ford, Clellen S., and Frank A. Beach. *Patterns of Sexual Behavior*. New York: Harper and Row, 1951.

Foucault, Michel. *The Order of Things*. New York: Pantheon, 1970.

Freud, Sigmund. "Female Sexuality." *The Complete Works of Sigmund Freud*. Vol 21, ed. James Strachey, 223-43. London: Hogarth, 1961.

Freud, Sigmund. "Femininity." *New Introductory Lectures in Psychoanalysis*, ed. James Strachey, 139-67. New York: Norton, 1965.

Freud, Sigmund. *A General Introduction to Psychoanalysis*. Garden City: Garden City, 1943.

Freud, Sigmund. "Some Psychical Consequences of the Anatomical Distinction between the Sexes." *The Complete Works of Sigmund Freud*. Vol 21, ed. James Strachey. London: Hogarth, 1961.

Gardiner, Jean. "Political Economy of Female Labor." Paper delivered at the "Sexual Divisions and Society" conference, British Sociological Association, 1974.

Gerstein, Ira. "Domestic Work and Capitalism." *Radical America* 7, no 4-5 (1973): 101-28.

Glasse, R.M. "The Mask of Venery." Paper presented at seventieth annual meeting of the American Anthropological Association, New York City, 1971.

Goodale, Jane, and Ann Chowning. "The Contaminating Woman." Paper presented at seventieth annual meeting of the American Anthropological Association, New York City, 1971.

Goody, Jack, and S. J. Tambiah. *Bridewealth and Dowry*. Cambridge: Cambridge University Press, 1973.

Gough, Ian. "Marx and Productive Labour." *New Left Review* 76 (1972): 47-72.

Hefner, Robert. "The *Tel Quel* Ideology: Material Practice upon Material Practice." *Substance* 8 (1974): 127-38.

Horney, Karen. "The Denial of the Vagina." *Feminine Psychology*, 147-61. Edited by Harold Kelman. New York: Norton, 1973.

Jakobson, Roman, and Morris Halle. *Fundamentals of Language*. The Hague: Mouton, 1971.

Jones, Ernest. "The Phallic Phase." *International Journal of Psychoanalysis* 14 (1933): 1-33.

Kelly, Raymond. "Witchcraft and Sexual Relations: An Exploration of the Social and Semantic Implications of the Structure of Belief." *Man and Woman in the New Guinea Highlands*, ed. Paul Brown and Georgeda Buchbinder, 36-53. Washington: American Anthropological Association, 1976.

Lacan, Jacques. *The Language of the Self: The function of Language in Psychoanalysis*. Translated by Anthony Wilden. Baltimore: Johns Hopkins University Press, 1968.

Lampl de Groot, Jeanne. "The Evolution of the Oedipus Complex in Women." *The Psychoanalytic Reader*, ed. R. Fleiss, 180-94. New York: International Universities Press, 1948.

Lampl de Groot, Jeanne. "Problems of Femininity." *Psychoanalytic Quarterly* 2 (1933): 489-518.

Langess, L.L. "Sexual Antagonism in the New Guinea Highlands: A Bena Bena Example." *Oceania* 37, no. 3 (1967): 161-77.

Laguia, Isabel, and John Dumoulin. "Towards a Science of Women's Liberation." NACLA Newsletter 6, no. 10 (1972): 3-20.

Lasch, Christopher. "Freud and Women." *New York Review of Books* 21, no. 15 (1974): 12-17.

Leach, Edmund. *Rethinking Anthropology*. New York: Humanities, 1971.

Lévi-Strauss, Claude. *The Elementary Structures of Kinship*. Translated by James Harle Bell, John Richard von Strurmer, and Rodney Needham. Boston: Beacon, 1969.

Lindenbaum, Shirley. "A Wife Is the Hand of the Man." Paper presented at the seventy-second annual meeting of the American Anthropological Association, Mexico City, 1973.

Malinowski, Bronislaw. "The Primitive Economics of the Trobriand Islanders." *Cultures of the Pacific*, ed. T. harding and B. Wallace, 51-62. New York: Free Press, 1970.

Malinowski, Bronislaw. *The Sexual Life of Savages*. London: Routledge and Kegan Paul, 1929.

Marmor, Judd. *Sexual Inversion*. London: Basic, 1965.

Marx, Karl. *Capital*. New York: International Publishers, 1972.

Marx, Karl. *Pre-capitalist Economic Formations*. New York: International Publishers, 1971.

Marx, Karl. *Theories of Surplus Value, Part 1*. Moscow: Progress, 1969.

Marx, Karl. *Wage-Labor and Capital.* New York: International Publishers, 1971.

Meggitt, M.J. "Male-Female Relationships in the Highlands of Australian New Guinea." *American Anthropologist* 66, no. 4, part 2 (1970): 204-24.

Mehlman, Jeffrey. *French Freud: Structural Studies in Psychoanalysis,* no. 48. New Haven: Yale French Studies, 1972.

Mitchell, Juliet. *Psychoanalysis and Feminism: Freud, Reich, Laing, and Women.* New York: Pantheon, 1974.

Mitchell, Juliet. *Women's Estate.* New York: Vintage, 1971.

Murphy, Robert. "Social Structure and Sex Antagonism." *Southwesst Journal of Anthropology* 15, no. 1 (1959): 81-96.

Plath, Sylvia. "Daddy." *Ariel: The Restored Edtion,* 64-66. New York: Harper Collins, 2004.

Rappaport, Roy, *Pigs for the Ancestors: Ritual in the Ecology of a New Guinea People.* New Haven: Yale University Press, 1975.

Read, Kenneth. "The Nama Cult of the Central Highlands, New Guinea." *Oceania* 23, no. 1 (1953): 1-25.

Reay, Marie. *The Kuma.* London: Cambridge University Press, 1959.

Rowntree, M., and J. Rowntree. "More on the Political Economy of Women's Liberation." *Monthly Review* 21, no. 8 (1970): 26-32.

Sahlins, Marshall. "The Origins of Society." *Scientific American* 203 (1960): 76-87.

Schneider, David M., and Kathleen Gough, eds. *Matrilineal Kinship.* Berkeley: University of California Press, 1961.

Scott, John Finley. "The Role of Collegiate Sororities in Maintaining Class and Ethnic Endogamy." *American Sociological Review* 30, no. 4 (1965): 415-26.

Strathern, Marily. *Women in Between.* New York: Seminar, 1972.

Thompson, E. P. *The Making of the English Working Class.* New York: Vintage, 1963.

Thurnwald, Richard. "Banaro Society." *Memoirs of the American Anthropological Association* 3, no. 4 (1916): 251-391.

Tiger, Lionel, and Robin Fox. *The Imperial Animal.* New yhork: Holt, Reinhart and Winston, 1971.

Van Baal, J. *Dema.* The hague: Nijhoff, 1966.

Vogel, Lise. "The Earthly Family." *Radical America* 7, no. 4-5 (1973): 9-50.

Wilden, Anthony. "Lacan and the Discourse of the Other." *The Language of the Self: The function of Language in Psychoanalysis,* by Jacques Lacan, 157-311. Baltimore: Johns Hopkins University Press, 1968.

Wittig, Monique. *Les Guérillères.* New York: Avon, 1973.

Wolff, Charlotte. *Love between Women.* London: Duckwortyh, 1971.

Yalmon, Nur. "On the Purity of women in the Castes of Ceylon and Malabar." *Journal of the Royal Anthropological Institute* 93, no. 1 (1963): 25-58.

Peter Brooks

American (1938-)

Freud's Masterplot (1977)

The sense of beginning, then, is determined by the sense of an ending. And if we inquire further into the nature of the ending, we no doubt find that it eventually has to do with the human end, with death.

In one of his best essays in "narratology," where he is working toward a greater formalization of principles advanced by Vladimir Propp and Viktor Shklovsky, Tzvetan Todorov elaborates a model of narrative transformation whereby narrative plot *(le récit)* is constituted in the tension of two formal categories, difference and resemblance.[1] Transformation—a change in a predicate term common to beginning and end—represents a synthesis of difference and resemblance; it is, we might say, the same-but-different. Now "the same-but-different" is a common (and if inadequate, not altogether false) definition of metaphor. If Aristotle affirmed that the master of metaphor must have an eye for resemblances, modern treatments of the subject have affirmed equally the importance of difference included within the operation of resemblance, the chief value of the metaphor residing in its "tension." Narrative operates as metaphor in its affirmation of resemblance, in that it brings into relation different actions, combines them through perceived similarities (Todorov's common predicate term), appropriates them to a common plot, which implies the rejection of merely contingent (or unassimilable) incident or action. The plotting of meaning cannot do without metaphor, for meaning in plot is the structure of action in closed and legible wholes. Metaphor is in this

---

[1] Tzvetan Todorov, "Les Transformations narratives," in *Poétique de la prose* (Paris: Seuil, 1971), p. 240. Todorov's terms *récit* and *histoire* correspond to the Russian Formalist distinction between *sjužet* and *fabula*. In English, we might use with the same sense of distinctions: narrative *plot* and *story*.I wish at the outset of this essay to express my debt to two colleagues whose thinking has helped to clarify my own: Andrea Bertolini and David A. Miller. It is to the latter that I owe the term "the narratable."

sense totalizing. Yet it is equally apparent that the key figure of narrative must in some sense be not metaphor but metonymy: the figure of contiguity and combination, the figure of syntagmatic relations.[2] The description of narrative needs metonymy as the figure of movement, of linkage in the signifying chain, of the slippage of the signified under the signifier. That Jacques Lacan has equated metonomy and desire is of the utmost pertinence, since desire must be considered the very motor of narrative, its dynamic principle.

The problem with "the same-but-different" as a definition of narrative would be the implication of simultaneity and stasis in the formulation. The postulation of a static model indeed is the central deficiency of most formalist and structuralist work on narrative, which has sought to make manifest the structures of narrative in spatial and atemporal terms, as versions of Lévi-Strauss's "atemporal matrix structure."[3] Todorov is an exception in that, faithful to Propp, he recognizes the need to consider sequence and succession as well as the paradigmatic matrix. He supplements his definition with the remark: "Rather than a 'coin with two faces,' [transformation] is an operation in two directions: it affirms at once resemblance and difference; it puts time into motion and suspends it, in a single movement; it allows discourse to acquire a meaning without this meaning becoming pure information; in a word, it makes narrative possible and reveals its very definition."[4] The image of a double operation upon time has the value of returning us to the evident but frequently eluded fact that narrative meanings are developed in time, that any narrative partakes more or less of what Proust called "un jeu formidable . . . avec le Temps," and that this game of time is not merely in the world of reference (or in the *fabula*) but as well in the narrative, in the *sjužet*, be it only that the meanings developed by narrative *take time:* the time of reading.[5]

2   See Roman Jakobson, "Two Types of Language and Two Types of Aphasic Disturbances," in Jakobson and Halle, *Fundamentals of Language* (The Hague: Mouton, 1956). Todorov in a later article adds to "transformation" the term "succession," and sees the pair as definitional of narrative. He discusses the possible equation of these terms with Jakobson's "metaphor" and "metonymy," to conclude that "the connection is possible but does not seem necessary." (Todorov, "The Two Principles of Narrative," *Diacritics*, Fall, 1971, p. 42.) But there seem to be good reasons to maintain Jakobson's terms as "master tropes" referring to two aspects of virtually any text.

3   See Claude Lévi-Strauss, "La Structure et la forme," *Cahiers de l'institut de science économique appliquée*, 99, série M, no. 7 (1960), p. 29. This term is cited with approval by A. J. Greimas in *Sémantique structurale* (Paris: Larousse, 1966) and Roland Barthes, in "Introduction à l'analyse structurale des récits," *Communications* 8 (1966).

4   Todorov, "Les Transformations narratives," *Poétique de la prose*, p. 240. Translations from the French, here and elsewhere, are my own.

5   Proust's phrase is cited by Gerard Genette in "Discours du récit," *Figures III* (Paris: Seuil, 1972), p. 182. Whereas Barthes maintains in "Introduction à l'analyse structurale des récits" that time belongs only to the referent of narrative, Genette gives attention to the time of reading and its necessary linearity. See pp. 77-78.

If at the end of a narrative we can suspend time in a moment where past and present hold together in a metaphor which may be the very recognition which, said Aristotle, every good plot should bring, that moment does not abolish the movement, the slidings, the errors and partial recognitions of the middle. As Roland Barthes points out, in what so far must be counted our most satisfactory dynamic analysis of plot, the proairetic and hermeneutic codes—code of actions, code of enigmas and answers—are irreversible: their interpretation is determined linearly, in sequence, in one direction.[6]

Ultimately—Barthes writes elsewhere—the passion that animates us as readers of narrative is the passion for (of) meaning.[7] Since for Barthes meaning (in the "classical" or "readable" text) resides in full predication, completion of the codes in a "plenitude" of signification, this passion appears to be finally a desire for the end. It is at the end—for Barthes as for Aristotle—that recognition brings its illumination, which then can shed retrospective light. The function of the end, whether considered syntactically (as in Todorov and Barthes) or ethically (as in Aristotle) or as formal or cosmological closure (as in Barbara H. Smith or Frank Kermode) continues to fascinate and to baffle. One of the strongest statements of its determinative position in narrative plots comes in a passage from Sartre's *La Nausée* which bears quotation once again. Roquentin is reflecting on the meaning of "adventure" and the difference between living and narrating. When you narrate, you appear to start with a beginning. You say, "It was a fine autumn evening in 1922. I was a notary's clerk in Marommes." But, says Roquentin:

> In reality you have started at the end. It was there, invisible and present, it is what gives these few words the pomp and value of a beginning. "I was out walking, I had left the town without realizing it, I was thinking about my money troubles." This sentence, taken simply for what it is, means that the man was absorbed, morose, a hundred miles from an adventure, exactly in a mood to let things happen without noticing them. But the end is there, transforming everything. For us, the man is already the hero of the story. His moroseness, his money troubles are much more precious than ours, they are all gilded by the light of future passions. And the story goes on in the reverse: instants have stopped piling themselves up in a haphazard way one on another, they are caught up by the end of the story which draws them and each one in its turn draws the instant preceding it: "It was night, the street was deserted." The sentence is thrown out negligently, it seems superfluous; but we don't let

---

[6] See Roland Barthes, *S/Z* (Paris: Seuil, 1970), p. 37.
[7] "Introduction à l'analyse structurale des récits," p. 27.

ourselves be duped, we put it aside: this is a piece of information whose value we will understand later on. And we feel that the hero has lived all the details of this night as annunciations, as promises, or even that he has lived only those that were promises, blind and deaf to all that did not herald adventure. We forget that the future wasn't yet there; the man was walking in a night without premonitions, which offered him in disorderly fashion its monotonous riches, and he did not choose.[8]

The beginning in fact presupposes the end. The very possibility of meaning plotted through time depends on the anticipated structuring force of the ending: the interminable would be the meaningless. We read the incidents of narration as "promises and annunciations" of final coherence: the metaphor reached through the chain of metonymies. As Roquentin further suggests, we read only those incidents and signs which can be construed as promise and annunciation, enchained toward a construction of significance—those signs which, as in the detective story, appear to be *clues* to the underlying intentionality of event.

The sense of beginning, then, is determined by the sense of an ending. And if we inquire further into the nature of the ending, we no doubt find that it eventually has to do with the human end, with death. In *Les Mots,* Sartre pushes further his reflection on ends. He describes how in order to escape contingency and the sense of being unjustified he had to imagine himself as one of the children in *L'Enfance des hommes illustres,* determined, as promise and annunciation, by what he would become for posterity. He began to live his life retrospectively, in terms of the death that alone would confer meaning and necessity on existence. As he succinctly puts it, "I became my own obituary."[9] All narration is obituary in that life acquires definable meaning only at, and through, death. In an independent but convergent argument, Walter Benjamin has claimed that life assumes transmissible form only at the moment of death. For Benjamin, this death is the very "authority" of narrative: we seek in fictions the knowledge of death, which in our own lives is denied to us. Death—which may be figural but in the classic instances of the genre is so often literal—quickens meaning: it is the "flame," says Benjamin, at which we warm our "shivering" lives.[10]

We need to know more about this death-like ending which is nonetheless animating of meaning in relation to initiatory desire, and about how the

[8] Jean-Paul Sartre, *La Nausée* (Paris: Livre de Poche, 1957), pp. 62-63.

[9] Sartre, *Les Mots* (Paris: Gallimard, 1968), p. 171.

[10] Walter Benjamin, "The Storyteller," in *Illuminations,* translated by Harry Zohn (New York: Schocken Books, 1969), p. 101.

interrelationship of the two determines, shapes, necessitates the middle—Barthes's "dilatory space" of retard, postponement—and the kinds of vacillation between illumination and blindness that we find there. If the end is recognition which retrospectively illuminates beginning and middle, it is not the exclusive truth of the text, which must include the processes along the way—the processes of "transformation"—in their metonymical complexity. If beginning is desire, and is ultimately desire for the end, between lies a process we feel to be necessary (plots, Aristotle tells us, must be of "a certain length") but whose relation to originating desire and to end remains problematic. It is here that Freud's most ambitious investigation of ends in relation to beginnings may be of help—and may suggest a contribution to a properly dynamic model of plot.

We undertake, then, to read *Beyond the Pleasure Principle* as an essay about the dynamic interrelationship of ends and beginnings, and the kind of processes that constitute the middle. The enterprise may find a general sort of legitimation in the fact that *Beyond the Pleasure Principle* is in some sense Freud's own masterplot, the text in which he most fully lays out a total scheme of how life proceeds from beginning to end, and how each individual life in its own way repeats the masterplot. Of Freud's various intentions in this text, the boldest—and most mysterious—may be to provide a theory of comprehension of the dynamic of the life-span, its necessary duration and its necessary end, hence, implicitly, a theory of the very narratability of life. In his pursuit of his "beyond," Freud is forced to follow the implications of argument—"to throw oneself into a line of thought and follow it wherever it leads," as he says late in the essay—to ends that he had not originally or consciously conceived.[11] *Beyond the Pleasure Principle* shows the very plotting of a masterplot made necessary by the structural demands of Freud's thought, and it is in this sense that we shall attempt to read it as a model for narrative plot.

Narrative always makes the implicit claim to be in a state of repetition, as a going over again of a ground already covered: a *sjužet* repeating the *fabula*, as the detective retraces the tracks of the criminal.[12] This claim to an act of repetition—"I sing," "I tell"—appears to be initiatory of narrative. It is equally initiatory of *Beyond the Pleasure Principle*; it is the first problem and

[11] Sigmund Freud, "Beyond the Pleasure Principle" (1920), in *The Standard Edition of the Complete Psychological Works of Sigmund Freud,* ed. James Strachey (London: Hogarth Press, 1955), 18, 59. Subsequent page references will be given between parentheses in the text.

[12] J. Hillis Miller, in "Ariadne's Web" (unpublished manuscript), notes that the term *diegesis* suggests that narrative is a retracing of a journey already made. On the detective story, see Tzvetan Todorov, "Typologie du roman policier," *Poétique de la prose,* pp. 58-59.

clue that Freud confronts. Evidence of a "beyond" that does not fit neatly into the functioning of the pleasure principle comes first in the dreams of patients suffering from war neuroses, or from the traumatic neuroses of peace: dreams which return to the moment of trauma, to relive its pain in apparent contradiction of the wish-fulfillment theory of dreams. This "dark and dismal" example is superseded by an example from "normal" life, and we have the celebrated moment of child's play: the toy thrown away, the reel on the string thrown out of the crib and pulled back, to the alternate exclamation of *fort* and *da*. When he has established the equivalence between making the toy disappear and the child's mother's disappearance, Freud is faced with a set of possible interpretations. Why does the child repeat an unpleasurable experience? It may be answered that by staging his mother's disappearance and return, the child is compensating for his instinctual renunciation. Yet the child has also staged disappearance alone, without reappearance, as a game. This may make one want to argue that the essential experience involved is the movement from a passive to an active role in regard to his mother's disappearance, claiming mastery in a situation which he has been compelled to submit to.

Repetition as the movement from passivity to mastery reminds us of "The Theme of the Three Caskets," where Freud, considering Bassanio's choice of the lead casket in *The Merchant of Venice*—the correct choice in the suit of Portia—decides that the choice of the right maiden in man's literary play is also the choice of death; by this choice, he asserts an active mastery of what he must in fact endure. "Choice stands in the place of necessity, of destiny. In this way man overcomes death, which he has recognized intellectually."[13] If repetition is mastery, movement from the passive to the active; and if mastery is an assertion of control over what man must in fact submit to—choice, we might say, of an imposed end—we have already a suggestive comment on the grammar of plot, where repetition, taking us back again over the same ground, could have to do with the choice of ends.

But other possibilities suggest themselves to Freud at this point. The repetition of unpleasant experience—the mother's disappearance—might be explained by the motive of revenge, which would yield its own pleasure. The uncertainty which Freud faces here is whether repetition can be considered a primary event, independent of the pleasure principle, or whether there is always some direct yield of pleasure of another sort involved. The pursuit of this doubt takes Freud into the analytic experience, to his discovery of patients' need to repeat, rather than simply remember, repressed material:

---

[13] Freud, "The Theme of the Three Caskets" (1913), *Standard Edition*, 12, 299.

the need to reproduce and to "work through" painful material from the past as if it were present. The analyst can detect a "compulsion to repeat," ascribed to the unconscious repressed, particularly discernable in the transference, where it can take "ingenious" forms. The compulsion to repeat gives patients a sense of being fatefully subject to a "perpetual recurrence of the same thing"; it suggests to them pursuit by a daemonic power. We know also, from Freud's essay on "The Uncanny," that this feeling of the daemonic, arising from involuntary repetition, is a particular attribute of the literature of the uncanny.[14]

Thus in analytic work (as also in literary texts) there is slim but real evidence of a compulsion to repeat which can over-ride the pleasure principle, and which seems "more primitive, more elementary, more instinctual than the pleasure principle which it over-rides" (23). We might note at this point that the transference itself is a metaphor, a substitutive relationship for the patient's infantile experiences, and thus approximates the status of a text. Now repetition is so basic to our experience of literary texts that one is simultaneously tempted to say all and to say nothing on the subject. To state the matter baldly: rhyme, alliteration, assonance, meter, refrain, all the mnemonic elements of fictions and indeed most of its tropes are in some manner repetitions which take us back in the text, which allow the ear, the eye, the mind to make connections between different textual moments, to see past and present as related and as establishing a future which will be noticeable as some variation in the pattern. Todorov's "same but different" depends on repetition. If we think of the trebling characteristic of the folk tale, and of all formulaic literature, we may consider that the repetition by three constitutes the minimal repetition to the perception of series, which would make it the minimal intentional structure of action, the minimum plot. Narrative must ever present itself as a repetition of events that have already happened, and within this postulate of a generalized repetition it must make use of specific, perceptible repetitions in order to create plot, that is, to show us a significant interconnection of events. Event gains meaning by repeating (with variation) other events. Repetition is a *return* in the text, a doubling back. We cannot say whether this return is a return *to* or a return *of*: for instance, a return to origins or a return of the repressed. Repetition through this ambiguity appears to suspend temporal process, or rather, to subject it to an indeterminate shuttling or oscillation which binds different moments together as a middle which might turn forward or back. This inescapable middle is suggestive of the daemonic. The relation of

---

[14] See Freud, "The Uncanny" *(Das Unheimliche)* (1919), in *Standard Edition*, 17, 219-52.

narrative plot to story may indeed appear to partake of the daemonic, as a kind of tantalizing play with the primitive and the instinctual, the magic and the curse of reproduction or "representation." But in order to know more precisely the operations of repetition, we need to read further in Freud's text.

"What follows is speculation" (24). With this gesture, Freud, in the manner of Rousseau's dismissal of the facts in the *Discourse on the Origins of Inequality,* begins the fourth chapter and his sketch of the economic and energetic model of the mental apparatus: the system Pcpt-Cs and Ucs, the role of the outer layer as shield against excitations, and the definition of trauma as the breaching of the shield, producing a flood of stimuli which knocks the pleasure principle out of operation. Given this situation, the repetition of traumatic experiences in the dreams of neurotics can be seen to have the function of seeking retrospectively to master the flood of stimuli, to perform a mastery or binding of mobile energy through developing the anxiety whose omission was the cause of the traumatic neurosis. Thus the repetition compulsion is carrying out a task that must be accomplished *before* the dominance of the pleasure principle can begin. Repetition is hence a primary event, independent of the pleasure principle and more primitive. Freud now moves into an exploration of the theory of the instincts.[15] The instinctual is the realm of freely mobile, "unbound" energy: the "primary process," where energy seeks immediate discharge, where no postponement of gratification is tolerated. It appears that it must be "the task of the higher strata of the mental apparatus to bind the instinctual excitation reaching the primary process" before the pleasure principle can assert its dominance over the psychic economy (34-35). We may say that at this point in the essay we have moved from a postulate of repetition as the assertion of mastery (as in the passage from passivity to activity in the child's game) to a conception whereby repetition works as a process of *binding* toward the creation of an energetic constant-state situation which will permit the emergence of mastery, and the possibility of postponement.

That Freud at this point evokes once again the daemonic and the uncanny nature of repetition, and refers us not only to children's play but as well to their demand for exact repetition in storytelling, points our way back to literature. Repetition in all its literary manifestations may in fact work as a "binding," a binding of textual energies that allows them to be mastered by putting

---

[15] I shall use the term "instinct" since it is the translation of *Trieb* given throughout the Standard Edition. But we should realize that "instinct" is inadequate and somewhat misleading, since it loses the sense of "drive" associated with the word *Trieb*. The currently accepted French translation, *pulsion,* is more to our purposes: the model that interests me here might indeed be called "pulsional."

them into serviceable form within the energetic economy of the narrative. Serviceable form must in this case mean perceptible form: repetition, repeat, recall, symmetry, all these journeys back in the text, returns to and returns of, that allow us to bind one textual moment to another in terms of similarity or substitution rather than mere contiguity. Textual energy, all that is aroused into expectancy and possibility in a text—the term will need more definition, but corresponds well enough to our experience of reading—can become usable by plot only when it has been bound or formalized. It cannot otherwise be plotted in a course to significant discharge, which is what the pleasure principle is charged with doing. To speak of "binding" in a literary text is thus to speak of any of the formalizations (which, like binding, may be painful, retarding) that force us to recognize sameness within difference, or the very emergence of a *sjužet* from the material of *fabula*.

We need at present to follow Freud into his closer inquiry concerning the relation between the compulsion to repeat and the instinctual. The answer lies in "a universal attribute of instincts and perhaps of organic life in general," that "*an instinct is an urge inherent in organic life to restore an earlier state of things*" (36). Instincts, which we tend to think of as a drive toward change, may rather be an expression of "the conservative nature of living things." The organism has no wish to change; if its conditions remained the same, it would constantly repeat the very same course of life. Modifications are the effect of external stimuli, and these modifications are in turn stored up for further repetition, so that, while the instincts may give the appearance of tending toward change, they "are merely seeking to reach an ancient goal by paths alike old and new" (38). Hence Freud is able to proffer, with a certain bravado, the formulation: "*the aim of all life is death.*" We are given an evolutionary image of the organism in which the tension created by external influences has forced living substance to "diverge ever more widely from its original course of life and to make ever more complicated *détours* before reaching its aim of death" (38-49). In this view, the self-preservative instincts function to assure that the organism shall follow its own path to death, to ward off any ways of returning to the inorganic which are not immanent to the organism itself. In other words, "the organism wishes to die only in its own fashion." It must struggle against events (dangers) which would help it to achieve its goal too rapidly—by a kind of short-circuit.

We are here somewhere near the heart of Freud's masterplot for organic life, and it generates a certain analytic force in its superimposition on fictional plots. What operates in the text through repetition is the death instinct, the drive toward the end. Beyond and under the domination of the pleasure principle is this baseline of plot, its basic "pulsation," sensible or audible through the repetitions which take us back in the text. Repetition can take us both backwards and forwards because these terms have become reversible: the end is a time before the beginning. Between these two moments of quiescence, plot itself stands as a kind of divergence or deviance, a postponement in the discharge which leads back to the inanimate. For plot starts (must give the illusion of starting) from that moment at which story, or "life," is stimulated from quiescence into a state of narratability, into a tension, a kind of irritation, which demands narration. Any reflection on novelistic beginnings shows the beginning as an awakening, an arousal, the birth of an appetency, ambition, desire or intention.[16] To say this is of course to say— perhaps more pertinently—that beginnings are the arousal of an intention in reading, stimulation into a tension. (The specifically erotic nature of the tension of writing and its rehearsal in reading could be demonstrated through a number of exemplary texts, notably Rousseau's account, in *The Confessions*, of how his novel *La Nouvelle Héloïse* was born of a masturbatory reverie and its necessary fictions, or the very similar opening of Jean Genet's *Notre-Dame des fleurs;* but of course the sublimated forms of the tension are just as pertinent.) The ensuing narrative—the Aristotelean "middle"—is maintained in a state of tension, as a prolonged deviance from the quiescence of the "normal"—which is to say, the unnarratable—until it reaches the terminal quiescence of the end. The development of a narrative shows that the tension is maintained as an ever more complicated postponement or *détour* leading back to the goal of quiescence. As Sartre and Benjamin compellingly argued, the narrative must tend toward its end, seek illumination in its own death. Yet this must be the right death, the correct end. The complication of the *détour* is related to the danger of short-circuit: the danger of reaching the end too quickly, of achieving the im-proper death. The improper end indeed lurks throughout narrative, frequently as the wrong choice: choice of the wrong casket, misapprehension of the magical agent, false erotic object-choice. The development of the subplot in the classical novel usually suggests (as William Empson has intimated) a different solution to the problems worked through by the main plot, and often illustrates the danger of short-circuit.[17] The subplot stands as one means of warding off the danger of short-circuit, assuring that the main plot will continue through to the right end. The desire of the text (the desire of reading) is hence desire for the end, but desire for

---

[16] On the beginning as intention, see Edward Said, *Beginnings: Intention and Method* (New York: Basic Books, 1975). It occurs to me that the exemplary narrative beginning might be that of Kafka's *Metamorphosis:* waking up to find oneself transformed into a monstrous vermin.

[17] See William Empson, "Double Plots," in *Some Versions of Pastoral* (New York: New Directions, 1960), pp. 25-84.

the end reached only through the at least minimally complicated *détour,* the intentional deviance, in tension, which is the plot of narrative.

Deviance, *détour,* an intention which is irritation: these are characteristics of the narratable, of "life" as it is the material of narrative, of *fabula* become *sjužet.* Plot is a kind of arabesque or squiggle toward the end. It is like Corporal Trim's arabesque with his stick, in *Tristram Shandy,* retraced by Balzac at the start of *La Peau de chagrin* to indicate the arbitrary, transgressive, gratuitous line of narrative, its deviance from the straight line, the shortest distance between beginning and end—which would be the collapse of one into the other, of life into immediate death. Freud's text will in a moment take us closer to understanding of the formal organization of this deviance toward the end. But it also at this point offers further suggestions about the beginning. For when he has identified both the death instincts and the life (sexual) instincts as conservative, tending toward the restoration of an earlier state of things, Freud feels obliged to deconstruct the will to believe in a human drive toward perfection, an impulsion forward and upward: a force which—he here quotes *Faust* as the classic text of man's forward striving— "*ungebändigt immer vorwärts dringt.*" The illusion of the striving toward perfection is to be explained by instinctual repression and the persisting tension of the repressed instinct, and the resulting difference between the pleasure of satisfaction *demanded* and that which is *achieved,* a difference which "provides the driving factor which will permit of no halting at any position attained" (36). This process of subtraction reappears in modified form in the work of Lacan, where it is the difference between *need* (the infant's need for the breast) and *demand* (which is always demand for recognition) that gives as its result *desire,* which is precisely the driving power, of plot certainly, since desire for Lacan is a metonymy, the forward movement of the signifying chain. If Roman Jakobson is able, in his celebrated essay, to associate the metonymic pole with prose fiction (particularly the nineteenth-century novel)—as the metaphoric pole is associated with lyric poetry it would seem to be because the meanings peculiar to narrative inhere (or, as Lacan would say, "insist") in the metonymic chain, in the drive of desire toward meaning in time.[18]

The next-to-last chapter of *Beyond the Pleasure Principle* cannot here be rehearsed in detail. In brief, it leads Freud twice into the findings of biology, first on the track of the origins of death, to find out whether it is a necessary or merely a contingent alternative to interminability, then in pursuit of the origins of sexuality, to see whether it satisfies the description

[18] See Jakobson, "Two Types of Language . . .". See, in Lacan's work, especially "Le Stade du miroir" and "L'Instance de la lettre dans l'inconscient," in *Écrits* (Paris: Seuil, 1966).

of the instinctual as conservative. Biology can offer no sure answer to either investigation, but it offers at least metaphorical confirmation of the necessary dualism of Freud's thought, and encouragement to reformulate his earlier opposition of ego instincts to sexual instincts as one between life instincts and death instincts, a shift in the grouping of oppositional forces which then allows him to reformulate the libidinal instincts themselves as the Eros "of the poets and philosophers" which holds all living things together, and which seeks to combine things in ever greater living wholes. Desire would then seem to be totalizing in intent, a process tending toward combination in new unities: metonymy in the search to become metaphor. But for the symmetry of Freud's opposition to be complete, he needs to be able to ascribe to Eros, as to the death instinct, the characteristic of a need to restore an earlier state of things. Since biology will not answer, Freud, in a remarkable gesture, turns toward myth, to come up with Plato's Androgyne, which precisely ascribes Eros to a search to recover a lost primal unity which was split asunder. Freud's apologetic tone in this last twist to his argument is partly disingenuous, for we detect a contentment to have formulated the forces of the human masterplot as "philosopher and poet." The apology is coupled with a reflection that much of the obscurity of the processes Freud has been considering "is merely due to our being obliged to operate with the scientific terms, that is to say with the figurative language, peculiar to psychology" (60). *Beyond the Pleasure Principle*, we are to understand, is not merely metapsychology, it is also mythopoesis, necessarily resembling "an equation with two unknown quantities" (57), or, we might say, a formal dynamic the terms of which are not substantial but purely relational. We perceive that *Beyond the Pleasure Principle* is itself a plot which has formulated that dynamic necessary to its own *détour*.

The last chapter of Freud's text recapitulates, but not without difference. He returns to the problem of the relationship between the instinctual processes of repetition and the dominance of the pleasure principle. One of the earliest and most important functions of the mental apparatus is to bind the instinctual impulses which impinge upon it, to convert freely mobile energy into a quiescent cathexis. This is a preparatory act on behalf of the pleasure principle, which permits its dominance. Sharpening his distinction between a *function* and a *tendency*, Freud argues that the pleasure principle is a "tendency operating in the service of a function whose business it is to free the mental apparatus entirely from excitation or to keep the amount of excitation in it constant or to keep it as low as possible" (62). This function is concerned "with the most universal endeavour of all living substance—namely to return to the quiescence of the inorganic world." Hence one can consider "binding" to be a preliminary function which prepares the excitation for its final elimination in the pleasure of discharge. In this manner, we could say that the repetition compulsion and the death instinct serve the pleasure principle; in a larger sense, the pleasure principle, keeping watch on the invasion of stimuli from without and especially from within, seeking their discharge, serves the death instinct, making sure that the organism is permitted to return to quiescence. The whole evolution of the mental apparatus appears as a taming of the instincts so that the pleasure principle— itself tamed, displaced—can appear to dominate in the complicated *détour* called life which leads back to death. In fact, Freud seems here at the very end to imply that the two antagonistic instincts serve one another in a dynamic interaction which is a perfect and self-regulatory economy which makes both end and *détour* perfectly necessary and interdependent. The organism must live in order to die in the proper manner, to die the right death. We must have the arabesque of plot in order to reach the end. We must have metonymy in order to reach metaphor.

We emerge from reading *Beyond the Pleasure Principle* with a dynamic model which effectively structures ends (death, quiescence, non-narratability) against beginnings (Eros, stimulation into tension, the desire of narrative) in a manner that necessitates the middle as *détour,* as struggle toward the end under the compulsion of imposed delay, as arabesque in the dilatory space of the text. We detect some illumination of the necessary distance between beginning and end, the drives which connect them but which prevent the one collapsing back into the other: the way in which metonymy and metaphor serve one another, the necessary temporality of the same-but-different which to Todorov constitutes the narrative transformation. The model suggests further that along the way of the path from beginning to end—in the middle—we have repetitions serving to bind the energy of the text in order to make its final discharge more effective. In fictional plots, these bindings are a system of repetitions which are returns to and returns of, confounding the movement forward to the end with a movement back to origins, reversing meaning within forward-moving time, serving to formalize the system of textual energies, offering the possibility (or the illusion) of "meaning" wrested from "life."

As a dynamic-energetic model of narrative plot, then, *Beyond the Pleasure Principle* gives an image of how "life," or the *fabula,* is stimulated into the condition of narrative, becomes *sjužet:* enters into a state of deviance and *détour* (ambition, quest, the pose of a mask) in which it is maintained for a certain time, through an at least minimally complex extravagance, before returning to the quiescence of the non-narratable. The energy generated by deviance, extravagance, excess—an energy which belongs to the textual hero's career and to the readers' expectation, his desire of and for the text—maintains

the plot in its movement through the vacillating play of the middle, where
repetition as binding works toward the generation of significance, toward
recognition and the retrospective illumination which will allow us to grasp
the text as total metaphor, but not therefore to discount the metonymies that
have led to it. The desire of the text is ultimately the desire for the end, for that
recognition which is the moment of the death of the reader in the text. Yet
recognition cannot abolish textuality, does not annul the middle which, in its
oscillation between blindness and recognition, between origin and endings,
is the truth of the narrative text.

It is characteristic of textual energy in narrative that it should always be
on the verge of premature discharge, of short-circuit. The reader experiences
the fear—and excitation—of the improper end, which is symmetrical to—
but far more immediate and present than—the fear of endlessness. The
possibility of short-circuit can of course be represented in all manner of
threats to the protagonist or to any of the functional logics which demand
completion; it most commonly takes the form of temptation to the mistaken
erotic object choice, who may be of the "Belle Dame sans merci" variety,
or may be the too-perfect and hence annihilatory bride. Throughout the
Romantic tradition, it is perhaps most notably the image of incest (of the
fraternal-sororal variety) which hovers as the sign of a passion interdicted
because its fulfillment would be too perfect, a discharge indistinguishable
from death, the very cessation of narrative movement. Narrative is in a state
of temptation to over-sameness, and where we have no literal threat of incest
(as in Chateaubriand, or Faulkner), lovers choose to turn the beloved into a
soul-sister so that possession will be either impossible or mortal: Werther
and Lotte, for instance, or, at the inception of the tradition, Rousseau's *La
Nouvelle Héloïse*, where Saint-Preux's letter to Julie following their night
of love begins: "Mourons, ô ma douce amie." Incest is only the exemplary
version of a temptation of short-circuit from which the protagonist and the
text must be led away, into *détour*, into the cure which prolongs narrative.

It may finally be in the logic of our argument that repetition speaks in
the text of a return which ultimately subverts the very notion of beginning
and end, suggesting that the idea of beginning presupposes the end, that the
end is a time before the beginning, and hence that the interminable never
can be finally bound in a plot. Analysis, Freud would eventually discover, is
inherently interminable, since the dynamics of resistance and the transference
can always generate new beginnings in relation to any possible end.[19] It is the
role of fictional plots to impose an end which yet suggests a return, a new

---

[19] See Freud, "Analysis Terminable and Interminable" (1937), in *Standard Edition*, 23, 216-
   53.

beginning: a rereading. A narrative, that is, wants at its end to refer us back to its middle, to the web of the text: to recapture us in its doomed energies.

One ought at this point to make a new beginning, and to sketch the possible operation of the model in the study of the plot of a fiction. One could, for instance, take Dickens's *Great Expectations*. One would have to show how the energy released in the text by its liminary "primal scene"— Pip's terrifying meeting with Magwitch in the graveyard—is subsequently bound in a number of desired but unsatisfactory ways (including Pip's "being bound" as apprentice, the "dream" plot of Satis House, the apparent intent of the "expectations"), and simultaneously in censored but ultimately more satisfying ways (through all the returns of the repressed identification of Pip and his convict). The most salient device of this novel's "middle "is literally the journey back—from London to Pip's home town—a repeated return to apparent origins which is also a return of the repressed, of what Pip calls "that old spell of my childhood." It would be interesting to demonstrate that each of Pip's choices in the novel, while consciously life-furthering, forward oriented, in fact leads back, to the insoluble question of origins, to the palindrome of his name, so that the end of the narrative—its "discharge"— appears as the image of a "life" cured of "plot," as celibate clerk for Clarrikers.

Pip's story, while ostensibly the search for progress, ascension, and metamorphosis, may after all be the narrative of an attempted homecoming: of the effort to reach an assertion of origin through ending, to find the same in the different, the time before in the time after. Most of the great nineteenth-century novels tell this same tale. Georg Lukács has called the novel "the literary form of the transcendent homelessness of the idea," and argued that it is in the discrepancy between idea and the organic that time, the process of duration, becomes constitutive of the novel as of no other genre:

> Only in the novel, whose very matter is seeking and failing to find the essence, is time posited together with the form: time is the resistance of the organic — which possesses a mere semblance of life — to the present meaning, the will of life to remain within its own completely enclosed immanence. . . . In the novel, meaning is separated from life, and hence the essential from the temporal; we might almost say that the entire inner action of the novel is nothing but a struggle against the power of time.[20]

The understanding of time, says Lukács, the transformation of the struggle against time into a process full of interest, is the work of memory—or more

---

[20] Georg Lukács, *The Theory of the Novel*, trans. Anna Bostock (Cambridge, Mass.: MIT Press, 1971), p. 122.

precisely, we could say with Freud, of "remembering, repeating, working through." Repetition, remembering, reënactement are the ways in which we replay time, so that it may not be lost. We are thus always trying to work back through time to that transcendent home, knowing of course that we cannot. All we can do is subvert or, perhaps better, pervert time: which is what narrative does.[21]

To forgo any true demonstration on a novel, and to bring a semblance of conclusion, we may return to the assertion, by Barthes and Todorov, that narrative is essentially the articulation of a set of verbs. These verbs are no doubt ultimately all versions of desire. Desire is the wish for the end, for fulfillment, but fulfillment delayed so that we can understand it in relation to origin, and to desire itself. The story of Scheherezade is doubtless the story of stories. This suggests that the tale as read is inhabited by the reader's desire, and that further analysis should be directed to that desire, not (in the manner of Norman Holland) his individual desire and its origins in his own personality, but his transindividual and intertextually determined desire as a reader. Because it concerns ends in relation to beginnings and the forces that animate the middle in between, Freud's model is suggestive of what a reader engages when he responds to plot. It images that engagement as essentially dynamic, an interaction with a system of energy which the reader activates. This in turn suggests why we can read *Beyond the Pleasure Principle* as a text concerning textuality, and conceive that there can be a psychoanalytic criticism of the text itself that does not become—as has usually been the case—a study of the psychogenesis of the text (the author's unconscious), the dynamics of literary response (the reader's unconscious), or the occult motivations of the characters (postulating an "unconscious" for them). It is rather the superimposition of the model of the functioning of the mental apparatus on the functioning of the text that offers the possibility of a psychoanalytic criticism. And here the superimposition of Freud's psychic masterplot on the plots of fiction seems a valid and useful maneuver. Plot mediates meanings with the contradictory human world of the eternal and the mortal. Freud's masterplot speaks of the temporality of desire, and speaks to our very desire for fictional plots.

---

[21] Genette discusses Proust's "perversion" of time in "Discours du récit," p. 182. "Remembering, Repeating, and Working Through" *(Erinnern, Wiederholen und Durcharbeiten)* (1914) is the subject of one of Freud's papers on technique. See *Standard Edition*, 12, 145-56.

Edward Said

Palestinian-American (1935-2003)

From the Introduction to
Orientalism (1978)

The imaginative examination of things Oriental was based more or less exclusively upon a sovereign Western consciousness out of whose unchallenged centrality an Oriental world emerged, first according to general ideas about who or what was an Oriental, then according to a detailed logic governed not simply by empirical reality but by a battery of desires, regressions, investments, and projections.

I have begun with the assumption that the Orient is not an inert fact of nature. It is not merely there, just as the Occident itself is not just there either: We must take seriously Vico's great observation that men make their own history, that what they can know is what they have made, and extend it to geography: as both geographical and cultural entities—to say nothing of historical entities—such locales, regions, geographical sectors as "Orient" and "Occident" are man-made. Therefore as much as the West itself, the Orient is an idea that has a history and a tradition of thought, imagery, and vocabulary that have given it reality and presence in and for the West. The two geographical entities thus support and to an extent reflect each other.

Having said that, one must go on to state a number of reasonable qualifications. In the first place, it would be wrong to conclude that the Orient was essentially an idea, or a creation with no corresponding reality. When Disraeli said in his novel *Tancred* that the East was a career, he meant that to be interested in the East was something bright young Westerners would find to be an all-consuming passion; he should not be interpreted as saying that the East was only a career for Westerners. There were—and are—cultures and nations whose location is in the East, and their lives, histories, and customs have a brute reality obviously greater than anything that could be said about them in the West. About that fact this study of Orientalism has very little to contribute, except to acknowledge it tacitly. But the phenomenon of Orientalism as I study it here deals principally, not with a correspondence between Orientalism and Orient, but with the internal consistency of Orientalism and its ideas about the Orient (the East as career) despite or beyond any correspondence, or lack thereof, with a "real" Orient. My point is that Disraeli's statement about the East refers mainly to that created consistency, that regular constellation of ideas as the pre-eminent thing about the Orient, and not to its mere being, as Wallace Stevens's phrase has it.

A second qualification is that ideas, cultures, and histories cannot seriously be understood or studied without their force, or more precisely their configurations of power, also being studied. To believe that the Orient was created—or, as I call it, "Orientalized"—and to believe that such things happen simply as a necessity of the imagination, is to be disingenuous. The relationship between Occident and Orient is a relationship of power, of domination, of varying degrees of a complex hegemony as is quite accurately indicated in the title of K. M. Panikkar's classic *Asia and Western Dominance*. The Orient was Orientalized not only because it was discovered to be "Oriental" in all those ways considered commonplace by an average nineteenth-century European, but also because it *could be*—that is, submitted to being—*made* Oriental. There is very little consent to be found, for example, in the fact that Flaubert's encounter with an Egyptian courtesan produced a widely influential model of the Oriental woman; she never spoke of herself, she never represented her emotions, presence, or history. He spoke for and represented her. He was foreign, comparatively wealthy, male, and these were historical facts of domination that allowed him not only to possess Kuchuk Hanem physically but to speak for her and tell his readers in what way she was "typically Oriental." My argument is that Flaubert's situation of strength in relation to Kuchuk Hanem was not an isolated instance. It fairly stands for the pattern of relative strength between East and West, and the discourse about the Orient that it enabled.

This brings us to a third qualification. One ought never to assume that the structure of Orientalism is nothing more than a structure of lies or of myths which were the truth about them to be told, would simply blow away. I myself believe that Orientalism is more particularly valuable as a sign of European-Atlantic power over the Orient then it is as a veridic discourse about the Orient (which is what, in its academic or scholarly form, it claims to be). Nevertheless, what we must respect and try to grasp is the sheer knitted-together strength of Orientalist discourse, its very close ties to the enabling socio-economic and political institutions, and its redoubtable durability. After all, any system of ideas that can remain unchanged as teachable wisdom (in academies, books, congresses, universities, foreign-service institutes) from the period of Ernest Renan in the late 1840s until the present in the United States must be something more formidable than a mere collection of lies. Orientalism, therefore, is not an airy European fantasy about the Orient but a created body of theory and practice in which, for many rations, there has been a considerable material investment. Continued investment made Orientalism, as a system of knowledge about the Orient, an accepted grid for filtering through the Orient into Western consciousness, just as that same investment multiplied—indeed, made truly productive—the statements proliferating out from Orientalism into the general culture.

Gramsci has made the useful analytic distinction between civil and political society in which the former is made up of voluntary (or atleast rational and noncoercive) affiliations like schools, families, and unions, the latter of state institutions (the army, the police, the central bureaucracy) whose role in the polity is direct domination. Culture, of course, is to be found operating within civil society, where the influence of ideas, of institutions, and of other persons works not through domination but by what Gramsci calls consent. In any society not totalitarian, then, certain cultural forms predominate over others, just as certain ideas are more influential than others; the form of this cultural leadership is what Gramsci has identified as *hegemony*, an indispensable concept for any understanding of cultural life in the industrial West. It is hegemony, or rather the result of cultural hegemony at work, that gives Orientalism the durability and the strength I have been speaking about so far. Orientalism is never far from what Denys Hay has called the idea of Europe,[1] a collective notion identifying "us" Europeans as against all "those" non-Europeans, and indeed it can be argued that the major component in European culture is precisely what made that culture hegemonic both in and outside Europe: the idea of European identity as a superior one in comparison with all the non-European peoples and cultures. There is in addition the hegemony of European ideas about the Orient, themselves reiterating European superiority over Oriental backwardness usually overriding the possibility that a more independent, or more skeptical, thinker might have had different views on the matter.

In a quite constant way, Orientalism depends for its strategy on this flexible *positional* superiority, which puts the Westerner in a whole series of possible relationships with the Orient without ever losing him the relative upper hand. And why should it have been otherwise, especially during the period of extraordinary European ascendancy from the late Renaissance

[1] Denys Hay, *Europe: the Emergence of an Idea*, 2nd ed. (Edinburgh: Edinburgh University Press, 1968)

to the present? The scientist, the scholar, the missionary, the trader, or the soldier was in, or thought about, the Orient because he could be there, or could think about it, with very little resistance on the Orient's part. Under the general heading of knowledge of the Orient, and within the umbrella of Western hegemony over the Orient during the period from the end of the eighteenth century, there emerged a complex Orient suitable for study in the academy, for display in the museum, for reconstruction in the colonial office, for theoretical illustration in anthropological, biological, linguistic, racial, and historical theses about mankind and the universe, for instances of economic and sociological theories of development, revolution, cultural personality, national or religious character. Additionally, the imaginative examination of things Oriental was based more or less exclusively upon a sovereign Western consciousness out of whose unchallenged centrality an Oriental world emerged, first according to general ideas about who or what was an Oriental, then according to a detailed logic governed not simply by empirical reality but by a battery of desires, regressions, investments, and projections. If we can point to great Orientalist works of genuine scholarship like Silvestre de Sacy's *Chrestomathie arabe* or Edward William Lane's *Account of the Manners and Customs of the Modern Egyptians*, we need also to note that Renan's and Gobineau's racial ideas came out of the same impulse, as did a great many Victorian pornographic novels (see the analysis by Steven Marcus of "The Lustful Turk"[2]).

And yet, one must repeatedly ask oneself whether what matters in Orientalism is the general group of ideas overriding the mass of material—about which who could deny that they were shot through with doctrines of European superiority, various kinds of racism, imperialism, and the like, dogmatic views of "the Oriental" as a kind of ideal and unchanging abstraction?—or the much more varied work produced by almost uncountable individual writers, whom one would take up as individual instances of authors dealing with the Orient. In a sense the two alternatives, general and particular, are really two perspectives on the same material: in both instances one would have to deal with pioneers in the field like William Jones, with great artists like Nerval or Flaubert. And why would it not be possible to employ both perspectives together, or one after the other? Isn't there an obvious danger of distortion (of precisely the kind that academic Orientalism has always been prone to) if either too general or too specific a level of description is maintained systematically?

---

[2] Steven Marcus, *The Other Victorians: A Study of Sexuality and Pornography in Mid-Nineteenth Century England* (1966; reprint ed., New York: Bantam Books, 1967), pp. 200-19.

My two fears are distortion and inaccuracy, or rather the kind of inaccuracy produced by too dogmatic a generality and too positivistic a localized focus. In trying to deal with these problems I have tried to deal with three main aspects of my own contemporary reality that seem to me to point the way out of the methodological or perspectival difficulties I have been discussing, difficulties that might force one, in the first instance, into writing a coarse polemic on so unacceptably general a level of description as not to be worth the effort, or in the second instance, into writing so detailed and atomistic a series of analyses as to lose all track of the general lines of force informing the field, giving it its special cogency. How then to recognize individuality and to reconcile it with its intelligent, and by no means passive or merely dictatorial, general and hegemonic context?

I mentioned three aspects of my contemporary reality: I must explain and briefly discuss them now, so that it can be seen how I was led to a particular course of research and writing.

1. *The distinction between pure and political knowledge.* It is very easy to argue that knowledge about Shakespeare or Wordsworth is not political whereas knowledge about contemporary China or the Soviet Union is. My own formal and professional designation is that of "humanist," a title which indicates the humanities as my field and therefore the unlikely eventuality that there might be anything political about what I do in that field. Of course, all these labels and terms are quite unnuanced as I use them here, but the general truth of what I am pointing to is, I think, widely held. One reason for saying that a humanist who writes about Wordsworth, or an editor whose specialty is Keats, is not involved in anything political is that what he does seems to have no direct political effect upon reality in the everyday sense. A scholar whose field is Soviet economics works in a highly charged area where there is much government interest, and what he might produce in the way of studies or proposals will be taken up by policymakers, government officials, institutional economists, intelligence experts. The distinction between "humanists" and persons whose work has policy implications, or political significance, can be broadened further by saying that the former's ideological color is a matter of incidental importance to politics (although possibly of great moment to his colleagues in the field, who may object to his Stalinism or fascism or too easy liberalism), whereas the ideology of the latter is woven directly into his material—indeed, economics, politics, and sociology in the modern academy are ideological sciences—and therefore taken for granted as being "political."

Nevertheless the determining impingement on most knowledge produced in the contemporary West (and here I speak mainly about the United States) is that it be nonpolitical, that is, scholarly, academic, impartial, above partisan or small-minded doctrinal belief. One can have no quarrel with such an ambition in theory, perhaps, but in practice the reality is much more problematic. No one has ever devised a method for detaching the scholar from the circumstances of life, from the fact of his involvement (conscious or unconscious) with a class, a set of beliefs, a social position, or from the mere activity of being a member of a society. These continue to bear on what he does professionally, even though naturally enough his research and its fruits do attempt to reach a level of relative freedom from the inhibitions and the restrictions of brute, everyday reality. For there is such a thing as knowledge that is less, rather than more, partial than the individual (with his entangling and distracting life circumstances) who produces it. Yet this knowledge is not therefore automatically nonpolitical.

Whether discussions of literature or of classical philology are fraught with—or have unmediated—political significance is a very large question that I have tried to treat in some detail elsewhere. What I am interested in doing now is suggesting how the general liberal consensus that "true" knowledge is fundamentally nonpolitical (and conversely, that overtly political knowledge is not "true" knowledge) obscures the highly if obscurely organized political circumstances obtaining when knowledge is produced. No one is helped in understanding this today when the adjective "political" is used as a label to discredit any work for daring to violate the protocol of pretended suprapolitical objectivity. We may say, first, that civil society recognizes a gradation of political importance in the various fields of knowledge. To some extent the political importance given a field comes from the possibility of its direct translation into economic terms; but to a greater extent political importance comes from the closeness of a field to ascertainable sources of power in political society. Thus an economic study of long-term Soviet energy potential and its effect on military capability is likely to be commissioned by the Defense Department, and thereafter to acquire a kind of political status impossible for a study of Tolstoi's early fiction financed in part by a foundation. Yet both works belong in what civil society acknowledges to be a similar field, Russian studies, even though one work may be done by a very conservative economist, the other by a radical literary historian. My point here is that "Russia" as a general subject matter has political priority over nicer distinctions such as "economics" and "literary history," because political society in Gramsci's sense reaches into such realms of civil society as the academy and saturates them with significance of direct concern to it.

I do not want to press all this any further on general theoretical grounds: it seems to me that the value and credibility of my case can be demonstrated by being much more specific, in the way, for example, Noam Chomsky has studied the instrumental connection between the Vietnam War and the notion of objective scholarship as it was applied to cover state-sponsored military research. Now because Britain, France, and recently the United States are imperial powers, their political societies impart to their civil societies a sense of urgency, a direct political infusion as it were, where and whenever matters pertaining to their imperial interests abroad are concerned. I doubt that it is controversial, for example, to say that an Englishman in India or Egypt in the later nineteenth century took an interest in those countries that was never far from their status in his mind as British colonies. To say this may seem quite different from saying that all academic knowledge about India and Egypt is somehow tinged and impressed with, violated by, the gross political fact—and yet *that is what I am saying* in this study of Orientalism. For if it is true that no production of knowledge in the human sciences can ever ignore or disclaim its author's involvement as a human subject in his own circumstances, then it must also be true that for a European or American studying the Orient there can be no disclaiming the main circumstances of *his* actuality: that he comes up against the Orient as a European or American first, as an individual second. And to be a European or an American in such a situation is by no means an inert fact. It meant and means being aware, however dimly, that one belongs to a power with definite interests in the Orient, and more important, that one belongs to a part of the earth with a definite history of involvement in the Orient almost since the time of Homer.

Put in this way, these political actualities are still too undefined and general to be really interesting. Anyone would agree to them without necessarily agreeing also that they mattered very much, for instance, to Flaubert as he wrote *Salammbô*, or to H. A. R. Gibb as he wrote *Modern Trends in Islam*. The trouble is that there is too great a distance between the big dominating fact, as I have described it, and the details of everyday life that govern the minute discipline of a novel or a scholarly text as each is being written. Yet if we eliminate from the start any notion that "big" facts like imperial domination can be applied mechanically and deterministically to such complex matters as culture and ideas, then we will begin to approach an interesting kind of study. My idea is that European and then American interest in the Orient was political according to some of the obvious historical accounts of it that I have given here, but that it was the culture that created that interest, that acted dynamically along with brute political, economic, and military rationales to make the Orient the varied and complicated place that it obviously was in the field I call Orientalism.

Therefore, Orientalism is not a mere political subject matter or field that is reflected passively by culture, scholarship, or institutions; nor is it a large and diffuse collection of texts about the Orient; nor is it representative and expressive of some nefarious "Western" imperialist plot to hold down the

"Oriental" world. It is rather a *distribution* of geopolitical awareness into aesthetic, scholarly, economic, sociological, historical, and philological texts; it is an *elaboration* not only of a basic geographical distinction (the world is made up of two unequal halves, Orient and Occident) but also of a whole series of "interests" which, by such means as scholarly discovery, philological reconstruction, psychological analysis, landscape and sociological description, it not only creates but also maintains; it *is*, rather than expresses, a certain *will* or *intention* to understand, in some cases to control, manipulate, even to incorporate, what is a manifestly different (or alternative and novel) world; it is, above all, a discourse that is by no means in direct, corresponding relationship with political power in the raw, but rather is produced and exists in an uneven exchange with various kinds of power, shaped to a degree by the exchange with power political (as with a colonial or imperial establishment), power intellectual (as with reigning sciences like comparative linguistics or anatomy, or any of the modern policy sciences), power cultural (as with orthodoxies and canons of taste, texts, values), power moral (as with ideas about what "we" do and what "they" cannot do or understand as "we" do). Indeed, my real argument is that Orientalism is—and does not simply represent—a considerable dimension of modern political-intellectual culture, and as such has less to do with the Orient than it does with "our" world.

Ihab Hassan

Egyptian-American (1925-2015)

Toward a Concept of Postmodernism (1987)

The battle of the books is also an ontic battle against death.

The strains of silence in literature, from Sade to Beckett, convey complexities of language, culture, and consciousness as these contest themselves and one another. Such eerie music may yield an experience, an intuition, of postmodernism but no concept or definition of it. Perhaps I can move here toward such a concept by putting forth certain queries. I begin with the most obvious: can we really perceive a phenomenon, in Western societies generally and in their literatures particularly, that needs to be distinguished from modernism, needs to be named? If so, will the provisional rubric "postmodernism" serve? Can we then—or even should we at this time—construct of this phenomenon some probative scheme, both chronological and typological, that may account for its various trends and counter-trends, its artistic, epistemic, and social character? And how would this phenomenon—let us call it postmodernism—relate itself to such earlier modes of change as turn-of-the-century avant-gardes or the high modernism of the twenties? Finally, what difficulties would inhere in any such act of definition, such a tentative heuristic scheme?

I am not certain that I can wholly satisfy my own questions, though I can assay some answers that may help to focus the larger problem. History, I take it, moves in measures both continuous and discontinuous. Thus the prevalence of postmodernism today, if indeed it prevails, does not suggest that ideas of institutions of the past cease to shape the present. Rather, traditions develop, and even types suffer a sea change. Certainly, the powerful cultural assumptions generated by, say, Darwin, Marx, Bauldelaire, Nietzsche, Cezanne, Debussy, Freud, and Einstein still pervade the Western mind. Certainly those assumptions have been reconceived, not once but many times—else history would repeat itself, forever the same. In this perspective postmodernism may appear as a significant revision, if not an original èpistemé, of twentieth-century Western societies.

Some names, piled here pell-mell, may serve to adumbrate postmodernism, or at least suggest its range of assumptions: Jacques Derrida, Jean-Francois Lyotard (philosophy), Michel Foucault, Hayden White (history), Jacques Lacan, Gilles Deleuze, R. D. Laing, Norman O. Brown (psychoanalysis), Herbert Marcuse, Jean Baudrillard, Jurgen Habermas (political philosophy), Thomas Kuhn, Paul Feyerabend (philosophy of science), Roland Barthes, Julia Kristeva, Wolfgang Iser, the "Yale Critics" (literary theory), Merce Cunningham, Alwin Nikolais, Meredith Monk (dance), John Cage, Karlheinz Stockhausen, Pierre Boulez (music), Robert Rauschenberg, Jean Tinguely, Joseph Beuys (art), Robert Venturi, Charles Jencks, Brent Bolin (architecture), and various authors from Samuel Beckett, Eugene Ionesco, Jorge Luis Borges, Max Bense, and Vladimir Nabokov to Harold Pinter, B. S. Johnson, Rayner Heppenstall, Christine Brooke-Rose, Helmut Heissenbuttel, Jurgen Becker, Peter Handke, Thomas Bernhardt, Ernest Jandl, Gabriel Garcia Márquez, Julio Cortázar, Alain RobbeGrillet, Michel Butor, Maurice Roche, Philippe Sollers, and, in America, John Barth, William Burroughs, Thomas Pynchon, Donald Barthelme, Walter Abish, John Ashbery, David Antin, Sam Shepard, and Robert Wilson. Indubitably, these names are far too heterogenous to form a movement, paradigm, or school. Still, they may evoke a number of related cultural tendencies, a constellation of values, a repertoire of procedures and attitudes. These we call postmodernism. Whence this term? Its origin remains uncertain, though we know that Federico de Onis used the word *postmodernismo* in his *Antologia de la poesia española e hispanoamericana* (1882-1932), published in Madrid in 1934; and Dudley Fitts picked it up again in his *Anthology of Contemporary Latin-American Poetry* of 1942.[1] Both meant thus to indicate a minor reaction to modernism already latent within it, reverting to the early twentieth century. The term also appeared in Arnold Toynbee's *A Study of History* as early as D.C. Somervell's first-volume abridgement in 1947. For Toynbee, Post-Modernism designated a new historical cycle in Western civilization, starting around 1875, which we now scarcely begin to discern. Somewhat later, during the fifties, Charles Olson often spoke of postmodernism with more sweep than lapidary definition.

But prophets and poets enjoy an ample sense of time, which few literary scholars seem to afford. In 1959 and 1960, Irving Howe and Harry Levin

---

[1]   For the best history of the term postmodernism see Michael Kohler, "'Postmodernismus': Ein begriffsgeschichtlicher Oberblick," *Amerikastudien*, vol. 22, no. 1 (1977). That same issue contains other excellent discussions and bibliographies on the term; see particularly Gerhard Hoffmann, Alfred Hornung, and Rudiger Kunow, "'Modern', 'Postmodern' and 'Contemporary as Criteria for the Analysis of 20th Century Literature."

wrote of postmodernism rather disconsolately as a falling off from the great modernist movement.[2] It remained for Leslie Fiedler and myself, among others, to employ the term during the sixties with premature approbation, and even with a touch of bravado.[3] Fiedler had it in mind to challenge the elitism of the high modernist tradition in the name of popular culture. I wanted to explore the impulse of self-unmaking which is part of the literary tradition of silence. Pop and silence, or mass culture and deconstruction, or Superman and Godot—or as I shall later argue, immanence and indeterminacy—may all be aspects of the postmodern universe. But all this must wait upon more patient analysis, longer history.

Yet the history of literary terms serves only to confirm the irrational genius of language. We come closer to the question of postmodernism itself by acknowledging the psychopolitics, if not the psychopathology, of academic life. Let us admit it: there is a will to power in nomenclature, as well as in people or texts. A new term opens for its proponents a space in language. A critical concept or system is a "poor" poem of the intellectual imagination. The battle of the books is also an ontic battle against death. That may be why Max Planck believed that one never manages to convince one's opponents—not even in theoretical physics!—one simply tries to outlive them. William James described the process in less morbid terms: novelties are first repudiated as nonsense, then declared obvious, then appropriated by former adversaries as their own discoveries.

I do not mean to take my stand with the postmoderns against the (ancient) moderns. In an age of frantic intellectual fashions, values can be too recklessly voided, and tomorrow can quickly preempt today or yesteryear. Nor is it merely a matter of fashions; for the sense of supervention may express some cultural urgency that partakes less of hope than fear. This much we recall: Lionel Trilling entitled one of his most thoughtful works *Beyond Culture* (1965); Kenneth Boulding argued that "postcivilization" is an essential part of *The Meaning of the 20th Century* (1964); and George Steiner could have subtitled his essay, *In Bluebeard's Castle* (1971); "Notes Toward the Definition of Postculture." Before them, Roderick Seidenberg published his *Post-Historic*

---

[2] Irving Howe, "Mass Society and Postmodern Fiction," *Partisan Review*, vol. 26, no. 3 (Summer 1959), reprinted in his *Decline of the New* (New York, 1970), 190-207; and Harry Levin, "What Was Modernism?", *Massachusetts Review*, vol. 1, no. 4 (August 1960), reprinted in *Refractions* (New York, 1966), 271-295.

[3] Leslie Fiedler, "The New Mutants," *Partisan Review*, vol. 32, no. 4 (Fall 1965), reprinted in his *Collected Essays*, vol. 2 (New York, 1971), 379400; and Ihab Hassan, "Frontiers of Criticism: Metaphors of Silence," *Virginia Quarterly*, vol. 46, no. 1 (Winter 1970). In earlier essays I had also used the term "Anti-literature" and "the literature of silence" in a proximate sense; see, for instance Ihab Hassan, "The Literature of Silence," *Encounter*, vol. 28, no. 1 (January 1967), and pp. 3-22 above.

Man exactly in mid-century; and most recently, I have myself speculated, in *The Right Promethean Fire* (1980), about the advent of a posthumanist era. As Daniel Bell put it: "It used to be that the great literary modifier was the word beyond. . . . But we seem to have exhausted the beyond, and today the sociological modifier is post."[4]

My point here is double: in the question of postmodernism, there is a will and counter-will to intellectual power, an imperial desire of the mind, but this will and desire are themselves caught in a historical moment of supervention, if not exactly of obsolescence. The reception or denial of postmodernism thus remains contingent on the psychopolitics of academic life—including the various dispositions of people and power in our universities, of critical factions and personal frictions, of boundaries that arbitrarily include or exclude—no less than on the imperatives of the culture at large. This much, reflexivity seems to demand from us at the start.

But reflection demands also that we address a number of conceptual problems that both conceal and constitute postmodernism itself. I shall try to isolate ten of these, commencing with the simpler, moving toward the more intractable.

1. The word postmodernism sounds not only awkward, uncouth; it evokes what it wishes to surpass or suppress, modernism itself. The term thus contains its enemy within, as the terms romanticism and classicism, baroque and rococo, do not. Moreover, it denotes temporal linearity and connotes belatedness, even decadence, to which no post-modernist would admit. But what better name have we to give this curious age? The Atomic, or Space, or Television, Age? These technological tags lack theoretical definition. Or shall we call it the Age of Indetermanence (indeterminacy + immanence) as I have half-antically proposed?[5] Or better still, shall we simply live and let others live to call us what they may?

2. Like other categorical terms—say poststructuralism, or modernism, or romanticism for that matter—postmodernism suffers from a certain semantic instability: that is, no clear consensus about its meaning exists among scholars. The general difficulty is compounded in this case by two factors: (a) the relative youth, indeed brash adolescence, of the term postmodernism, and (b) its semantic kinship to more current terms, themselves equally unstable. Thus some critics mean by postmodernism what others call avant-gardism or even neo-avant-gardism, while still

---

4   Daniel Bell, *The Coming of Post-Industrial Society* (New York, 1973), 53.
5   See pp. 46-83 [in *The Postmodern Turn.*]

others would call the same phenomenon simply modernism. This can make for inspired debates.[6]

3. A related difficulty concerns the historical instability of many literary concepts, their openness to change. Who, in this epoch of fierce misprisions, would dare to claim that romanticism is apprehended by Coleridge, Pater, Lovejoy, Abrams, Peckham, and Bloom in quite the same way? There is already some evidence that postmodernism, and modernism even more, are beginning to slip and slide in time, threatening to make any diacritical distinction between them desperate.[7] But perhaps the phenomenon, akin to Hubble's "red shift" in astronomy, may someday serve to measure the historical velocity of literary concepts.

4. Modernism and postmodernism are not separated by an Iron Curtain or Chinese Wall; for history is a palimpsest, and culture is permeable to time past, time present, and time future. We are all, I suspect, a little Victorian, Modern, and Postmodern, at once. And an author may, in his or her own lifetime, easily write both a modernist and postmodernist work. (Contrast Joyce's *Portrait of the Artist as a Young Man* with his *Finnegans Wake.*) More generally, on a certain level of narrative abstraction, modernism itself may be rightly assimilated to romanticism, romanticism related to the enlightenment, the latter to the renaissance, and so back, if not to the Olduvai Gorge, then certainly to ancient Greece.

5. This means that a "period," as I have already intimated, must be perceived in terms both of continuity and discontinuity, the two perspectives being

---

[6] Matei Calinescu, for instance, tends to assimilate "postmodern" to "neo-avant-garde" and sometimes to "avant-garde," in *Faces of Modernity: Avant-Garde, Decadence, Kitsch* (Bloomington, 1977), though later he discriminates between these terms thoughtfully, in "Avant-Garde, Neo-AvantGarde, and Postmodernism," unpublished manuscript. Miklos Szabolcsi would identify "modern" with "avant-garde" and call "postmodern" the "neo-avant-garde," in "Avant-Garde, Neo-Avant-Garde, Modernism: Questions and Suggestions," *New Literary History*, vol. 3, no 1 (Autumn 1971); while Paul de Man would call "modern" the innovative element, the perpetual "moment of crisis" in the literature of every period, in "Literary History and Literary Modernity," in *Blindness and Insight* (New York, 1971), chapter 8; in a similar vein, William V Spanos employs the term "postmodernism" to indicate "not fundamentally a chronological event, but rather a permanent mode of human understanding," in "De-Struction and the Question of Postmodern Literature: Towards a Definition," *Par Rapport*, vol. 2, no. 2 (Summer 1979), 107. And even John Barth, as inward as any writer with postmodernism, now argues that postmodernism is a synthesis yet to come, and what we had assumed to be postmodernism all along was only late modernism, in "The Literature of Replenishment: Post modernist Fiction," *Atlantic Monthly* 245, no. 1 (January 1980).

[7] In my own earlier and later essays on the subject, I can discern such a slight shift. See "POSTmodernISM," pp. 25-45 above, "Joyce, Beckett, and the Postmodern Imagination," *TriQuarterly* 34 (Fall 1975), and "Culture, Indeterminacy, and Immanence," pp. 46-83 above.

complementary and partial. The Apollonian view, rangy and abstract, discerns only historical conjunctions; the Dionysian feeling, sensuous though nearly purblind, touches only the disjunctive moment. Thus postmodernism, by invoking two divinities at once, engages a double view. Sameness and difference, unity and rupture, filiation and revolt, all must be honored if we are to attend to history, apprehend (perceive, understand) change, both as a spatial, mental structure and as a temporal, physical process, both as pattern and unique event.

6. Thus a "period" is generally not a period at all; it is rather both a diachronic and synchronic construct. Postmodernism, again, like modernism or romanticism, is no exception; it requires both historical and theoretical definition. We would not seriously claim an inaugural "date" for it as Virginia Woolf pertly did for modernism, though we may sometimes woefully imagine that postmodernism began "in or about September, 1939." Thus we continually discover "antecedents" of postmodernismin Sterne, Sade, Blake, Lautreamont, Rimbaud, Jarry, Tzara, Hofmannsthal, Gertrude Stein, the later Joyce, the later Pound, Duchamp, Artaud, Roussel, Bataille, Broch, Queneau, and Kafka. What this really indicates is that we have created in our mind a model of postmodernism, a particular typology of culture and imagination, and have proceeded to "rediscover" the affinities of various authors and different moments with that model. We have, that is, reinvented our ancestors-and always shall. Consequently, "older" authors can be postmodern—Kafka, Beckett, Borges, Nabokov, Gombrowicz—while "younger" authors needs not be so—Styron, Updike, Capote Irving Doc, Irving, Doctorow, Gardner.

7. As we have seen, any definition of postmodernism calls upon a four-fold vision of complementarities, embracing continuity and discontinuity, diachrony and synchrony. But a definition of the concept also requires a dialectical vision; for defining traits are often antithetical, and to ignore this tendency of historical reality is to lapse into single vision and Newton's sleep. Defining traits are dialectical and also plural; to elect a single trait as an absolute criterion of postmodern grace is to make of all other writers preterites.[8] Thus we cannot simply rest—as I have sometimes done—on the assumption that postmodernism is antiformal,

---

[8] Though some critics have argued that postmodernism is primarily "temporal" and others that it is mainly "spatial," it is in the particular relation between these single categories that postmodernism probably reveals itself. See the two seemingly contradictory views of William V Spanos, "The Detective at the Boundary," in *Existentialism* 2, ed. William V Spanos (New York, 1976), 163-89; and Jurgen Peper, "Postmodernismus: Unitary Sensibility," *Amerikastudien*, vol. 22, no. 1 (1977).

anarchic, or decreative; for though it is indeed all these, and despite its fanatic will to unmaking; it also contains the need to discover a "unitary sensibility" (Sontag), to "cross the border and close the gap" (Fiedler), and to attain, as I have suggested, an immanence of discourse, an expanded noetic intervention, a "neo-gnostic immediacy of mind."[9]

8. All this leads to the prior problem of periodization which is also that of literary history conceived as a particular apprehension of change. Indeed, the concept of postmodernism applies some theory of innovation, renovation, novation, or simply change. But which one? Heraclitean? Darwinian? Marxist? Freudian? Kuhnian? Viconian? Derridean? Eclectic?[10] Or is a "theory of change" itself an oxymoron best suited to ideologues intolerant of the ambiguities of time? Should postmodernism, then, be left—at least for the moment— unconceptualized, a kind of literary-historical "difference" or "trace?"[11]

9. Postmodernism can expand into a still large problem: is it only an artistic tendency or also a social phenomenon, perhaps even a mutation in Western humanism? If so, how are the various aspects of this phenomenon—psychological, philosophical, economic, political—joined or disjoined? In short, can we understand postmodernism in literature without some attempt to perceive the lineaments of a postmodern society, a Toynbeean postmodernity, or future Foucauldian épistémè, of which the literary tendency I have been discussing is but a single, elitist strain?[12]

---

[9] Susan Sontag, "One Culture and the New Sensibility," in *Against Interpretation* (New York, 1967), 293-304; Leslie Fiedler, "Cross the Border-Close the Gap," in *Collected Essays*, vol. 2 (New York, 1971), 461-85; and Ihab Hassan, "The New Gnosticism," *Paracriticism: Seven Speculations of the Times* (Urbana, 1975), chapter 6.

[10] For some views of this, see Ihab Hassan and Sally Hassan, eds. *Innovation/Renovation: Recent Trends and Reconceptions in Western Culture* (Madison, Wis., 1983).

[11] At stake here is the idea of literary periodicity, challenged by current French thought. For other views of literary and historical change, including "hierarchic organization" of time, see Leonard Meyer, *Music, the Arts and Ideas* (Chicago, 1967), 93, 102; Calinescu, *Faces of Modernity*, 147ff; Ralph Cohen, "Innovation and Variation: Literary Change and Georgic Poetry," in Ralph Cohen and Murray Krieger, *Literature and History* (Los Angeles, 1974); and my *Paracriticisms*, chapter 7. A harder question is one Geoffrey Hartman asks: "With so much historical knowledge, how can we avoid historicism, or the staging of history as a drama in which epiphanic raptures are replaced by epistemic ruptures?" Or, again, how can we "formulate a theory of reading that would be historical rather than historicist"? *Saving the Text: Literature/Derrida/Philosophy* (Baltimore, 1981), xx.

[12] Writers as different as Marshall McLuhan and Leslie Fiedler have explored the media and pop aspects of postmodernism for two decades, thought their efforts are now out of fashion in some circles. The difference between postmodernism, as a contemporary artistic tendency, and postmodernity, as a cultural phenomenon, perhaps even an era of history, is discussed by Richard E. Palmer in "Postmodernity and Hermeneutics," *Boundary* 2, vol. 5, no. 2 (Winter 1977).

10. Finally, though not least vexing, is postmodernism as an honorific term, used insidiously to valorize writers, however disparate, whom we otherwise esteem, to hail trends, however discordant which we somehow approve? Or is it, on the contrary, a term of opprobrium and objurgation? In short, is postmodernism a descriptive as well as evaluative or normative category of literary thought? Or does it belong, as Charles Altieri notes, to that category of "essentially contested concepts" in philosophy that never wholly exhaust their constitutive confusions?[13]

No doubt, other conceptual problems lurk in the matter of postmodernism. Such problems, however, cannot finally inhibit the intellectual imagination, the desire to apprehend our historical presence in noetic constructs that reveal our being to ourselves. I move, therefore, to propose a provisional scheme that the literature of silence, from Sade to Beckett, seems to envisage, and do so by distinguishing, tentatively, between three modes of artistic change in the last hundred years. I call these avant-garde, modern, and postmodern, though I realize that all three have conspired together to that "tradition of the new" that, since Baudelaire, brought "into being an art whose history regardless of the credos of its practitioners, has consisted of leaps from vanguard to vanguard, and political mass movements whose aim has been the total renovation not only of social institutions but of man himself."[14]

By avant-garde, I means those movements that agitated the earlier part of our century, including Pataphysics, Cubism, Futurism, Dadaism, Surrealism, Suprematism, Constructivism, Merzism, de Stijl—some of which I have already discussed in this work. Anarchic, these assaulted the bourgeoisie with their art, their manifestoes, their antics. But their activism could also turn inward, becoming suicidal—as happened later to some postmodernists like Rudolf Schwartzkogler. Once full of brio and bravura, these movements have all but vanished now, leaving only their story, at once fugacious and exemplary. Modernism, however, proved more stable, aloof, hieratic, like the French Symbolism from which it derived; even its experiments now seem olympian. Enacted by such "individual talents" as Valéry, Proust, and Gide, the early Joyce, Yeats, and Lawrence, Rilke, Mann, and Musil, the early Pound, Eliot, and Faulkner, it commanded high authority, leading Delmore Schwartz

[13] Charles Altieri, "Postmodernism: A Question of Definition," *Par Rapport*, vol. 2, no. 2 (Summer 1979), 90. This leads Altieri to conclude: "The best one can do who believes himself post-modern . . . is to articulate spaces of mind in which the confusions cannot paralyze because one enjoys the energies and glimpses of our condition which they produce," p. 99.

[14] Harold Rosenberg, *The Tradition of the New* (New York, 1961), 9.

to chant in Shenandoah: "Let us consider where the great men are/ Who will obsess the child when he can read. . ." But if much of modernism appears hieratic, hypotactical, and formalist, postmodernism strikes us by contrast as playful, paratactical, and deconstructionist. In this it recalls the irreverent spirit of the avantgarde, and so carries sometimes the label of neo-avant-garde. Yet postmodernism remains "cooler," in McLuhan's sense, than older vanguards—cooler, less cliquish, and far less aversive to the pop, electronic society of which it is a part, and so hospitable to kitsch.

Can we distinguish postmodernism further? Perhaps certain schematic differences from modernism will provide a start:

Modernism	Postmodernism
Romanticism/Symbolism	Pataphysics/Dadaism
Form (conjunctive, closed)	Antiform (disjunctive, open)
Purpose	Play
Design	Chance
Hierarchy	Anarchy
Mastery/Logos	Exhaustion/Silence
Art Object/Finished Work	Process/Performance/Happening
Distance	Participation
Creation/Totalization	Decreation/Deconstruction
Synthesis	Antithesis
Presence	Absence
Centering	Dispersal
Genre/Boundary	Text/Intertext
Semantics	Rhetoric
Paradigm	Syntagm
Hypotaxis	Parataxis
Metaphor	Metonymy
Selection	Combination
Root/Depth	Rhizome/Surface
Interpretation/Reading	Against Interpretation/Misreading
Signified	Signifier
Lisible (Readerly)	Scriptible (Writerly)
Narrative/Grande Histoire	Anti-narrative/Petite Histoire
Master Code	Idiolect
Symptom	Desire
Type	Mutant
Genital/Phallic	Polymorphous/Androgynous
Paranoia	Schizophrenia
Origin/Cause	Difference-Differance/Trace
God the Father	The Holy Ghost
Metaphysics	Irony
Determinancy	Indeterminancy
Transcendence	Immanence

The preceding table draws on ideas in many fields—rhetoric, linguistics, literary theory, philosophy, anthropology, psychoanalysis, political science, even theology—and draws on many authors European and American—aligned with diverse movements, groups, and views. Yet the dichotomies this table represents remain insecure, equivocal. For differences shift, defer, even collapse; concepts in any one vertical column are not all equivalent; and inversions and exceptions, in both modernism and postmodernism, abound. Still, I would submit that rubrics in the right column point to the postmodern tendency, the tendency of indetermanence, and so may bring us closer to its historical and theoretical definition.

The time has come, however, to explain a little that neologism: "indetermanence:" I have used that term to designate two central, constitutive tendencies in postmodernism: one of indeterminancy, the other of immanence. The two tendencies are not dialectical; for they are not exactly antithetical; nor do they lead to a synthesis. Each contains its own contradictions, and alludes to elements of the other. Their interplay suggests the action of a "polylectic," pervading postmodernism. Since I have discussed this topic at some length earlier, I can avert to it here briefly.[15]

By indeterminacy, or better still, indeterminacies, I mean a complex referent that these diverse concepts help to delineate: ambiguity, discontinuity, heterodoxy, pluralism, randomness, revolt, perversion, deformation. The latter alone subsumes a dozen current terms of unmaking: decreation, disintegration, deconstruction, decenterment, displacement, difference, discontinuity, disjunction, disappearance, decomposition, de-definition, demystification, detotalization, delegitimization—let alone more technical terms referring to the rhetoric of irony, rupture, silence. Through all these signs moves a vast will to unmaking, affecting the body politic, the body cognitive, the erotic body, the individual psyche—the entire realm of discourse in the West. In literature alone our ideas of author, audience, reading, writing, book, genre, critical theory, and of literature itself, have all suddenly become questionable. And in criticism? Roland Barthes speaks of literature as "loss," "perversion," "dissolution"; Wolfgang Iser formulates a theory of reading based on textual "blanks"; Paul de Man conceives rhetoric—that is, literature—as a force that "radically suspends logic and opens up vertiginous possibilities of referential aberration"; and Geoffrey Hartman affirms that "contemporary criticism aims at the hermeneutics of indeterminacy."[16]

---

[15] See pp. 65-72 [in *The Postmodern Turn*]. Also, my "Innovation/Renovation: Toward a Cultural Theory of Change," *Innovation/Renovation*, chapter 1.

[16] See, for instance, Roland Barthes and Maurice Nadeau, *Sur la litterature* (Paris, 1980), 7, 16, 19f, 41; Wolfgang Iser, *The Act of Reading* (Baltimore, 1978), passim; Paul de Man, *Allegories of Reading* (New Haven, Conn., 1979), 10; and Geoffrey H. Hartman, *Criticism in the Wilderness* (New Haven, 1980), 41.

Such uncertain diffractions make for vast dispersals. Thus I call the second major tendency of postmodernism immanences, a term that I employ without religious echo to designate the capacity of mind to generalize itself in symbols, intervene more and more into nature, act upon itself through its own abstractions and so become, increasingly, immediately, by its own environment. This noetic tendency may be evoked further by such sundry concepts as diffusion, dissemination, pulsion, interplay, communication, interdependence, which all derive from the emergence of human beings as language animals, *homo pictor* or *homo significans*, gnostic creatures constituting themselves, and determinedly their universe, by symbols of their own making. Is "this not the sign that the whole of this configuration is about to topple, and that man is in the process of perishing as the being of language continues to shine ever brighter upon our horizon?" Foucault famously asks.[17] Meanwhile, the public world dissolves as fact and fiction blend, history becomes derealized by media into a happening, science takes its own models as the only accessible reality, cybernetics confronts us with the enigma of artificial intelligence, and technologies project our perceptions to the edge of the receding universe or into the ghostly interstices of matter.[18] Everywhere—even deep in Lacan's "lettered unconscious," more dense than a black hole in space—everywhere we encounter that immanence called Language, with all its literary ambiguities, epistemic conundrums, and political distractions.[19]

No doubt these tendencies may seem less rife in England, say, than in America or France where the term postmodernism, reversing the recent

---

[17] Michel Foucault, *The Order of Things* (New York, 1970), 386.

[18] "Just as Pascal sought to throw the dice with God . . . so do the decisions theorists, and the new intellectual technology, seek their own tableau entier-the compass of rationality itself," Daniel Bell remarks in "Technology, Nature, and Society," in *Technology and the Frontiers of Knowledge* (Garden City, 1975), 53. See also the more acute analysis of "l'informatique" by Jean-Francois Lyotard, *La Condition postmoderne* (Paris, 1979, passim).

[19] This tendency also makes the abstract, conceptual, and irrealist character of so much postmodern art. See Suzi Gablik, *Progress in Art* (New York, 1977), whose argument was prefigured by Ortega y Gasset, *The Dehumanization of Art* (Princeton, 1968). Note also that Ortega presaged the gnostic or noetic tendency to which I refer here in 1925: "Man humanizes the world, injects it, impregnates it with his own ideal substance and is finally entitled to imagine that one day or another, in the far depths of time, this terrible outer world will become so saturated with man that our descendants will be able to travel through it as today we mentally travel through our own most inmost selves—he finally imagines that the world, without ceasing to be like the world, will one day be changed into something like a materialized soul, and, as in Shakespeare's *Tempest*, the winds will blow at the bidding of Ariel, the spirit of ideas," p. 184.

direction of poststructuralist flow, has now come into use.[20] But the fact
in most developed societies remains: as an artistic, philosophical, and
social phenomenon, postmodernism veers toward open, playful, optative,
provisional (open in time as well as in structure or space), disjunctive, or
indeterminate forms, a discourse of ironies and fragments, a "white ideology"
of absences and fractures, a desire of diffractions, an invocation of complex,
articulate silences. Postmodernism veers towards all these yet implies
a different, if not antithetical, movement toward pervasive procedures,
ubiquitous interactions, immanent codes, media, languages. Thus our earth
seems caught in the process of planetization, transhumanization, even as it
breaks up into sects, tribes, factions of every kind. Thus, too, terrorism and
totalitarianism, schism and ecumenism, summon one another, and authorities
decreate themselves even as societies search for new grounds of authority.
One may well wonder: is some decisive historical mutation—involving art
and science, high and low culture, the male and female principles, parts and
wholes, involving the One and the Many as pre-Socratics used to say—active
in our midst? Or does the dismemberment of Orpheus prove no more than
the mind's need to make but one more construction of life's mutabilities and
human mortality?

And what construction lies beyond, behind, within, that construction?

---

[20] Though postmodernism and poststructuralism cannot be identified, they clearly
reveal many affinities. Thus in the course of one brief essay, Julia Kristeva comments
on both immanence and indeterminacy in terms of her own: "postmodernism is that
literature which writes itself with the more or less conscious intention of expanding the
signifiable, and thus human, realm"; and again: "At this degree of singularity, we are
faced with idiolects, proliferating uncontrollably." Julia Kristeva, "Postmodernism?" in
Romanticism, Modernism, Postmodernism, ed. Harry R. Garvin (Lewisberg, Pa. 1980),
137, 141.

Gayatri Chakravorty Spivak

Indian (1942-)

Can the Subaltern Speak? (1988)

The question is not of female participation in insurgency, or the ground rules of the sexual division of labor, for both of which there is "evidence." It is, rather, that, both as object of colonialist historiography and as subject of insurgency, the ideological construction of gender keeps the male dominant.

Let us now move to consider the margins (one can just as well say the silent, silenced center) of the circuit marked out by this epistemic violence, men and women among the illiterate peasantry, Aboriginals, and the lowest strata of the urban subproletariat. According to Foucault and Deleuze (in the First World, under the standardization and regimentation of socialized capital, though they do not seem to recognize this) and mutatis mutandis the metropolitan "third world feminist" only interested in resistance within capital logic, the oppressed, if given the chance (the problem of representation cannot be bypassed here), and on the way to solidarity through alliance politics (a Marxist thematic is at work here) *can speak and know their conditions.* We must now confront the following question: On the other side of the international division of labor from socialized capital, inside *and* outside the circuit of the epistemic violence of imperialist law and education supplementing an earlier economic text, *can the subaltern speak?*

We have already considered the possibility that, given the exigencies of the inauguration of colonial records, the instrumental woman (the Rani of Sirmur) is not fully written.

Antonio Gramsci's work on the "subaltern classes" extends the class-position/class-consciousness argument isolated in *The Eighteenth Brumaire.* Perhaps because Gramsci criticizes the vanguardistic position of the Leninist intellectual, he is concerned with the intellectual's rôle in the subaltern's cultural and political movement into the hegemony. This movement must be made to determine the production of history as narrative (of truth). In texts such as *The Southern Question,* Gramsci considers the movement of historical-political economy in Italy within what can be seen as an allegory of reading taken from or prefiguring an international division of labor.[1] Yet an account of the phased development of the subaltern is thrown out of joint when his cultural macrology is operated, however remotely, by the epistemic interference with legal and disciplinary definitions accompanying the imperialist project. When I move, at the end of this essay, to the question of woman as subaltern, I will suggest that the possibility of collectivity itself is persistently foreclosed through the manipulation of female agency.

The first part of my proposition that the phased development of the subaltern is complicated by the imperialist project is confronted by the "Subaltern Studies" group. They *must* ask, Can the subaltern speak? Here we are within Foucault's own discipline of history and with people who acknowledge his influence. Their project is to rethink Indian colonial historiography from the perspective of the discontinuous chain of peasant insurgencies during the colonial occupation. This is indeed the problem of "the permission to narrate" discussed by Said.[2] As Ranajit Guha, the founding editor of the collective, argues,

> The historiography of Indian nationalism has for a long time been dominated by elitism—colonialist elitism and bourgeois-nationalist elitism . . . shar[ing] the prejudice that the making of the Indian nation and the development of the consciousness—nationalism—which confirmed this process were exclusively or predominantly elite achievements. In the colonialist and neo-colonialist historiographies these achievements are credited to British colonial rulers, administrators, policies, institutions, and culture; in the nationalist and neo-nationalist writings—to Indian elite personalities, institutions, activities and ideas.[3]

Certain members of the Indian elite are of course native informants for first-world intellectuals interested in the voice of the Other. But one must nevertheless insist that the colonized subaltern *subject* is irretrievably heterogeneous.

Against the indigenous elite we may set what Guha calls "the *politics* of the people," both outside ("this was an *autonomous* domain, for it neither originated from elite politics nor did its existence depend on the latter") and

---

[1] Antonio Gramsci, *The Southern Question,* tr. Pasquale Verdicchio (West Lafayette, Ind.: Bordighera, Inc., 1995). As usual, I am using "allegory of reading" in the sense suggested by Paul de Man.

[2] Edward W. Said, "Permission to Narrate," *London Review of Books* (16 Feb. 1984).

[3] Guha, *Subaltern Studies,* (Delhi: Oxford Univ. Press, 1982), 1:1.

inside ("it continued to operate vigorously in spite of [colonialism], adjusting itself to the conditions prevailing under the Raj and in many respects developing entirely new strains in both form and content") the circuit of colonial production. I cannot entirely endorse this insistence of determinate vigor and full autonomy, for practical historiographic exigencies will not allow such endorsements to privilege subaltern consciousness. Against the possible charge that his approach is essentialist, Guha constructs a definition of the people (the place of that essence) that can be only an identity-in-differential. He proposes a dynamic stratification grid describing colonial social production at large. Even the third group on the list, the buffer group, as it were, between the people and the great macro-structural "dominant groups, is itself defined as a place of in-betweenness. The classification falls into: "dominant foreign groups," and "dominant indigenous groups at the all-India and at the regional and local levels" representing the elite; and "[t]he social groups and elements included in [the terms 'people' and 'subaltern classes'] represent[ing] *the demographic difference between the total Indian population and all those whom we have described as the 'elite.'"*[4]

"The task of research" projected here is "to investigate, identify and measure the *specific* nature and degree of the *deviation* of [the] elements [constituting item 3] from the ideal and situate it historically." "Investigate, identify, and measure the specific": a program could hardly be more essentialist and taxonomic. Yet a curious methodological imperative is at work. I have argued that, in the Foucault-Deleuze conversation, a postrepresentationalist vocabulary hides an essentialist agenda. In subaltern studies, because of the violence of imperialist epistemic, social, and disciplinary inscription, a project understood in essentialist terms must traffic in a radical textual practice of differences. The object of the group's investigation, in this case not even of the people as such but of the floating buffer zone of the regional elite—is a *deviation* from an *ideal*—the people or subaltern—which is itself defined as a difference from the elite. It is toward this structure that the research is oriented, a predicament rather different from the self-diagnosed transparency of the first-world radical intellectual. What taxonomy can fix such a space? Whether or not they themselves perceive it in fact Guha sees

[4] Ibid., pp. 4, 8. The usefulness of this tightly defined term was largely lost when *Selected Subaltern Studies* was launched in the United States under Spivak's initiative (New York: Oxford Univ. Press, 1988). Guha, ed., *A Subaltern Studies Reader* (Minneapolis: Univ. of Minnesota Press, 1997) is now a corrective. In the now generalized usage, it is precisely this notion of the subaltern inhabiting a space of difference that is lost in statements such as the following: "The subaltern is force fed into appropriating the master's culture" (Emily Apter, "French Colonial Studies and Postcolonial Theory," *Sub-Stance* 76/77, vol. 24, nos. 1–2 [1995]: 178); or worse still, Jameson's curious definition of subalternity as "the experience of inferiority" ("Marx's Purloined Letter," *New Left Review* 209 [1994]: 95).

his definition of "the people" within the master slave dialectic their text articulates the difficult task of rewriting its own conditions of impossibility as the conditions of its possibility. "At the regional and local levels [the dominant indigenous groups] . . . if belonging to social strata hierarchically inferior to those of the dominant all-Indian groups *acted in the interests of the latter and not in conformity to interests corresponding truly to their own social being*."[5] When these writers speak, in their essentializing language, of a gap between interest and action in the intermediate group, their conclusions are closer to Marx than to the self conscious naivete of Deleuze's pronouncement on the issue, Guha, like Marx, speaks of interest in terms of the social rather than the libidinal being.

The Name of-the-Father imagery in *The Eighteenth Brumaire* can help to emphasize that, on the level of class or group action, "true correspondence to own being" is as artificial or social as the patronymic.

It is to this intermediate group that the second woman in this chapter belongs. The pattern of domination is here determined mainly by gender rather than class. The subordinated gender following the dominant within the challenge of nationalism while remaining caught within gender oppression is not an unknown story.

For the (gender-unspecified) "true" subaltern group, whose identity is its difference, there is no unrepresentable subaltern subject that can know and speak itself; the intellectual's solution is not to abstain from representation. The problem is that the subject's itinerary has not been left traced so as to offer an object of seduction to the representing intellectual. In the slightly dated language of the Indian group, the question becomes, How can we touch the consciousness of the people, even as we investigate their politics? With what voice-consciousness can the subaltern speak?

My question about how to earn the "secret encounter" with the contemporary hill women of Sirmur is a practical version of this. The woman of whom I will speak in this section was not a "true" subaltern, but a metropolitan middle class girl. Further, the effort she made to write or speak her body was in the accents of accountable reason, the instrument of self-conscious responsibility. Still her Speech Act was refused. She was made to unspeak herself posthumously, by other women. In an earlier version of this chapter, I had summarized this historical indifference and its results as: the subaltern cannot speak.

The critique by Ajit K. Chaudhury, a West Bengali Marxist, of Guha's search for the subaltern consciousness can be taken as representative of a moment of

---

5   Guha, *Subaltern Studies*, 1:1.

the production process that includes the subaltern.[6] Chaudhury's perception that the Marxist view of the transformation of consciousness involves the knowledge of social relations seems, in principle, astute. Yet the heritage of the positivist ideology that has appropriated orthodox Marxism obliges him to add this rider: "This is not to belittle the importance of understanding peasants' consciousness or workers' consciousness *in its pure form.* This enriches our knowledge of the peasant and the worker and, possibly, throws light on how a particular mode takes on different forms in different regions, *which is considered a problem of second order importance in classical Marxism.*"[7]

This variety of "internationalist Marxism," which believes in a pure, retrievable form of consciousness only to dismiss it, thus closing off what in Marx remain moments of productive bafflement, can at once he the occasion for Foucault's and Deleuze's rejection of Marxism *and* the source of the critical motivation of the subaltern studies groups. All three are united in the assumption that there is a pure form of consciousness. On the French scene, there is a shuttling of signifiers: "the unconscious" or "the subject-in-oppression" clandestinely fills the space of "the pure form of consciousness." in orthodox "internationalist" intellectual Marxism, whether in the First World or the Third, the pure form of consciousness remains, paradoxically, a material effect, and therefore a second-order problem. This often earns it the reputation of racism and sexism. In the subaltern studies group it needs development according to the unacknowledged terms of its own articulation.

Within the effaced itinerary of the subaltern subject, the track of sexual difference is doubly effaced.[8] The question is not of female participation in insurgency, or the ground rules of the sexual division of labor, for both of which there is "evidence." It is, rather, that, both as object of colonialist historiography and as subject of insurgency, the ideological construction of gender keeps the male dominant. If, in the contest of colonial production, the subaltern has no history and cannot speak, the subaltern as female is even more deeply in shadow.

In the first part of this chapter we meditate upon an elusive female figure called into the service of colonialism. In the last part we will look at a comparable figure in anti-colonialist nationalism. The regulative

---

[6] Since then, in the disciplinary fallout after the serious electoral and terrorist argumentation of Hindu nationalism in India, more alarming charges have been leveled at the group. See Aijaz Ahmad, *In Theory: Classes, Nations, Literatures* (New York: Verso, 1992), pp. 68, 194, 207–11; and Sumit Sarkar, "The Fascism of the Sangh Parivar," *Economic and Political Weekly*, 30 Jan. 1993, pp. 163–67.

[7] Ajit K. Chaudhury, "New Wave Social Science," *Frontier* 16–24 (28 Jan. 1984), p. 10. Emphasis mine.

[8] I do not believe that the recent trend of romanticizing anything written by the Aboriginal or outcaste ("dalit" = oppressed) intellectual has lifted the effacement.

psychobiography of widow self-immolation will be pertinent in both cases. In the interest of the invaginated spaces of this book, let us remind ourselves of the gradual emergence of the new subaltern in the New World Order.

The contemporary international division of labor is a displacement of the divided field of nineteenth-century territorial imperialism. Put in the abstractions of capital logic, in the wake of industrial capitalism and mercantile conquest, a group of countries, generally first-world, were in the position of investing capital; another group, generally third-world, provided the field for investment, both through the subordinate indigenous capitalists and through their ill-protected and shifting labor force. In the interest of maintaining the circulation and growth of industrial capital (and of the concomitant task of administration within nineteenth-century territorial imperialism), transportation, law, and standardized education systems were developed— even as local industries were destroyed or restructured, land distribution was rearranged, and raw material was transferred to the colonizing country. With so-called decolonization, the growth of multinational capital, and the relief of the administrative charge, "development" did not now involve wholesale state-level legislation and establishing education *systems* in a comparable way. This impedes the growth of consumerism in the former colonies. With modern telecommunications and the emergence of advanced capitalist economics at the two edges of Asia, maintaining the international division of labor serves to keep the supply of cheap labor in the periphery. The implosion of the Soviet Union in 1989 has smoothed a way to the financialization of the globe. Already in the mid-seventies, the newly electronified stock exchanges added to the growth of telecommunication, which allowed global capitalism to emerge through export-based subcontracting and postfordism. "Under this strategy, manufacturers based in developed countries subcontract the most labor intensive stages of production, for example, sewing or assembly, to the Third World nations where labor is cheap. Once assembled, the multinational re imports the goods—under generous tariff exemptions—to the developed country *instead of selling them to the local market.*" Here the link to training in consumerism is almost snapped. "While global recession has markedly slowed trade and investment worldwide since 1979, international subcontracting has boomed. . . . In these cases, multinationals are freer to resist militant workers, revolutionary upheavals, and even economic downturns."[9]

Human labor is not, of course, intrinsically "cheap" or "expensive." An absence of labor laws (or a discriminatory enforcement of them), a totalitarian

---

[9]   "Contracting Poverty," *Multinational Monitor* 4.8 (Aug. 1983):8. This report was
     contributed by John Cavanagh and Joy Hackel, who work on the International
     Corporations Project at the Institute for Policy Studies. Emphasis mine.

state (often entailed by development and modernization in the periphery), and minimal subsistence requirements on the part of the worker will ensure "cheapness." To keep this crucial item intact, the urban proletariat in what is now called the "developing" nations must not be systematically trained in the ideology of consumerism (parading as the philosophy of a classless society) that, against all odds, prepares the ground for resistance through the coalition politics Foucault mentions (*FD* 216). This separation from the ideology of consumerism is increasingly exacerbated by the proliferating phenomena of international subcontracting.

In the post-Soviet world, the Bretton Woods organizations, together with the United Nations, are beginning to legislate for a monstrous North/ South global state, which is coming into being as micrologically as the trade controlled colonial state that was mentioned earlier. If Macaulay had spoken of a class of persons, Indian in blood and colour, but English in taste, in opinions, in morals, and in intellect; and Marx of the capitalist as *Faust's* "mechanical man," there is now an impersonal "Economic Citizen," site of authority and legitimation, lodged in finance capital markets and transnational companies.[10] And if under postfordism and international subcontracting, unorganized or permanently casual female labor was already becoming the mainstay of world trade, in contemporary globalization, the mechanism of "aid" is supported by the poorest women of the South, who form the base of what I have elsewhere called globe-girdling struggles (ecology, resistance to "population *control*"), where the boundary between global and local becomes indeterminate. This is the ground of the emergence of the new subaltern—rather different from the nationalist example we will consider later. To confront this group is not only to represent (*vertreten*) them globally in the absence of infrastructural support, but also to learn to represent (*darstellen*) ourselves. This argument would take us into a critique of a disciplinary anthropology and the relationship between elementary pedagogy and disciplinary formation. It would also question the implicit demand, made by intellectuals who choose the "naturally articulate" subject of oppression, that such a subject come through a history that is a foreshortened mode-of-production narrative.

Not surprisingly, some members of *indigenous dominant* groups in the "developing" countries, members of the local bourgeoisie, find the language of alliance politics attractive. Identifying with forms of resistance plausible in advanced capitalist countries is often of a piece with that elitist bent of bourgeois historiography described by Ranajit Guha.

---

[10] Saskia Sassen, "On Economic Citizenship," in *Losing Control? Sovereignty in An Age of Globalization* (New York: Columbia Univ. Press, 1996), pp. 31–58.

Belief in the plausibility of global alliance politics is increasingly prevalent among women of dominant social groups interested in "international feminism" in the "developing" nations as well as among well-plated Southern diaspories in the North. At the other end of the scale, those most separated from any possibility of an alliance among "women, prisoners, conscripted soldiers, hospital patients, and homosexuals" (*FD* 216) are the females of the urban subproletariat. In their case, the denial and withholding of consumerism and the structure of exploitation is compounded by patriarchal social relations.

That Deleuze and Foucault ignored both the epistemic violence of imperialism and the international division of labor would matter less if they did not, in closing, touch on third-world issues. In France it is impossible to ignore the problem of their *tiers monde,* the inhabitants of the erstwhile French African colonies. Deleuze limits his consideration of the Third World to these old local and regional indigenous elite who are, ideally, subaltern. In this context, references to the maintenance of the surplus army of labor fall into reverse ethnic sentimentality. Since he is speaking of the heritage of nineteenth-century territorial imperialism, his reference is to the nation-state rather than the globalizing center:

> French capitalism needs greatly a floating signifier of unemployment. In this perspective, we begin to see the unity of the forms of repression: restrictions on immigration, once it is acknowledged that the most difficult and thankless jobs go to immigrant workers; repression in the factories, because the French must reacquire the "taste" for increasingly harder work; the struggle against youth and the repression of the educational system. (*FD* 211–12)

This is certainly an acceptable analysis. Yet it shows again that the Third World can enter the resistance program of an alliance politics directed against a "*unified* repression" only when it is confined to the third-world groups that are directly accessible to the First World.[11] This benevolent

---

[11] The mechanics of the invention of the Third World as signifier are susceptible to the type of analysis directed at the constitution of race as a signifier in Carby, *Empire.* In the contemporary conjuncture, in response to the augmentation of Eurocentric migration as the demographic fallout of postcoloniality, neocolonialism, end of the Soviet Union, and global financialization, the South (the Third World of yore, with shifting bits of the old Second World thrown in) is being reinvented as the South-in-the-North. Even so brilliant a book as Etienne Balibar and Immanuel Wallerstein, *Race, Nation, Class: Ambiguous Identities,* tr. Chris Turner (New York: Verso, 1991) starts from this invention as unquestioned premise.

first-world appropriation and reinscription of the Third World as an Other is the founding characteristic of much third worldism in the U.S. human sciences today.

Foucault continues the critique of Marxism by invoking geographical discontinuity. The real mark of "geographical (geopolitcal) discontinuity" is the international division of labor. But Foucault uses the term to distinguish between exploitation (extraction and appropriation of surplus value; read, the field of Marxist analysis) and domination ("power" studies) and to suggest the latter's greater potential for resistance based on alliance politics. He cannot acknowledge that such a monist and unified access to a conception of "power" (methodologically presupposing a Subject of-power) is made possible by a certain stage in exploitation, for his vision of geographical discontinuity is geopolitically specific to the First World:

> This geographical discontinuity of which you speak might mean perhaps the following: as soon as we struggle against *exploitation,* the proletariat not only leads the struggle but also defines its targets, its methods, its places and its instruments; and to ally oneself with the proletariat is to consolidate with its positions, its ideology, it is to take up again the motives for their combat. This means total immersion (in the Marxist project). But if it is against *power* that one struggles, then all those who acknowledge it as intolerable can begin the struggle wherever they find themselves and in terms of their own activity (or passivity). In engaging in this struggle that is *their own,* whose objectives they clearly understand and whose methods they can determine, they enter into the revolutionary process. As allies of the proletariat, to be sure, because power is exercised the way it is in order to maintain capitalist exploitation. They genuinely serve the cause of the proletariat by fighting in those places where they find themselves oppressed. Women, prisoners, conscripted soldiers, hospital patients, and homosexuals have now begun a specific struggle against the particular form of power, the constraints and controls, that are exercised over them. (FD 216)

This is an admirable program of localized resistance. Where possible, this model of resistance is not an alternative to, but can complement, macrological struggles along "Marxist" lines. Yet if its situation is universalized, it accommodates unacknowledged privileging of the subject. Without a theory of ideology, it can lead to a dangerous utopianism. And, if confined to migrant struggles in Northern countries, it can work against global social justice.

The topographical reinscription of imperialism never specifically informed Foucault's presuppositions. Notice the omission of the fact, in the following passage, that the new mechanism of power in the seventeenth and eighteenth centuries (the extraction of surplus value without extra-economic coercion is its marxist description) is secured *by means of* territorial imperialism the Earth and its products—"elsewhere." The representation of sovereignty is crucial in these theaters: "in the seventeenth and eighteenth centuries, we have the production of an important phenomenon, the emergence, or rather the invention, of a new mechanism of power possessed of highly specific procedural techniques . . . which is also, I believe, absolutely incompatible with the relations of sovereignty. This new mechanism of power is more dependent upon bodies and what they do than the Earth and its products" (*PK* 104).

Sometimes it seems as if the very brilliance of Foucault's analysis of the centuries of European imperialism produces a miniature version of that heterogeneous phenomenon: management of space—but by doctors; development of administrations—but in asylums; considerations of the periphery—but in terms of the insane, prisoners, and children. The clinic, the asylum, the prison, the university—all seem to be screen-allegories that foreclose a reading of the broader narratives of imperialism. (One could open a similar discussion of the ferocious motif of "deterritorialization" in Deleuze and Guattari.) "One can perfectly well not talk about something because one doesn't know about it," Foucault might murmur (*PK* 66). Yet we have already spoken of the sanctioned ignorance that every critic of imperialism must chart.

By contrast, the early Derrida seemed aware of ethnocentrism in the production of knowledge.[12] (We have seen this in his comments on Kant quoted in Chapter 1. Like "empirical investigation, . . . tak[ing] shelter in the field of grammatological knowledge" obliges "operat[ing] through 'examples,'" *OG* 75.)

---

[12] Subsequently, as I indicate at length elsewhere (*Outside*, pp. 113–15; "Ghostwriting," pp. 69–71, 82) his work in these areas has speculated with the tendencies of computing migrancy or displacement as an origin (see page 17); in the figure of the absolute *arrivant*, of the marrano, and, most recently, in his seminars, hospitality. He would figure the indigenous subaltern, from the perspective of the metropolitan hybrid, as a correlative of cultural conservatism, topological archaism, ontopological nostalgia (*Specters*, p. 82). Here, too, he speculates with already existing tendencies. Just as pedigreed Marxists have been told, by Derrida among others, that Marx must be read in Marx's way, *as if* the reader were haunted by Marx's ghost; so might one deconstruct deconstruction (as Klein Freuded Freud): do not accuse, do not excuse, make it "your own," turn it around and use with no guarantees except that this formula too will become useless tomorrow—or in the moment of its saying: "each time that ethnocentrism is precipitately and ostentatiously reversed, some effort silently hides behind all the spectacular effects to consolidate an inside and to draw from it some domestic benefit."

The examples Derrida lays out—to show the limits of grammatology as a positive science—come from the appropriate ideological self-justification of an imperialist project. In the European seventeenth century, he writes, there were three kinds of "prejudices" operating in histories of writing which constituted a "symptom of the crisis of European consciousness" (*OG* 75): the "theological prejudice," the "Chinese prejudice," and the "hieroglyphist prejudice." The first can be indexed as: God wrote a primordial or natural script: Hebrew or Greek. The second: Chinese is a perfect *blueprint* for philosophical writing, but it is only a blueprint. True philosophical writing is "independen[t] with regard to history" (*OG* 79) and will sublate Chinese into an easy-to-learn script that will supersede actual Chinese. The third: that the Egyptian script is too sublime to be deciphered.

The first prejudice preserves the "actuality" of Hebrew or Greek; the last two ("rational" and "mystical," respectively) collude to support the first, where the center of the logos is seen as the Judaeo Christian God (the appropriation of the Hellenic Other through assimilation is an earlier story)—a "prejudice" still sustained in efforts to give the cartography of the Judaeo-Christian myth the status of geopolitical history:

> The concept of Chinese writing thus functioned as a sort of *European hallucination*. . . . This functioning obeyed a rigorous necessity. . . . It was not disturbed by the knowledge of Chinese script . . . which was then available. . . . A "*hieroglyphirst prejudice*" had produced the same effect of *interested blindness*. Far from proceeding . . . from ethnocentric scorn, the occultation takes the form of an hyperbolical admiration. We have not finished demonstrating the necessity of this pattern. Our century is not free from it; each time that ethnocentrism is precipitately and ostentatiously reversed, some effort silently hides behind all the spectacular effects to *consolidate an inside* and to draw from it some domestic benefit. (*OG* 80; Derrida italicizes only "hieroglyphist prejudice")

This pattern operates the culturalist excuse for Development encountered, for example, in John Rawls's *Political Liberalism,* as it does all unexamined metropolitan hybridism.[13]

Derrida closes the chapter by showing again that the project of grammatology is obliged to develop *within* the discourse of presence. It is not just a critique of presence but an awareness of the itinerary of the discourse of

---

[13] John Rawls, *Political Liberalism* (New York: Columbia Univ. Press, 1993).

presence in one's *own* critique, a vigilance precisely against too great a claim for transparency. The word "writing" as the name of the object and model of grammatology is a practice "only within the *historical* closure, that is to say within the limits of science and philosophy" (*OG* 93).

Derrida calls the ethnocentrism of the European science of writing in the late seventeenth and early eighteenth centuries a symptom of the general crisis of European consciousness. It is, of course, part of a larger symptom, or perhaps the crisis itself, the slow turn from feudalism to capitalism via the first waves of capitalist imperialism. The itinerary of recognition through assimilation of the Other can he more interestingly traced, it seems to me, in the imperialist constitution of the colonial subject and the foreclosure of the figure of the "native informant."

Abbreviations

FD = Michel Foucault, *Language, Counter-Memory, Practice: Selected Essays and Interviews,* tr. Donald Bouchard and Sherry Simon (Ithaca: Cornell University Press, 1977), pp. 205–17.

OG = Jacques Derrida, *Of Grammatology,* trans. Gayatri Chakravorty Spivak (Baltimore: The Johns Hopkins University Press, 1976).

PK = Michel Foucault, "On Popular Justice: A Discussion with Maoists," in *Power/Knowledge: Selected Interviews and Other Writings, 1972–1977,* ed. Colin Gordon (New York: Pantheon, 1980).

Judith Butler

American (1956-)

From Interiority to Gender Performatives (1990)

If gender attributes, however, are not expressive but performative then these attributes effectively constitute the identity they are said to express or reveal. The distinction between expression and performativeness is crucial.

In *Discipline and Punish* Foucault challenges the language of internalization as it operates in the service of the disciplinary regime of the subjection and subjectivation of criminals.[1] Although Foucault objected to what he understood to be the psychoanalytic belief in the "inner" truth of sex in *The History of Sexuality*, he turns to a criticism of the doctrine of internalization for separate purposes in the context of his history of criminology. In a sense, *Discipline and Punish* can be read as Foucault's effort to rewrite Nietzsche's doctrine of internalization in *On the Genealogy of Morals* on the model of *inscription*. In the context of prisoners, Foucault writes, the strategy has been not to enforce a repression of their desires, but to compel their bodies to signify the prohibitive law as their very essence, style, and necessity. That law is not literally internalized, but incorporated, with the consequence that bodies are produced which signify that law on and through the body; there the law is manifest as the essence of their selves, the meaning of their soul, their conscience, the law of their desire. In effect, the law is at once fully

---

[1] Parts of the following discussion were published in two different contexts, in my "Gender Trouble, Feminist Theory, and Psychoanalytic Discourse," in *Feminism/Postmodernism*, ed. Linda J. Nicholson (New York; Routledge, 1989) and "Performative Acts and Gender Constitution: An Essay in Phenomenology and Feminist Theory," *Theatre Journal*, Vol. 20, No. 3, Winter 1988.

manifest and fully latent, for it never appears as external to the bodies it subjects and subjectivates. Foucault writes:

> It would be wrong to say that the soul is an illusion, or an ideological effect. On the contrary, it exists, it has a reality, it is produced permanently *around, on, within,* the body by the functioning of a power that is exercised on those that are punished. (my emphasis)[2]

The figure of the interior soul understood as "within" the body is signified through its inscription *on* the body, even though its primary mode of signification is through its very absence, its potent invisibility. The effect of a structuring inner space is produced through the signification of a body as a vital and sacred enclosure. The soul is precisely what the body lacks; hence, the body presents itself as a signifying lack. That lack which *is* the body signifies the soul as that which cannot show. In this sense, then, the soul is a surface signification that contests and displaces the inner/outer distinction itself, a figure of interior psychic space inscribed *on* the body as a social signification that perpetually renounces itself as such. In Foucault's terms, the soul is not imprisoned by or within the body, as some Christian imagery would suggest, but "the soul is the prison of the body."[3]

The redescription of intrapsychic processes in terms of the surface politics of the body implies a corollary redescription of gender as the disciplinary production of the figures of fantasy through the play of presence and absence on the body's surface, the construction of the gendered body through a series of exclusions and denials, signifying absences. But what determines the manifest and latent text of the body politic? What is the prohibitive law that generates the corporeal stylization of gender, the fantasied and fantastic figuration of the body? We have already considered the incest taboo and the prior taboo against homosexuality as the generative moments of gender identity, the prohibitions that produce identity along the culturally intelligible grids of an idealized and compulsory heterosexuality. That disciplinary production of gender effects a false stabilization of gender in the interests of the heterosexual construction and regulation of sexuality within the reproductive domain. The construction of coherence conceals the gender discontinuities that run rampant within heterosexual, bisexual, and gay and lesbian contexts in which gender does not necessarily follow from sex, and desire, or sexuality generally, does not seem to follow from gender—indeed, where none of these dimensions of significant

---

[2] Michel Foucault, *Discipline and Punish: the Birth of the Prison,* trans. Alan Sheridan (New York: Vintage, 1979), p. 29.

[3] Ibid., p. 30.

corporeality express or reflect one another. When the disorganization and disaggregation of the field of bodies disrupt the regulatory fiction of heterosexual coherence, it seems that the expressive model loses its descriptive force. That regulatory ideal is then exposed as a norm and a fiction that disguises itself as a developmental law regulating the sexual field that it purports to describe.

According to the understanding of identification as an enacted fantasy or incorporation, however, it is clear that coherence is desired, wished for, idealized, and that this idealization is an effect of a corporeal signification. In other words, acts, gestures, and desire produce the effect of an internal core or substance, but produce this *on the surface* of the body, through the play of signifying absences that suggest, but never reveal, the organizing principle of identity as a cause. Such acts, gestures, enactments, generally construed, are *performative* in the sense that the essence or identity that they otherwise purport to express are *fabrications* manufactured and sustained through corporeal signs and other discursive means. That the gendered body is performative suggests that it has no ontological status apart from the various acts which constitute its reality. This also suggests that if that reality is fabricated as an interior essence, that very interiority is an effect and function of a decidedly public and social discourse, the public regulation of fantasy through the surface politics of the body, the gender border control that differentiates inner from outer, and so institutes the "integrity" of the subject. In other words, acts and gestures, articulated and enacted desires create the illusion of an interior and organizing gender core, an illusion discursively maintained for the purposes of the regulation of sexuality within the obligatory frame of reproductive heterosexuality. If the "cause" of desire, gesture, and act can be localized within the "self" of the actor, then the political regulations and disciplinary practices which produce that ostensibly coherent gender are effectively displaced from view. The displacement of a political and discursive origin of gender identity onto a psychological "core" precludes an analysis of the political constitution of the gendered subject and its fabricated notions about the ineffable interiority of its sex or of its true identity.

If the inner truth of gender is a fabrication and if a true gender is a fantasy instituted and inscribed on the surface of bodies, then it seems that genders can be neither true nor false, but are only produced as the truth effects of a discourse of primary and stable identity. In *Mother Camp: Female Impersonators in America,* anthropologist Esther Newton suggests that the structure of impersonation reveals one of the key fabricating mechanisms through which the social construction of gender takes place.[4] I would suggest

---

[4] See the chapter "Role Models" in Esther Newton, *Mother Camp: Female Impersonators in America* (Chicago: University of Chicago Press, 1972).

as well that drag fully subverts the distinction between inner and outer psychic space and effectively mocks both the expressive model of gender and the notion of a true gender identity. Newton writes:

> At its most complex, [drag] is a double inversion that says, "appearance is an illusion." Drag says [Newton's curious personification] "my 'outside' appearance is feminine, but my essence 'inside' [the body] is masculine." At the same time it symbolizes the opposite inversion; "my appearance 'outside' [my body, my gender] is masculine but my essence 'inside' [myself] is feminine."[5]

Both claims to truth contradict one another and so displace the entire enactment of gender significations from the discourse of truth and falsity.

The notion of an original or primary gender identity is often parodied within the cultural practices of drag, cross-dressing, and the sexual stylization of butch/femme identities. Within feminist theory, such parodic identities have been understood to be either degrading to women, in the case of drag and cross-dressing, or an uncritical appropriation of sex-role stereotyping from within the practice of heterosexuality, especially in the case of butch/femme lesbian identities. But the relation between the "imitation" and the "original" is, I think, more complicated than that critique generally allows. Moreover, it gives us a clue to the way in which the relationship between primary identification—that is, the original meanings accorded to gender—and subsequent gender experience might be reframed. The performance of drag plays upon the distinction between the anatomy of the performer and the gender that is being performed. But we are actually in the presence of three contingent dimensions of significant corporeality: anatomical sex, gender identity, and gender performance. If the anatomy of the performer is already distinct from the gender of the performer, and both of those are distinct from the gender of the performance, then the performance suggests a dissonance not only between sex and performance, but sex and gender, and gender and performance. As much as drag creates a unified picture of "woman" (what its critics often oppose), it also reveals the distinctness of those aspects of gendered experience which are falsely naturalized as a unity through the regulatory fiction of heterosexual coherence. *In imitating gender, drag implicitly reveals the imitative structure of gender itself as well as its contingency.* Indeed, part of the pleasure, the giddiness of the performance is in the recognition of a radical contingency in the relation between sex and gender in the face

---

[5] Ibid., p. 103.

of cultural configurations of causal unities that are regularly assumed to be natural and necessary. In the place of the law of heterosexual coherence, we see sex and gender denaturalized by means of a performance which avows their distinctness and dramatizes the cultural mechanism of their fabricated unity.

The notion of gender parody defended here does not assume that there is an original which such parodic identities imitate. Indeed, the parody is *of* the very notion of an original; just as the psychoanalytic notion of gender identification is constituted by a fantasy of a fantasy, the transfiguration of an Other who is always already a "figure" in that double sense, so gender parody reveals that the original identity after which gender fashions itself is an imitation without an origin. To be more precise, it is a production which, in effect that is, in its effect—postures as an imitation. This perpetual displacement constitutes a fluidity of identities that suggests an openness to resignification and recontextualization; parodic proliferation deprives hegemonic culture and its critics of the claim to naturalized or essentialist gender identities. Although the gender meanings taken up in these parodic styles are clearly part of hegemonic, misogynist culture, they are nevertheless denaturalized and mobilized through their parodic recontextualization. As imitations which effectively displace the meaning of the original, they imitate the myth of originality itself. In the place of an original identification which serves as a determining cause, gender identity might be reconceived as a personal/cultural history of received meanings subject to a set of imitative practices which refer laterally to other imitations and which, jointly, construct the illusion of a primary and interior gendered self or parody the mechanism of that construction.

According to Fredric Jameson's "Postmodernism and Consumer Society," the imitation that mocks the notion of an original is characteristic of pastiche rather than parody:

> Pastiche is, like parody, the imitation of a peculiar or unique style, the wearing of a stylistic mask, speech in a dead language: but it is a neutral practice of mimicry, without parody's ulterior motive, without the satirical impulse, without laughter, without that still latent feeling that there exists something *normal* compared to which what is being imitated is rather comic. Pastiche is blank parody, parody that has lost it humor.[6]

The loss of the sense of "the normal," however, can be its own occasion for laughter, especially when "the normal," "the original" is revealed to be a copy,

---

[6] Fredric Jameson, "Postmodernism and Consumer Society," in *The Anti-Aesthetic: Essays on Postmodern Culture*, ed. Hal Foster (Port Townsend, WA.: Bay Press, 1983), p. 114.

and an inevitably failed one, an ideal that no one *can* embody. In this sense, laughter emerges in the realization that all along the original was derived.

Parody by itself is not subversive, and there must be a way to understand what makes certain kinds of parodic repetitions effectively disruptive, truly troubling, and which repetitions become domesticated and recirculated as instruments of cultural hegemony. A typology of actions would clearly not suffice, for parodic displacement, indeed, parodic laughter, depends on a context and reception in which subversive confusions can be fostered. What performance where will invert the inner/outer distinction and compel a radical rethinking of the psychological presuppositions of gender identity and sexuality? What performance where will compel a reconsideration of the *place* and stability of the masculine and the feminine? And what kind of gender performance will enact and reveal the performativity of gender itself in a way that destabilizes the naturalized categories of identity and desire.

If the body is not a "being," but a variable boundary, a surface whose permeability is politically regulated, a signifying practice within a cultural field of gender hierarchy and compulsory heterosexuality, then what language is left for understanding this corporeal enactment, gender, that constitutes its "interior" signification on its surface? Sartre would perhaps have called this act "a style of being," Foucault, "a stylistics of existence." And in my earlier reading of Beauvoir, I suggest that gendered bodies are so many "styles of the flesh." These styles all never fully self-styled, for styles have a history, and those histories condition and limit the possibilities. Consider gender, for instance, as *a corporeal style,* an "act," as it were, which is both intentional and performative, where *"performative"* suggests a dramatic and contingent construction of meaning.

Wittig understands gender as the workings of "sex," where "sex" is an obligatory injunction for the body to become a cultural sign, to materialize itself in obedience to a historically delimited possibility, and to do this, not once or twice, but as a sustained and repeated corporeal project. The notion of a "project," however, suggests the originating force of a radical will, and because gender is a project which has cultural survival as its end, the term *strategy* better suggests the situation of duress under which gender performance always and variously occurs. Hence, as a strategy of survival within compulsory systems, gender is a performance with clearly punitive consequences. Discrete genders are part of what "humanizes" individuals within contemporary culture; indeed, we regularly punish those who fail to do their gender right. Because there is neither an "essence" that gender expresses or externalizes nor an objective ideal to which gender aspires, and because gender is not a fact, the various acts of gender create the idea of gender, and without those acts, there would be no gender at all. Gender is, thus, a construction that regularly conceals its genesis; the tacit collective agreement to perform, produce, and sustain discrete and polar genders as cultural fictions is obscured by the credibility of those productions—and the punishments that attend not agreeing to believe in them; the construction "compels" our belief in its necessity and naturalness. The historical possibilities materialized through various corporeal styles are nothing other than those punitively regulated cultural fictions alternately embodied and deflected under duress.

Consider that a sedimentation of gender norms produces the peculiar phenomenon of a "natural sex" or a "real woman" or any number of prevalent and compelling social fictions, and that this is a sedimentation that over time has produced a set of corporeal styles which, in reified form, appear as the natural configuration of bodies into sexes existing in a binary relation to one another. If these styles are enacted, and if they produce the coherent gendered subjects who pose as their originators, what kind of performance might reveal this ostensible "cause" to be an "effect"?

In what senses, then, is gender an act? As in other ritual social dramas, the action of gender requires a performance that is *repeated*. This repetition is at once a reenactment and reexperiencing of a set of meanings already socially established; and it is the mundane and ritualized form of their legitimation.[7] Although there are individual bodies that enact these significations by becoming stylized into gendered modes, this "action" is a public action. There are temporal and collective dimensions to these actions, and their public character is not inconsequential; indeed, the performance is effected with the strategic aim of maintaining gender within its binary frame—an aim that cannot be attributed to a subject, but, rather, must be understood to found and consolidate the subject.

Gender ought not to be construed as a stable identity or locus of agency from which various acts follow; rather, gender is an identity tenuously constituted in time, instituted in an exterior space through a *stylized repetition of acts*. The effect of gender is produced through the stylization of the body and, hence, must be understood as the mundane way in which bodily gestures, movements, and styles of various kinds constitute the illusion of an abiding gendered self. This formulation moves the conception of gender off the ground of a substantial model of identity to one that requires a conception of gender as a constituted *social temporality*. Significantly, if gender is instituted through acts which are internally discontinuous, then the *appearance of substance* is

---

[7] See Victor Turner, *Dramas, Fields and Metaphors* (Ithaca: Cornell University Press, 1974). See also Clifford Geertz, "Blurred Genres: The Refiguration of Thought," in *Local Knowledge, Further Essays in Interpretive Anthropology* (New York: Basic Books, 1983).

precisely that, a constructed identity, a performative accomplishment which the mundane social audience, including the actors themselves, come to believe and to perform in the mode of belief. Gender is also a norm that can never be fully internalized; "the internal" is a surface signification, and gender norms are finally phantasmatic, impossible to embody. If the ground of gender identity is the stylized repetition of acts through time and not a seemingly seamless identity, then the spatial metaphor of a "ground" will be displaced and revealed as a stylized configuration, indeed, a gendered corporealization of time. The abiding gendered self will then be shown to be structured by repeated acts that seek to approximate the ideal of a substantial ground of identity, but which, in their occasional *dis*continuity, reveal the temporal and contingent groundlessness of this "ground." The possibilities of gender transformation are to be found precisely in the arbitrary relation between such acts, in the possibility of a failure to repeat, a de-formity, or a parodic repetition that exposes the phantasmatic effect of abiding identity as a politically tenuous construction.

If gender attributes, however, are not expressive but performative then these attributes effectively constitute the identity they are said to express or reveal. The distinction between expression and performativeness is crucial. If gender attributes and acts, the various ways in which a body shows or produces its cultural signification, are performative, then there is no preexisting identity by which an act or attribute might be measured; there would be no true or false, real or distorted acts of gender, and the postulation of a true gender identity would be revealed as a regulatory fiction. That gender reality is created through sustained social performances means that the very notions of an essential sex and a true or abiding masculinity or femininity are also constituted as part of the strategy that conceals gender's performative character and the performative possibilities for proliferating gender configurations outside the restricting frames of masculinist domination and compulsory heterosexuality.

Genders can be neither true nor false, neither real nor apparent, neither original nor derived. As credible bearers of those attributes, however, genders can also be rendered thoroughly and radically *incredible.*

Slavoj Žižek

Slovenian (1949-)

The Real of Sexual Difference (2002)

There is no 'big Other' guaranteeing the consistency of the symbolic space within which we dwell: there are just contingent, punctual and fragile points of stability.

1 The 'formulae of sexuation'

Roger Ebert's *The Little Book of Hollywood Clichés*[1] contains hundreds of stereotypes and obligatory scenes—from the famous 'Fruit Cart' rule (during any chase scene involving a foreign or an ethnic locale, a fruit cart will be overturned and an angry peddler will run into the middle of the street to shake his fist at the hero's departing vehicle) and the more refined 'Thanks, but No Thanks' rule (when two people have just had a heart-to-heart conversation, as Person A starts to leave room, Person B tentatively says 'Bob [or whatever A's name is]?' and Person A pauses, turns, and says 'Yes?' and then Person B says, 'Thanks') to the 'Grocery Bag' rule (whenever a scared, cynical woman who does not want to fall in love again is pursued by a suitor who wants to tear down her wall of loneliness, she goes grocery shopping; her grocery bags then break, and the fruits and vegetables fall, either to symbolize the mess her life is in or so the suitor can help her pick up the pieces of her life, or both). This is what the 'big Other', the symbolic substance of our lives, is: a set of unwritten rules that effectively regulate our speech and acts, the ultimate guarantee of Truth to which we have to refer even when lying or trying to deceive our partners in communication, precisely in order to be successful in our deceit.

---

[1]   See Roger Ebert, *The Little Book of Hollywood Clichés*, London, Virgin Books, 1995.

We should bear in mind, however, that in the last decades of his teaching, Lacan twice severely qualified the status of the big Other:

- first in the late 1950s, when he emphasized the fact that the 'quilting point' (or 'button tie')—the quasi-transcendental master-signifier that guarantees the consistency of the big Other—is ultimately a fake, an empty signifier without a signified. Suffice it to recall how a community functions: the master-signifier that guarantees the community's consistency is a signifier whose signified is an enigma for the members themselves—nobody really knows what it means, but each of them somehow presupposes that others know it, that it has to mean 'the real thing', and so they use it all the time. This logic is at work not only in politico-ideological links (with different terms for the *Cosa Nostra*: our nation, revolution, and so on), but even in some Lacanian communities, where the group recognizes itself through the common use of some jargon-laden expressions whose meaning is not clear to anyone, be it 'symbolic castration' or 'divided subject'—everyone refers to them, and what binds the group together is ultimately their shared *ignorance*. Lacan's point, of course, is that psychoanalysis should enable the subject to *break* with this safe reliance on the enigmatic master-signifier.
- and second, and even more radically, in *Seminar XX*, when Lacan developed the logic of the 'not-all' (or 'not-whole') and of the exception constitutive of the universal. The paradox of the relationship between the series (of elements belonging to the universal) and its exception does not reside merely in the fact that 'the exception grounds the [universal] rule', that is, that every universal series involves the exclusion of an exception (all men have inalienable rights, with the exception of madmen, criminals, primitives, the uneducated, children, etc.). The properly dialectical point resides, rather, in the way a series and exceptions directly coincide: the series is always the series of 'exceptions', that is, of entities that display a certain exceptional quality that qualifies them to belong to the series (of heroes, members of our community, true citizens, and so on). Recall the standard male seducer's list of female conquests: each is 'an exception', each was seduced for a particular *je ne sais quoi*, and the series is precisely the series of these exceptional figures.[2]

---

[2] I owe this point to a conversation with Alenka Zupančič. To give another example: therein also resides the deadlock of the 'open marriage' relationship between Jean-Paul Sartre and Simone de Beauvoir: it is clear, from reading their letters, that their 'pact' was effectively asymmetrical and did not work, causing de Beauvoir many traumas. She expected that, although Sartre had a series of other lovers, she was nonetheless the Exception, the one true love connection, while to Sartre, it was not that she was just one in the series but that she was precisely one *of the exceptions*—his series was a series of women, each of whom was 'something exceptional' to him.

The same matrix is at work in the shifts in the Lacanian notion of the symptom. What distinguishes the last stage of Lacan's teaching from the previous ones is best approached through the changed status of this notion. Previously a symptom was a pathological formation to be (ideally, at least) dissolved in and through analytic interpretation, an index that the subject had somehow and somewhere compromised his desire, or an index of the deficiency or malfunctioning of the symbolic Law that guarantees the subject's capacity to desire. In short, symptoms were the series of exceptions, disturbances and malfunctionings, measured by the ideal of full integration into the symbolic Law (the Other). Later, however, with his notion of the universalized symptom, Lacan accomplished a paradoxical shift from the 'masculine' logic of Law and its constitutive exception to a 'feminine' logic, in which there is *no* exception to the series of symptoms—that is, in which there are *only* symptoms, and the symbolic Law (the paternal Name) is ultimately just one (the most efficient or established) in the series of symptoms.

This is, according to Jacques-Alain Miller, Lacan's universe in *Seminar XX*: a universe of the radical split (between signifier and signified, between *jouissance* of the drives and *jouissance* of the Other, between masculine and feminine), in which no *a priori* Law guarantees the connection or overlapping between the two sides, so that only partial and contingent knots-symptoms (quilting points, points of gravitation) can generate a limited and fragile coordination between the two domains. From this perspective, the 'dissolution of a symptom', far from bringing about a nonpathological state of full desiring capacity, leads instead to a total psychotic catastrophe, to the dissolution of the subject's entire universe. There is no 'big Other' guaranteeing the consistency of the symbolic space within which we dwell: there are just contingent, punctual and fragile points of stability.[3]

One is tempted to claim that the very passage from Judaism to Christianity ultimately obeys the matrix of the passage from the 'masculine' to the

---

[3] The difference between these two notions of the symptom, the particular distortion and the universalized symptom ('sinthome'), accounts for the two opposed readings of the last shot of Hitchcock's *Vertigo* (Scottie standing at the precipice of the church tower, staring into the abyss in which Judy-Madeleine, his absolute love, vanished seconds ago): some interpreters see in it the indication of a happy ending (Scottie finally got rid of his agoraphobia and is able fully to confront life), while others see in it utter despair (if Scottie survives the second loss of Judy-Madeleine, he will stay alive as one of the living dead). It all hinges upon how we read Lacan's statement that 'woman is a symptom of man'. If we use the term *symptom* in its traditional sense (a pathological formation that bears witness to the fact that the subject betrayed his desire), then the final shot effectively points toward a happy ending: Scottie's obsession with Judy-Madeleine was his 'symptom', the sign of his ethical weakness, so his rectitude is restored when he gets rid of her. However, if we use the term *symptom* in its more radical sense, that is, if Judy-Madeleine is his *sinthome*, then the final shot points toward a catastrophic ending: when Scottie is deprived of his *sinthome*, his entire universe falls apart, losing its minimal consistency.

'feminine' formulae of sexuation. Let us clarify this passage apropos of the opposition between the *jouissance* of the drives and the *jouissance* of the Other, elaborated by Lacan in *Seminar XX*, which also is sexualized according to the same matrix. On the one hand, we have the closed, ultimately solipsistic circuit of drives that find their satisfaction in idiotic masturbatory (auto-erotic) activity, in the perverse circulating around *objet a* as the object of a drive. On the other hand, there are subjects for whom access to *jouissance* is much more closely linked to the domain of the Other's discourse, to how they not so much talk as are talked about: erotic pleasure hinges, for example, on the seductive talk of the lover, on the satisfaction provided by speech itself, not just on the act in its stupidity. Does this contrast not explain the long-observed difference as to how the two sexes relate to cybersex? Men are much more prone to use cyberspace as a masturbatory device for their lone playing, immersed in stupid, repetitive pleasure, while women are more prone to participate in chat rooms, using cyberspace for seductive exchanges of speech.

Do we not encounter a clear case of this opposition between the masculine phallic-masturbatory *jouissance* of the drive and the feminine *jouissance* of the Other in Lars von Trier's *Breaking the Waves*? Confined to his hospital bed, Jan tells Bess that she must make love to other men and describe her experiences to him in detail—this way, she will keep awake his will to live. Although she will be physically involved with other men, the true sex will occur in their conversation. Jan's *jouissance* is clearly phallic-masturbatory: he uses Bess to provide him with the fantasmatic screen that he needs in order to be able to indulge in solipsistic, masturbatory *jouissance*, while Bess finds *jouissance* at the level of the Other (symbolic order), that is, in her words. The ultimate source of satisfaction for her is not the sexual act itself (she engages in such acts in a purely mechanical way, as a necessary sacrifice) but the way she *reports* on it to the crippled Jan.

Bess's *jouissance* is a *jouissance* 'of the Other' in more than one way: it is not only enjoyment in words but also (and this is ultimately just another aspect of the same thing) in the sense of utter alienation—her enjoyment is totally alienated/externalized in Jan as her Other. That is, it resides entirely in her awareness that she is enabling the Other to enjoy. (This example is crucial insofar as it enables us to dispense with the standard misreading of Lacan, according to which feminine *jouissance* is a mystical beatitude beyond speech, exempted from the symbolic order—on the contrary, it is women who are immersed in the order of speech *without exception*.)[4]

---

[4] For a closer reading of *Breaking the Waves*, see Slavoj Žižek, 'Death and the Maiden', in *The Žižek Reader*, ed. Elizabeth Wright and Edmond Wright, Oxford, Blackwell, 1998, pp. 206–21.

How does this allow us to shed new light on the tension between Judaism and Christianity? The first paradox to take note of is that the vicious dialectic between Law and its transgression elaborated by St Paul is the invisible third term, the 'vanishing mediator' between Judaism and Christianity. Its spectre haunts both of them, although neither of the two religious positions effectively occupies its place: on the one hand, Jews are *not yet* there, that is, they treat the Law as the written Real, which does not engage them in the vicious, superego cycle of guilt; on the other hand, as St Paul makes clear, the basic point of Christianity proper is to *break out* of the vicious superego cycle of the Law and its transgression via Love. In *Seminar VII,* Lacan discusses the Paulinian dialectic of the Law and its transgression at length. Perhaps we should thus read this Paulinian dialectic along with its corollary, the *other* paradigmatic passage by St Paul, the one on love from I Corinthians 13:

If I speak in the tongues of mortals and of angels, but do not have love, I am a noisy gong or a clanging cymbal. And if I have prophetic powers, and understand all mysteries and all knowledge, and if I have all faith, so as to remove mountains, but do not have love, I am nothing. If I give away all my possessions, and if I hand over my body so that I may boast [alternative translation: 'may be burned'], but do not have love, I gain nothing . . .

Love never ends. But as for prophecies, they will come to an end; as for tongues, they will cease; as for knowledge, it will come to an end. For we know only in part, and we prophesy only in part; but when the complete comes, the partial will come to an end . . . For now we see in a mirror, dimly, but then we will see face to face. Now I know only in part; then I will know fully, even as I have been fully known. And now faith, hope and love abide, these three; and the greatest of these is love.

Crucial here is the clearly paradoxical place of Love with regard to the All (to the completed series of knowledge or prophesies). First, St Paul claims that there is love, even if we possess *all* knowledge—then, in the second paragraph, he claims that there is love only for *incomplete* beings, that is, beings possessing incomplete knowledge. When I will 'know fully as I have been fully . . . known', will there still be love? Although, unlike knowledge, 'love never ends', it is clearly only 'now' (while I am still incomplete) that 'faith, hope and love abide'.

The only way out of this deadlock is to read the two inconsistent claims according to Lacan's feminine formulas of sexuation: even when it is 'all' (complete, with no exception), the field of knowledge remains in a way not-all, incomplete. Love is not an exception to the All of knowledge but rather a 'nothing' that renders incomplete even the complete series or field of knowledge. In other words, the point of the claim that, even if I were to possess all knowledge, without love, I would be nothing, is not simply that *with* love I am 'something'. For in love, *I also am nothing*, but as it were a Nothing humbly aware of itself, a Nothing paradoxically made rich through the very awareness of its lack. Only a lacking, vulnerable being is capable of love: the ultimate mystery of love is therefore that incompleteness is in a way higher than completion.

On the one hand, only an imperfect, lacking being loves: we love because we do not know everything. On the other hand, even if we were to know everything, love would inexplicably still be higher than complete knowledge. Perhaps the true achievement of Christianity is to elevate a loving (imperfect) Being to the place of God, that is, the place of ultimate perfection. Lacan's extensive discussion of love in *Seminar XX* is thus to be read in the Paulinian sense, as opposed to the dialectic of the Law and its transgression. This latter dialectic is clearly 'masculine' or phallic: it involves the tension between the All (the universal Law) and its constitutive exception. Love, on the other hand, is 'feminine': it involves the paradoxes of the not-All.

2 Sexual difference as a zero-institution

The notion of sexual difference that underlies the formulae of sexuation in *Seminar XX* is strictly synonymous with Lacan's proposition that 'there's no such thing as a sexual relationship'. Sexual difference is not a firm set of 'static' symbolic oppositions and inclusions/exclusions (heterosexual normativity that relegates homosexuality and other 'perversions' to some secondary role) but the name of a deadlock, a trauma, an open question—something that *resists* every attempt at its symbolization. Every translation of sexual difference into a set of symbolic opposition(s) is doomed to fail, and it is this very 'impossibility' that opens up the terrain of the hegemonic struggle for what 'sexual difference' will mean. What is barred is *not* what is excluded under the present hegemonic regime.[5]

---

[5] The gap that forever separates the Real of an antagonism from (its translation into) a symbolic opposition becomes palpable in a surplus that emerges apropos of every such translation. Say the moment we translate class antagonism into the opposition of classes *qua* positive, existing social groups (bourgeoisie versus working class), there is always, for structural reasons, a surplus, a third element that does not 'fit' this opposition (e.g., lumpenproletariat). And, of course, it is the same with sexual difference *qua* real: this means that there is always, for structural reasons, a surplus of 'perverse' excess over 'masculine' and 'feminine' as two opposed symbolic identities. One is even tempted to say

How, then, are we to understand the 'ahistorical' status of sexual difference? Perhaps an analogy to Claude Lévi-Strauss's notion of the 'zero-institution' might be of some help here. I am referring to Lévi-Strauss's exemplary analysis, in *Structural Anthropology*, of the spatial disposition of buildings among the Winnebago, one of the Great Lakes tribes. The tribe is divided into two sub-groups ('moieties'), 'those who are from above' and 'those who are from below'. When we ask an individual to draw the ground-plan of their village (the spatial disposition of cottages), we obtain two quite different answers, depending on which sub-group they belong to. Both groups perceive the village as a circle. For one sub-group, however, there is within this circle another circle of central houses, so that we have two concentric circles, while for the other sub-group, the circle is split into two by a clear dividing line. In other words, a member of the first sub-group (let us call it 'conservative-corporatist') perceives the ground-plan of the village as a ring of houses more or less symmetrically disposed around the central temple, whereas a member of the second ('revolutionary-antagonistic') sub-group perceives his or her village as two distinct heaps of houses, separated by an invisible frontier.[6]

Lévi-Strauss's central point here is that this example should in no way entice us into cultural relativism, according to which the perception of social space depends on which group the observer belongs to: the very splitting into the two 'relative' perceptions implies a hidden reference to a constant. This constant is not the objective, 'actual' disposition of buildings but rather a traumatic kernel, a fundamental antagonism the inhabitants of the village were unable to symbolize, account for, 'internalize' or come to terms with: an imbalance in social relations that prevented the community from stabilizing into a harmonious whole. The two perceptions of the ground-plan are simply two mutually exclusive endeavours to cope with this traumatic antagonism, to heal its wound via the imposition of a balanced symbolic structure.

Is it necessary to add that things are exactly the same with respect to sexual difference? 'Masculine' and 'feminine' are like the two configurations of houses in the Lévi-Straussian village. In order to dispel the illusion that our 'developed' universe is not dominated by the same logic, suffice it to recall the splitting of our political space into Left and Right: a leftist and a

---

that the symbolic/structural articulation of the Real of an antagonism is always a triad; today, for example, class antagonism appears, within the edifice of social difference, as the triad of 'top class' (the managerial, political and intellectual elite), 'middle class' and the non-integrated 'lower class' (immigrant workers, the homeless, etc.).

6 Claude Lévi-Strauss, 'Do Dual Organizations Exist?', in *Structural Anthropology, Volume 1*, trans. Claire Jacobson and Brooke Grundfest-Schoepf, New York, Basic Books, 1963, pp. 131–63.

rightist behave exactly like members of the opposite sub-groups of the Lévi-Straussian village. They not only occupy different places within the political space, each of them perceives differently the very disposition of the political space—a leftist as a field that is inherently split by some fundamental antagonism, a rightist as the organic unity of a Community disturbed only by foreign intruders.

However, Lévi-Strauss makes a further crucial point here: since the two sub-groups nonetheless form one and the same tribe, living in the same village, this identity has to be symbolically inscribed somehow. Now how is that possible, if none of the tribe's symbolic articulations—none of its social institutions—are neutral, but are instead overdetermined by the fundamental and constitutive antagonistic split? It is possible through what Lévi-Strauss ingeniously calls the 'zero-institution'—a kind of institutional counterpart to 'mana', the empty signifier with no determinate meaning, since it signifies only the presence of meaning as such, in opposition to its absence. This zero-institution has no positive, determinate function— its only function is the purely negative one of signalling the presence and actuality of social institution as such in opposition to its absence, that is, in opposition to presocial chaos. It is the reference to such a zero-institution that enables all members of the tribe to experience themselves as members of the same tribe.

Is not this zero-institution ideology at its purest, that is, the direct embodiment of the ideological function of providing a neutral, all-encompassing space in which social antagonism is obliterated and all members of society can recognize themselves? And is not the struggle for hegemony precisely the struggle over how this zero-institution will be overdetermined, coloured by some particular signification? To provide a concrete example: is not the modern notion of the nation a zero-institution that emerged with the dissolution of social links grounded in direct family or traditional symbolic matrixes—that is, when, with the onslaught of modernization, social institutions were less and less grounded in naturalized tradition and more and more experienced as a matter of 'contract'?[7] Of special importance here is the fact that national identity is experienced as at least minimally 'natural', as a belonging grounded in 'blood and soil' and, as such, opposed to the 'artificial' belonging to social institutions proper (state, profession, and so on). Premodern institutions functioned as 'naturalized' symbolic entities (as institutions grounded in unquestionable traditions),

---

[7] See Rastko Močnik, 'Das "Subjekt, dem unterstellt wird zu glauben" und die Nation als eine Null-Institution', in *Denk-Prozesse nach Althusser*, ed. H. Boke, Hamburg, ArgumentVerlag, 1994, pp. 87–99.

and the moment institutions were conceived of as social artifacts, the need arose for a 'naturalized' zero-institution that would serve as their neutral common ground.

Returning to sexual difference, I am tempted to risk the hypothesis that the same zero-institution logic should perhaps be applied not only to the unity of a society, but also to its antagonistic split. What if sexual difference is ultimately a kind of zero-institution of the social split of humankind, the naturalized, minimal zero-difference, a split that, prior to signalling any determinate social difference, signals this difference as such? The struggle for hegemony would then, once again, be the struggle for how this zero-difference is overdetermined by other particular social differences.

It is against this background that one should read an important, although usually overlooked, feature of Lacan's schema of the signifier. Lacan replaces the standard Saussurian scheme (above the bar the word 'arbre', and beneath it the drawing of a tree) with the two words 'gentlemen' and 'ladies' next to each other above the bar and two identical drawings of a door below the bar. In order to emphasize the differential character of the signifier, Lacan first replaces Saussure's single signifier schema with a pair of signifiers: the opposition gentlemen/ladies—that is, sexual difference. But the true surprise resides in the fact that, at the level of the imaginary referent, *there is no difference*: Lacan does not provide some graphic index of sexual difference, such as the simplified drawings of a man and a woman, as are usually found on the doors of most contemporary restrooms, but rather *the same* door reproduced twice. Is it possible to state in clearer terms that sexual difference does not designate any biological opposition grounded in 'real' properties but a purely symbolic opposition to which nothing corresponds in the designated objects—nothing but the Real of some undefined X that cannot ever be captured by the image of the signified?

Returning to Lévi-Strauss's example of the two drawings of the village, let us note that it is here that we can see in what precise sense the Real intervenes through anamorphosis. We have first the 'actual', 'objective' arrangement of the houses and then the two different symbolizations that both distort the actual arrangement anamorphically. However, the 'real' here is not the actual arrangement but the traumatic core of the social antagonism that distorts the tribe members' view of the actual antagonism. The Real is thus the disavowed X on account of which our vision of reality is anamorphically distorted. (Incidentally, this three-level apparatus is strictly homologous to Freud's three-level apparatus for the interpretation of dreams: the real kernel of the dream is not the dream's latent thought, which is displaced onto or translated into the explicit texture of the dream, but the unconscious desire which inscribes itself through the very distortion of the latent thought into the explicit texture.)

The same is true of today's art scene: in it, the Real does *not* return primarily in the guise of the shocking brutal intrusion of excremental objects, mutilated corpses, shit, and so on. These objects are, for sure, out of place—but in order for them to be out of place, the (empty) place must already be there, and this place is rendered by 'minimalist' art, starting with Kazimir Malevich. Therein resides the complicity between the two opposed icons of high modernism, Malevich's *The Black Square on the White Surface* and Marcel Duchamp's display of readymade objects as works of art. The underlying notion of Duchamp's elevation of an everyday common object into a work of art is that being a work of art is not an inherent property of the object. It is the artist himself who, by pre-empting the (or, rather, *any*) object and locating it at a certain place, makes it a work of art—being a work of art is not a question of 'why' but 'where'. What Malevich's minimalist disposition does is simply render—or isolate—this place as such, an empty place (or frame) with the proto-magic property of transforming any object that finds itself within its scope into a work of art. In short, there is no Duchamp without Malevich: only after art practice isolates the frame/place as such, emptied of all of its content, can one indulge in the readymade procedure. Before Malevich, a urinal would have remained just a urinal, even if it was displayed in the most distinguished gallery.

The emergence of excremental objects that are out of place is thus strictly correlative to the emergence of the place without any object in it, of the empty frame as such. Consequently, the Real in contemporary art has three dimensions, which somehow repeat the Imaginary–Symbolic–Real triad within the Real. The Real is first there as the anamorphic stain, the anamorphic distortion of the direct image of reality—as a distorted image, a pure semblance that 'subjectivizes' objective reality. Then the Real is there as the empty place, as a structure, a construction that is never actual or experienced as such but can only be retroactively constructed and has to be presupposed as such—the Real as symbolic construction. Finally, the Real is the obscene, excremental Object out of place, the Real 'itself'. This last Real, if isolated, is a mere fetish whose fascinating/captivating presence masks the structural Real, in the same way that, in Nazi anti-Semitism, the Jew as an excremental Object is the Real that masks the unbearable 'structural' Real of social antagonism. These three dimensions of the Real result from the three modes by which one can distance oneself from 'ordinary' reality: one submits this reality to anamorphic distortion; one introduces an object that has no place in it; and one subtracts or erases all content (objects) of reality, so that all that remains is the very empty place that these objects were filling.

3 'Post-secular thought'? No, thanks!

In *Seminar XX*, Lacan massively rehabilitates the religious problematic (Woman as one of the names of God, etc.). However, against the background of the properly Lacanian notion of the Real, it is easy to see why the so-called 'post-secular' turn of deconstruction, which finds its ultimate expression in a certain kind of Derridean appropriation of Lévinas, is totally incompatible with Lacan, although some of its proponents try to link the Lévinasian Other to the Lacanian Thing. This post-secular thought fully concedes that modernist critique undermined the foundations of onto-theology, the notion of God as the supreme Entity, and so on. Its point is that the ultimate outcome of this deconstructive gesture is to clear the slate for a new, undeconstructable form of spirituality, for the relationship to an unconditional Otherness that precedes ontology. What if the fundamental experience of the human subject is not that of self-presence, of the force of dialectical mediation-appropriation of all Otherness, but of a primordial passivity, sentiency, of responding, of being infinitely indebted to and responsible for the call of an Otherness that never acquires positive features but always remains withdrawn, the trace of its own absence? One is tempted to evoke here Marx's famous quip about Proudhon's *Poverty of Philosophy* (instead of actual people in their actual circumstances, Proudhon's pseudo-Hegelian social theory gives these circumstances themselves, deprived of the people who bring them to life):[8] instead of the religious matrix with God at its heart, post-secular deconstruction gives us this matrix itself, deprived of the positive figure of God that sustains it.

The same configuration is repeated in Derrida's 'fidelity' to the spirit of Marxism: 'Deconstruction has never had any sense or interest, in my view at least, except as a radicalization, which is also to say in the tradition of, a certain Marxism, in a certain spirit of Marxism.'[9] The first thing to note here (and of which Derrida is undoubtedly aware) is how this 'radicalization' relies on the traditional opposition between Letter and Spirit: reasserting the authentic spirit of the Marxist tradition means to leave behind its letter (Marx's particular analyses and proposed revolutionary measures, which are irreducibly tainted by the tradition of ontology) in order to save from the ashes the authentic messianic promise of emancipatory liberation. What cannot but strike the eye is the uncanny proximity of such 'radicalization' to

---

[8] Karl Marx, *The Poverty of Philosophy*, New York, International Publishers, 1963, p. 105 [eds].

[9] Jacques Derrida, *Spectres of Marx: The State of Debt, the Work of Mourning and the New International*, trans. Peggy Kamuf, New York and London, Routledge, 1994, p.92.

(a certain common understanding of) Hegelian sublation (*Aufhebung*): in the messianic promise, the Marxian heritage is 'sublated', that is, its essential core is redeemed through the very gesture of overcoming/renouncing its particular historical shape. And—herein resides the crux of the matter, that is, of Derrida's operation—the point is not simply that Marx's particular formulation and proposed measures are to be left behind and replaced by other, more adequate formulations and measures but rather that the messianic promise that constitutes the 'spirit' of Marxism is betrayed by *any* particular formulation, by *any* translation into determinate economico-political measures. The underlying premise of Derrida's 'radicalization' of Marx is that the more 'radical' these determinate economico-political measures are (up to the Khmer Rouge or Sendero Luminoso killing fields), the less they are effectively radical and the more they remain caught in the metaphysical ethico-political horizon. In other words, what Derrida's 'radicalization' means is in a way (more precisely, practically speaking) its exact opposite: the renunciation of any actual radical political measures.

The 'radicality' of Derridean politics involves the irreducible gap between the messianic promise of the 'democracy to come' and all of its positive incarnations: on account of its very radicality, the messianic promise forever remains a promise—it cannot ever be translated into a set of determinate, economico-political measures. The inadequacy between the abyss of the undecidable Thing and any particular decision is irreducible: our debt to the Other can never be reimbursed, our response to the Other's call never fully adequate. This position should be opposed to the twin temptations of unprincipled pragmatism and totalitarianism, which both suspend the gap: while pragmatism simply reduces political activity to opportunistic manoeuvring, to limited strategic interventions in contextualized situations, dispensing with any reference to transcendent Otherness, totalitarianism identifies the unconditional Otherness with a particular historical figure (the Party *is* historical Reason embodied directly).

In short, we see here the problematic of totalitarianism in its specific deconstructionist twist: at its most elementary—one is almost tempted to say ontological—level, 'totalitarianism' is not simply a political force that aims at total control over social life, at rendering society totally transparent, but a short-circuit between messianic Otherness and a determinate political agent. The 'to come [*à venir*]' is thus not simply an additional qualification of democracy but its innermost kernel, what makes democracy a democracy: the moment democracy is no longer 'to come' but pretends to be actual— fully actualized—we enter totalitarianism.

To avoid a misunderstanding: this 'democracy to come' is, of course, not simply a democracy that promises to arrive in the future, but all arrival is forever postponed. Derrida is well aware of the 'urgency', of the 'now-ness', of the need for justice. If anything is foreign to him, it is the complacent postponement of democracy to a later stage in evolution, as in the proverbial Stalinist distinction between the present 'dictatorship of the proletariat' and the future 'full' democracy, legitimizing the present terror as creating the necessary conditions for the later freedom. Such a 'two stage' strategy is for him the very worst form of ontology; in contrast to such a strategic economy of the proper dose of (un)freedom, 'democracy to come' refers to the unforeseeable emergencies/outbursts of ethical responsibility, when I am suddenly confronted with an urgency to answer the call, to intervene in a situation that I experience as intolerably unjust. However, it is symptomatic that Derrida nonetheless retains the irreducible opposition between such a spectral experience of the messianic call of justice and its 'ontologization', its transposition into a set of positive legal and political measures. Or, to put it in terms of the opposition between ethics and politics, what Derrida mobilizes here is the gap between ethics and politics:

> On the one hand, ethics is left defined as the infinite responsibility of unconditional hospitality. Whilst, on the other hand, the political can be defined as the taking of a decision without any determinate transcendental guarantees. Thus, the hiatus in Levinas allows Derrida both to affirm the primacy of an ethics of hospitality, whilst leaving open the sphere of the political as a realm of risk and danger.[10]

The ethical is thus the (back)ground of undecidability, while the political is the domain of decision(s), of taking the full risk of crossing the hiatus and translating this impossible ethical request of messianic justice into a particular intervention that never lives up to this request, that is always unjust toward (some) others. The ethical domain proper, the unconditional spectral request that makes us absolutely responsible and cannot ever be translated into a positive measure/intervention, is thus perhaps not so much a formal a priori background/frame of political decisions but rather their inherent, indefinite *différance*, signalling that no determinate decision can fully 'hit its mark'.

This fragile, temporary unity of unconditional, ethical injunction and pragmatic, political interventions can best be rendered by paraphrasing Kant's famous formulation about the relationship between reason and experience: 'If ethics without politics is empty, then politics without ethics is

---

[10] Simon Critchley, *Ethics–Politics–Subjectivity: Essays on Derrida, Lévinas and Contemporary French Thought*, London and New York, Verso, 1999, p.275.

blind.'[11] Elegant as this solution is (ethics is here the condition of possibility *and* the condition of impossibility of the political, for it simultaneously opens up the space for political decision as an act without a guarantee in the big Other and condemns it to ultimate failure), it is to be opposed to the act in the Lacanian sense, in which the distance between the ethical and the political collapses.

Consider the case of Antigone. She can be said to exemplify the unconditional fidelity to the Otherness of the Thing that disrupts the entire social edifice. From the standpoint of the ethics of *Sittlichkeit*, of the mores that regulate the intersubjective collective of the polis, her insistence is effectively 'mad', disruptive, evil. In other words, is not Antigone—in the terms of the deconstructionist notion of the messianic promise that is forever 'to come'—a proto-totalitarian figure? With regard to the tension (which provides the ultimate coordinates of ethical space) between the Other *qua* Thing, the abyssal Otherness that addresses us with an unconditional injunction, and the Other *qua* Third, the agency that mediates my encounter with others (other 'normal' humans)—where this Third can be the figure of symbolic authority but also the 'impersonal' set of rules that regulate my exchanges with others—does not Antigone stand for the exclusive and uncompromising attachment to the Other *qua* Thing, eclipsing the Other *qua* Third, the agency of symbolic mediation/reconciliation? Or, to put it in slightly ironic terms, is not Antigone the anti-Habermas par excellence? No dialogue, no attempt to convince Creon of the good reasons for her acts through rational argumentation, but just the blind insistence on her right. If anything, the so-called 'arguments' are on Creon's side (the burial of Polynices would stir up public unrest, etc.), while Antigone's counterpoint is ultimately the tautological insistence: 'Okay, you can say whatever you like, it will not change anything—I stick to my decision!'

This is no fancy hypothesis: some of those who read Lacan as a proto-Kantian effectively (mis)read Lacan's interpretation of Antigone, claiming that he condemns her unconditional insistence, rejecting it as the tragic, suicidal example of losing the proper distance from the lethal Thing, of directly immersing oneself in the Thing.[12] From this perspective, the opposition between Creon and Antigone is one between unprincipled pragmatism and totalitarianism: far from being a totalitarian, Creon acts like a pragmatic state politician, mercilessly crushing any activity that would

---

[11] *Ibid.*, p.283.
[12] See Rudolf Bernet, 'Subjekt and Gesetz in der Ethik von Kant und Lacan', in *Ethik und Psychoanalyse*, ed. Hans-Dieter Gondek and Peter Widmer, Frankfurt, Fischer Verlag, 1994, pp. 15–27.

destabilize the smooth functioning of the state and civil peace. Moreover, is not the very elementary gesture of sublimation 'totalitarian', insofar as it consists in elevating an object into the Thing (in sublimation, something—an object that is part of our ordinary reality—is elevated into the unconditional object that the subject values more than life itself)? And is not this short-circuit between a determinate object and the Thing the minimal condition of 'ontological totalitarianism'? Is not, as against this short-circuit, the ultimate ethical lesson of deconstruction the notion that the gap that separates the Thing from any determinate object is irreducible?

4 The other: Imaginary, symbolic and real

The question here is whether Lacan's 'ethics of the Real'—the ethics that focuses neither on some imaginary Good nor on the pure symbolic form of a universal Duty—is ultimately just another version of this deconstructive-Levinasian ethics of the traumatic encounter with a radical Otherness to which the subject is infinitely indebted. Is not the ultimate reference point of what Lacan himself calls the ethical Thing the neighbour, *der Nebenmensch*, in his abyssal dimension of irreducible Otherness that can never be reduced to the symmetry of the mutual recognition of the Subject and his Other, in which the Hegelian-Christian dialectic of intersubjective struggle finds its resolution, that is, in which the two poles are successfully mediated?

Although the temptation to concede this point is great, it is *here* that one should insist on how Lacan accomplishes the passage from Law to Love, in short, from Judaism to Christianity. For Lacan, the ultimate horizon of ethics is *not* the infinite debt toward an abyssal Otherness. The act is for him strictly correlative to the suspension of the 'big Other', not only in the sense of the symbolic network that forms the 'substance' of the subject's existence but also in the sense of the absent originator of the ethical Call, of the one who addresses us and to whom we are irreducibly indebted and/or responsible, since (to put it in Levinasian terms) our very existence is 'responsive'—that is, we emerge as subjects in response to the Other's Call. The (ethical) act proper is *neither* a response to the compassionate plea of my neighbourly *semblable* (the stuff of sentimental humanism) *nor* a response to the unfathomable Other's call.

Here, perhaps, we should risk reading Derrida against Derrida himself. In *Adieu to Emmanuel Lévinas*, Derrida tries to dissociate decision from its usual metaphysical predicates (autonomy, consciousness, activity, sovereignty, and so on) and think of it as the 'other's decision in me': 'Could it not be argued that, without exonerating myself in the least, decision and responsibility are always *of the other*? They always come back or come down to the other, from the other, even if it is the other in me?'[13] When Simon Critchley tries to explicate this Derridean notion of 'the other's decision in me' with regard to its political consequences, his formulation displays a radical ambiguity:

> Political decision is made *ex nithilo*, and is not deduced or read off from a pre-given conception of justice or the moral law, as in Habermas, say, and yet it is not arbitrary. It is the demand provoked by the other's decision in me that calls forth political invention, that provokes me into inventing a norm and taking a decision.[14]

If we read these lines closely, we notice that we suddenly have *two* levels of decision: the gap is not only between the abyssal ethical Call of the Other and my (ultimately always inadequate, pragmatic, calculated, contingent, unfounded) decision how to translate this Call into a concrete intervention. Decision itself is split into the 'other's decision in me', and my decision to accomplish some pragmatic political intervention as my answer to this other's decision in me. In short, the first decision is identified with/as the injunction of the Thing in me to decide; it is a *decision to decide*, and it still remains my (the subject's) responsibility to translate this decision to decide into a concrete actual intervention—that is, to 'invent a new rule' out of a singular situation where this intervention has to obey pragmatic/strategic considerations and is never at the level of decision itself.

Does this distinction of the two levels apply to Antigone's act? Is it not rather that her decision (to insist unconditionally that her brother have a proper funeral) is precisely an *absolute* one in which the two dimensions of decision *overlap*? This is the Lacanian act in which the abyss of absolute freedom, autonomy and responsibility coincides with an unconditional necessity: I feel obliged to perform the act as an automaton, without reflection (I simply *have* to do it, it is not a matter of strategic deliberation). To put it in more 'Lacanian' terms, the 'other's decision in me' does *not* refer to the old structuralist jargonladen phrases on how 'it is not I, the subject, who is speaking, it is the Other, the symbolic order itself, which speaks through me, so that I am spoken by it', and other similar babble. It refers to something much more radical and unheard of: what gives Antigone such unshakeable, uncompromising fortitude to persist in her decision is precisely the *direct* identification of her particular/determinate desire with the Other's (Thing's)

---

[13] Jacques Derrida, *Adieu to Emmanuel Levinas*, trans. Pascale-Anne Brault and Michael Naas, Stanford, Stanford University Press, 1999, p. 23.

[14] Critchley. *Ethics–Politics–Subjectivity*, p. 277.

injunction/call. Therein lies Antigone's monstrosity, the Kierkegaardian 'madness' of decision evoked by Derrida: Antigone does not merely relate to the Other-Thing; for a brief, passing moment of decision, she *is* the Thing directly, thus excluding herself from the community regulated by the intermediate agency of symbolic regulations.

The topic of the 'other' must be submitted to a kind of spectral analysis that renders visible its imaginary, symbolic and real aspects. It perhaps provides the ultimate case of the Lacanian notion of the 'Borromean knot' that unites these three dimensions. First there is the imaginary other—other people 'like me', my fellow human beings with whom I am engaged in mirror-like relationships of competition, mutual recognition, and so on. Then there is the symbolic 'big Other'—the 'substance' of our social existence, the impersonal set of rules that coordinate our existence. Finally there is the Other *qua* Real, the impossible Thing, the 'inhuman partner', the Other with whom no symmetrical dialogue, mediated by the symbolic Order, is possible. It is crucial to perceive how these three dimensions are linked. The neighbour [*Nebenmensch*] as the Thing means that, beneath the neighbour as my *semblable*, my mirror image, there always lurks the unfathomable abyss of radical Otherness, a monstrous Thing that cannot be 'gentrified'. Lacan indicates this dimension already in *Seminar III*:

> And why [the Other] with a capital O? No doubt for a delusional reason, as is the case whenever one is obliged to provide signs that are supplementary to what language offers. That delusional reason is the following. 'You are my wife'—after all, what do you know about it? 'You are my master'—in point of fact, are you so sure? Precisely what constitutes the foundational value of this speech is that what is aimed at in the message, as well as what is apparent in the feint, is that the other is there as absolute Other. Absolute, that is to say that he is recognized but that he isn't known. Similarly, what constitutes the feint is that ultimately you do not know whether it's a feint or not. It's essentially this unknown in the otherness of the Other that characterizes the speech relation at the level at which speech is spoken to the other.[15]

Lacan's early 1950s notion of 'founding speech', of the statement that confers on you a symbolic title and thus makes you what you are (wife or master), usually is perceived as an echo of the theory of performatives (the link between Lacan and Austin was Émile Benveniste, the author of the notion

---

[15] Jacques Lacan, *The Seminar of Jacques Lacan III: The Psychoses, 1955–56*, ed. Jacques-Alain Miller, trans. Russell Grigg, New York, W. W. Norton, 1993, pp. 37–8.

of performatives). However, it is clear from the above quote that Lacan is aiming at something more: we need to resort to performativity, to symbolic engagement, precisely and only insofar as the other whom we encounter is not only the imaginary *semblable* but also the elusive absolute Other of the Real Thing with whom no reciprocal exchange is possible. In order to render our co-existence with the Thing minimally bearable, the symbolic order *qua* Third, the pacifying mediator, has to intervene: the 'gentrification' of the homely Other-Thing into a 'normal fellow human' cannot occur through our direct interaction but presupposes a third agency to which we both submit— there is no intersubjectivity (no symmetrical, shared relation between humans) without the impersonal symbolic Order. So no axis between the two terms can subsist without the third one: if the functioning of the big Other is suspended, the friendly neighbour coincides with the monstrous Thing (Antigone); if there is no neighbour to whom I can relate as a human partner, the symbolic Order itself turns into the monstrous Thing that directly parasitizes upon me (like Daniel Paul Schreber's God, who directly controls me, penetrating me with the rays of *jouissance*); if there is no Thing to underpin our everyday, symbolically regulated exchange with others, we find ourselves in a 'flat', aseptic Habermasian universe in which subjects are deprived of their hubris of excessive passion, reduced to lifeless pawns in the regulated game of communication. Antigone–Schreber–Habermas: a truly uncanny ménage à trois.

5 Historicism and the real

How, then, can we answer Judith Butler's well-known objection that the Lacanian Real involves the opposition between the (hypostasized, proto-transcendental, prehistorical and presocial) 'symbolic order', that is, the 'big Other', and 'society' as the field of contingent socio-symbolic struggles? Her main arguments against Lacan can be reduced to the basic reproach that Lacan hypostasizes some historically contingent formation (even if it is Lack itself) into a proto-transcendental presocial formal *a priori*. However, this critical line of reasoning only works if the (Lacanian) Real is silently reduced to a prehistorical a priori symbolic norm: only in this case can Lacanian sexual difference be conceived of as an ideal prescriptive norm, and all concrete variations of sexual life be conceived of as constrained by this non-thematizable, normative condition. Butler is, of course, aware that Lacan's 'il n'y a pas de rapport sexuel' means that any 'actual' sexual relationship is always tainted by failure. However, she interprets this failure as the failure of the contingent historical reality of sexual life fully to actualize the symbolic norm: the ideal is still there, even when the bodies in question—contingent and historically formed—do not conform to the ideal.

I am tempted to say that, in order to get at what Lacan is aiming at with his 'il n'y a pas de rapport sexuel', one should begin by emphasizing that, far from serving as an implicit symbolic norm that reality can never reach, sexual difference as real/impossible means precisely that there is no such norm: sexual difference is that 'bedrock of impossibility' on account of which every 'formalization' of sexual difference fails. In the sense in which Butler speaks of 'competing universalities', one can thus speak of competing symbolizations/normativizations of sexual difference: if sexual difference may be said to be 'formal', it is certainly a strange form—a form whose main result is precisely that it undermines every universal form that aims at capturing it.

If one insists on referring to the opposition between the universal and the particular, between the transcendental and the contingent/pathological, then one could say that sexual difference is the paradox of a particular that is more universal than universality itself—a contingent difference, an indivisible remainder of the 'pathological' sphere (in the Kantian sense of the term), that always somehow derails or destabilizes normative ideality itself. Far from being normative, sexual difference is thus pathological in the most radical sense of the term: a contingent stain that all symbolic fictions of symmetrical kinship positions try in vain to obliterate. Far from constraining in advance the variety of sexual arrangements, the Real of sexual difference is the traumatic cause that sets in motion their contingent proliferation.[16]

This notion of the Real also enables me to answer Butler's reproach that Lacan hypostasizes the 'big Other' into a kind of prehistorical transcendental *a priori*. For as we have already seen, when Lacan emphatically asserts that 'there is no big Other', his point is precisely that there is no *a priori* formal structural scheme exempted from historical contingencies: there are only contingent, fragile, inconsistent configurations. (Furthermore, far from clinging to paternal symbolic authority, the 'Name-of-the-Father' is for Lacan a fake, a semblance that conceals this structural inconsistency.) In other words, the claim that the Real is inherent to the Symbolic is strictly equivalent to the claim that 'there is no big Other': the Lacanian Real is

---

[16] I rely here, of course, on Joan Copjec's pathbreaking 'Sex and the Euthanasia of Reason', in *Read My Desire: Lacan among the Historicists*, Cambridge MA, MIT Press, 1995, pp.201– 36. It is symptomatic how this essay on the philosophical foundations and consequences of the Lacanian notion of sexual difference is silently passed over in numerous feminist attacks on Lacan.

that traumatic 'bone in the throat' that contaminates every ideality of the symbolic, rendering it contingent and inconsistent.

For this reason, far from being opposed to historicity, the Real is its very 'ahistorical' ground, the a priori of historicity itself. We can thus see how the entire topology changes from Butler's description of the Real and the 'big Other' as the prehistorical a priori to their actual functioning in Lacan's edifice. In her critical portrait, Butler describes an ideal 'big Other' that persists as a norm, although it is never fully actualized, the contingencies of history thwarting its full imposition, while Lacan's edifice is instead centred on the tension between some traumatic 'particular absolute', some kernel resisting symbolization, and the 'competing universalities' (to use Butler's appropriate term) that endeavour in vain to symbolize/normalize it. The gap between the symbolic a priori Form and history/sociality is utterly foreign to Lacan. The 'duality' with which Lacan operates is not the duality of the a priori form/norm, the symbolic Order and its imperfect historical realization: for Lacan, as well as for Butler, there is *nothing* outside of contingent, partial, inconsistent symbolic practices, no 'big Other' that guarantees their ultimate consistency. However, in contrast to Butler and historicism, Lacan grounds historicity in a different way: not in the simple empirical excess of 'society' over symbolic schemas but in the resisting kernel *within* the symbolic process itself.

The Lacanian Real is thus not simply a technical term for the neutral limit of conceptualization. We should be as precise as possible here with regard to the relationship between trauma as real and the domain of socio-symbolic historical practices: the Real is neither presocial nor a social effect. Rather, the point is that the Social itself is *constituted* by the exclusion of some traumatic Real. What is 'outside the Social' is not some positive a priori symbolic form/norm but merely its negative founding gesture itself.

In conclusion, how are we to counter the standard postmodern rejection of sexual difference as a 'binary' opposition? One is tempted to draw a parallel to the postmodern rejection of the relevance of class antagonism: class antagonism should not, according to this view, be 'essentialized' into the ultimate, hermeneutic point of reference to whose 'expression' all other antagonisms can be reduced, for today we are witnessing the thriving of new, multiple political (class, ethnic, gay, ecological, feminist, religious) subjectivities, and the alliance between them is the outcome of the open, thoroughly contingent, hegemonic struggle. However, philosophers as different as Alain Badiou and Fredric Jameson have pointed out, regarding today's multiculturalist celebration of the diversity of lifestyles, how this thriving of differences relies on an underlying One, that is, on the radical obliteration of Difference, of the antagonistic gap.[17] The same goes for the standard postmodern critique of sexual difference as a 'binary opposition' to be deconstructed: 'there are not only two sexes, but a multitude of sexes and sexual identities'. In all of these cases, the moment we introduce 'thriving multitude', what we effectively assert is the exact opposite: underlying all-pervasive Sameness. In other words, the notion of a radical, antagonistic gap that affects the entire social body is obliterated. The non-antagonistic Society is here the very global 'container' in which there is enough room for all of the multitudes of cultural communities, lifestyles, religions and sexual orientations.[18]

[17] Alain Badiou, in his *Deleuze: The Clamor of Being*, trans. Louise Burchill, Minneapolis, University of Minnesota Press, 2000, fully emphasizes how Deleuze, the philosopher of the thriving rhizomatic multitude, is at the same time the most radical monist in modern philosophy, the philosopher of Sameness, of the One that pervades all differences— not only at the level of the content of his writings but already at the level of his formal procedure. Is not Deleuze's style characterized by an obsessive compulsion to assert the same notional pattern or matrix in all the phenomena he is analysing, from philosophical systems to literature and cinema?

[18] There is already a precise *philosophical* reason antagonism has to be a dyad, that is, why the 'multiplication' of differences amounts to the reassertion of the underlying One. As Hegel emphasized, each genus has ultimately only two species, that is, the specific difference is ultimately the difference between the genus itself and its species 'as such'. Say in our universe sexual difference is not simply the difference between the two species of the human genus but the difference between one term (man) that stands for the genus as such and the other term (woman) that stands for the Difference within the genus as such, for its specifying, particular moment. So in a dialectical analysis, even when we have the appearance of multiple species, we always have to look for the exceptional species that directly gives body to the genus as such: the true Difference is the 'impossible' difference between this species and all others.

Lee Edelman

American (1953–)

The Future is Kid Stuff: Queer Theory, Disidentification, and the Death Drive (1998)

Fuck the social order and the figural children paraded before us as its terroristic emblem….Fuck the whole network of symbolic relations and the future that serves as its prop.

Allow me, by way of introduction, to call your attention to a recent, minor, and short-lived political controversy, one that citizens of the United States have been rightly unwilling to fret about amid all the other incidents by which the press would have us be scandalized. According to an article in the *New York Times*, a series of public service announcements featuring President and Mrs. Clinton and sponsored by the Ad Council, a nonprofit organization, have "raise[d] questions about where politics stops and public service begins" (Bennet A18). These "questions," for those who have chosen to raise them, center on a fear that these commercial spots, however briefly and unexpectedly caught in the glare of the media spotlight, might burnish the President's image, and thus increase his political clout, insofar as they show him in a role construed as inherently non-political. By depicting the President, in the words of the *Times*, as "a concerned, hard-working parent," one who attends to the well-being of children unable to protect themselves, these public service announcements on behalf of the "Coalition for America's Children" could have the effect of heightening his moral stature with the American electorate, or so fears Alex Castellanos, a Republican media consultant. "This is the father picture," he fulminates in the pages of the *Times*, "this is the daddy bear, this is the head of the political household. There's nothing that helps him more" (Bennet A18).

But what helps him most in this public appeal for parental involvement with children is the social consensus that such an appeal is *distinct* from the realm of politics; indeed, though these public service announcements conclude with a rhetorical flourish evocative of an ongoing political campaign ("We're fighting for the children. Whose side are you on?"), that rhetoric is intended precisely to assert that this issue *has* only one side. And while such apparently self-evident one-sidedness—the affirmation of so uncontested, because so uncontroversial, a cultural value as that condensed in the figure of the child whose innocence cries out for defense—is precisely what ought to distinguish the public service spots from the more volatile discourse of political persuasion, I want to suggest that this is also what makes them so oppressively, and so dangerously, political: political not in the partisan terms implied by the media consultant, but political in a far more insidious way; political insofar as the universalized fantasy subtending the image of the child coercively shapes the structures within which the "political" itself can be thought. For politics, however radical the means by which some of its practioners seek to effect a more desirable social order, is conservative insofar as it necessarily works to *affirm* a social order, defining various strategies aimed at actualizing social reality and transmitting it into the future it aims to bequeath to its inner child. What, in that case, would it signify *not* to be "fighting for the children"? How, then, to take the *other* "side" when to take a side at all necessarily constrains one to take the side of, by virtue of taking a side within, a political framework that compulsively returns to the child as the privileged ensign of the future it intends?

In what follows I want to interrogate the politics that informs the pervasive trope of the child as figure for the universal value attributed to political futurity and to pose against it the impossible project of a queer oppositionality that would oppose itself to the structural determinants of politics as such, which is also to say, that would oppose itself to the logic of opposition. This paradoxical formulation suggests the energy of resistance—the characteristically perverse resistance informing the work of queer theory—to the substantialization of identities, especially as defined through opposition, as well as to the political fantasy of shaping history into a narrative in which meaning succeeds in revealing itself, *as itself*, through time. By attempting to resist that coercive faith in political futurity, while refusing as well any hope for the sort of dialectical access to meaning that such resistance, as quintessential political gesture, holds out, I mean to insist that politics is always a politics of the signifier, and that queer theory's interventions in the reproduction of dominant cultural logics must never lose sight of its figural relation to the vicissitudes of signification. Queer theory, as a particular story of where storytelling fails, one that takes the value and burden of that failure upon itself, occupies, I want to suggest, the impossible "other" side where narrative realization and derealization overlap. The rest of this paper aspires to explain the meaning and implications of that assertion, but to do so it must begin by tracing some connections between politics and the politics of the sign.

Like the network of signifying relations Lacan described as the symbolic, politics may function as the register within which we experience social reality, but only insofar as it compels us to experience that reality in the form of a fantasy: the fantasy, precisely, of form as such, of an order, an organization, assuring the stability of our identities as subjects and the consistency of the cultural structures through which those identities are reflected back to us in recognizable form. Though the material conditions of human experience may indeed be at stake in the various conflicts by means of which differing political perspectives vie for the power to name, and by naming to shape, our collective reality, the ceaseless contestation between and among their competing social visions expresses a common will to install as reality itself one libidinally-subtended fantasy or another and thus to avoid traumatically confronting the emptiness at the core of the symbolic "reality" produced by the order of the signifier. To put this otherwise: politics designates the ground on which imaginary relations, relations that hark back to a notion of the self misrecognized as enjoying an originary fullness—an undifferentiated presence that is posited retroactively and therefore lost, one might say, from the start—compete for symbolic fulfillment within the dispensation of the signifier. For the mediation of the signifier alone allows us to *articulate* these imaginary relations, though always at the price of introducing the distance that precludes their realization: the distance inherent in the chain of ceaseless deferrals and mediations to which the very structure of the linguistic system must give birth. The signifier, as alienating and meaningless token of our symbolic construction as subjects, as token, that is, of our subjectification through subjection to the prospect of meaning; the signifier, by means of which we always inhabit the order of the Other, the order of a social and linguistic reality articulated from somewhere else; the signifier, which calls us into meaning by seeming to call us to ourselves, only ever confers upon us a sort of *promissory* identity, one with which we never succeed in fully coinciding because we, as subjects of the signifier, can only be signifiers ourselves: can only ever aspire to catch up to—to close the gap that divides and by dividing calls forth—ourselves as subjects. Politics names those processes, then, through which the social subject attempts to secure the conditions of its consolidation by identifying with what is outside it in order to bring it into the presence, deferred perpetually, of itself.

Thus, if politics in the symbolic is always a politics *of* the symbolic, operating in the name, and in the direction, of a future reality, the vision it hopes to realize is rooted in an imaginary past. This not only means that politics conforms to the temporality of desire, to what we might call the inevitable historicity of desire—the successive displacements forward of figures of meaning as nodes of attachment, points of intense metaphoric investment, produced in the hope, however vain, of filling the gap within the subject that the signifier installs—but also that politics is a name for the temporalization of desire, for its translation into a narrative, for its teleological representation. Politics, that is, by externalizing and configuring in the fictive form of a narrative, allegorizes or elaborates sequentially those overdeterminations of libidinal positions and inconsistencies of psychic defenses occasioned by the intractable force of the drives unassimilable to the symbolic's logic of interpretation and meaning-production, drives that carry the destabilizing force of what insists outside or beyond, because foreclosed by, signification. These drives hold the place of what meaning misses in much the same way that the signifier, in its stupidity, its intrinsic meaninglessness, preserves at the heart of the signifying order the irreducible void that order as such undertakes to conceal. Politics, in short, gives us history as the staging of a dream of self-realization through the continuous negotiation and reconstruction of reality itself; but it does so without acknowledging that the future to which it appeals marks the impossible place of an imaginary past exempt from the deferrals intrinsic to the symbolic's signifying regime.

Small wonder then that the post-Kantian era of the universal subject should produce as the figure of politics, because also as the figure of futurity collapsing undecidably into the past, the image of the child as we know it. Historically constructed, as numerous scholars, including Phillipe Aries, Lawrence Stone, and James Kincaid, have made clear, to serve as the figural repository for sentimentalized cultural identifications, the child has come to embody for us the telos of the social order and been enshrined as the figure for whom that order must be held in perpetual trust. The image itself, however, in its coercive universalization, works to discipline political discourse by consigning it always to accede in advance to the reality of a collective futurity whose figurative status we are never permitted to acknowledge or address. From Delacroix's iconic image of Liberty urging us into a brave new world of revolutionary hope, her bare breast making each spectator the unweaned child to whom it belongs, to the equally universalized waif in the logo that performs in miniature the "politics" of the mega-musical *Les Miz*, we are no more able to conceive of a politics without a fantasy of the future than we are able to conceive of a future without the figure of the child.

And so, for example, when P. D. James, in her novel, *The Children of Men*, attempts to imagine the social effects of a future in which the human race has suffered a seemingly absolute loss of the capacity to reproduce, her narrator not only, predictably enough, attributes this reversal of biological fortune to

the putative crisis of sexual values in late twentieth-century democracies—
"Pornography and sexual violence on film, on television, in books, in life had
increased and became more explicit but less and less in the West we made
love and bred children" (James 10), he declares—but also gives voice to the
ideological truism that governs our investment in the child as emblem of
fantasmatic futurity: "without the hope of posterity, for our race if not for
ourselves, without the assurance that we being dead yet live," her narrator
notes, "all pleasures of the mind and senses sometimes seem to me no more
than pathetic and crumbling defences shored up against our ruins" (13).
While the plangent allusion to "The Waste Land" here may recall another
of its well-known lines, one for which, apparently, we have Vivienne Eliot to
thank, "What you get married for if you don't want children?," it also brings
out the function of the child as prop of the secular theology upon which our
common reality rests—the secular theology that shapes at once the meaning
of our collective narratives and our collective narratives of meaning. Charged,
after all, with the task of assuring "that we being dead yet live," the child, as
if by nature, indeed as the living promise of a natural transcendence of the
limits of nature itself, exudes the very pathos from which the narrator of
The Children of Men recoils when mirrored back in the non-reproductive
"pleasures of the mind and senses." For the "pathetic" quality he projectively
locates in all such forms of enjoyment exposes the fetishistic figurations of
the child that the narrator offers against them as legible in terms identical
to those whereby pleasures pursued in the absence of "hope of posterity"
are scorned: legible, that is, as nothing more than so many "pathetic and
crumbling defences shored up against our ruins." Indeed, how better to
characterize the narrative project of the text itself, which ends as any reader
not born yesterday expects, with renewal of the barren world through the
miracle of birth.

And if the author of *The Children of Men*, like the parents of mankind's
children, succumbs without struggle to the mystifications of the all-
pervasive, self-congratulatory, and strategically misrecognized narcissism
endlessly animating pronatalism, why should we be the least bit surprised
when her narrator insists, with what fully deserves to be characterized as
a "straight face," that "sex totally divorced from procreation has become
almost meaninglessly acrobatic" (167)? Which is, of course, to say no
more than that sexual practice will be made to allegorize the vicissitudes
of meaning so long as the heterosexually-specific alibi of reproductive
necessity covers up the drive *beyond* meaning that drives the symbolic's
machinery of sexual meaningfulness and erotic relationality. The child whose
pure possibility suffices to spirit away the naked truth of heterosexual sex,
seeming to impregnate heterosexuality itself with the future of signification

by bestowing upon it the cultural burden of signifying the future, figures an identification with an always about-to-be-realized identity—an identity intent on disavowing the threat to the symbolic order of meaning that inheres in a structure of desire that drives us to seek fulfillment in a meaning unable, *as* meaning, to fulfill us: unable, that is, to close the gap in identity that "meaning" means.

The consequences of such a compulsory identification both of and with the child as the culturally pervasive emblem of the motivating end, albeit endlessly postponed, of every political vision *as a vision of futurity,* must weigh upon the consideration of a queer oppositional politics. For the only queerness that queer sexualities could ever hope to claim would spring from their determined opposition to this underlying structure of the political— their opposition, that is, to the fantasmatic ambition of achieving symbolic closure through the marriage of identity to futurity in order to reproduce the social subject. Conservatives, of course, understand this in ways most liberals never can, since conservatism profoundly imagines the radical rupturing of the social fabric, while liberalism conservatively clings to a faith in its limitless elasticity. The discourse of the right thus tends toward a greater awareness of, and an insistence on, the figural logics implicit in the social relations we inhabit and enact, while the discourse of the left tends to understand better the capacity of the symbolic to accommodate change by displacing those figural logics onto history as the unfolding of narrative sequence.

Consider, for example, a local moment from the ongoing campaign around abortion. Not long ago, on a much-traveled corner in Cambridge, Massachusetts, opponents of the legal right to abortion posted an enormous image of a full-term fetus on a rented billboard accompanied by a simple and unqualified assertion: "It's not a choice; it's a child." Many critics, Barbara Johnson among them, have detailed with powerful insight how such anti-abortion polemics simultaneously rely on and generate tropes that animate, by personifying, the fetus, determining in advance the answer to the juridical question of its personhood by the terms with which the fetus, and thus the question, is addressed. Rather than attempting a deconstruction of this rhetorical instance, however (rather, that is, than note, for example, the collocation of the objectifying pronoun, "it," and the quintessentially humanizing epithet, "child," in order to see how this fragment of discourse maintains the undecidability it seems intended to resolve, casting doubt, therefore, on the truth of its statement by the form of its enunciation), I want to focus instead, for a moment, on the ideological truth its enunciation, unintentionally perhaps, makes clear.

For as strange as it may seem for a gay man to say this, when I first encountered that billboard in Cambridge I read it as addressed to me. The sign, after all, might as well have pronounced, and with the same absolute and invisible authority that testifies to the successfully accomplished work of ideological naturalization, the divine injunction: "Be fruitful and multiply." Like an anamorphotic distortion that only comes into focus when approached from an angle, the slogan acquired, through the obliquity of my subjective relation to it, a logic that served to articulate together the common stake in opposition to abortion and to the practice of queer sexualities—a common stake well understood (if only as the literalization of a figural identity) by radical groups like the one behind the January 1997 bombings of a lesbian bar and an abortion clinic in Atlanta. For the billboard, in this exemplary of the truths that right-wing discourse makes evident, understood what left-wing discourse prefers to keep concealed: that the true compulsion, the imperative that affords us as subjects no meaningful choice, is the compulsion to embrace our own futurity in the privileged form of the child and thereby to imagine the present as pregnant with the child of our identifications, as pregnant, that is, with a meaning to fill up the hole in the signifying order opened up by the distance, the internal division, produced through our subjection to the symbolic's logic of "meaning" itself.

Thus the left no more than the right will speak in *favor* of abortion; it, as the billboard cannily notes, aligns itself only with choice. And who, indeed, would speak *for* abortion, who would speak against reproduction, against futurity, and hence against life? Who would destroy the child and with it the sustaining fantasy of somehow bridging the signifying gap (a fantasy that serves to protect us against the violence of the drives insofar as it distracts us from seeing how thoroughly it compels us to enact them)? The right once again knows the answer, knows that the true oppositional politics implicit in the practice of queer sexualities lies not in the liberal discourse, the patient negotiation, of tolerances and rights, important as these undoubtedly are to all of us still denied them, but rather in the capacity of queer sexualities to figure the radical dissolution of the contract, in every sense social and symbolic, on which the future as guarantee against the return of the real, and so against the insistence of the death drive, depends. It is in this sense that we should listen to, and even perhaps be instructed by, the readings of queer sexualities produced by the forces of reaction. However much we might wish, for example, to reverse the system of values informing the following quotation from Donald Wildmon, founder and head of the deeply reactionary American Family Association, we would surely do well to consider it less as hyperbolic rant and more as a reminder of the disorientation that queer oppositionality entails: "Acceptance or indifference to the homosexual movement will result in society's destruction by allowing civil order to be redefined and by plummeting ourselves, our children and grandchildren into an age of godlessness. Indeed, the very foundation of Western Civilization is at stake" (Wildmon). Before the standard discourse of liberal pluralism spills from our lips, before we supply once more the assurance that ours is another kind of love but a love like his nonetheless, before we piously invoke the litany of our glorious contributions to civilizations of East and West alike, dare we take a moment and concede that Mr. Wildmon might be right, that the queerness of queer theory should tend precisely toward such a redefinition of civil order itself through a rupturing of our foundational faith in the reproduction of futurity?

It is true, of course, that the ranks of lesbian, gay, bisexual, and transgendered parents swell larger now than the belly sufficient to house that anti-abortion billboard's poster child for children. And nothing intrinsic to the constitution of persons who identify as lesbian, gay, bisexual, transgendered, transsexual, or queer predisposes them to resist the appeal of the future, to refuse the temptation to reproduce, or to place themselves outside or against the acculturating logic of the symbolic; neither, indeed, is there any ground we could stand on outside of that logic. But politics, construed as oppositional or not, never rests on essential identities; it centers, instead, on the figurality that is always essential *to* identity, and thus on the figural relations in which social identities are always inscribed. And so, when I argue, as I intend to do here, that the burden of queerness is to be located less in the assertion or reification of an oppositional political identity than in opposition to politics as the fantasy of realizing, in an always indefinite future, imaginary identities foreclosed by the fact of our constitutive subjection to the signifier, I am not suggesting a platform or position from which queer subjects or queer sexualities might finally and truly become themselves, as if they could somehow manage thereby to realize their essential queerness. I am suggesting instead that the efficacy of queerness, its strategic value, resides in its capacity to expose as figural the symbolic reality that invests us as subjects insofar as it simultaneously constrains us in turn to invest ourselves in *it*, to cling to its fictions as reality, since we are only able to live within, and thus may be willing to die to maintain, the figures of meaning that pass as the very material of literal truth.

The child, in the historical epoch of our current epistemological regime, is the figure for that compulsory investment in the misrecognition of figure; it takes its place on the social stage like every adorable Annie gathering her limitless funds of pluck to "stick out her chin/ and grin/ and say/ 'Tomorrow,/ tomorrow,/ I love you tomorrow,/ you're only a day away.'" And lo and behold, as viewed through the distorting prism of the tears she calls forth, the figure of this child seems to shimmer with the iridescent promise of Noah's rainbow, serving, like the rainbow, as the pledge of a covenant to shield us against the threat of apocalypse now—or apocalypse later. Recall, for example, the end of *Philadelphia*, Jonathan Demme's cinematic atonement for what some construed as the homophobia of *The Silence of the Lambs*. After saintly Tom Hanks, last seen on his deathbed in an oxygen mask that slyly alludes to, if only by virtue of troping upon, Hannibal Lecter's more memorable muzzle, has shuffled off this mortal coil to stand, as we are led to suppose, before a higher law, we find ourselves in, if not at, his wake surveying a room in his family home crowded with children and pregnant women whose reassuringly bulging bellies, lingered upon by the camera, displace the bulging basket (unseen) of the HIV-positive gay man (unseen) from whom, as the filmic text suggests, in a cinema given over, unlike the one in which we sit taking in *Philadelphia*, to explicit depictions of gay male sex, our Tom himself was infected by the virus that finally cost him his life. And when, in the film's final sequence, we look at the videotaped representation of our dead hero as a boy, can the tears that this shot would solicit fail to burn with an indignation directed not only against the homophobic world that sought to crush the man this boy was destined to become, but also against the homosexual world within which boys like this grow up to have crushes on other men? For the cult of the child permits no shrines to the queerness of boys or girls, since queerness, for the culture at large, as for *Philadelphia* in particular, is understood as bringing children and childhood to an end. The occasion of a gay man's death thus provides a perfect opportunity to unleash once more the disciplinary force of the figure of the child performing the mandatory cultural labor of social reproduction, a force we encounter continuously as the lives, the speech, and the freedoms of adults, especially queer adults, continue to suffer restriction out of deference to imaginary children whose futures, as if they were permitted to have them except insofar as they consist in transmitting them to children of their own, could only be endangered by the social disease as which queer sexualities register. Nor should we forget the extent to which AIDS, for which to this day the most effective name to be associated with the appropriation of funds in the U.S. Congress is that of a child, Ryan White, reinforces a much older linkage, as old as the gay-inflection given to the Biblical narrative of Sodom, between practices of gay sexuality and disappropriation from the promise of futurity, a linkage on which Anita Bryant could draw in waging her anti-gay campaign under the rubric of "Save Our Children."

While lesbians and gay men by the thousands work for the right to marry, to serve in the military, to adopt and raise children of their own, the right simply opens its closet and asks us to kneel at the shrine of the child: the child who might be subjected to physical or intellectual molestation; the child who might witness lewd or inappropriately intimate behavior; the child who might discover information about queer sexualities on the internet; the child who might choose a provocative book from the shelves of the public library; the child, in short, who might find an enjoyment that would nullify the figural value invested by the force of adult desire in the child as unmarked by the adult's adulterating implication in desire itself; the child, that is, compelled to image, for the satisfaction of adults, an imaginary fullness thought to want, and thus to want for, nothing. As Lauren Berlant puts it cogently in the introduction to *The Queen of America Goes to Washington City*, "a nation made for adult citizens has been replaced by one imagined for fetuses and children" (1). On every side, the present enjoyment of our liberties as citizens is eclipsed by the lengthening shadow of the child whose phantasmatic freedom to develop unmarked by encounters with an "otherness" of which its parents either do not or *should* not approve, unimpaired by any collision with the reality of alien desires, terroristically holds us all in check and determines that political discourse conform to the logic of a narrative in which history unfolds the future for a figural child who must never grow up. That child, immured in an innocence seen as continuously under seige, embodies a fantasy unable to withstand the queerness of queer sexualities precisely insofar as it promises the perpetuation of the same, the return, by way of the future, to an imaginary past. It denotes, in this, the *homo*sexuality intrinsic to the proper functioning of the heterosexual order: the erotically charged investment in the sameness of identity that is guaranteed oppositionally and realized in the narrative of reproductive futurity. And so, the radical right insists, the battle to preserve what Michael Warner describes as "heteronormativity" amounts to a life and death struggle over the future of the child whose ruin feminists, queers, and pro-choice activists intend.

Indeed, according to the bomb-making guide produced by the so-called Army of God, the group that claimed, correctly or not, responsibility for attacks on an abortion clinic and a lesbian bar in Atlanta, their purpose was to "disrupt and ultimately destroy Satan's power to kill our children, God's children" (Sack A13).

While we continue to refute the lies that pervade these insidious right-wing diatribes, do we also have the courage to acknowledge, and embrace, their correlative truths? Are we willing, as queers, to be sufficiently oppositional to the structural logic of opposition—oppositional, that is, to the logic by which political engagement serves always as the medium for reproducing our social reality—to accept that the figural burden of queerness, the burden that queerness is phobically produced in order to represent, is that of the agency of disfiguration that punctures the fictions of the symbolic, shattering its persistent fantasy of recapturing a lost imaginary unity, by obtruding upon it the void of what remains necessarily unsymbolizable, the gap or wound of the real that insists as a death drive within the symbolic? Not that we are—or, indeed, could be—committed to living outside the figures that constitute the symbolic; but perhaps we can begin to explore the possibilities of acceding to our construction as figures bodying forth, within the logic of narrative, the dissolution of that very logic.

The death drive, after all, refers to an energy of mechanistic compulsion whose structural armature exceeds the specific object, the specific content, toward which we might feel that it impels us. That object, that content, is never "it," and could never, possessed, truly satisfy; for the drive itself insists, and whatever the thing to which we mistakenly interpret its insistence to pertain, it is always only a grammatical placeholder deceiving us into reading the drive's compulsive insistence as transitive. But the structural mandate of the drive within the order of the symbolic produces that content, that thing, as mere displacement: as allegorization, within the governing logic of narrative transitivity, of its own differential force. That is why Lacan can declare that "if everything that is immanent or implicit in the chain of natural events may be considered as subject to the so-called death drive, it is only because there is a signifying chain" (1992, 212). And we can locate this reading of the death drive in terms of the figural economy inherent in the "chain of natural events" central to narrative if we conceptualize the play and place of the death drive in relation to a theory of irony, that queerest of rhetorical devices, especially as construed by Paul de Man. Proposing that "any theory of irony is the undoing, the necessary undoing, of any theory of narrative," de Man asserts a tension between irony as a particular trope and narrative as the representational mode he construes as the allegory of tropes, as the attempt to account for trope systematically by reading it as the site of a meaning that reflects a dialetical consciousness confronting its status as subject to the signifier (176–77). The corrosive force of irony carries a charge for de Man quite similar to that of the death drive for Lacan. "Words have a way of saying things which are not at all what you want them to say, " de Man observes; "There is a machine there, a text machine, an implacable determination and a total arbitrariness . . . which inhabits words on the level of the play of the signifier, which undoes any narrative consistency of lines, and which undoes the reflexive and dialectical model, both of which are, as you know, the basis of any narration" (181). This mindless violence of the textual machine, implacable and arbitrary, threatens, like a guillotine, to sever the integrity of narrative genealogy, recasting its narrative "chain of . . . events" as merely a "signifying chain" that inscribes in the realm of signification, along with unwanted meanings, the meaninglessness of the machinery that puts signification into play.

What is this but the death drive, which Barbara Johnson in a different context evokes as "a kind of unthought remainder . . . a formal overdetermination that is, in Freud's case, going to produce repetition or, in deconstruction's case, may inhere in linguistic structures that don't correspond to anything else" (98)? Irony may be one of the names for the force of that unthought remainder; queerness is surely another. Queer theory, then, should be viewed as a site at which a culturally repudiated irony, phobically displaced by the dominant culture onto the figure of the queer, is uncannily returned by those who propose to embrace such a figural identity with the *figuralization* of identity itself. Where the critical interventions of identitarian minorities, not excluding those seeking to substantialize the identities of lesbians, bisexuals, and gay men, may properly take shape as oppositional, reassuringly confronting the dominant order with the symmetrical image of its own achieved identity as social authority, queer theory's opposition, instead, is to the logic of oppositionality; its proper task the perpetual disappropriation of propriety.

It is not, therefore, a matter of either being or becoming, but rather of *embodying,* within the historical moment that imposes upon us such a figural association, the unsymbolizable remainder of the real produced by the order of meaning as the token of what that order is necessarily barred from being able to signify. One name given to this unnameable remainder by Lacan is "jouissance," occasionally translated as "enjoyment": the sense of a violent passage beyond the circumscriptions inherent in meaning that can have the effect, insofar as it gets attached, fetishistically, to a privileged object, of defining and congealing our experiential identities around fantasies of fulfillment through that object, but that also can function, insofar as it escapes such fetishistic reification, to rupture, or at least to seem to rupture, the consistency of a symbolic reality organized around the signifier as substantial identity, as name. Hence there is another name that can designate the unnameability to which the experience of jouissance can appear to give us access: "behind what is named, there is the unnameable," writes Lacan. "It is in fact because it is unnameable, with all the resonances you can give to this name, that it's akin to the quintessential unnameable, that is to say to death" (1991, 211). The death drive, then, manifests itself, though in radically different guises, in both versions of jouissance. To the extent that jouissance, as fantasmatic escape from the alienation intrinsic to meaning, and thus to the symbolic, lodges itself in an object on which our identities then come to depend, it produces those identities as mortifications, reenactments of the very constraints of meaning they were intended to help us escape. But to the extent that jouissance as a tear in the fabric of symbolic reality as we know it unravels the solidity of every object, including the object as which the subject necessarily takes itself, it evokes the death drive that always insists on the void both in and of the subject beyond its fantasy of self-realization in the domain of the pleasure principle.

Bound up with the first of these death drives we find the figure of the child, enacting the law of perpetual repetition as it fixes our identity through identification with the futurity of the social order; bound up with the second, the figure of the queer localizes that order's traumatic encounter with its own inescapable failure, its encounter, that is, with the illusory status of its faith in the future as suture, as balm for the wound as which the subject of the signifier experiences its alienation in meaning. In the preface to *Homographesis*, I wrote that "gay," understood "as a figure for the textuality, the rhetoricity, of the sexual . . . designates the gap or incoherence that every discourse of 'sexuality' or 'sexual identity' would master" (xv); I am now extending that claim by suggesting that queer sexualities, within the framework of the social text we inhabit, figure the gap in which the symbolic confronts what its discourse can never know. It is certainly the case that this production of the queer as the figural signifier of what the signifying system constitutively fails to name reassures by seeming to span the abyss opened up by the signifier itself, reassures by giving a name to the unnameable—a name such as "faggot," or "dyke," or "queer"—and construing in the form of an object what threatens the consistency of objects as such. But it is also the case that the righteous protestations against this figural positioning by those called upon historically to personify it, while enabling the gradual extension of rights and benefits to those denied them, *similarly* reassures by suggesting the seamless coherence of the symbolic, suggesting that its logic of narrative supersedes the corrosive force of our irony. For every expression of opposition to the figural status to which we are called affirms the triumph of history as story, as the narrative allegorization of the irony that is trope.

It may seem, from within this structure, that the symbolic can only win; but that, of course, is to ignore the fact that it also can only lose. For the division on which the subject rests, opening it to incursions of anxiety in which the reality conjured by the signifier quakes, can never be conjured away. The order of social reality demands some figural repository for what the structural logic of its articulation is destined to foreclose, for the fracture that persistently haunts it as the death within itself. By refusing to identify with this death drive, by refuting the tropology that aligns us with this disidentification from the logic of futurity, those of us occupying the place of the queer can only, at best, displace that figural burden onto someone else; only by making the ethical choice of acceding to that position, only by assuming the truth of our queer capacity to figure the undoing of the symbolic and the subject of the symbolic can we undertake the impossible project of imagining an oppositional political position exempt from the repetitive necessity of reproducing the politics of the signifier—the politics aimed at eliminating the gap opened up by the signifier itself—which can only return us, by way of the child, to the politics of reproduction.

In Boston last year, Cardinal Bernard Law, mistaking, or perhaps understanding too well, the authority of identity bestowed by the signifier that constitutes his own name, declared his opposition to domestic benefits assuring the availability of health care to same-sex partners of municipal workers by offering us the following piece of rancid piety in the sky: "Society has a special interest in the protection, care and upbringing of children. Because marriage remains the principal, and the best, frame-work for the nurture, education and socialization of children, the state has a special interest in marriage" (Slattery 68). If Cardinal Law, by adducing this bitter concentrate of a governing futurism so fully invested in the figure of the child that it manages to justify refusing health care to the adults that those children become, if Cardinal Law can thus give voice to the mortifying mantra of a communal jouissance committed to the fetishization of the child at the expense of whatever it renders queer, then we must respond not only by insisting on our right to enjoy on an equal footing the various prerogatives of the social order, not only by avowing our capacity to confirm the integrity of the social order by demonstrating the selfless and enduring love we bestow on the partners we'd gladly fly to Hawaii in order to marry or on the children we'd as eagerly fly to China or Guatemala in order to adopt, but also by saying explicitly what Law and the law of the symbolic he represents hear, more clearly even than we do perhaps, in every public avowal of queer sexuality or identity: fuck the social order and the figural children paraded before us as its terroristic emblem; fuck Annie; fuck the waif from *Les Miz*; fuck the poor innocent kid on the 'Net; fuck Laws both with capital "l"s and with small; fuck the whole network of symbolic relations and the future that serves as its prop.

Choosing to stand, as many of us do, outside the cycles of reproduction, choosing to stand, as we also do, by the side of those living and dying each day with the complications of AIDS, we know the deception of the societal lie that endlessly looks toward a future whose promise is always a day away. We can tell ourselves that with patience, with work, with generous contributions to lobbying groups, or generous participation in activist groups, or generous doses of political savvy and electoral sophistication, the future will hold a place for us—a place at the political table that won't have to come, as it were, at the cost of our place in the bed, or the bar, or the baths. But there are no *queers* in that future as there can be no future for queers. The future itself is kid stuff, reborn each day to postpone the encounter with the gap, the void, the emptiness, that gapes like a grave from within the lifeless mechanism of the signifier that animates the subject by spinning the gossamer web of the social reality within which that subject lives. If the fate of the queer is to figure the fate that cuts the thread of futurity, if the jouissance, the excess enjoyment, by which we are defined would destroy the other, fetishistic, identity-confirming jouissance through which the social order congeals around the rituals of its own reproduction, then the only oppositional status to which our queerness can properly lead us depends on our taking seriously the place of the death drive as which we figure and insisting, against the cult of the child and the political culture it supports, that we are not, to quote Guy Hocquenghem, "the signifier of what might become a new form of 'social organization'" (138), that we do not intend a new politics, a better society, a brighter future, since all of these fantasies reproduce the past, through displacement, in the form of the future by construing futurity itself as merely a form of reproduction. Instead we choose not to choose the child, as image of the imaginary past or as identificatory link to the symbolic future; we would bury the subject in the tomb that waits in the hollow of the signifier and pronounce at last the words we are condemned from the outset for having said anyway: that *we* are the advocates of abortion; that the child as figure of futurity must die; that we have seen the future and it's every bit as lethal as the past; and thus what is queerest about us, queerest within us, and queerest despite us, is our willingness to insist intransitively: to insist that the future stops here.

Acknowledgement

This paper was delivered at the Narrative conference at the University of Florida in April 1997. I wish to thank the other plenary speakers, Nancy Armstrong and Rey Chow, for their valuable comments and enjoyable company. I would also like to thank D. A. Miller, Diana Fuss, and Joseph Litvak for their generous readings of the text.

Works cited

Bennet, James. "Clinton, in Ad, Lifts Image of Parent." *New York Times.* 4 March 1997: New England Edition, A18.
Berlant, Lauren. *The Queen of America Goes to Washington City.* Durham: Duke Univ. Press, 1997.

de Man, Paul. *Aesthetic Ideology*. Edited by Andrzej Warminski. Minneapolis: Univ. of Minnesota Press, 1996.

Edelman, Lee. *Homographesis: Essays in Gay Literary and Cultural Theory*. New York: Routledge, 1994.

Hocquenghem, Guy. *Homosexual Desire*. Translated by Daniella Dangoor. Durham: Duke Univ. Press, 1993.

James, P. D. *The Children of Men*. New York: Warner Books, 1994.

Johnson, Barbara. *The Wake of Deconstruction*. Cambridge: Basil Blackwell, 1994.

Lacan, Jacques. *The Seminar of Jacques Lacan; Book II: The Ego in Freud's Theory and in the Technique of Psychoanalysis, 1954–1955*. Translated by Sylvana Tomaselli. New York: W. W. Norton: 1991.

Lacan, Jacques. *The Seminar of Jacques Lacan; Book VII: The Ethics of Psychoanalysis, 1959–1960*. Edited by Jacques-Alain Miller. Translated by Dennis Potter. New York: W. W. Norton, 1992.

Sack, Kevin. "Officials Look For Any Links in Bombings in Atlanta." *New York Times*. 2 February 1997: New England Edition, A13.

Slattery, Ryan. "Cardinal Law Urges Menino to Veto Bill Giving Benefits to City Workers' Partners." *Boston Sunday Globe*. 17 March 1996, 68.

Wildmon, Donald. "Hope '97 Tour to Counter Pro-Homosexual Philosophy in American Culture." Lkd. *American Family Association Action Alert*. <http://www.cfnweb.com/headline.htm> (25 February 1997).

Editor's Afterword: (Still) No Kingdom (of the Queer)

Queerness can never define an identity; it can only ever disturb one.
Lee Edelman, *No Future: Queer Theory and the Death Drive*

Queer, in its deconstructive sense, designates a kind of Derridean différance.
Carla Freccero, *Queer/Early/Modern*

It has been written *somewhere that deconstruction in the United States was successful among feminists and homosexuals. And there is always something sexual at stake in the resistance to deconstruction.*
Jacques Derrida, "Women in the Beehive"

Deconstruction, insofar as it insists on the necessary non-coincidence of the present with itself, is in fact in some senses the [queerest] of discourses imaginable.
Geoff Bennington, "Demanding History"

At the heart of something seemingly natural, self-identical, and proper, enabling or prolonging its functionality, stands something that is unnatural, or other, or improper, with the result that the so-called opposition between natural and unnatural, self and other, proper and improper is called into doubt, and what, by rights, should only be on one side of the equation is found to be already on the other. Such instabilities, **Derrida argued,** *are more common than it may be thought, and represent a grave and irreducible challenge to any concept of self-identity.*
Leslie Hill, *The Cambridge Introduction to Jacques Derrida*

As we know, as "**it has been written**," and as I have **boldly** emphasized in what you will have just (epigraphically) read, "**Derrida argued**."

Or, if you prefer, as I do, to obey the still regnant rhetorical convention and employ the present tense when describing what "has been written" (and so, in a sense, bring the dead back to life), then, as we might argue:

Derrida (still) writes.[1]

Without nostalgia (except perhaps for the Derridean phrase "without nostalgia" itself); without future (or perhaps with an unjustifiable embrace of Lee Edelman's *No Future*, refusing, heretical as the assertion may sound to certain Derrideans, any responsiveness to or responsibility for any future whatsoever); without "critical authority" or any desire to establish, inhabit, or exercise such, but also without much—it must be admitted—in the way of queer credibility, much less "Derridean" expertise (being only inexactly queer ourselves, Derrida and I, and my not having read anything like *his* every word), I (nonetheless) write that Derrida, though still, still writes, in a present tense that will have always already failed to be fully present or ever safely past or reassuringly *future anterior*, and so still sends trembles through "the heart" of anything "seemingly natural, self-identical, and proper," through "any concept of self-identity," through all the sedimented foundations of Western metaphysics, but also through all the coagulated institutions of heteronormativity, and, especially, through any heteronormatively determined, cisgendered "I" (if I—"a heterosexual" of sorts, not to mention a bit of a cissy—might venture to say so).

As much as any other adventurer in otherness, it was Derrida who helped to initiate and perpetuate these tremblings—helped, that is, to stir up gender trouble and proliferate critical queerness, helped, in other words, to queer theory. By (still) writing. By (still) having written. For example, that

> *différance* is not. It is not a present being, however excellent, unique, principal, or transcendent. It governs nothing, reigns over nothing, and nowhere exercises any authority. It is not announced by a capital letter. Not only is there **no kingdom of *différance***, but *différance* instigates the subversion of every kingdom. Which makes it obviously threatening and infallibly dreaded by everything within us that desires a kingdom, the past or future presence of a kingdom. And it is always in the name of a kingdom that one may reproach *différance* for wanting to reign. (*Margins* 21–22, bold emphasis mine)

---

[1]   This piece was written circa 2008, not very long after Derrida's demise in 2004—hence the somewhat elegiac references to Derrida's "stillness" here. The piece was written by invitation to be included in the volume *Derrida and Queer Theory*, edited by Christian Hite, and (finally) published by Punctum Books in 2017.

Obviously, the title of what I will have written here is drawn from this remarkable passage from "*Différance*."[2] As you'll note, I have in my kingdomless title substituted the word "queer" for the nonword "*différance*"—just as, in the epigraph from Geoffrey Bennington above, I have inserted the outrageously wrong word ("queerest") in the bracketed place where the proper words, the intended words, the authorized words (which were "most historical," in case you were wondering) should appear. Such catachreses invite the question of what makes the fungibility (though not the marriage) that I have arranged between the wrong word, the disturbing word, "queer," and the nonword/non-concept "*différance*," possible (if not, from a certain perspective, all too easy), as well as the question of *what* might abrade or even (of *who* might desire to) prohibit this alliance. And perhaps the problem of the very distinction between the *what* and the *who* will assume some importance here, whether I take the Freudian slogan *Wo Es war soll Ich werden* seriously to heart (as I pretty much *must*, if I am to become anything of an "I" at all) or whether "I" make(s) a complete hash of it (as I also unavoidably must, since "I" remains an other, or since, as Derrida's "I" remarks in *Glas*, "I—mark[s] the division" [165]).[3]

Or, as Derrida allows the questions to be posed in "*Différance*": "What differs? Who differs? What is *différance*" (*Speech* 141)? Or again, as Donald E. Hall titles a chapter in his book *Queer Theories*, "Who and What is Queer?" And yet:

> If we answered these questions even before examining them as questions, even before going back over them and questioning their form (even what seems to be most natural and necessary about them), we would fall below the level we have now reached. For if we accepted the form of the question in its own sense and syntax ("What?" "What is?" "Who is?"), we would have to admit that *différance* is derived, supervenient,

---

[2] In this piece I employ both the Alan Bass and the David Allison translations of "*Différance*" (from *Margins of Philosophy* and *Speech and Phenomena*, respectively), usually for the sake of sound alone (for example, "No *Kingdom* of the Queer" sounds much better to me than "No *Realm* of the Queer"). In one case, marked as such, I have mixed and modified the translations, trading Bass's "tyrant" for Allison's "king." Please note that the Bass translation, from *Margins of Philosophy*, is the one reprinted here in *Adventures*. Please also note that on page 114 of *Adventures* I have mixed translations again, changing Bass's "go on" to Allison's "begin again."

[3] *Wo Es war soll Ich werden*: usually, as in the *New Introductory Lectures*, "Where Id was, there shall Ego be" (*SE* 22:.80), but also, in Lacan's *Écrits*, "Where it was, I must come into being" (435) or again, to take a stab at it myself, "where a *what* was, a *who* must be established." With the line "'I' remains an other," I am alluding to Artur Rimbaud's grammatically deformed and self-alienating line "*Je est un autre*"—I *is* an other—which appears untranslated as the epigraph to the "Editor's Interlude" section in *Adventures*. To track Rimbaud's line down in the writings of Lacan, see Lesson Five: "You are not yourself"—*or I (think, therefore I) is an other*, in *Ten Lessons in Theory*.

controlled, and ordered from the starting point of a being-present, once capable of being something, a force, a state, or power in the world, to which we could give all kinds of names: a *what*, or being-present as a *subject*, a *who*. (*Speech* 145)

We will therefore *not* answer these questions or accept them in their given form, but merge and deform them—"What and who (queers) differs? What is (queer) *différance*?"—so as to let them provoke an alternative interrogative series. To wit:

What can we adventurers in theory—we who profess to know a *thing* or two about this *who/what* division as *internal to* and *constitutive of* subjectivity, as a difference not *between* subject and object but *within* the subject itself, we who claim to be conversant with the ins and outs of "deconstructive anti-identitarian critical and political practice" (Freccero 6)—what can we *decisively* say about "every*thing* within *us*" that desires a kingdom"? Can we confidently state that *whatever* this "everything within us" might end up being, it can't possibly be queer? That there can be "no kingdom of the queer" in exactly the same way as there can be "no kingdom of *différance*" and for exactly (or roughly) the same reasons? Can we conflate this (perhaps) anything-but-queer desire for a kingdom with what Derrida, in "Structure, Sign, and Play in the Discourse of the Human Sciences," calls the desire for "coherence in contradiction," for "a fundamental ground . . . a fundamental immobility and a reassuring certitude" (*Writing* 279)? Can we relate the fundamental ground of this desired epistemological and ontological kingdom not only to "the privilege accorded to consciousness," and thus to the "privilege accorded to the present," but also to the privilege accorded to *heterosex* as the reassuringly normative coherence of *erotic* contradiction, and so assert that "this privilege [i.e., heterosexual privilege] is the ether of metaphysics, the very element of our thought insofar as it is caught up in the language of metaphysics" (*Speech* 147), caught up in the language of heteronormativity, the pro-identitarian language of the desire (ours? theirs?) for a kingdom?[4] Does Lee Edelman's designation of queerness

---

[4] Note the variations on the words *coherence, contradiction,* and *consciousness* that appear in the following description of *heteronormativity* in Berlant and Warner's "Sex in Public":

By heteronormativity we mean the institutions, structures of understanding, and practical orientations that make heterosexuality seem not only coherent—that is, organized as a sexuality—but also privileged. Its coherence is always provisional, and its privilege can take several (sometimes contradictory) forms: unmarked, as the basic idiom of the personal and the social; or marked as a natural state; or projected as an ideal or moral accomplishment. It consists less of norms that could be summarized as a body of doctrine than of a sense of the rightness produced in contradictory manifestations—often unconscious, immanent to practice or to institutions. (547)

as that which "can never define an identity but . . . only ever disturb one" allow us to assert that queerness is not "incompatible with the theme of *différance*" (*Speech* 146) *as* that theme is elaborated in the writing called "*Différance*"? That queerness and *différance* are "the same without being identical" in that both can be said to "instigate the subversion of every kingdom"—particularly the kingdom of self-identity (but is there any other kind?)? In other words, allowing (at least provisionally) an intimate correspondence between queer disturbance and desedimenting *différance*, and given what Derrida signals, in the following, as the *regicidal* proximity of the latter, can there be any such entity or personage as "the queer who would be king"?

> The *a* of *différance* . . . cannot be heard; it remains silent, secret, and discrete, like a tomb.
>
> It is a tomb that (provided one knows how to decipher its legend) is not far from signaling the death of the tyrant. (*Speech* 132, translation modified)

Of course, contemporary homophobic popular culture—to cite one particularly blood-soaked example of it—knows exactly how to answer that last question, even in its appeals to ancient legend. For from the perspective of the 2007 film *The 300*, there can indeed be such an entity, such a personage: it's clear enough that this hyper-hetero-masculine (and so inadvertently self-queering) spectacle intends its antagonist, the marauding "Persian 'God-king' Xerxes," to be deciphered as a gigantic, invasive, raging *faggot*. Perhaps, in and for a certain political imaginary, all "strange gods" are queer.

As for myself, I hope, in what I will have ended up writing here, to have arrived, if not at my letter's destination, then at least "not far from signaling" some very different, non-homophobic responses to the questions my title provokes. "On the other hand, I must be excused if I refer, at least implicitly, to one or another of the texts that I have ventured to publish" (*Speech* 131). Actually, no, I must *not* be excused, must *refuse* to be forgiven, for these impending textual self-references; indeed, for what little I have ventured to publish on Derrida (the worst chapter of the book called *Male Matters*) I do not excuse myself, while for what I ("a heterosexual" of sorts) have ventured to publish on queer theory (a longer but not much better list of texts), you yourself must never forgive me.[5] Permit me, however, to point out that at some juncture in each one of my inexcusably and unjustifiably

---

[5] My unforgiveable texts are listed in all their abject glory in the Works Cited. Those attuned to my perverse textual narcissism will note that I've listed more of my own texts there than those of anyone else, including Derrida.

"straight queer" texts, there does come that necessary moment of attempted authorial self-justification (in the form, kicking it old-school, of the "review of scholarship"), the moment at which I am compelled to round up the (un)usual suspects, to trundle out an enabling assemblage of proper names (Butler, Berlant, Warner, Halperin, Hall, Sedgwick, Bersani, Edelman, Dean) and critical articulations, a battery of established renegade theorists and statements, each brandishing its own properly queer *bona fides*, its own "critically queer" authority, but each providing in its own way the condition of possibility (if not exactly its author's *intentional* justification or licensure) for the "straight queer" engagement yours truly is attempting to perform or inscribe.[6] I will not rehearse this necessary moment yet again here. I will submit, however, that each of these enabling articulations, if read closely, reveals itself to be a "deconstructive proposition." Conversely, it could be suggested that any deconstructive proposition, if read closely, will reveal itself to be queer, will out itself as queer. And if we follow this particular line of thought we come perilously close to the proposition (at once abyssally profound and radically flippant) that any proposition, if read closely, could turn out or come out to be deconstructive—and hence queer.

I will not hold back at the edge of this insignificant abyss but rather allow the "necessary moment" of which I write above to collapse (catachrestically) into the "moment" or "event" or "rupture" to which Derrida alludes at the beginning of "Structure, Sign, and Play," the moment that "presumably would have come about when the structurality of structure had to begin to be thought." As Derrida (still) writes:

> This was the moment in which language invaded the universal problematic, the moment when, in the absence of center or origin, everything became discourse . . . that is to say, a system in which the central signified, the original or transcendental signified, is never absolutely present outside a system of differences. The absence of the transcendental signified extends the domain and the play of signification infinitely. (*Writing* 280)

In other words, given language's invasion of the universal problematic, given "the linguistic turn" of the universal screw, it's always already "a queer planet." The world, in other words, is always already "queerer than ever."[7] The wrong

---

6   The relevant texts attributed to the mentioned proper names are given in the Works Cited.
7   I allude here to the title of Michael Warner's edited collection *Fear of a Queer Planet* and to his assertion, in the introduction to that volume, that the project of queer theory is to make "the world queerer than ever" (xxvii).

word "queer," like the nonword "*différance*," signifies the *disturbance* of identity that corresponds to the *absence* of the transcendental signified that *extends* the domain and the interplay of signification ad infinitum.

But "where and how does this decentering"—this queering, this *différance*, this *queerance*—"this notion of the structurality of structure, occur" (*Writing* 280)? If we respond to this question with the question "Where else and how else but *in the fucking text*?" then we acknowledge that the answers to the questions of where and how, as well as those of who and what, are nowhere (foundationally) but everywhere (figuratively) to be found. Language having invaded the universal problematic, the text, like "sex" of any all-too-human variety, has "no natural site" (*Writing* 280) or locus, no supernatural or transcendental guarantee. And if there is, as Derrida (still) writes, "no outside the text" (*Grammatology* 158), then human reality (the planet, the universal problematic, the world that must always "be made to mean") is also always already queer.[8]

Yes, to be sure, I am, totally and globally, profoundly and superficially— and with a nod toward what Madhavi Menon productively calls "queer universalism"—conflating *textuality*, which never confirms but only ever disturbs identity, with *human reality as such*, while thoroughly *saturating* that reality with queerness, or *queerance*, "itself."[9] I am suggesting, again, here, what I have already submitted in one or another of the aforementioned texts engaged with "queer theory" that I have ventured to publish, that theory "itself" is *queering*, that theory and/or Derrida and/or "the linguistic turn" turned or torqued or twisted me ("a heterosexual" cissy of sorts) into the queer thing that/who "I" is/am today, and, more specifically, that *literary* theory is *especially* queer, that *literature*, which never ceases to conceal/reveal the absence of natural locus, the missing transcendental signified, is in some senses the queerest of discourses imaginable.

The fact that others, recognizably queerer than I, have articulated similar arguments means, among other things, that something resembling the "necessary moment" of unjustifiable justification is about to be re-enacted after all. So: "Let us begin again" (*Speech* 142). Or rather, "Let us begin with the problem of signs and writing—since we are already in the midst of it"

---

8   The assertion that "the world must be made to mean" comes from Stuart Hall; I use this sentence as the guiding axiom/chapter title to Lesson One in *Ten Lessons in Theory*. Derrida's infamous claim that "there is nothing outside the text," from *Of Grammatology*, loosely cited above, is the guiding axiom/chapter title to Lesson Nine in *Ten Lessons*.

9   Menon's book's title—*Indifference to Difference: On Queer Universalism*—is compatible with some of the points I try to make at the very end of *Ten Lessons in Theory*. But her title also provokes a question that I will here leave hanging: Is indifference to the difference between "queer" and "not-queer" queer or not queer?

(*Speech* 138). In the introductory chapter, called "Prolepses," of her book *Queer/Early/Modern*, Carla Freccero writes that "the *queer* of this collection of critical interventions [i.e., her own] is difficult to define in advance."

> Over the past decade and a half, this term, as taken up by political movements and by the academy, has undergone myriad transformations and has been the object of heated definitional as well as political debates. . . . It is a term that, here, does have something to do with a critique of literary critical and historical presumptions of sexual and gender (hetero) normativity, in cultural contexts and in textual subjectivities. It also has something to do with the sexual identities and positionalities, as well as the subjectivities, that have come to be called lesbian, gay, and transgender, but also perverse and narcissistic—that is, queer. At times, *queer* continues to exploit its productive indeterminacy as a word used to designate that which is odd, strange, aslant; in this respect, I will argue that all textuality, when subjected to close reading, can be said to be queer. (5)

A bit further on, in a chapter called "Always Already Queer (French) Theory," Freccero illuminates and explains that title by writing:

> *Queer*, in its deconstructive sense, designates a kind of Derridean *différance*, occupying an interstitial space between binary oppositions . . . . This use of *queer* finds its energy from the way the term works to undo the binary between *straight* and *gay*, operating uncannily between but also elsewhere. *Queer*—precisely by marking out the space and time of *différance*—can thus show how the two, gay and straight, are inter-implicated and how they differ from themselves from within. . . . Meanwhile, *queer* can also be a grammatical perversion, a misplaced pronoun, the wrong proper name; it is what is strange, odd, funny, not quite right, improper. Queer is what is and is not there, what disaggregates the coherence of the norm from the very beginning and is ignored in the force to make sense out of the unintelligibilities of grammar and syntax. . . .
>
> It is in this sense that queer theory seems French, that French-influenced poststructuralist theory is already queer in the U.S. context. . . . The "linguistic turn" in French theory . . . not only facilitates the rise of queer theory as a literary cultural practice in the United States, but also lends an "always already" quality to the activity of queering. French theory has, in other words, made possible the demonstration of how tropological dimensions of language subvert the

very heteronormativity of Western logocentrism and thus, for example, how desire and identification may be unfixed from their sexually differentiated and opposed poles. Indeed, *queer* may be said to emerge spectrally in deconstructive critique. (18–19)

Conversely, of course, it might be said that *deconstruction* emerges spectrally in *queer* critique. Or, as Freccero's commentary would seem to allow, both deconstruction and queering—deconstruction *as* queering, differing/deferring as *queerance*—emerge spectrally in and as *literary critique*, the radical critique of "normal" human reality that literature, arguably, always already enacts. Freccero insinuates as much when she suggests that "if one were being playfully adjectival . . . one might call English departments departments of queer studies" (18). But the funny thing about Freccero's playful resignification of the English department—other than the fact that it generously queers every member of said department simply by virtue of each member's being a studiously close reader (while we all know that some of our most studious colleagues don't read all *that* closely)—the funny thing is that it resembles (without being identical to) a certain half-serious comment I once tossed off in a text called "Moments of Productive Bafflement, or, Defamiliarizing Graduate Studies in English." In that text (the first part of its title cops a line from Spivak's "Can the Subaltern Speak?"), I somehow manage never to mention the word "queer," but I do "playfully" suggest that "if I [as a Director of Graduate Studies in English] had my way, if I could institutionalize my slightest whims [if I were, perhaps, a tyrant or a king], I would . . . call the studies which I am supposed to direct 'Graduate Studies in Defamiliarization'" (25).

Now, in pointing out this superficial resemblance, am I suggesting that queering (English departments) and defamiliarizing (Graduate Studies in English) are "the same" or at least related activities, and so (given that literary formalism, at least in its Russian variation, posits defamiliarization as constituting the very "literariness" of literature itself) further attempting to lubricate the insertion of *queerance* into "the text" and textuality into "the queer"? "There is no simple answer to such a question" (*Speech* 153). I will say, however, that comparing Freccero's adjectival play to my own institutional whimsy at least allows me to get the word "defamiliarization" on the table, and so keep the question of the queerness of literature and the literariness of queerness alive. But of course it isn't as if "defamiliarization" wasn't already *on* the table, at least in the sense that this word has a history of showing up in discussions of both deconstruction and "queering" (particularly when the gerund indicates not "turning into a homosexual" but rather otherwise "making strange"). Moreover, since "defamiliarization" does in fact hold a formalist (albeit Russian) pedigree, the word tends to factor into charges of "apolitical formalism" routinely leveled against both deconstruction and queer theory.

My concern here is not to insist that defamiliarizing, deconstructing, queering, writing, and making art (not to mention "having sex") are all exactly "the same" activity, but to allow that all of these activities can be said to perform mutually supportive work in the ongoing "labor of ambiguating categories of identity" (Berlant and Warner, 345). To *fully* demonstrate that allowance, that performance, that hard (but anti-coagulating or de-reifying) collective labor, would require more temporalizing/spatializing (i.e., *writing*) than I can allow myself here. Were I to attempt such a demonstration, however, I might begin by revisiting the old question of why Derrida insists that "*différance* is neither a *word* nor a *concept*" (*Speech* 130). I might suggest that while today, for us, it is no longer entirely accurate to say that *différance* is not a word (for we can locate it as such in multiple dictionaries, not excluding, say, Julian Wolfreys's *Critical Keywords in Literary and Cultural Theory*), the claim that *différance* is not a concept still obtains, and for all the reasons Derrida gives (although, for the reasons he gives and in the sense that he means, even the claim that *différance* is not a word might still prove persuasive). And, were I actually demonstrating this point, which I swear I'm not, I might point to the moment in "*Différance*" where Derrida explains himself in this regard, where he quotes Saussure to the effect that "in language there are only differences *without positive terms*," and then suggests that

> The first consequence to be drawn from this is that the signified concept is never present to itself in an adequate presence that would refer only to itself. Every concept is necessarily and essentially inscribed in a chain or a system, within which it refers to another and to other concepts, by the systematic play of differences. Such a play, then—*différance*—is no longer simply a concept but the possibility of conceptuality, of the conceptual system and process in general. For the same reason, *différance*, which is not a concept, is not a mere word; that is, it is not what we represent to ourselves as the calm and present self-referential unity of a concept and sound. (*Speech* 140)

I would then reach further back into the history of the linguistic turn, the history of the questioning of conceptuality's possibility, to *Nietzsche*— but not without sneaking in Donald Hall's description of this figure as a "proto-postmodernist" and "proto-queer" philosopher "who took up most intensely the late nineteenth century challenge to received notions of normality" (56, 58)—and I would no doubt trot out the famous passage in "On Truth and Lie in an Nonmoral Sense" in which Nietzsche happily deconstructs "the formation of concepts."[10] I would then be compelled to visit, if only in a footnote, the aptly defamiliarizing, epistemologically devastating moment in Book Five of *The Gay Science*—the section called *"The origin of our concept of 'knowledge'"*[11]—but not without alluding to Nietzsche's influence on Viktor Shklovsky (who as you know first broke the news about defamiliarization) and to the manner in which Shklovsky's essay "Art as Technique" is explicitly formulated as an anti-epistemological intervention.[12] I would then probably make the gesture of linking Shklovsky's emphasis on "the principle of phonetic 'roughening' of poetic language," his claim that "the language of poetry is . . . a difficult, *roughened*, impeded

---

[10] Here's where Nietzsche reveals that concepts are formed through the forgetting or erasure or repression of differences, if not of *différance*:

> Let us further consider the formation of concepts in particular. Every word instantly becomes a concept precisely insofar as it is not supposed to serve as a reminder of the unique and entirely individual original experience to which it owes its origin; but rather, a word becomes a concept insofar as it simultaneously has to fit countless more or less similar cases—which means, purely and simply, cases which are never equal and altogether unequal. Every concept arises from the equation of unequal things. Just as it is certain that one leaf is never totally the same as another, so it is certain that the concept "leaf" is formed by an arbitrarily discarding these individual differences by forgetting the distinguishing concepts. (*The Nietzsche Reader*, 117; see also the Nietzsche selection in this volume; you can read more about this passage and its place in the genealogy of deconstruction in Lesson Nine of *Ten Lessons*.)

[11] Here's the defamiliarizing bit from *Gay Science*:

> What is it that the common people take for knowledge? What do they want when they want "knowledge"? Nothing more than this: Something strange is to be reduced to something *familiar*. And we philosophers—have we really meant *more* than this when we have spoken of knowledge? What is familiar means what we are used to so that we no longer marvel at it, our everyday, some rule in which we are stuck, anything at all in which we feel at home. Look, isn't our need for knowledge precisely this need for the familiar, the will to uncover under everything strange, unusual, and questionable something that no longer disturbs us? Is it not the *instinct of fear* that bids us to know? And is the jubilation of those who attain knowledge not the jubilation over the restoration of a sense of security? (*The Nietzsche Reader*, 368; you can read more about this passage and its place in the genealogy of poststructuralism in Lessons Five and Nine of *Ten Lessons*.)

[12] And here's the "anti-epistemological" bit from "Art as Technique," with what I take to be the resistance to epistemology emphasized (by me) at the end: "Art exists that one may recover the sensation of life; it exists to make one feel things, to make the stone *stony*. The purpose of art is to impart the sensation of things as they are perceived and *not as they are known*" (Shklovsky, p. 55 in *Adventures*). But here's a question: Why, in the latter part of an essay that posits "defamiliarization" as the defining formal protocol of literary technique—that is, the technique that produces the very literariness of literature—does Shklovsky spend so much time talking about *sex*? A possible answer: because human sex is *fucking strange*.

language" (783, my emphasis) to Donald Hall's reference to queer theory's persistent "questionings and *abrasions* of normality" (54, my emphasis). Then, having roughly traded *defamiliarization* for *queering* by virtue of nothing better than a linguistic similarity, I would more than likely bring the problem of conceptuality back into the mix by quoting Julian Wolfreys's aforementioned *Critical Keywords* to the effect that

> the mobility of "queer," its resistance to definition and its affirmation of that in identity which is irreducible to any heteronormative domestication calls into question the efficacy of any categorization . . . . Moreover, such affirmation implies a critique of the limits of normative concepts, if not the act of conceptualization itself. (202–03)

And of course the mobile implications of this quotation would allow me to circle metaleptically back to Derrida and to suggest that there was, after all, something always already queer about his insistence that *différance* is neither a word nor a concept.

It's really too bad that I can't perform this demonstration, because it might very well have made the case that "*Queer*, in its deconstructive sense, designates a kind of Derridean *différance*" (Freccero 18), that defamiliarizing, deconstructing, queering, and making artful sentences can all be said to perform mutually supportive, identity-disturbing work, or play, the sort of work-play or word-play that troubles any calm and present self-referential unity.

What, then, about the aforementioned/unmentioned "having sex"? At the end of the day, shouldn't "queer" pertain in some specific way to the practice of sex or the question of sexuality? Derrida specifies with sufficient vagueness that "there is always something sexual at stake in the resistance to deconstruction" ("Women" 148). Although I would doubt the inverted form of this proposition—doubt, that is, that there is anything deconstructive in the resistance to having sex—I *would* say that there is everything deconstructive in the resistance to having *a* sex, having to have or to be *one* sex, having to have one identifiable "sexual orientation," having the "truth" of one's sexual or erotic or corporeal being-in-the-world reduced to one specific identity category or another. And since categorization is the essential act of heteronormative conceptualization *qua* domestication *qua* naturalization *qua* reification, to the extent that deconstruction resists all that, to *that* extent deconstruction plays its part in queerness as "resistance to regimes of the normal" (Warner xxvi), "which makes it obviously threatening and infallibly dreaded by everything within us that desires a kingdom," and which, finally (but without finale—or, better, without ever letting be be finale of seem) makes it seem evident that while there may somewhere be an empire, and perhaps even an emperor, of ice cream, there can be no kingdom of the queer, if only because there can be no queer without catachresis.[13]

Or, as Derrida (still) (queerly) writes,

"Let us begin again."

Works Cited

Bennington, Geoff. "Demanding History." In *Post-structuralism and the Question of History*, ed. Derek Attridge, Geoff Bennington, and Robert Young, 15–29. Cambridge: Cambridge University Press, 1987.

Berlant, Lauren, and Michael Warner. "Sex in Public." *Critical Inquiry* 24, no. 2 (1998): 547–66.

Bersani, Leo. *Homos*. Cambridge: Harvard University Press, 1995.

Butler, Judith. *Bodies That Matter: On the Discursive Limits of "Sex"*. New York: Routledge, 1993.

Dean, Tim. *Beyond Sexuality*. Chicago: University of Chicago Press, 2000.

Derrida, Jacques. *Glas*. Translated by John P. Leavey and Richard Rand. Lincoln: University of Nebraska Press, 1986.

Derrida, Jacques. *Margins of Philosophy*. Translated by Alan Bass. Chicago: University of Chicago Press, 1982.

Derrida, Jacques. *Of Grammatology*. Corrected Edition. Translated by Gayatri Spivak. Baltimore: Johns Hopkins University Press, 1997.

Derrida, Jacques. *Speech and Phenomena*. Translated by David Allison. Evanston, IL: Northwestern University Press, 1973.

Derrida, Jacques. "Women in the Beehive: A Seminar with Jacques Derrida." *Differences: A Journal of Feminist Cultural Studies* 16, no. 3 (2005): 139–57.

Derrida, Jacques. *Writing and Difference*. Translated by Alan Bass. Chicago: University of Chicago Press, 1978.

Edelman, Lee. *No Future: Queer Theory and the Death Drive*. Durham: Duke University Press, 2004.

Freccero, Carla. *Queer/Early/Modern*. Durham: Duke University Press, 2006.

Freud, Sigmund. *The Standard Edition of the Complete Psychological Works*. 24 vols. Translated by James Strachey. London: Hogarth, 1953–74.

Hall, Donald E. *Queer Theories*. New York: Palgrave-Macmillan, 2003.

Halperin, David. *Saint Foucault: Towards a Gay Hagiography*. New York and Oxford: Oxford University Press, 1995.

---

[13] Apologies to Wallace Stevens, to whose poem "The Emperor of Ice Cream" I have here alluded for no good reason.

Hill, Leslie. *The Cambridge Introduction to Jacques Derrida*. Cambridge:
   Cambridge University Press, 2007.
Lacan, Jacques. *Écrits: The First Complete Translation in English*. Translated by
   Bruce Fink. New York: Norton, 2006.
Menon, Madhavi. *Indifference to Difference: On Queer Universalism*.
   Minneapolis and London: University of Minnesota Press, 2015.
Nietzsche, Friedrich. *The Nietzsche Reader*, ed. Keith Ansell Pearson and
   Duncan Large. Malden, MA, and Oxford, UK: Blackwell Publishing, 2006.
Sedgwick, Eve Kofosky. *Tendencies*. Durham: Duke University Press, 1993.
Shklovsky, Viktor. "Art as Technique." In *The Critical Tradition: Classic Texts and
   Contemporary Trends*, ed. David Richter, 3rd edition, 775–85. New York:
   Bedford-St. Martin's, 2007.
Thomas, Calvin. "Crossing the Streets, Queering the Sheets; or, 'Do You Want
   to Save the Changes to Queer Heterosexuality?'" Foreword to *Straight Writ
   Queer: Non-normative Expressions of Heterosexual Desire in Literature*, ed.
   Richard Fantina, 1–8. Ashville and London: McFarland Press, 2006.
Thomas, Calvin. "Is Straight Self-Understanding Possible?" *Transformations: The
   Journal of Inclusive Scholarship and Pedagogy* 13, no. 2 (Fall 2002): 17–24.
Thomas, Calvin. *Male Matters: Masculinity, Anxiety, and the Male Body on the
   Line*. Urbana: University of Illinois Press, 2006.
Thomas, Calvin. *Masculinity, Psychoanalysis, Straight Queer Theory: Essays
   on Abjection in Literature, Mass Culture, and Film*. New York: Palgrave-
   Macmillan, 2008.
Thomas, Calvin. "Moments of Productive Bafflement: or, Defamiliarizing
   Graduate Studies in English," *Pedagogy: Critical Approaches to Teaching
   Literature, Language, Composition, and Culture* 5, no. 1 (Winter 2005):
   19–35.
Thomas, Calvin. "On Being Post-Normal: Heterosexuality After Queer Theory,"
   in *The Ashgate Companion to Queer Theory*, eds. Michael O"Rourke and
   Noreen Giffney. London: Ashgate, 2008.
Thomas, Calvin. "Straight with a Twist: Queer Theory and the Subject
   of Heterosexuality." In *Genders 26: The Gay 90s: Disciplinary and
   Interdisciplinary Formations in Queer Studies*, ed. Thomas Foster, Carol
   Siegel, and Ellen E. Berry, 83–115. New York: New York University Press,
   1997. Reprinted in *Straight with a Twist: Queer Theory and the Subject of
   Heterosexuality*, ed. Calvin Thomas, with Joseph O. Aimone and Catherine
   A. F. MacGillivray, 11–44. Urbana: University of Illinois Press, 2000.
Thomas, Calvin. *Ten Lessons in Theory: An Introduction to Theoretical Writing*.
   New York and London: Bloomsbury Academic, 2013.
Warner, Michael. "Introduction." *Fear of a Queer Planet: Queer Politics and
   Social Theory*, ed. Michael Warner, vii–xxxi. Minneapolis: University of
   Minnesota Press, 1993.
Wolfreys, Julian. *Critical Keywords in Literary and Cultural Theory*. New York:
   Palgrave-Macmillan, 2006.

Index